TRAILS OF THE SMOKY HILL

TRAILS OF THE SMOKY HILL

From Coronado to the Cow Towns

by

WAYNE C. LEE

and

HOWARD C. RAYNESFORD

THE CAXTON PRINTERS, LTD.
Caldwell, Idaho
1980

Library of Congress Cataloging in Publication Data

Lee, Wayne C
Trails of the Smoky Hill.

Bibliography: p.
Includes index.
1. Smoky Hill Valley, Colo. and Kan. — History.
2. Butterfield Overland Trail. 3. Overland Mail
Company — History. 4. Frontier and pioneer life —
Smoky Hill Valley, Colo. and Kan. I. Raynesford,
Howard C., joint author. II. Title.
F687.S84L43 1980 978.1'1 78-67199
ISBN 0-87004-276-9

Printed and bound in the United States of America
by
The Caxton Printers, Ltd., Caldwell, Idaho 83605
133631

Dedicated to:
ARTHUR CARMODY and KIRK RAYNESFORD,
whose great interest in preserving
the history of
The Smoky Hill River Trails
has been an inspiration to me
in the research and writing
of this book.

CONTENTS

ILLUSTRATIONS

MAPS

PREFACE

A SECTION OF THE PAST as monumental as the history of the Smoky Hill River cannot be contained within the covers of one book. This volume is not intended to give a definitive description of every historical event that took place along the river but rather to present an overall view of one of the most action-packed areas in the dramatic era of our developing frontier. For those who want more details of certain episodes, the notes and bibliography will direct them to more detailed accounts of these events.

Many rivers and many trails have received more publicity than the Smoky Hill River and the trails that ran along its blood-soaked banks. But few were more important to the settlement of the plains between the Missouri River and the Rocky Mountains, and none was more hotly contested by the Indian than the Smoky Hill River Valley, the center of the greatest buffalo pasture in the world. Here the Indian made a desperate stand against the tide of white civilization. The miners, merchants, and settlers who traveled the trails did so at great risk, and those who strove to keep the trails open laid their lives on the line every day.

The white man with his vast reserve of weapons and warriors eventually won the right to live on the great buffalo pastures along the Smoky Hill and turn them into wheatfields, and the trails were gradually forgotten. But there were some who did not forget. Howard C. Raynesford was one.

Few men spend forty years digging into the history of one event; when a dedicated historian does, it usually means that generations to come will benefit from his findings. Howard C. Raynesford (1876-1967) spent the last forty odd years of his ninety-one digging into the history of the Butterfield Overland Despatch, correcting some of the errors in the history that had been handed down and unearthing a great deal that had sunk unheralded into the forgotten past.

He and his son, Kirk, a civil engineer, located and mapped many of the old B.O.D. station sites while it was still possible to find them. By 1950 there probably was no other man alive who knew as much about the Butterfield Overland Despatch through western Kansas as Howard Raynesford did.

Because of the help I received from his maps, mileage charts, and what he wrote about the B.O.D., and because I feel he has certainly earned the thanks of all historians of the American West, I am listing him as coauthor of this book in the hope that he will receive a small portion of the recognition he deserves. Without the information that he preserved on the B.O.D. through western Kansas, the section of this book on the Butterfield Overland Despatch would not be nearly as complete.

ACKNOWLEDGMENTS

WHEN A WRITER UNDERTAKES to record a historical panorama of any area he must enlist a great many people to help him uncover and assemble the facts. I was fortunate to find so many wonderful people willing to sacrifice time and labor to help me find and fit together the pieces of history of the Smoky Hill River from Coronado to the cow towns.

Senator Arthur Carmody of Trenton, Nebraska, not only went with me on many trips along the old B.O.D. Trail, walking over the station sites and visualizing the happenings that occurred there, but he opened up his great library of western history books and helped me find the ones I needed for my research. Occasionally our wives Grace Carmody and Pearl Lee, went along and helped in the research, both on the trail and in the museums and libraries.

My thanks go to Kirk Raynesford of Big Bear Lake, California, son of Howard Raynesford, the man who spent forty-four years researching the B.O.D. Kirk made his father's manuscript, the result of that research, available to me.

Nyle S. Miller, executive director emeritus of the Kansas State Historical Society, and Joseph W. Snell, the present executive director, guided me to much information I needed. Mr. Snell not only gave me every possible aid in the historical society's museum and library, for which I want to thank both him and his staff, but also loaned me several books from his personal library that helped me find many obscure items that I probably would not have found otherwise.

Leigh DeLay, historian, Nebraska State Historical Society, who once lived and researched along the Smoky Hill River, sent me many items and articles pertaining to the area and helped me locate pictures I needed.

Marjorie Wright and Dorothy Janke, both of Russell Springs, Kansas, did a great deal of research for me, sending me any item they found that they thought I could use. They live within fifty yards of the old B.O.D. Trail, and their interest in its history is boundless.

Mrs. Harold DeBacker of Boulder, Colorado, is a great-granddaughter of David Butterfield, and she gave me clippings and pictures of David Butterfield's family. Some of these may be the only such pictures in existence, since she and her children are the only descendants of David Butterfield.

Douglas and Mary Allyn Philip of Hays, Kansas, own a ranch through which the B.O.D. ran. The site of Big Creek Station is only a half-mile from their home. Doug and Mary Allyn took me over a long stretch of the B.O.D. Trail, pointing out places where history was made.

The late Ward Philip guided me to Threshing Machine Canyon on the B.O.D. and pointed out the places where many interesting events occurred.

Many historians along the Smoky Hill

River were a big help to me. Leslie Linville of Colby, Kansas, grew up on a farm on the banks of the Smoky Hill, and he went with me on several research trips along the river.

Dave Grusing of Colby, Kansas, lives on a ranch that includes the area believed to be the site of Turkey Leg's camp, where Bill Comstock was killed and Sharp Grover wounded. He showed me things he had found to substantiate that belief and took me over the area.

Mike Baughn of Brewster, Kansas, sent me innumerable clippings and other items of great value to me.

Elnor Brown, librarian at Imperial, Nebraska, helped me find books that I needed in my research, at times bringing in books that were not available locally.

Nellie Darnell, curator of the Butterfield Trail Museum in Russell Springs, Kansas, showed me items in the museum vaults that are seldom seen and that filled little gaps in the story of the Smoky Hill. Ruth Rains, curator of the Fort Wallace Museum, was also most helpful.

George Jelinek of Ellsworth, Kansas, a true historian of his area, gave me articles and clippings of Ellsworth's history that proved very valuable.

There are so many more that I cannot name them all, but I will never forget their help. To all of them I say thanks.

TRAILS OF THE SMOKY HILL

THE RIVER

IT ISN'T A GREAT RIVER in size; it's not the longest river on the plains by any means; but it holds its own with any river in importance in the rise of the Great Plains to the pinnacle of production and stability in our country.

From prehistoric times the watershed of this nearly six-hundred-mile-long river, from its source in Colorado to its junction with the Republican to form the Kansas River, has contained the finest country, nearly fifty-eight thousand square miles of it, in all the Great Plains east of the Rocky Mountains. Its valley was a favorite pasture of the buffalo, and so it was a main source of food supply for many tribes of plains Indians. Most of these tribes made regular trips into this hunting paradise for their annual needs. Although all tribes claimed it as their own, none could solidify its claim. The result was that many fierce battles were fought along its banks between tribes — long before, as well as after, the white man appeared on the river.

The river was known by some of the plains Indians as Chetolah, by others as Okesee-Sebo. The early French and English explorers designated it the River of the Padoucas, but eventually it became known as the Smoky Hill. Some historians say it got this name because of the hazy or smoky appearance of its dark shale hills. George Bird Grinnell maintained that the cottonwood grove known as Big Timbers was the origin of the name.

This was a very large grove of immense cottonwood trees on the Smoky Hill in an almost treeless sea of grass very close to what is now the Colorado-Kansas state line. It was a favorite camping place of the Indians. Over a thousand of them under Black Kettle camped here early in 1864, and it was the place of refuge for the same Black Kettle and other survivors of the Chivington Massacre on Sand Creek in November of that year.

The trees were very tall and dense with no underbrush and could be seen for a great distance, looking much like a cloud of smoke. Capt. John C. Fremont took particular note of this outstanding landmark in 1844 when he searched out the river's source and followed its flow to its junction with the Republican River. To Lieutenant Fitch's party, surveying the route for the Butterfield Overland Despatch in 1865, this grove appeared on the horizon like a smoky hill or large blue mound. The station built there was officially called Blue Mound by that company, even though it was generally spoken of as Big Timbers.

For much of its course in western Kansas the Smoky Hill River is just a small stream flowing in a wide sandy bed, with most of its flow under the surface. In floodtime, however, it carries an enormous amount of water. Toward central Kansas, the visible flow of water becomes much greater. Before the white man came, the river carried much more water because the rainfall, running off the unbroken prairies, swelled the stream instead of

Courtesy the Kansas State Historical Society, Topeka *From Gardner Collection*

Mushroom Rock on Alum Creek

Photo by Leslie Linville

Monument Rock

soaking into cultivated fields as it does now.

Immense herds of buffalo once roamed the prairies on either side of the Smoky Hill. It is said that some herds, twenty to thirty miles across, contained hundreds of thousands. After a hot day a herd like that could drink an astonishing amount of water. The year 1868 was especially dry. Many small streams dried up, limiting the buffalo's water supply to the larger streams. After a very hot day one of these herds, estimated at more than twenty miles wide, plunged into the Smoky Hill River where it was quite wide in McPherson County. As each wave of animals drank its fill, another wave of thirsty animals crowded in, pushing the first one out on the opposite bank. They actually drank the river dry before the last of the herd had satisfied itself.[1]

The scenery along the Smoky Hill is quite spectacular in places, even today. Its hazy gray shale hills, especially in Ellis and Trego counties, remind the traveler of small mountains. It was in these hills that the Smoky Hill gold craze centered, about the beginning of the twentieth century.

In Ellsworth County there are the odd Mushroom Rock and Fremont's Table. A large deposit of exceptionally pure volcanic lava is in Trego County, as well as the Cedar Bluffs on which an isolated heavy stand of cedars grows. In Gove County there is the majestic Castle Rock, and about thirty miles farther west are the castlelike Monuments, guarded by the protective Chief Smoky, the carved-by-nature Sphinx of the Prairies. Farther west, in Logan County, are found some interesting chalk beds, in which many of the world's finest specimens of prehistoric sea monsters have been found

These landmarks registered the progress

Photo by Leslie Linville

Chief Smoky, Monument Rock

of the early pioneer as he drove his freight wagon or prairie schooner along the Smoky Hill toward his golden dream to the west. Today they can take the modern traveler backward into the exciting, dramatic history of the river's past.

NOTES

1. *Greenley County Republican* (Tribune, Kans.) July, 1932.

THE TRAIL

AT THE BEGINNING the trail was merely a means of reaching an end, an unpleasant, dangerous but necessary journey through what was called the Great American Desert. Beyond beckoned the goldfields of the mountains or trade with the far-off cities of New Mexico or free land and a new home for the settlers. Many travelers spoke disparagingly of this section of the journey. As early as 1806 Lt. Zebulon Pike, marching from St. Louis through the length of Kansas to the Rocky Mountains on his way to Santa Fe, recorded this observation: "As the vast plains are incapable of cultivation, they will prove of great benefit to the United States, not only in restricting its population to certain limits and thus keeping the Union intact, but also providing a barrior against invasion from that quarter." Sixty years later another traveler insisted that "the great plains could never be other than the vast wilderness they are."

However, Pike himself had begun the chain of events that eventually belied his words. In writing of Santa Fe he had awakened and activated the American's appetite for lucrative trading and bartering, and that impassable and protective "barrier" was soon pierced by an open trail. As other parts of the West became focal points for the traveler (places like California, Utah, Oregon, and Colorado) many trails came into being. The Smoky Hill Trail, however, was the shortest and most direct route from the Missouri River through this wilderness.

Atchison, the eastern end of the Smoky Hill Trail, though farther north than Kansas City, was about twelve miles farther west and added little to the travel time of the westward-bound emigrant. Atchison had a natural wharf for boats, which not only came up the Missouri from St. Louis but also down from the north with freight that had been brought from the east by the only northern railroad to reach the river at Council Bluffs. The Smoky Hill route to Denver laid out by David A. Butterfield, as 116 miles shorter than any other and traversed a country whose terrain offered an excellent roadbed, with almost no sand and with watering places every few miles.

When settlement of the country began, it naturally appeared along the trail. Travelers, for one reason or another, stopped and settled down, often forming the nucleus for a town. Before the settlements, however, the entire plains country was a battleground, with an implacable enemy who gave no quarter and fought by none of the recognized rules of civilized warfare.

The Smoky Hill Trail, which ran the full length of Smoky Hill Valley and beyond, was considered the most dangerous crossing of the plains. Not a mile of that two-hundred-odd-mile section of the trail that crossed western Kansas escaped repeated conflicts with the hostiles. It took a type of determination and perseverance that we seldom see today to change that country into the "breadbasket of the world."

I.

TRAILS OF THE EXPLORERS

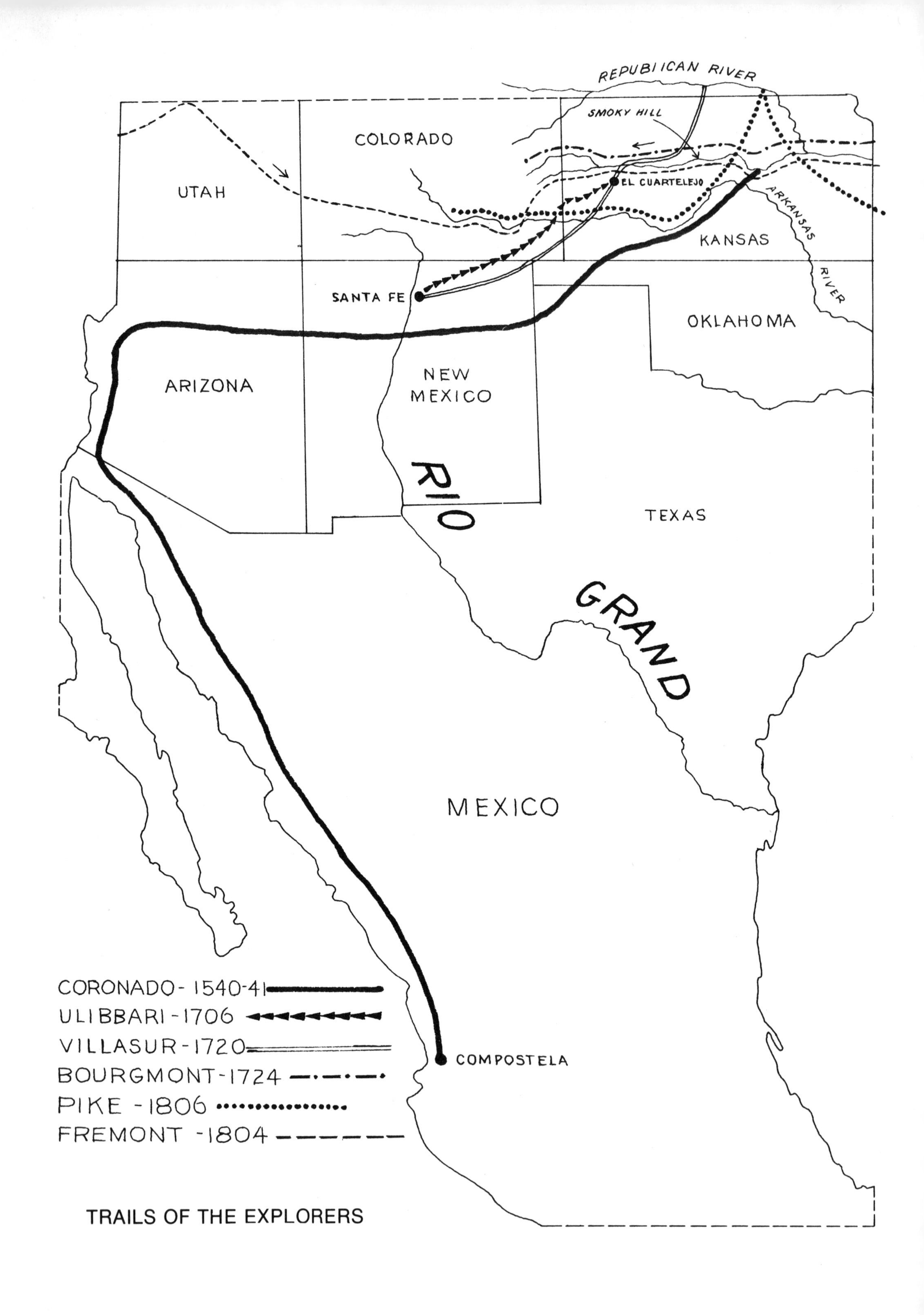

TRAILS OF THE EXPLORERS

CHAPTER 1

FROM CORONADO TO FREMONT

NO ONE IS QUITE SURE who was the first white man to set eyes on the valley of the Smoky Hill River. Francisco Vasquez de Coronado is generally given credit for being the first white explorer to visit the Smoky Hill. He was sent on his venture to find the fabulously rich seven cities of Cibola by Viceroy Mendoza, after Mendoza had heard the report of the first white man to cross the continent from east to west, Alvar Nunez Cabeza de Vaca.[1]

Coronado had come to New Spain with Mendoza in 1535 when he was twenty-five years old. Mendoza had appointed him governor of the province of Nueva Galicia.

Coronado agreed to make the journey to the seven cities of Cibola and began his expedition from Compostela in the present Mexican state of Nayarit near the West Coast in February of 1540.

He traveled northwest across the present state of Sonora until he reached the Colorado River. Turing east past the Grand Canyon, he eventually came to a desert that sapped the strength of his command and caused many men to desert. Then they met the first of the messengers from what Coronado was sure was one of the cities of Cibola.

Suspecting their friendship to be a blind for an ambush, Coronado watched for the trap and avoided it. Angry at their trickery he advanced, determined to take the city, more for the food he knew would be there than for the gold he hoped to find.

The pueblo was not easily taken, however. Twice Coronado himself was felled by rocks thrown from the top of the pueblo, but he got up each time to lead his men eventually to victory.[2]

They found food but no gold, just a few bits of impure turquoise. Coronado did not give up. The gold might be in one of the other cities of Cibola. It would take historians to establish the fact that Cibola was merely the land of the Zuni Indians.

Crossing the Rio Grande, Coronado went into winter quarters in the fall of 1540. It was while he was here that he met a plains Indian called the Turk[3] and heard from him of the rich cities of Quivira to the north and east. He hired the Turk to guide him there.

In the spring they moved out, crossing what are now the panhandles of Texas and Oklahoma, and came into Kansas, traveling over forty days to reach the Arkansas River. Somewhere along the river or just to the north of it, they reached the first of the cities of Quivira.

It was another disappointment. No gold. One of Coronado's men described the village as huts made of straw — probably grass and reeds from the river. The people raised corn and beans and melons. He called them a brutish people.[4]

While here, Coronado heard of another kingdom to the northwest, presumably ruled by a white man. Coronado made arrangements to meet this man. From the scanty reports of this meeting it is thought to have taken place on the banks of the Smoky Hill River.[5] Relics of Coronado's expedition found by archeologists in recent years confirm the fact that Coronado did reach central Kansas, probably as far north as the Smoky Hill.

With the discouraging report brought back to new Spain by Coronado, the interest of the Spaniards in the vast lands to the northeast dwindled. It wasn't until 1706 that another Spaniard got far enough north to reach the Smoky Hill Valley. Juan de Ulibarri was sent from Santa Fe to bring back a band of Picuries who had fled from New Mexico to escape Spanish rule. Ulibarri found the Picuries at El Cuartelejo. In his wandering, trying to find El Cuartelejo, Ulibarri may have gotten as far north as the Smoky Hill River.

There is sharp controversy among historians as to the exact location of El Cuartelejo. Some, using the league scale of the Spanish who traveled to the place, have located it in the vicinity of southern Lincoln County or western Kiowa County in Colorado.[6] Others, using the same scale, have located it in Scott County, Kansas.[7] Excavations at the latter site are now included in a state park. The Colorado site has never been pinpointed.

With war in Europe between Spain and the combined forces of England and France threatening to spill over into the New World, Viceroy Valero of New Spain ordered Governor Valverde at Santa Fe to take some soldiers to El Cuartelejo in January 1720 to repel any French advance. Once a defense was established there, Valverde was to advance to the northwest in search of the French.[8]

Valverde placed this task in the hands of his lieutenant general, Don Pedro de Villasur. Villasur left Santa Fe in June, crossed the Arkansas River on rafts, and eventually came to El Cuartelejo.[9]

Finding no French near El Cuartelejo, Villasur moved on toward the Rio Jesus Maria, the Platte River. Shortly after leaving El Cuartelejo, the soldiers crossed the Smoky Hill River, probably traveling for some time along its northern banks to the Pawnee Trail, which they followed to the Platte River.[10] While others since Coronado may have viewed segments of the Smoky Hill, it seems likely that Villasur got the first good look at quite a stretch of the valley.

On the Platte, Villasur met with disaster. He mistook a big camp of Indians for friendlies and was ambushed. They proved to be Pawnees, allies of the French.[11] Only a few of Villasur's men escaped. They spent months nursing their wounds and making their way back to El Cuartelejo — and from there to Santa Fe to report to Governor Valverde.

In 1724 Etienne Veniard de Bourgmont, an officer in the French army, led an expedition from the Missouri River all the way to the headwaters of the Smoky Hill, in what is now eastern Colorado. He was probably the first white man to explore the entire length of the river.[12] Bourgmont loved the country. Writing about it later he called it "the most beautiful land in the world."

French traders moved up and down the Smoky Hill River in the years that followed, but it wasn't until after the

Courtesy the Kansas State Historical Society, Topeka

Scott County — El Cuartelejo

Louisiana Purchase that American adventurers took their turn at exploring the valley.

The first was Zebulon Montgomery Pike. He was sent in 1806 by Gen. James Wilkinson to explore the headwaters of the rivers to the west. There seems little doubt that Lieutenant Pike was on or near the Smoky Hill River on this exploration trip. He sighted the peak that was given his name.

He was arrested by the Spanish for encroachment on their territory and was taken to Santa Fe but soon released. He was killed by an exploding powder magazine at York, Canada, during the War of 1812; he was only thirty-three years old.

It was left to the Great Pathfinder to be the first to explore the length of the Smoky Hill River in the name of the United States. John Charles Fremont became a second lieutenant when he was twenty-five and married Jessie Benton in 1841 when he was twenty-eight. This marriage had a great deal to do with his career, since she was the daughter of U.S. Senator Thomas Hart Benton. Senator Benton didn't approve of the marriage at first but soon became an ardent supporter of Fremont. His influence helped secure governmental approval and backing for some of Fremont's explorations.

In 1842, with Kit Carson as guide, Fremont officially mapped the route to Oregon by way of South Pass. His report

Courtesy the Kansas State Historical Society, Topeka

Zebulan Pike

Courtesy the Kansas State Historical Society, Topeka

John C. Fremont

upon his return was widely received. Fremont's wife helped him write it. This report was instrumental in securing his next assignment — again to Oregon, then through California, and back the southern way to explore the rivers of Kansas.

All of Fremont's exploring expeditions were outfitted at, started out from, and returned to, the mouth of the Kaw River, now called the Kansas. The Kansas River is actually a short river; the name applies to the stream formed by the confluence of the Republican and the Smoky Hill rivers at Junction City, Kansas. It flows into the Missouri River at Kansas City.

The government "permitted" the first expedition, although readily taking the credit for its accomplishments. The second expedition was actually revoked after being approved by the War Department because Fremont proposed to take along a small mountain howitzer. His wife, Jessie, however, received the message after Fremont was with his company preparing to leave. Instead of forwarding the message to her husband she sent word to him to leave immediately.[13] He knew nothing of the order until he returned from his trip fifteen months later.

This expedition took Fremont and his men to Fort Vancouver and then to the Great Basin, of which the Great Salt Lake is the center. This was followed by a forty-day struggle through winter snows to reach the Sacramento Valley. Starved and nearly frozen, they spent the rest of the winter there and then headed east. By the first of July they were at Bent's Fort on the Arkansas River in eastern Colorado. From there Fremont's goal was to explore the Smoky Hill River.

Fremont made a detailed report of his travels and accompanied it with a good map of the area covered. From these, his course as he traveled east can be easily followed. His report states:

> On the 5th of July we resumed our journey [from Bent's Fort] down the Arkansas and encamped about twenty miles below the fort. Agreeable to your instructions which required me to complete as far as practicable our examination of the Kansas River [Smoky Hill River], I left at this encampment the Arkansas River, taking a northeasterly direction across the elevated dividing grounds which separate that river from the waters of the Platte. On the 7th we crossed a large stream about 40 yards wide and one or two feet deep, flowing with a lively current on a sandy bed.[14] Beyond this stream we traveled over high and level prairies, halting at small ponds and holes of water.
>
> On the morning of the 8th, we encamped in a cottonwood grove on the banks of a sandy stream where there was water in holes sufficient for the camp. Here several hollows or dry creeks with sandy beds met together, forming the head of a stream which afterward proved to be the Smoky Hill fork of the Kansas River.

Fremont's map shows this camp to be in Colorado, about twenty miles west of the Kansas line. On July 9 he camped about eight miles east of the Colorado-Kansas line. On the tenth he was near the present town of Wallace; on the twelfth, somewhere near Russell Springs. On the thirteenth he camped somewhere east of Jerome near the mouth of Plum Creek; on the fourteenth, near the mouth of Indian Creek near Alanthus. At this camp his report states:

> We were encamped in a pleasant evening on a high level prairie, the stream [Smoky] being less than a hundred yards broad. During the night, we had a succession of thunder storms with heavy and continuous rain and toward morning the water suddenly burst over the banks, flooding the bottom and becoming a large river five or six hundred yards in breadth. The darkness of the night and the incessant rain had concealed from the guard the rise of the water and the river broke into the camp so suddenly that the baggage was instantly covered and all our perishable collection almost utterly ruined and the hard labor of many months destroyed in a moment.

On the sixteenth they camped near the mouth of Page Creek (now under Cedar Bluff Reservoir). They moved on the next day and his report continues:

> On the 17th, we discovered a large village of Indians encamped at the mouth of a handsomely

wooded stream on the right bank of the river. Readily inferring from the nature of the encampment that they were Pawnee Indians and confidently expecting good treatment from a people who received an annuity from the Government, we proceeded directly to the village where we found assembled nearly all the Pawnee tribes, who were returning from crossing of the Arkansas where they had met the Kiowa and Comanche Indians. We were received by them with unfriendly rudeness and characteristic insolence which they never fail to display whenever they find an occasion for doing so with impunity. The little that remained of our goods was distributed among them but proved entirely insufficient to satisfy their greedy rapacity; and after some delay and considerable difficulty we succeeded in extricating ourselves from the village and encamped on the river about fifteen miles below.

From the tone of Fremont's report it seems obvious he did not realize the danger that threatened him and his party of twenty-six men. It was two months before the gravity of the situation came to light, and then it was uncovered by accident. Major Wharton was visiting several Pawnee villages along the Platte and Loup Rivers in what in now Nebraska and found some Indians who had been at the confrontation with Fremont on the Smoky Hill. These Indians told Wharton that all the Pawnee tribes on the Smoky Hill had agreed to attack Fremont and his men except the Loups. Two years earlier Fremont had befriended these Loups, and they held out for letting him go in peace. Had it not been for these few Loups there on the Smoky Hill River, Fremont and his men would have been massacred.

Even considering his narrow escapes from starvation, freezing, and many forms of violent death in his travels over the western half of the United States, it is probable that John Charles Fremont had never come closer to death than he did that July day on the Smoky Hill River.

NOTES

1. C. W. Ceram, *The First American: A Story of North American Archeology* (New York: Harcourt Brace Jovanovich, 1971), p. 35.
2. Ibid., pp. 50–51.
3. For more about the Turk, consult the *Encyclopedia Americana*, vol, 23, p. 100.
4. Alfred Barnaby Thomas, *After Coronado* (Norman: Univ. of Oklahoma Press, 1935), pp. 5–6.
5. Floyd Benjamin Streeter, *The Kaw* (New York: Farrar & Rinehart, 1941), p. 26.
6. Thomas, *After Coronado*, p. 270.
7. *Nebraska History*, vol. 7, no. 3, July-September 1924, pp. 84–85.
8. Thomas, *After Coronado*, p. 34.
9. Ibid., p. 37.
10. *Nebraska History*, vol. 7, no. 3, July-September 1924, p. 82. M. A. Shine describes the route he thinks Villasur took from Santa Fe to the Platte River and gives his reasons for assuming this. It disagrees completely with A. B. Thomas's route, although each cites the same distance charts to prove his conviction. It all hinges on the location of El Cuartelejo. If Thomas is correct in stating that El Cuartelejo is in either Lincoln or Kiowa County, Colorado, then Villasur's course from El Cuartelejo to the Platte would be through eastern Colorado, and the expedition would barely have touched the headwaters of the Smoky Hill. But if Shine is correct (and he has corroboration from such historians as Professor H. T. Martin and Addison E. Sheldon — see *Nebraska History*, vol. 6, no. 1, January-March 1923) then El Cuartelejo is in Scott County, Kansas, and Villasur's route from there would have taken him along the Smoky Hill River to the Pawnee Trail and then north to the Platte. The ruins in the Scott County State Park definitely point to Pueblo Indians, and the Kansas State Historical Society has identified them as the ruins of El Cuartelejo.
11. Thomas, *After Coronado*, p. 38; *Nebraska History*, vol. 6, no. 1, January-March 1923, pp. 1–32; *Nebraska History*, vol. 7, no. 3, July-September 1924, pp. 66-96.
12. Streeter, *The Kaw*, p. 27.
13. For more on this subject see *Encyclopedia Americana*, vol. 12, p. 59.
14. The map shows this stream to be the Big Sandy.

II.

TRAILS OF THE GOLD SEEKERS

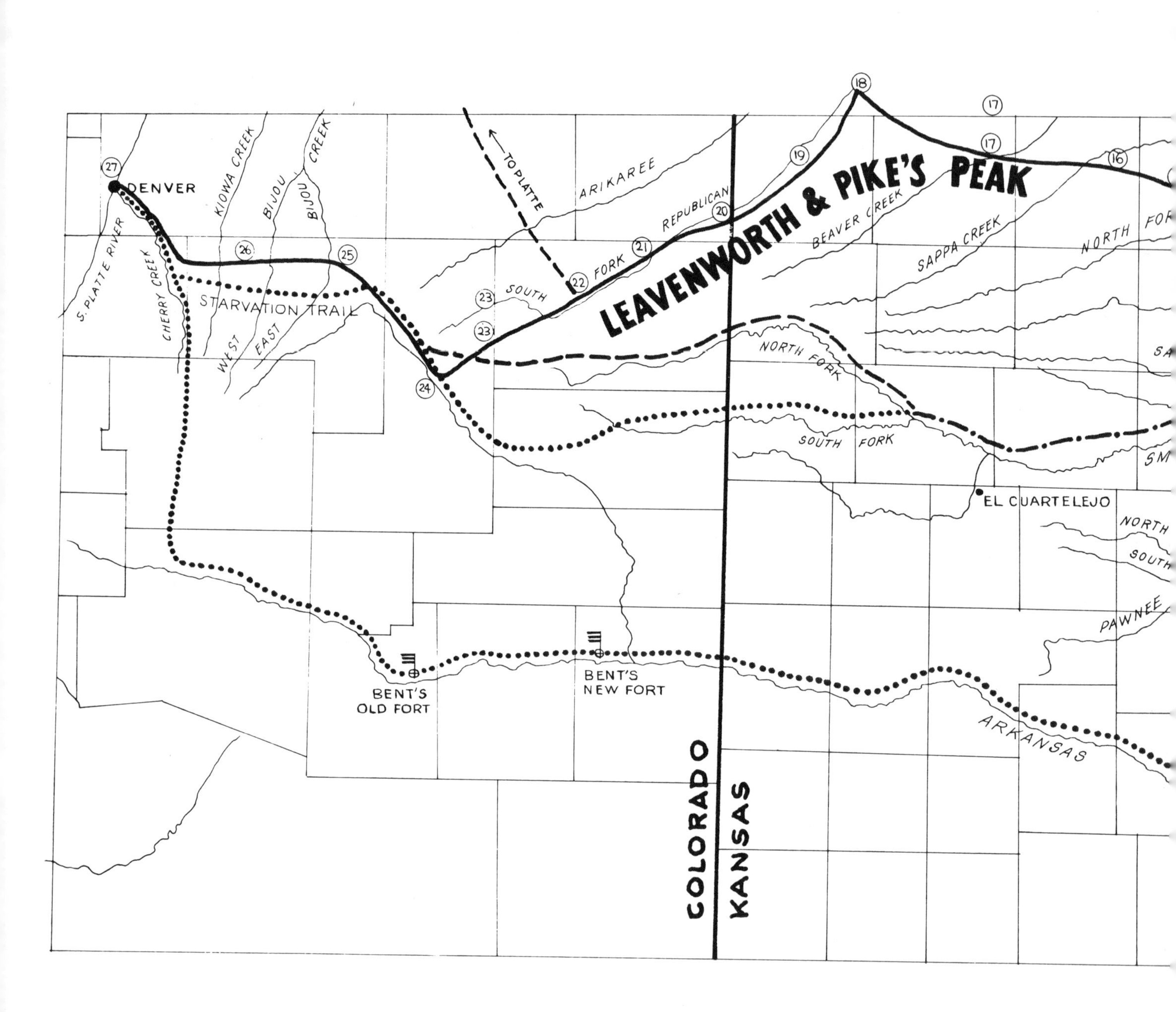

LEAVENWORTH & PIKE'S PEAK
DENVER
S. PLATTE RIVER
CHERRY CREEK
KIOWA CREEK
BIJOU
BIJOU
CREEK
WEST
EAST
STARVATION TRAIL
TO PLATTE
ARIKAREE
REPUBLICAN
SOUTH
FORK
BEAVER CREEK
SAPPA CREEK
NORTH FORK
SOUTH FORK
EL CUARTELEJO
NORTH
SOUTH
PAWNEE
BENT'S OLD FORT
BENT'S NEW FORT
ARKANSAS
COLORADO
KANSAS
16
17
17
18
19
20
21
22
23
23
24
25
26
27

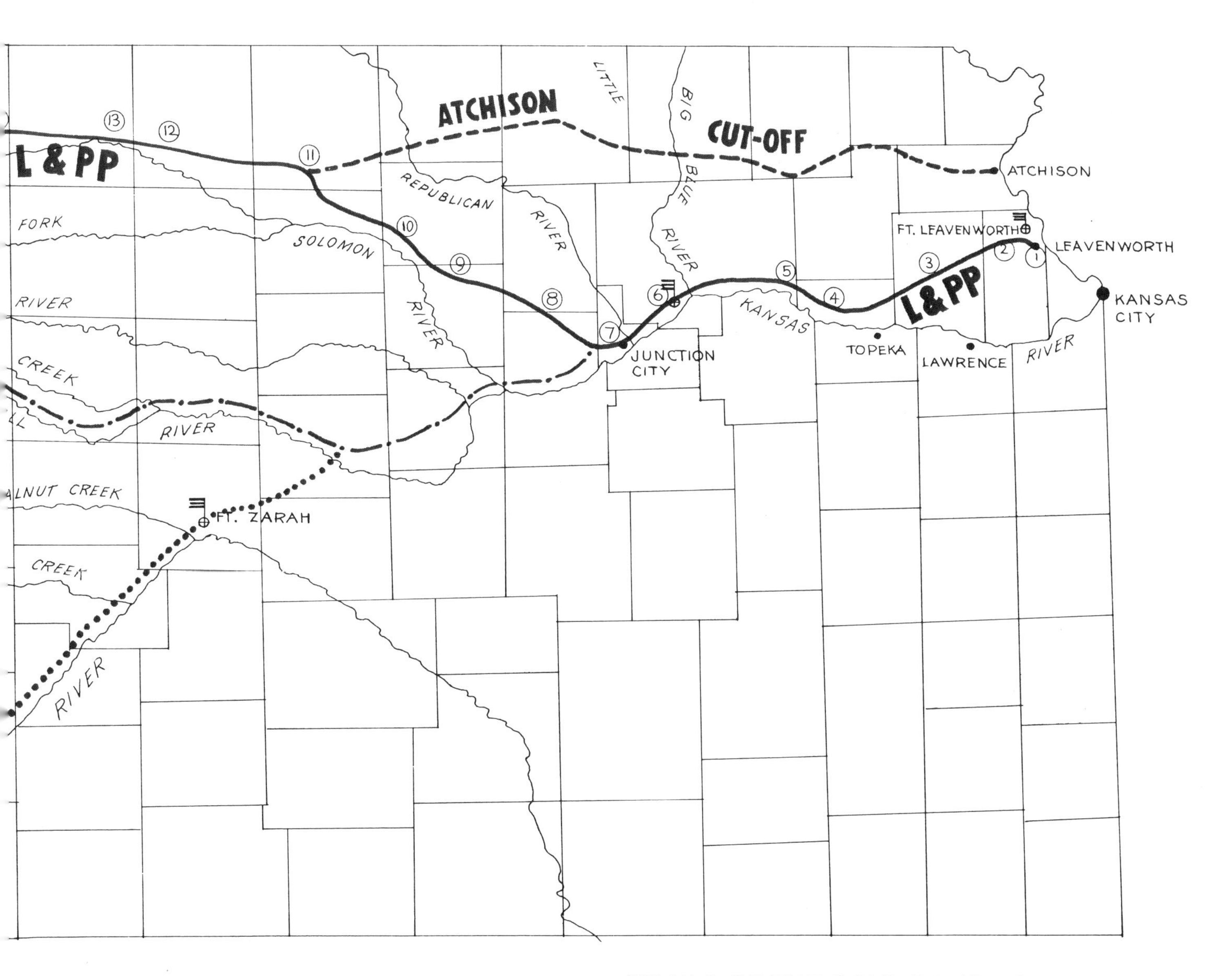

TRAILS OF THE GOLD SEEKERS

C H A P T E R 2

SURVEYING THE L&PP

AMERICA WAS SETTLED by pioneers who marched resolutely toward the virgin lands to the west, seeking a free life and a fortune. Pike and Fremont followed. Then gold was discovered in California, and from that moment nothing could stem the westward tide.

In the early 1850s Cherokee Indians had brought stories back to Georgia of gold along Cherry Creek in the Rocky Mountains, but not many took them seriously. One man, W. Green Russell, did. But if was not until the early spring of 1858 that he was able to get some other men interested enough to make an expedition to the mountains to see for themselves.

Russell had prospected for gold in Georgia and also in California when he followed the rush there in 1849. His group of prospectors didn't find a great deal at Cherry Creek. Most of the group went back East. Some stayed with Russell, and they found several hundred dollars worth of flour gold in the South Platte River. A trader named Cantrell took some of the gold-bearing soil from Russell's camp back to Westport, where it was checked by an experienced miner. He found gold in it, and the news spread like wildfire.[1]

The discovery of gold in the Rocky Mountains of western Kansas Territory presented a problem for the gold seeker from eastern Kansas who wanted to get to the fields as quickly as possible. There were already two established routes to the mountains, but both took the traveler far out of his way to Cherry Creek.

A verse published by the *Kansas Tribune* of Topeka spurred on the men who were impatient to get rich as quickly as possible.

A Call to the Mines
by Floy

Hurra for Pike's Peak! Hurra for Pike's Peak!
A rich El Dorado has lately been found,
Far, far to the westward, and near Cherry Creek;
Where gold in abundance is scattered around.
Ah! Hurra for pike's peak!

Hurra for Pike's Peak! Hurra for Peak's Peak!
There's gold in the mountain, there's gold in the vale,
There's plenty for all who are willing to seek —
Believe me; believe me — 'tis no idle tale
Come, hurra for Pike's Peak![2]

The fact that the gold was not exactly in the shadow of Pike's Peak had little significance to the man in eastern Kansas with his face set eagerly to the west. As people in the midsection of the country later thought of Los Angeles, San Francisco, and Portland as neighboring cities on the West Coast, so people in the mid-nineteenth century thought of Pike's Peak as representing all the mountain range of Colorado. The goldfields of Cherry Creek and directly to the west became known as the gold fields of Pike's Peak, although the peak was seventy miles to the south.

One established road to the area was up the Oregon Trail to Jules' trading post on the South Platte River at the Upper

California Crossing, leaving the Oregon Trail there and following the South Platte to the goldfields on Cherry Creek where that creek ran into the South Platte. The aggravating thing about this trail was that it was over a hundred miles out of the way, taking the traveler far to the north before bringing him back.

The other established trail was almost as far out of the way to the south. Here the traveler went southwest on the Santa Fe Trail, following the Arkansas River to the west finally leaving it and turning north past Pike's Peak to Cherry Creek.

The immediate cry was for a direct route to the goldfields. The Smoky Hill River pointed almost directly from the new City of Kansas, growing up near Westport Landing, to the shack towns of Auraria City and Denver City on the banks of Cherry Creek. Before any planning was done, campsites located, or wood and water found, men began pouring up the Smoky Hill, eyes ablaze with dreams of great riches at the end of the trail.

Others, more practical but still in a tremendous hurry, decided on a route to the north of the Smoky Hill, where they felt certain there would be wood and water and plenty of game. One of the dreamers who had his eyes on this route was William H. Russell, of the freighting firm of Russell, Majors, and Waddell. Russell was the plunger of the three partners, and he wanted to get into the business of moving the great stream of men and supplies that would be going west. His partners, however, were not so enthusiastic about the idea.

The three partners were so different that it was obvious business rather than personalities had brought them together. William Waddell was a businessman, as was Russell, but a conservative one. Alexander Majors was a freighter. He had taken freight trains to Santa Fe and to lonely army posts on the plains and had shown a profit for his efforts each time.

Russell, Majors, and Waddell are well remembered for their freight lines, and many think of them all as freighters, but neither Russell nor Waddell ever drove a freight wagon across the plains.

Both Waddell and Majors saw the impracticality of a stage and freight line directly through Kansas to Denver. There

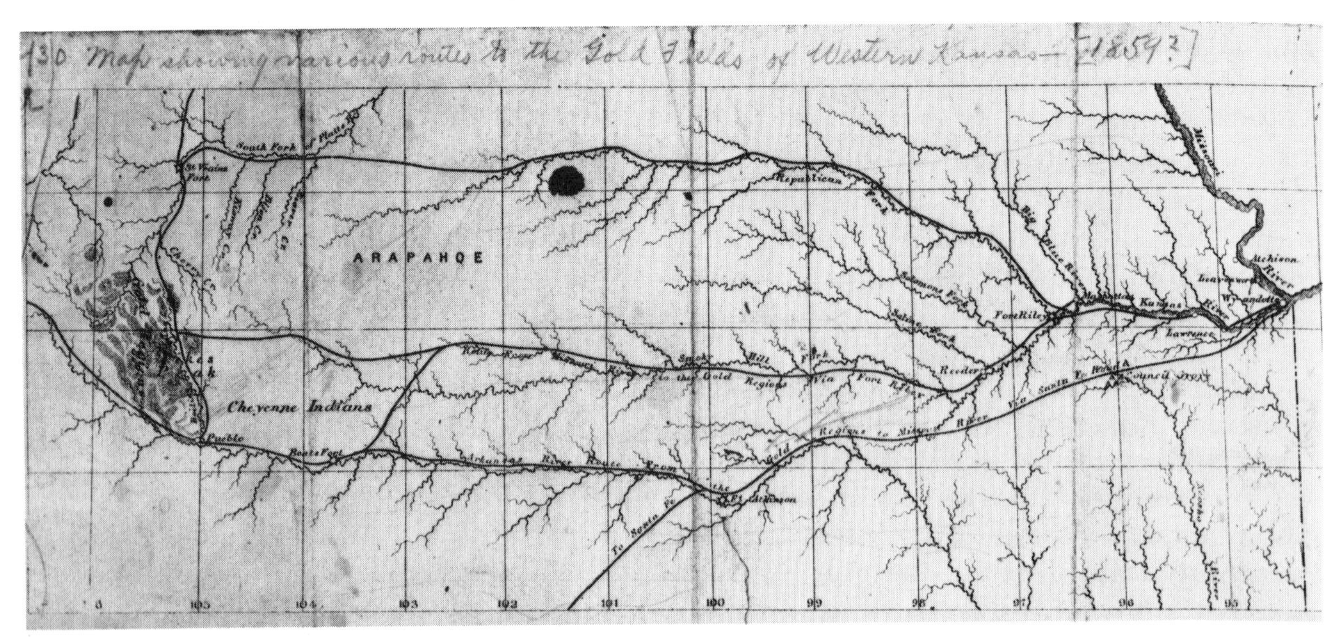

Courtesy the Kansas State Historical Society, Topeka

Map showing various routes to the goldfields of western Kansas about 1859

Courtesy the Kansas State Historical Society, Topeka

William B. Wadell copied from *Empire on Wheels* by Settle and Settle.

Courtesy the Kansas State Historical Society, Topeka

Alexander Majors copied from *Empire on Wheels* by Settle and Settle.

had not yet been enough exploration made west of the Missouri. The little that had been done suggested that the land was an arid wasteland, unfit for habitation and incapable of supporting the traveler.

William Hepburn Russell was forty-six when he got the idea of a stage and freight line directly from eastern Kansas to the goldfields. He was born on January 31, 1812, in Burlington, Vermont.[3] His father fought in the War of 1812 and died while in service, so William was brought up by his mother and his stepfather, Oliver Bangs.

In 1828 the family moved from Vermont to northwestern Missouri, where William, at sixteen, immediately got a job at a store in Liberty. He soon left that job for one with the famous Aull Brothers, who had a store in Liberty. Within two years he had been promoted to Lexington, Missouri, where he was second in command to James Aull in the big store there. One year later, when he was nineteen, he became manager of the store.[4]

On June 9, 1835, when he was twenty-three years old, he married Harriet Elliott Warder, the daughter of a self-styled preacher, the Reverend John Warder. Warder answered to no one on what he preached. He built his own church on his own land and there held sway. But he was well thought of in the community, and Russell's marriage to his daughter assured Russell of general acceptance and recognition.[5]

Russell's rise in the business world was phenomenal. He took his first step into the freighting business in 1847 in partnership with James Bullard, sending a wagon train of goods to Santa Fe.[6]

Courtesy the Kansas State Historical Society, Topeka

William H. Russell

In 1850 Russell formed a partnership with James Brown and John S. Jones and began freighting to Santa Fe.[7] This apparently was the start of Russell's partnership with John Jones that was to culminate in the Leavenworth and Pike's Peak Express Company of 1858 and 1859.

Russell signed a partnership agreement with Majors and Waddell on December 28, 1854, forming one of the greatest freighting firms the West was to know. [8] The firm went into business on January 1, 1855. The partners based their headquarters in the budding town of Leavenworth, Kansas, and opened several businesses there, including a store, warehouse, blacksmith and wagon shop, a packing plant, a sawmill on Shawnee Creek, and a lumberyard. They also built a home office for the company and corrals for their oxen. The packing plant was meant primarily to provide meat for their wagon trains running out of Leavenworth.

Fortune smiled on the partners of the new freighting firm. They showed a good profit in 1855 and 1856. In 1857 they lost fourteen trains in a disastrous attempt to supply General Johnston's army in Utah. Russell's claim against the government for losses resulting from this disaster totaled almost a half million dollars.[9]

The government never reimbursed the firm for its losses in Utah. This was the first blow that eventually led to the downfall of the company in 1860 and 1861.[10]

Russell's reaction to any backset was to seek another venture which he was certain would bring in more money than the company had lost in the previous adventure. He saw golden glory and enormous profits in the trail that would take passengers and freight directly to the goldfields from the center of population in eastern Kansas. His partners, however, didn't see the same golden rainbow and they withdrew.

Russell persisted, and finally the partners granted him enough money to set up his stage and freight line to Denver City. However, it was on a ninety-day basis. That short time limit didn't deter Russell. He was sure the money would be rolling in before then.

John S. Jones, Russell's partner in this venture, was a veteran freighter on the plains with ten years of experience behind him. He had worked as a subcontractor for Russell, Majors, and Waddell ever since the company had begun operation in 1855.[11]

Newspapers leaped on the story of the new stage and freight line to be established by such veterans of the business as Russell and Jones. The press played it up, creating additional excitement among the people in eastern Kansas who wanted to reap some of the golden harvest of this great boom. Those who did not propose to go to the goldfields figured to sell supplies to the travelers who did go. A stage line from their city would mean a great explosion of business.

It was not clearly stated where the stage line would originate, and this created vicious competition for the site. The town that got the eastern terminal of the stage line would soon be a city that could look down on its struggling neighbors like a mountain peak looking down on the valley below.

Kansas City was in favor of the Jones and Russell line but insisted that the logical and sensible route would be on the Santa Fe Trail, turning northwest to Denver where the main trail turned southwest to Santa Fe. The towns along the Missouri to the north of Kansas City favored the Oregon Trail and up the South Platte to Denver City.

It was the towns in the middle that were fighting for the shortcut. Atchison, St. Joseph, and Leavenworth would all gain considerably if the new road took the direct route to the goldfields. They screamed through their newspapers about the time and miles that would be saved if the road went directly west. Leavenworth in particular put forth its strongest arguments.

"It's the only direct route to the gold mines, whereon a road can be established with wood and water, throughout the whole distance. The valley of the Smoky Hill Fork affords these facilities. It heads within thirty miles[12] of Pike's Peak, and flows nearly due east, to its confluence with the Kansas River, and the line produced would touch our city. This gives our route an advantage of 120 miles over all others."[13]

Another Leavenworth newspaper shouted back at cities that played down Leavenworth's claim of being the most advantageous jumping-off place: "It has been demonstrated a thousand times that the route to the gold mines from our city is the shortest, best supplied with wood, water and grass, and most agreeable to travel. The road is direct and even camping grounds are scattered at intervals of from five to twenty miles. The streams are all bridged and supplies at hand."[14]

By early March of 1859 Jones and Russell had settled on Leavenworth as the starting point for their road to the goldfields. They had also decided on a road along the divide between the Smoky Hill River and the Republican River. One of the Leavenworth papers, the *Herald*, was ecstatic about the choice of Leavenworth for the jumping-off place and also about the future of the enterprise.

In late March the *Herald* headlined the activities of Jones and Russell, saying that John S. Jones was in town and had hired a hundred men the first day to work for the stage line. It stated that he had already sent seven men, under the command of Col. William J. Preston, to survey the road and mark it. Twenty-seven stations were to be established, twenty-five miles apart, and six men would be stationed at each one. Four of them would be drivers and two would be permanent custodians of the station. Five wagons would be started immediately, hauling forage for the livestock. As soon as the grass was good enough, twenty-five oxteams would start out with provisions for the stations.[15]

Colonel Preston[16] and his party of seven men left Leavenworth on March 15. Their plans were for the entire company to stay together until they reached the halfway mark, where two of the men would turn back to Leavenworth to guide the first wagons over the trail they had marked. The timetable called for the rest of the crew to continue the survey to Denver City then come back over the trail and meet the wagons at the halfway mark and guide them on to the goldfields. This would guarantee the fastest possible beginning of practical use of the trail.

Among the men with Colonel Preston was C. F. Smith. He became a very important member of the party because he kept a daily journal of their work and location of the stations. His report gives a day-by-day account of the trip, the kind of weather they encountered, the topography of the country, and the areas where they decided the route would not be good.

They started out with a wagon and had no trouble with it until after they left the established road at Junction City on March 19. Here they turned north and west, keeping to the divide between the Smoky Hill and the Republican. Five days later, on the twenty-fourth, they decided to abandon the wagon. They were not satisfied with their progress, seldom making more than twenty-five miles a day. It took too long to find crossings for the wagon on the small creeks and dry washes.

They made packs for their mules and proceeded by horseback, making much better time. Smith still reported that the road would be an easy one to travel, even though their own wagon had been a source of frustration.

On March 27 they sent two of their men back to guide the first express trains out on the road to set up stations and equip them. The next day they were hit by a six-inch snowstorm that impeded their progress and made traveling miserable. They saw signs of Indians that day, which didn't improve their peace of mind.

They followed the South Fork of the Republican to its headwaters, then cut straight west. The course from here to the junction of the good road down Cherry Creek to the South Platte was not one they could recommend. There was a scarcity of both wood and water. Coming back from Denver they tried a route farther to the north to a junction with the Republican River and were better satisfied with it.[17]

They had set out to find a course directly through to the goldfields that would be shorter and better watered than the Smoky Hill River just to the south. There was some question as to the availability of wood and water along the Smoky Hill course, but there could be little question as to the distance traveled over the two routes. The course laid out by Colonel Preston was many miles longer than a direct route along the Smoky Hill River would have been.

Courtesy the Kansas State Historical Society, Topeka

From Gardner Colletion #91

St. Mary's Mission, Kansas

The route had twenty-seven stations as originally planned, Station No. 1 being Leavenworth and Station No. 27 being Denver City. Station No. 2 was still in Leavenworth County near the little town of Easton on Stranger Creek. Station No. 3 was in Jefferson County on Delaware Creek, often called Grasshopper Creek then. Station No. 4 was in Shawnee County, west of Topeka near Silver Lake.

Station No. 5 was at St. Mary's in the southeastern corner of Pottawatomie County. Station No. 6 was at Manhattan in Riley County. Station No. 7 was at Junction City in Geary County. It was called Davis County then. Station No. 8 was near Chapman Creek in southwestern Clay County.

From here the road moved out into territory that was not yet divided into coun-

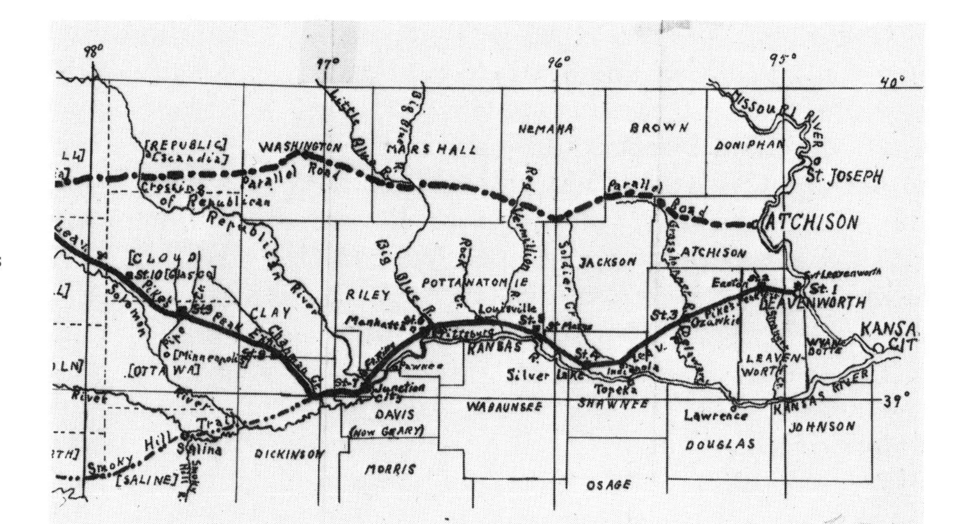

Courtesy the Kansas State
Historical Society, Topeka

Route of the Leavenworth & Pike's Peak Express, 1859 (1 of 3 parts).

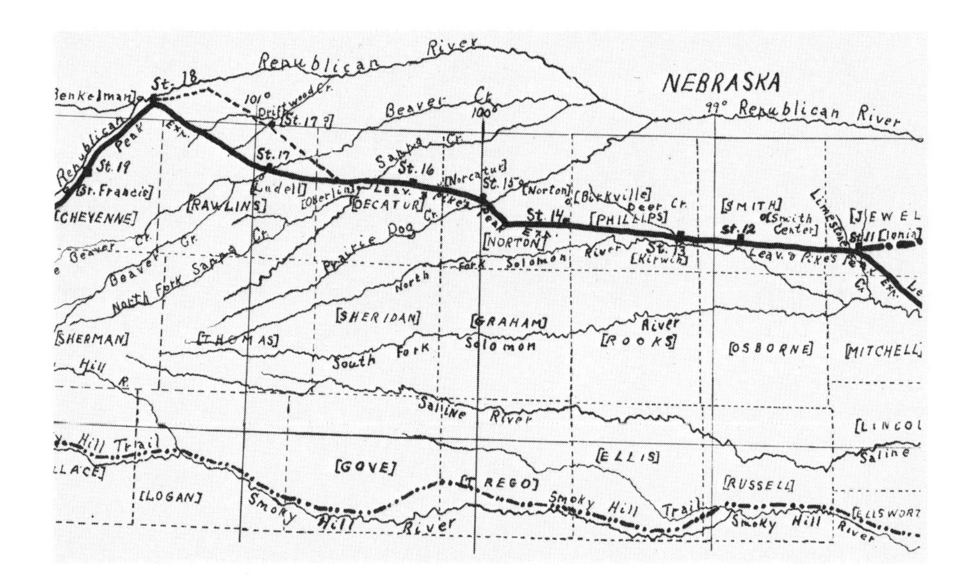

Courtesy the Kansas State
Historical Society, Topeka

Route of the Leavenworth & Pike's Peak Express, 1859 (2 of 3 parts).

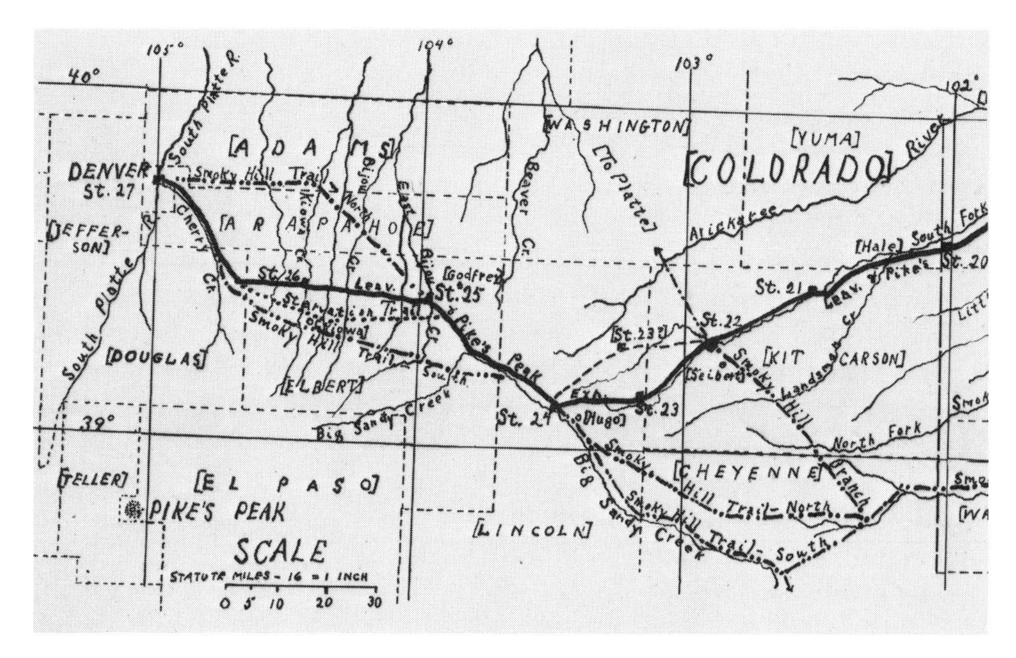

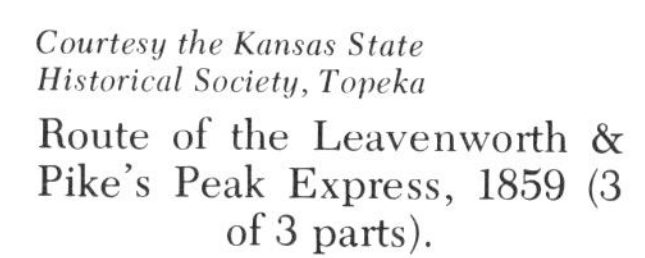

Courtesy the Kansas State
Historical Society, Topeka

Route of the Leavenworth & Pike's Peak Express, 1859 (3 of 3 parts).

ties. Station No. 9 was in what is now Ottawa County, north and a bit east of Minneapolis. No 10 was in southwestern Cloud County close to the Solomon River at present Glasco. Station No. 11 was in Limestone Creek in southwestern Jewell County, near Ionia. From here the road turned straight west, with Station No. 12 on the North Fork of the Solomon in Smith County, southwest of Smith Center.

Station No. 13 was only a short distance from No. 12, just across the line into Phillips County near present Kirwin. Station No. 14 was right on the county line between Phillips and Norton counties, some distance north of the Solomon River as the road began cutting across the various streams running into the Republican River. Station No. 15 was on Prairie Dog Creek in west central Norton County, southwest of Norton.

Station No. 16 was between Prairie Dog Creek and Sappa Creek in east central Decatur County. From there the road crossed Sappa Creek and reached Station No. 17 on Beaver Creek, a short distance northeast of Ludell. Some descriptions of the road suggest that the trail west of Station No. 16 may have turned more to the northwest and that Station No. 17 was actually on the Nebraska-Kansas border on Driftwood Creek.

Station No. 18 was on the Republican River near present Benkleman in Dundy County, Nebraska. This was the farthest north that the road went and was actually north of its goal, Denver City. It was this detour to the north that made it so much longer than the direct route up the Smoky Hill Valley.

The road southwest from Station No. 18 followed the South Fork of the Republican River, with Station No. 19 near the center of Cheyenne County Kansas, a little northeast of St. Francis. Station No. 20 was still on the south bank of the South Fork of the Republican, almost on the Colorado-Kansas state line.

Station No. 21 was still on the South Fork of the Republican in north central Kit Carson County, Colorado. Station No. 22 was farther southwest in west central Kit Carson County, a short distance northwest of Seibert. Here one branch of the Smoky Hill Trail crossed the Leavenworth and Pike's Peak Express Trail. This was one of the early mistakes of the Smoky Hill travelers. As they learned later, their best route after hitting the headwaters of the Smoky Hill River was to continue on either to the southwest or straight west until they hit Big Sandy Creek. The earliest travelers on the Smoky Hill Trail did not know this, and when water in the Smoky River disappeared completely they turned northwest toward Denver across a dry, desolate country.

Station No. 23 was southwest, on the now practically dry Republican River just across the county line into Lincoln County. Descriptions of the route and stations present a possibility that Station No. 23 might have been straight west of No. 22. If so, it would have been a dry upland station in Lincoln County south of Arickaree Creek. Whichever location is correct, the two route descriptions come together again at Station No. 24 on Big Sandy Creek in Lincoln County, northwest of Hugo.

At Station No. 24 the trail turned sharply to the northwest again, following Big Sandy Creek to the point where that stream comes in from the southwest, then leaving the Sandy and continuing northwest until it hit East Bijou Creek in northeastern Elbert County. There Station No. 25 was established. Station No. 26 was almost straight west, in northwestern Elbert County on Kiowa Creek. From there the trail ran straight until it hit Cherry Creek, then turned northwest down that creek until it reached Denver City, Station No. 27.

It wasn't long after Colonel Preston had returned with his complete survey of the route that Atchison decided on a shortcut from that city to the main trail.[18] It would be shorter, the backers insisted, and would save time. They didn't mention the great advantage such a shortcut would give to Atchison as a jumping-off place. The cutoff that was surveyed did shorten the distance to the goldfields by many miles, heading almost directly west from Atchison and connecting with Colonel Preston's trail at Station No. 11 in Jewell County.

But the Leavenworth and Pike's Peak Express Company had its base in Leavenworth, and the cutoff from Atchison remained just that, a cutoff. It never became a heavily traveled road.

NOTES

1. Calvin W. Gower, "Kansas Territory and the Pike's Peak Gold Rush: Governing the Gold Region," *Kansas Historical Quarterly* (Autumn 1966), pp. 292–3.
2. *Kansas Tribune* (Topeka), 20 January 1859.
3. Raymond W. Settle and Mary Lund Settle, "The Early Careers of William Bradford Waddell and William Hepburn Russell: Frontier Capitalists" *Kansas Historical Quarterly* (Winter 1960), p. 359.
4. Ibid., p. 362.
5. Mary Lund Settle and Raymond W. Settle, *Saddles and Spurs* (New York: Bonanza Books, 1960), p. 2.
6. Settle, "Careers of Waddell and Russell," p. 365.
7. Ibid., p. 367.
8. Ibid., p. 373.
9. Ibid., p. 378.
10. Ibid., p. 380.
11. George A. Root and Russell K. Hickman, "Pike's Peak Express Companies," *Kansas Historical Quarterly* (August 1944), p. 169.
12. This is optimistic advertising. It is nearer one hundred and thirty miles from the headwaters of the Smoky Hill to Pike's Peak.
13. *Leavenworth (Kan.) Herald*, 8 January 1859.
14. *Leavenworth Times*, 4 February 1859. This was highly exaggerated optimism. At this time the route wasn't properly surveyed or marked. The little streams running into the Smoky Hill were not bridged until about 1861. There were stretches of the Smoky Hill Trail as traced in 1859 where there was neither wood nor water.
15. *Leavenworth* (Kans.) *Herald*, 26 March 1859.
16. Root and Hickman,"Pike's Peak Express Companies," p. 173. William J. Preston was a U.S. deputy marshal commissioned a lieutenant colonel in the Kansas militia by Governor Shannon.
17. Ibid., C. F. Smith's daily journal is reprinted verbatim on pages 174 through 180.
18. Ibid., p. 181.

CHAPTER 3

THE L&PP IN KANSAS

THE HEADQUARTERS for the Leavenworth and Pike's Peak Express was located just outside the city, between the city and the fort. Horace Greeley got a look at it when he made his first trip over the L&PP to Denver in 1859 shortly after the line was inaugurated. He wrote the following description of it:

> Such acres of wagons! Such pyramids of extra axletrees! Such herds of oxen! Such regiments of drivers and other employees! No one who does not see can realize how vast a business this is, nor how immense are its outlays as well as its income. I presume this great firm has at this hour two millions of dollars invested in stock, mainly in oxen, mules and wagons.[1]

Russell, Majors, and Waddell had a long-standing rule against their drivers using profanity.[2] Although it was admitted by everyone, except to the face of one of their employers, that profanity and mudholes were almost impossible to separate, most drivers agreed to the rule when they hired on. Otherwise they usually failed to get the job.

It was reported that one driver applied for a job and was interviewed by one of the three partners, who asked him if he could drive oxen.

"Yep," he said. "I can drive oxen to hell and back."

"Well," the interviewer said. "I'm afraid I can't use you then. Our firm doesn't make that point."

Not everybody was satisfied with the route laid out by Colonel Preston. E. D. Boyd made the trip to Denver City late in May in 1859. His report of the trip, printed in *Freedom's Champion* at Atchison, was anything but complimentary concerning the route laid out. He gave a big boost to the Atchison cutoff, saying it was at least sixty-five miles closer to Atchison from the spot where the cutoff met the main road than it was to Leavenworth from the same point.

> Very poor judgment has been displayed, in my opinion, in the location of the stage road.[3] . . . It is a constant succession of ascents and descents and is very crooked. No time was taken to examine routes and consequently the best has not been selected. . . . Colonel Preston could not tell the latitude of any point on the road; did not know the magnetic variation, and said the road did not touch Nebraska. The men employed at Station 18 and 19 supposed that they were in Arapahoe County, Kansas, till I told them differently.[4]

Beverly D. Williams was assigned the task of setting up the stations along the route mapped out by Colonel Preston. It was a monumental task and had to be

Courtesy the Kansas State Historical Society, Topeka
From Gardner Collection #51

Fort Leavenworth, Kansas

done in a hurry, since thousands of emigrants were waiting very impatiently for the route to be established so they could get to the goldfields.

Williams started his first train in two sections, the first leaving Leavenworth on March 28 and the second half following four days later on April 1. The first section arrived at Junction City, Station No. 7 on the route, on April 12. When the second section caught up with it they repacked for the trip across the plains. It was a huge undertaking. The local paper reported: "Four hundred and fifty mules; one hundred and twenty men and women; and forty wagons constitutes this advance train and many more on the road, followed by thousands of emigrants!"[5]

Even Williams admitted that the road would be much shorter once it was straightened out. He felt the distance from Leavenworth to Denver could be reduced from 689 miles to about 500.[6]

Home stations, the stations where the coach passengers were to eat and often where they were to spend the night, were equipped with milk cows as well as barns, corrals, and extra horses for the team changes on the coaches. The *Leavenworth Times* reported that eighty milk cows accompanied the families and equipment taken out to locate the stations between Leavenworth and Denver.[7]

Some of the men deserted after seeing the desolate country they had been assigned to. Most of these desertions occurred in the barren reaches of the upper Republican River, where both wood and water were scarce items. At the relay stations where only teams were changed and no meals or rooms were furnished for the passengers, only men were stationed; life for them promised to be very boring.

The first stagecoach was scheduled to leave Leavenworth on April 10, but the departure date was delayed because the Concord coaches failed to arrive. This touched off a series of stories in papers of rival towns around Leavenworth, denouncing the whole Leavenworth and Pike's Peak Express company as a fraud. A Kansas City paper called it "a humbug —

Courtesy the Kansas State Historical Society, Topeka *From Gardner Collection #69*

Oxteam at Tonganoxie on Branch Road, between Leavenworth and Lawrence, Kansas.

one of those well conceived schemes, got up by a few speculators to make a little money out of the sale of city lots, etc., and which, in the end, is calculated to do the West a serious injury." It also stated: "There is no such route, and no such facilities for taking emigrants to the mines."[8]

However, the coaches did arrive, and the departure date was set for Monday, April 18. Albert D. Anderson accompanied Horace Greeley on his trip to the goldfields and wrote a detailed description of the Concord Coach as it appeared to him:

> It is covered with duck and canvas, the driver sitting in front, at a slight elevation above the passengers. Bearing no weight upon the roof, it is less top-heavy than the old-fashioned stagecoach for mud holes and mountainsides, where to preserve the center of gravity, with Falstaff's instinct, becomes a great matter. Like human travelers on life's highway, it goes best under a heavy load. Empty, it jolts and pitches like a ship in a raging sea; filled with passengers and balanced by a proper distribution of baggage in the "boot" behind, and under the driver's feet before, its motion is easy and elastic.[9]

These new stagecoaches for the L&PP road were the first Concords in Kansas.[10] The first two coaches to leave Leavenworth were sent off by a huge, cheering crowd. The feeling was the two coaches traveling together would be safer from Indian attack and also that it would be convenient for helping each other in case of breakdown on the rough road.

The reports all state that the coaches made good time getting to Denver. However, the arrival date of May 7 shows that twenty days had elapsed since the coaches left Leavenworth.[11] Later the trips were made much faster than that.

The return trip was made in ten days, in contrast to the twenty it had taken to get to Denver. The coaches left Denver on May 10 and arrived in Leavenworth on May 20. They were greeted by a huge celebration that had been planned for many days. A big parade had been scheduled, with each organization in town assigned a certain spot in the marching order.

The celebration consumed almost all day on May 21. The parade was more than a mile long, headed by the two coaches and the bands. Everything went as planned except for a runaway cannon. It had been dragged along in the parade to be fired occasionally to voice enthusiasm. At one point it broke loose and rolled down the slope into the crowd. Except for a milk wagon blocking its path, a catastrophe could have occurred. As it was there were only a few injuries and a street full of spilled milk.[12]

Much of the return stampede of disgruntled, disappointed, and starving miners heading back to civilization took place in late April and May of 1859, just as soon as travel was possible on the plains. Most of the exodus from the tarnished Bonanza of the goldfields took place over the Platte River Road.

The travelers moving over the new Leavenworth and Pike's Peak Express road saw few of these failures.[13] The exodus from the goldfields around Cherry Creek began before the L&PP road was well enough established to encourage many travelers to venture over it in their desire to reach the safety of civilization.

Most of those leaving the land of broken dreams pulled out before John Gregory came down from the hills to announce his strike. Those who were planning to head for home but had not yet joined the panic-driven crowd fleeing eastward had second thoughts about the wisdom of leaving this potential bonanza. Many of them faced westward instead and joined the rush to the mountains, into the area now anchored by Central City.[14]

The passengers arriving on the Leavenworth and Pike's Peak stages heard of Gregory's strike up in the mountains, and those who were seeking a fast fortune headed into the hills. The gold being brought down from the new strike gave stability at last to the new twin cities on Cherry Creek.

All was not roses for the new express route, however. The warring cities in eastern Kansas had not declared peace. Those who had been bypassed by the new route leaped with glee on the stories of discouragement coming from the goldfields, calling the whole thing a humbug.[15] Those stories were slow in reaching the Missouri River; some of them were printed in papers as late as June, long after gold had been discovered in the mountains. The *St. Joseph Gazette* called the Jones and Russell express "an arrant humbug" but later changed its tune to encourage emigrants to head for the goldfields.[16]

The original announcement that the coaches would leave every day, probably two at a time, proved too optimistic. The passengers who had been expected to crowd into the Leavenworth terminal begging for a place on a coach headed for the goldfields did not materialize. The coaches did travel in pairs and often in small groups for safety, but they left on a schedule that was erratic, to say the least. Once a week was nearer correct than once a day. Later the company announced that "one, two or three coaches will start every day if there are passengers enough to justify." However, it added that no coaches would leave except on Tuesdays unless there were at least six passengers.[17] A companion in the coach with Horace Greeley on his trip to Denver, Albert D. Richardson, kept a diary. He noted anything that struck his fancy. In one case he saw a little tent beside the road with big letters announcing that it was a "grocery." The coach stopped, and they went into the tent to get something to eat.

They found the owner asleep between two whiskey barrels. They roused him.

"Do you have any crackers?" they asked.

"Nary cracker."

"Any bread?"

"Any what?"

"Bread."

He was indignant. "No sir. I don't keep a bakery."

"Any ham?"

"No."

"Any figs?"

"No."

"Well, what do you have?"

"I have sardines, pickled oysters, smoking tobacco — and stranger, I have the best whiskey you ever seen since you was born!"[18]

Although Greeley reported at the end of the trip that nothing of importance happened on the way he did include an accident in the details of his journey.

Near Station 17 three Indians appeared and frightened the mules pulling the coach. The mules ran away, going over a steep bank and upsetting the coach. Greeley, seeing that it was going over,

Courtesy the Kansas State Historical Society, Topeka

Horace Greeley

leaped out, getting bruised and bumped as he hit the ground. The mules broke the front wheels off the coach and ran off with them. Greeley's partner stayed in the coach. After it had settled on its side he poked his head up through a window and was rescued. They were taken to the station nearby, and the women there patched up Richardson, who was slightly injured.[19] Station 17 was in Rawlins County, Kansas, near present Ludell.

Greeley visited the mines up in the mountains on this trip, and his report of the gold being found there finally quieted the cries of "humbug" back in eastern Kansas. Coaches began bringing cargoes of gold dust back from the mines, and the last doubter was silenced.

Jones and Russell charged $125 for a passenger from Leavenworth to Denver. This included twenty pounds of baggage if the passenger wanted to take that much. They also advertised for freight to haul to the mines:[20]

> Will contract with parties to deliver in Denver City any quantity of freight. Will start a train next week, and at least two or three a week during the summer, or as often as freight offers. Apply at my office, under the Planters Hotel. June 20th, 1859 John S. Jones.[21]

The first freight supply train arrived in Denver June 3, 1859,[22] and was most welcome. There were far too many people in Denver for the amount of supplies available. This train was loaded mostly with groceries. There were twenty-five wagons, each pulled by six mules.

Each trip the coaches made on the route from the Missouri to the goldfields was a challenge to the drivers. There had been both praise and complaint about the time taken to make the trip. The first trip had taken twenty days, and each successive trip was aimed at cutting that down.

Before the middle of June two coaches set out from Denver for the return trip to Leavenworth, determined to make it in seven days or less. An accident near Station 12 on the Solomon River in present-day Smith County cost them a day.

Beverly D. Williams, who had set up the stations along the route, was a passenger on this run. On the Solomon they came upon a vast herd of buffalo, miles wide. They were grazing in small herds, so the drivers kept the coaches running at a fast rate through the scattered buffalo.

The buffalo is not a creature to turn aside for anything in his way, and when a small group of them moved across the stage road on a collision course with one of the coaches, they didn't give it any priority. The mules pulling the coach panicked and turned with the buffalo, breaking into a wild run. The driver couldn't hold them. Beverly Williams tried to help him, but their combined efforts were useless.

When it became obvious to Williams that the mules were going to take the coach right over a steep embankment, he leaped for safety. He didn't quite make it, falling under the coach. The wheels ran over both his legs and one arm. Almost miraculously he was only bruised, suffering no broken bones. The coach and mules went over the embankment. The coach was only slightly damaged and none of the mules was injured. Two of them did break free, and it took a day to capture them. Including that delay the trip from Denver to Leavenworth took eight days, which was still a record.

It wasn't until late June, when schedules began being interrupted, that the general public became aware of a transaction that had taken place just four days after the first Leavenworth and Pike's Peak stagecoach reached Denver.[23]

On May 11, 1859, Jones, Russell and Company made a major transaction with J. M. Hockaday and company for the mail contract that Hockaday had been operating since 1859 from St. Joseph, Missouri, to Great Salt Lake City. With all the praise that Jones, Russell and Company had been receiving for opening up a short route to the goldfields in the Rocky Mountains, the firm apparently didn't want to dampen the enthusiasm by telling the public they had taken on the mail contract, which was going to necessitate changing the route.

Jones, Russell and Company agreed, upon purchasing the contract, to fulfill it as specified, and the contract called for the mail to be carried from St. Joseph to Fort Kearny in Nebraska and up the Platte River. To combine the mail contract with the Leavenworth and Pike's Peak Express route meant that the coaches would have to abandon the road through northern Kansas in favor of the Platte River Road. At Julesburg the mail would be carried to Salt Lake City on the Russell, Majors, and Waddell lines, which had been running for some time. The Leavenworth and Pike's Peak Express line would run on up the South Platte River to Denver. It would be the longer route that the original L&PP had tried to avoid, but it was a safe route, and it complied with the mail contract that was now a part of the Jones, Russell and Company business.

J. M. Hockaday had found that the operation of the mail contract line, which had been started in 1858, was too expensive, and he called his sale to Jones, Russell and Company a "forced sale."[24]

There were other reasons given for the abandonment of the original route of the Leavenworth and Pike's Peak road. Some said it was because of lack of wood and water along the route.[25] Jones and Russell gave no reason other than the mail contract they had bought. To fulfill that contract they had no choice but to move the route.

The change in routes was made in late June, moving horses, mules, and equipment to the Platte River Road. The first express destined for Denver to leave Leavenworth by way of the Platte River was on July 2, 1859.[26] The Leavenworth and Pike's Peak Express had made its last run along the divide between the Smoky Hill and Republican rivers in Kansas.

NOTES

1. Floyd Benjamin Streeter, *The Kaw* (New York: Farrar & Rinehart, 1941), p. 17.
2. Leroy R. Hafen, ed., *Overland Routes to the Gold Fields 1859* (Glendale, Calif.: Arthur H. Clark Co., 1942), p. 243. Of the firm of Russell, Majors, and Waddell, Alexander Majors was the religious one who was responsible for the rule against profanity.
3. *Freedom's Champion* (Atchison), 18 June 1859.
4. At the time this was written, all of what is now eastern Colorado was part of Kansas Territory, and Arapahoe County reached from the goldfields of the mountains east to what was soon to be the Colorado-Kansas border. The men in question at Stations 18 and 19 apparently thought they were farther south and west than they were. Station 18 was just north of the Kansas line in Dundy County, Nebraska, and No. 19 was in Cheyenne County, Kansas.
5. *Leavenworth* (Kans.) *Herald*, 16 April 1859. Taken from the Junction City Sentinel. The mules were for stocking the relay stations. The women were wives and cooks for home stations along the way.
6. George A. Root and Russell K. Hickman, "Pike's Peak Express Companies," *Kansas Historical Quarterly* (August 1944), p. 184.
7. Ibid., p. 225 footnote.
8. *Daily Journal of Commerce* (Kansas City), 13 April 1859. Others papers joined in the cry, such as the *St. Joseph Gazette*. The Leavenworth papers, naturally, replied with hot words to these accusations, defending the route.
9. Root and Hickman, "Pike's Peak Express Companies," p. 215.
10. Ibid., p. 187. These coaches were made by Abbot, Downing and Company of Concord, New Hampshire.
11. Streeter, *The Kaw*, p. 10.
12. Root and Hickman, "Pike's Peak Express Companies," p. 192–4.
13. Hafen, *Overland Routes*, p. 245. Horace Greeley reported that, in his trip over the L&PP, they met many oxteams pulling wagons loaded with Pike's Peakers coming back disheartened. This was likely before they reached Manhatten and the Blue River. The returning Pike's Peakers coming down the Blue River from the Platte River Road would travel east from Manhattan on the same road that westbound L&PP travelers would be using.
14. Stanley W. Zamonski and Teddy Keller, *The Fifty-Niners: A Denver Diary* (Denver: Sage Books, 1961), p. 32.
15. Root and Hickman, "Pike's Peak Express Companies," *Kansas Historical Quarterly*, November 1944, p. 213.
16. Ibid., p. 214.
17. *Leavenworth* (Kans.) *Daily Times*, 21 June 1859.
18. Hafen *Overland Routes*, p. 247.
19. Root and Hickman, "Pike's Peak Express Companies," p. 216. A more complete account of Greeley's experiences on this trip can be found in *Beyond the Mississippi*.
20. Ibid., p. 220.
21. Ibid. Planters Hotel was in Denver.
22. Special correspondent for the *Leavenworth Times* called the arrival of this freight train a real godsend because of the scarcity of everything in the new city of Denver.
23. Root and Hickman, "Pike's Peak Express Companies" *Kansas Historical Quarterly* (November 1945), p. 488.
24. Ibid., p. 489. Hockaday blamed the government for his dilemma because of the curtailment of mail service to semimonthly transportation and the subsequent reduction of pay. Hockaday owed huge sums of money and sold out rather than try to make the operation pay.
25. Streeter, *The Kaw*, p. 10.
26. Root and Hickman, "Pike's Peak Express Companies," p. 221.

CHAPTER 4

THE SMOKY HILL TRAIL IN 1859

THE FASTEST, MOST DIRECT ROUTE from the Missouri to the goldfields of the Rocky Mountains was almost due west, up the Smoky Hill River, but it wasn't used nearly as much as the Leavenworth and Pike's Peak Express route.

It wasn't because it hadn't been considered. In 1858, as soon as the reports of gold along Cherry Creek hit Kansas, editorials began bragging about the short, direct route up the Smoky Hill.

In September 1858 the people of Wyandotte[1] called a mass meeting to outline plans for making the town an outfitting point for people going over the Smoky Hill Trail to the new goldfields. They argued that "the true route is directly up the Kansas River and Smoky Hill Fork."[2]

Kansas City itself contended that the best route was along the Santa Fe Trail and up the Arkansas River. Leavenworth backed Wyandotte's claim that the Smoky Hill was the most direct route but disagreed that Wyandotte should be the outfitting point, claiming that advantage for itself. The *Junction City Sentinel* ran editorials about the advantages of the Smoky Hill route and featured a story about a man who had returned from the goldfields over the Smoky Hill route and declared the distance much shorter, the road better, and with plenty of wood, water, and game.[3]

Three guidebooks were published, all directing the traveler to the Smoky Hill River. One did caution that the road was not definitely opened to emigrants and suggested that caution be used until it was. The other two suggested that the traveler drop down to the Arkansas River after reaching the headwaters of the Smoky Hill.[4]

Claims were made that it was only 500 miles from the Missouri to the goldfields on Cherry Creek. Another claim was that it was 555 miles but that there were settlements for 250 of those miles, leaving only three hundred miles through the wilderness — a much shorter distance through unsettled areas than any other road offered.

One of the biggest incentives given to travelers to choose the Smoky Hill route was the statement that the road followed the banks of the river for all but 130 miles of the way. The suggested road that would follow the divide between the Smoky Hill and the Republican rivers (the Leavenworth and Pike's Peak) would depend for water on the small streams it crossed. The

Courtesy the Kansas State Historical Society, Topeka *From Gardner Collection*

Wyandotte — view

Smoky Hill route would have water all along the way. There would be no long, hard days of travel to make sure there would be water for camp. In many cases on the L&PP there would be dry camps, something every traveler detested and feared.

Feeling that most gold seekers still leaned toward the Platte River Road or the Santa Fe and the Arkansas route, the papers continued to hammer on the great advantages of the central route to the mountains. A Leavenworth paper recalled Fremont's report of the good road that could be made along the Smoky Hill River. The paper concluded: "Subsequent explorations have corroborated the view taken by the Great Explorer, and the bulk of the spring migration will, undoubtedly, select this as their main road."[5]

Glowing reports of men who had traveled the route and of its many advantages came from the *Lawrence Republican*, the *Wyandotte Commercial Gazette*, and the *Junction City Sentinel*, all aimed at encouraging the traveler to select the direct route along the Smoky Hill River. The *Sentinel* even concluded its article with a bit of poetry:

> Let Hercules do what he may
> The Smoky Hill route MUST have its day.[6]

This was in the winter of 1858 and 1859. Came the spring and the rude awakening. Travelers started out on the trail with high hopes of an easy, well-watered trail, with plenty of fuel and game. Those hopes were soon dashed. Beyond Fort Riley there was very little trail; hardly out of sight of civilization the trail was gone completely and the traveler was on his own. His only guide was the river along which he made his way — and the reports had admitted that it disappeared 130 miles short of the mountains. Worry and uncertainty had to raise their heads as the traveler moved up the river.

People who had never burned anything but wool and coal soon learned to burn "prairie coal," buffalo chips. They were the only thing on the prairie that would burn, other than the dry grass. When there was no rain and the sun dried the grass, that could be a source of worry to the traveler, too. Any of them who had ever seen a prairie fire, started by lightning or by Indians, never forgot the terror it instilled.

The Smoky Hill River supplied water for travelers for much of the distance across what is now Kansas. But as they neared the western end of the river the water disappeared for long stretches, appearing only in occasional pools or when a hole was dug in the dry riverbed. Often that hole took on the proportions of a small well before it yielded water.

Although there was no road laid out along the Smoky Hill there were many guidebooks to help the traveler. One of these guides was printed several times in the *Freedom's Champion* in Atchison, Kansas. Like Leavenworth, Atchison considered itself the perfect outfitting town for the Smoky Hill route directly to the goldfields of the Rockies. The guide that the *Freedom's Champion* published directed the traveler down to the Akansas River before water ran out in the Smoky Hill.

Many a traveler left the Missouri with this chart in his pocket, torn from an issue of the *Freedom's Champion:*

ROUTE FROM ATCHISON via the SMOKY HILL FORK ROUTE[7]

From Atchison to	Miles	Total	Remarks
Mormon Grove	3½		Junction of the great military road
Monrovia	8½	12	Provisions, entertainment and grass
Mouth of Bill's Creek	13	25	On the Grasshopper, wood and grass

ROUTE FROM ATCHISON via the SMOKY HILL FORK ROUTE[7]

From Atchison to	Miles	Total	Remarks
Territorial Road from Nebraska	15	40	Wood, water and grass
Soldier Creek	10	50	Wood and grass
Lost Creek	15	65	Wood and grass
Louisville	10	75	Water and grass
Manhattan City	12	87	Water, wood and grass
Ft. Riley	15	102	Water, wood and grass
Saline	52	154	Wood, water and grass
Pawnee Trail — Smoky Hill[8]	130	284	Grass and buffalo chips
Pawnee Fork	35	319	Grass and buffalo chips
Arkansas Crossing	35	354	Wood, water and grass
Bent's Fort	150	504	Wood, water and grass
Bent's Old Fort	40	544	Water and grass
Huerfano	40	584	Water and grass
Fontaine qui Bouille	15	599	Wood, water and grass
Crossing of same	18	617	Wood, water and grass
Jim's Camp	15	632	Water and grass
Brush Corral	12	644	Wood, water and grass
Head of Cherry Creek	26	670	Wood, water and grass
Crossing of same	35	705	From this point to the mines there is heavy timber and grass and water in abundance.
Mines	6	711	

There are several things in the guide that should have discouraged the traveler from taking this route. First, it took the traveler south to the Arkansas and then back north to the goldfields at Cherry Creek, making a distance of over seven hundred miles. That was about forty-five miles farther than the Platte River Road to Denver, which offered an established road to Julesburg Station and from there to Denver. It was simply a case of following the river with plenty of water at all times.

Second, there was the lack of wood at so many of the campgrounds. Likely there were plenty of buffalo chips, however, since there certainly had not been enough travelers over this trail to diminish the supply.

The most discouraging aspect about this guide was the long stretch between sites. For instance, it was 52 miles from Fort Riley to Salina, followed by 130 unchartered miles between Salina and the crossing of the Pawnee Trail, where the route left the Smoky Hill and turned south to follow the Arkansas. To the experienced traveler this could only mean that the road was not surveyed or camps established.

Many of the travelers followed this guide from the Missouri River to the point where it turned south from the Smoky Hill River to the Arkansas. There they simply set their own course west to the goldfields, thinking it would be well over one hundred miles shorter. In that respect they were correct. In their conviction that they could easily find plenty of water, fuel, and game, they were sadly mistaken. The result was pure disaster.

Shortly after travelers began moving west up the Smoky Hill Trail in the early spring of 1859, newspapers on both ends of the route began lamenting about the hardships of the trail. Kansas City papers reported the stories coming from the trail and concluded: "How often will it be necessary to tell the public that there is no road up the Smoky Hill?"[9]

At the other end, the first issue of the *Cherry Creek Pioneer* in Denver reported that several men coming up the trail had gotten lost because there were no markers.

It stated: "Any other route is better than the Smoky Hill road."[10]

Newspapers at both ends of the trail were full of gruesome stories of the tragedies among travelers along the Smoky Hill Trail.

The *Western Journal of Commerce* in Kansas City said that a man from Council Grove reported that a hundred men had become lost and wandered south from the Smoky Hill River, apparently losing their way shortly after leaving the established road at Junction City. According to the report the men robbed a trading post, beat up the man who owned it, and took about a hundred sacks of corn and all the flour and groceries on hand and headed west toward the goldfields.[11]

The *Rocky Mountain News* in Denver reported that men were arriving every day from the states by way of the Smoky Hill Trail and most of them were half-starved. One story reported that three men had starved to death on the trail. Still another story told by an emigrant, although it was unverified, told of seventeen men in one party who had starved to death on the trail. One emigrant reported that the remains of a hundred men could be found along the road.

An editorial in the *News* condemned the men and newspapers in the East that had encouraged people to start out on the Smoky Hill Trail with so few provisions, expecting to find a good road and good camps with plenty of wood and water. Instead, they had found no road at all, very little wood and, in many places, no water.[12]

Alfred D. Richardson, newspaper correspondent who made one of the early trips from the Missouri to Denver City on a Leavenworth and Pike's Peak Express coach, told of crossing the trail of Smoky Hill travelers after they had left the headwaters of the Smoky Hill and cut north to the Platte River. This was at Station 22 of the L&PP, in what is now western Kit Carson County. There was water in the Republican River here, after many miles in which the river ran underground.

Richardson complained about traveling twenty-five miles without seeing a drop of water until they reached Station 22. He described people who had come north from the Smoky Hill who had been without water for seventy-five miles and had suffered intensely. Some had burned their wagons, killed their dying stock and continued on foot themselves.[13]

Horace Greeley described the same place, Station 22, and the travelers coming north from the Smoky Hill. "Here is Station 22 and here are a so-called spring and one or two considerable pools. Here the thirsty men and teams which have been twenty-five miles without water on the Express Company's road, are met by those which have come up the longer and more southerly route by the Smoky Hill,[14] and which have traveled sixty miles since they last found water or shade. The Pike's Peakers from the Smoky Hill whom I met here, had driven their oxteams through the sixty miles at one stretch, the time required being two days and the intervening night."[15]

Another correspondent reported on his experiences at Station 22, where the Leavenworth and Pike's Peak Express road crossed the road of the Smoky Hill travelers on their way to the Platte. "I found a whole city of canvas, inhabited by weary emigrants who wanted to give themselves and stock a few day's rest. I conversed freely with such as had come via the Smoky Hill route, and they were all unanimous in their denunciations of the same. The Indians had burned off all the early grass and were themselves congregated in large numbers along the road and were overbearing and troublesome."[16]

NOTES

1. Wyandotte was later absorbed by Kansas City. About the only mark it left on the maps of today is Wyandotte County, of which Kansas City, Kansas, is the county seat.

2. *Western Weekly Argus* (Wyandotte, Kans. Terr.), 30 September 1858.
3. *Lawrence*, (Kans.) *Republican*, 7 October 1858. Quoted from the *Junction City Sentinel*.
4. Calvin W. Gower, "The Pike's Peak Gold Rush and the Smoky Hill Route, 1859–1860," *Kansas Historical Quarterly* (Summer 1959), p. 159.
5. *Leavenworth* (Kans.) *Weekly Times*, 19 March 1859.
6. *Junction City* (Kans.) *Sentinel*, copied by *Freedom's Champion*, 25 March 1859.
7. *Freedom's Champion* (Atchison). Printed and reprinted in several issues during the winter and spring of 1858–1859.
8. This one hundred and thirty mile stretch along the north side of the Smoky Hill River took the traveler to the crossing of the north-south Pawnee Trail, the spot where most historians think Villasur turned north in 1720 toward the Platte River where he was killed.
9. *Western Journal of Commerce* (Kansas City), 9 April 1859.
10. *Cherry Creek Pioneer* (Denver), 23 April 1859.
11. Gower, "Smoky Hill Route, 1859–1860," p. 161.
12. *Rocky Mountain News* (Denver), 7 May 1859.
13. George A. Root and Russell K. Hickman, "Pike's Peak Express Companies," *Kansas Historical Quarterly* (November 1944) p. 236; LeRoy R. Hafen, ed., *Overland Routes to the Gold Fields 1859* (Glendale, Calif.: Arthur H. Clark Company, 1942), p. 260.
14. Greeley was wrong here in saying that the Smoky Hill route was longer than the Leavenworth and Pike's Peak Express road. It was, in fact, many miles shorter. At this time, however, it was not surveyed, and the travelers, in desperation, took a longer detour north to the South Platte River to find water.
15. Horace Greeley, *Overland Journey*, pp. 107–9.
16. Root and Hickman, "Pike's Peak Express Companies," pp. 236–7.

CHAPTER 5

THE STARVATION TRAIL

PERHAPS THE MOST BIZARRE INCIDENT to be recorded about travelers along the Smoky Hill route that spring of 1859 (and one that helped condemn it as a death road) was one involving a group of men who left the Missouri River in late winter, taking the Smoky Hill route to the goldfields.

The three Blue brothers, Alexander, Daniel, and Charles, left their home in Whiteside County, Illinois, along with a cousin and a neighbor, on February 22, 1859, bound for the glittering goldfields in the Rockies.[1] Of the three brothers; only Alexander was married. He left behind a wife and four children, with dreams of being a rich man when he returned.

They traveled by rail and boat to Kansas City, where they bought a pony to use as a packhorse. They then made their way to Topeka, where they bought two hundred pounds of flour[2] and other things they thought they would need. Following the Kansas River they moved on until a blizzard drove them to shelter just after they crossed the Blue River.

Here they met nine other men who were going the same way. They joined forces and moved on after the storm. One of these men claimed to have been over the Smoky Hill Trail before, so the group elected him their captain to act as guide. They soon overtook two other men on foot who were from Ohio. These two joined the group, and now there were sixteen men.

The only horse in the party was the packhorse the Blue brothers had. The others carried their packs on their backs. At Fort Riley they debated about taking the Smoky Hill route or the route up the Republican, which some said was safer, with more water and wood. The Smoky Hill route was more than a hundred miles shorter, however, and the man who had been over the road said they could make it all right. With a driving eagerness to get to the goldfields, they elected to go over the Smoky Hill Trail.

After several days travel, being stopped once by another bad storm, they halted while the group that had joined them late went on a hunt; their supplies were low. The Blue brothers and their companions had plenty of provisions. They became impatient at the delay and soon decided to go ahead and let the others catch up with them once they had some buffalo meat.

This proved to be the first of several bad mistakes. They had proceeded only a couple of days when they began to argue about their course. They realized that someone was totally confused, but they didn't know which one. So they struck out in the direction voted most likely to be toward the river. They had kept to the high ground north of the river up to this point.

They traveled all day but found no river. Camping for the night they unpacked their horse and staked it out. The next morning the horse was gone. They looked for it for a while but realized that Indians probably had stolen it. Distributing their supplies among themselves they made backpacks and proceeded, moving now in the direction they knew was west, according to the sun. They estimated they were about halfway between Fort Riley and Denver. About the only good thing that happened to them was finding the river again. They now had water when they needed it.

After a few days travel, the oldest brother, Alexander, got sick. They had to stop for more than half a day before he was able to travel again. Their food ran low, and finally they threw away all their luggage except what they absolutely had to have.

Before they reached the headwaters of the Smoky Hill River they ate the last of their food. It is believed they took the North Fork of the Smoky where the two branches come together in western Kansas. The North Fork at this point has more water than the South Fork and promises to be the one with water to the west. Surveyors and later travelers learned this was not the case. The South Fork has flowing water in the wet season and pockets of water in most places in the dry season. The North Fork runs dry a short distance above the confluence of the two streams.

The party was able to dig into the riverbed and get water when needed, however, and there had been late snow that winter, so water was not a problem as it was for those who followed them in drier times of the year. Eventually they came to an area where there was water only from melting snow, and they realized they had reached the headwaters.

Here they paused and debated whether to push on to Denver or stop and hunt for meat. All their supplies were gone. They had been told at the start of their journey that it was only 55 miles from the headwaters of the Smoky Hill River to Denver. Everyone in the group believed this, and their decision was based on that belief. They were sure they could kill enough small game as they went along to keep them alive until they reached Denver. If they stopped and hunted they might lose a lot of time, and there was no assurance they would get anything, anyway. So the decision was made, and it proved to be another mistake. That 55 miles was, in truth, about 170 miles — across a dry, wind-swept prairie, where their chance of sneaking up close enough to kill any game was very slim.

Setting their course a little north of west, according to the sun, they moved out. Within a day a blizzard swept down on them. Hungry as they were they felt they didn't dare wait out the storm. They kept moving during the daylight hours, wrapping up in their blankets at night. They were wet and very weary, and pushing ahead in the snow sapped their strength.

When the sun finally came out after four or five days they discovered they had been traveling in a big circle and had gained practically nothing in their march toward Denver. Both Alexander and Charles Blue were near exhaustion. They had to rest before they could push on. All the group went ahead except the three Blue brothers and a man from Cleveland named Soley. The others were still able to travel and were afraid if they lost any time they too might become to weak to walk.

The four left behind moved ahead as fast as their strength would allow, but at a snail's pace through the snow. Their hunger grew, and they could think of little but food. They had to rest more and more often.

It was during one of these rests that the idea was advanced that if one of them should die the rest should consider eating his flesh to survive. Daniel Blue reported afterward that, even though they were starving, the very thought of such a thing made them sick. The idea persisted however and became part of their conversation whenever they rested. It finally was accepted as something that would be considered should one of them die. With each day, it became more apparent that some of them would never leave this barren prairie.

Soley was the first one to die. For three days the Blue brothers stayed there, too weak to bury the body or to move on. It had been Soley's last request that they eat his body to strengthen themselves and at last they did just that.

They moved on then, slowly for none of them had much strength left. Alexander Blue was the next to die. Daniel and Charles rebelled at the thought of eating their brother's flesh but finally succumbed to the pangs of hunger and the drive for self-preservation.

This nourishment allowed the two brothers to push on for a short distance toward the mountains. On clear mornings they could see the sun reflecting off the snow at the top of Pike's Peak to the southwest. The first sight of the mountain had cheered them with hope of reaching the settlements. Now its shining, snow-capped top was only a mockery.

They could travel little more than a mile a day. Finally Charles, the youngest of the brothers, dropped from exhaustion. He soon died, leaving only Daniel alive.

Daniel lost his desire to live after the death of the last of his brothers, yet hunger drove him to eat his flesh. Even that and the water from the stream nearby[3] were barely enough to keep him alive. He reached the point where he could no longer get to his feet, and he was sure he was dying. He sank into a stupor.

He was roused by an Indian touching him. The Indian and his two companions lifted him onto a horse and took him to their camp. The Indians were Arapahoe, and the brave and his squaw nursed the feeble white man until he was able to ride again. Then they took him to the Leavenworth and Pike's Peak Express road, which was just then coming into use. Daniel had heard nothing about it when he left the Missouri in early March.[4]

There was an Indian scare, and the people at the station where he was taken had to retreat to the station to the east. Daniel was put on the next coach going west. He rode into Denver on the second stage to reach the new town at the foot of the Rockies, arriving there on May 11.

The story that Daniel Blue had to tell[5] shocked even the hardy miners and residents of Denver, who were used to a rough life and daily death. Many a resolution was made not to travel back to the states on the Smoky Hill route.

When Blue's story reached travelers along the Missouri River it had the effect of putting a final taboo on the Smoky Hill Trail. One writer summed up the Smoky Hill fiasco of the spring of 1859 by saying it was an unexplored route where "grass and water proved woefully scarce and fearful suffering prevailed." Another writer, putting down his opinion a short time later, admitted the dangers of the trail that spring but predicted a better future for it. "That route will doubtless turn out as good in the end as either the Northern or Southern," he wrote. "But at the time of the Pike's Peak emigration it was but partially explored."[6]

Both writers saw the problem quite clearly, especially the latter when he said the route was only partially explored. A road across such a vast region for slow-moving traffic had to be well planned. Water must be located at frequent intervals, and food for both man and beast must be available along the way. The fact that neither was found by many emigrants moving over the Smoky Hill Trail did not prove for all time that neither was there;

they simply had not found it at the right time and place.

Although travel on the Smoky Hill practically stopped after the spring of 1859, it was not totally forgotten. It still remained the shortest route to the goldfields by more than a hundred miles. That meant several days' travel with an oxteam or even a fast mule team. If a traveler was going by foot, a hundred miles was a long, long distance.

Not everyone gave up on the route. They figured if they could find water and grass and fuel along the route and mark the camps, the Smoky Hill could become the most traveled route to the mountains. That was a guaranteed factor because of the time and distance saved.

A few travelers came back from the mountains over the Smoky Hill Trail in the fall of 1859, but the fact that they had no trouble did little to encourage people to consider the route for travel to the mountains in the future.

Then the people of Leavenworth began to agitate for a surveyed road along the Smoky Hill for the following year's travel. Letters to editors of newpapers in Leavenworth in February and March suggested that a party be organized as quickly as possible to survey and establish a road up the Smoky Hill to the goldfields. One writer gave a reason that made a great deal of sense to the people of Leavenworth. He said that a direct route from Leavenworth to the goldfields would secure for Leavenworth a lion's share of the business of outfitting the travelers to Denver. Otherwise, the rival cities along the Missouri River would continue to get that business.

Two bills came up in the territorial legislature that session proposing that the governing body take up the project. It excited much discussion but no concrete action — the action was going to be left to the people who wanted it most. Those people seemed to be in Leavenworth, the city that had the most to gain by a direct route up the Smoky Hill to Denver.

Much of the travel going over the northern route outfitted at cities other than Leavenworth, some as far north as Nebraska. All the travelers going over the southern route outfitted at Kansas City and took the Santa Fe Trail out of town. Now that the Leavenworth and Pike's Peak Express Company had abandoned its route across northern Kansas in favor of the mail route over the Oregon Trail, Leavenworth was left like the hole in the doughnut.

A few neighboring papers sided with Leavenworth in agitating for a surveyed road up the Smoky Hill. Others (rivals of Leavenworth for the business of outfitting travelers) ridiculed the idea, pointing out the suffering and even death that the Smoky Hill Road had brought to travelers the year before.

The *Rocky Mountain News* joined them, saying it "had been tried once over this fated *Smoky Hell* route with only too lamentable success, and its instigators stand today, in the sight of Heaven, guilty of manslaughter, to say the least." The article went on to suggest that the promotors of the idea travel over the Smoky Hill route themselves. "If they get through without eating each other up, some adventurous individuals may be induced to follow."[7]

The story of the Blue brothers' cannibalism had clearly not been forgotten.

The people of Leavenworth were not discouraged. Competition from Atchison and St. Joseph for supplying the emigrants taking the northern route to the mines was fierce, and all of Leavenworth's business was feeling the pinch of it. A Lawrence paper, backing Leavenworth's bid to open a good road up the Smoky Hill, pointed this out. It also predicted that the Pacific Railroad, already being talked about, would go up the Platte River in Nebraska if a good road were not opened along the Smoky Hill. Such a road could well induce the railroad to build along the shortest route to the mines.[8]

In late March W. Green Russell, originally from Georgia, who had been in the Pike's Peak region at the start of the gold rush, came to Leavenworth with a proposition. He would take a crew of men and explore the possibilities of a good road up the Smoky Hill River to Denver for $3,500. He would provide information about camping sites and give a complete guide to water, grass, and fuel all along the way. The people of Leavenworth jumped at the offer. At last they were going to get some action.

Russell's party made good time over the road, arriving in Denver early in May. Russell wrote his report and sent it back. It arrived in Leavenworth on May 15, and the town welcomed his favorable comments.

By now, however, they had had time to consider the entire picture. They realized it was going to take more than a good report of a survey to induce people to travel up a trail where suffering and death had been the reward of so many who had tried it the year before. A government road would have to be laid out, with definite camping sites and guaranteed watering places along the way.

The urgency of action was emphasized by a report published in the *Rocky Mountain News*. A correspondent for the *News* had reported from St. Louis that emigration to the goldfields was heavy again that spring but most of the flow was going through St. Joseph and over the northern route. The emigration from Atchison, Leavenworth, and Kansas City was far less than the spring before. "Leavenworth, especially, appears to be much less attractive as an outfitting point than last year," the report said.[9]

Kansas was watching a bill on its way through Congress in Washington. The bill to admit Kansas into the Union as a state breezed through the House on a 134-to-73 vote on April 11 and was sent on to the Senate. There it was relegated to the Senate Committee on Territories and disappeared in the mire of slow-moving legislation. On May 16 the Kansas statehood bill was reported back from committee without recommendation. No one had to be told that meant the end of the bill.

The people of Leavenworth swallowed their disappointment and proceeded to outfit an expedition to build a road up the Smoky Hill Valley. They estimated it would cost about $7,500. They asked the towns along the first part of the route to pay part of the cost, since it would benefit them if the road were put through. Leavenworth got together $2,000 to begin the work.

The towns along the route were enthusiastic about the idea, but money was very scarce. Some dug up what they could; some put up things other than money. Topeka offered to furnish five yoke of oxen and hoped to be able to contribute $500 later. Junction City put up $500 in bonds. Ogden contributed a yoke of oxen for the work, and Manhatten guaranteed $500. Auburn promised three yoke of oxen; Vermillion offered a mare for work; Lawrence launched a campaign and raised $155 in cash.[10]

With this much promised, Leavenworth issued $3,000 worth of bonds. It seemed that the project was well underwritten, so the expedition was authorized.

Henry Green, a lawyer who had lived in Leavenworth for six years, was chosen to head the road-building crew. Green was thirty-four years old and had come to Leavenworth from Virginia in 1854. There was some misgiving among backers because Green was not an experienced man on the prairies. But he was a leader, and among his crew was a guide, a surveyor, and an engineer. There were over forty workers in the crew and five wagons, with provisions for sixty days. They also took along plenty of guns and ammunition.

They left Leavenworth on June 18 and reached Topeka on the twenty-second. On June 26 they were in Manhattan, and Green told the editor of the *Manhatten Express* what they hoped to accomplish as they traveled west.

Green expected to bridge all streams that could not be forded easily, grade off the sharp banks of ravines so the decline would not be so steep, fill in the deepest parts of the ravines, move rocks out of the road, and set up some kind of markers along the way so travelers would have no trouble following the road. At the headwaters of the Smoky Hill he intended to make camp while a thorough search of the country ahead was made to assure the best and shortest route to Cherry Creek. The *Express* relayed this information to its readers, with emphasis on the importance of the road. Everyone was certain this road would be the forerunner of the railroad that would surely soon follow across the plains.[11]

There was a celebration for the road builders in Salina on July 4, and they reported no trouble in preparing an easy road for travelers. As the crew traveled west, reports were sent back describing the easy road they were building. Green was marking his road with big mounds of dirt, one about every mile, "so that there could be no trouble in finding it hereafter."

Reports finally reached Leavenworth that Green and his men had reached Denver after fifty-seven days on the road. Considering the work they were supposed to have done, that was very good time. The report from Green was encouraging, and Leavenworth began shouting to the world that a good road was completed for the traveler and that next year Leavenworth would be the center of emigrant outfitting as travelers took the shortest, fastest, and easiest road to the mines.

Green arrived back in Leavenworth on October 6. He reported that wood was scarce on much of the Smoky Hill route but that buffalo chips were plentiful. The longest stretch without water was twenty-two miles. Travelers could make that in one day, so there would be no dry camps.

Some travelers coming back from the mines for the winter took the Smoky Hill Road and declared it was shorter and easier to travel than the roads to the north and south. Leavenworth leaped on these statements with great enthusiasm and predicted a banner year in 1861.

One man returning in late October praised the road but issued a warning. He reported that herds of buffalo were destroying the mounds of dirt piled up by the road builders to mark the road and said if something wasn't done a new survey might have to be made.[12]

Enthusiasm remained high. However, spring was far away, and the rush to the Rockies up the Smoky Hill Valley was farther in the future than any one realized.

At the general election on November 6 Abraham Lincoln was elected to succeed James Buchanan as president in March, and there were rumbles of war echoing throughout the South. Kansas had the jitters. In early January Gen. W. S. Hancock put Fort Leavenworth on notice for mobilization to have the troops ready to move out quickly.

Finally, after more amendments and haggling, the bill admitting Kansas to the Union as a state was passed and signed

Courtesy the Kansas State Historical Society, Topeka *From Gardner Collection*

Topeka — Kansas Avenue

into law by President Buchanan on January 29, 1861.

In March eastern Kansas counties began raising their own militia regiments, and on April 12 the war began with the firing on Fort Sumter. Thoughts of getting rich in the goldfields of the Rockies were crowded out by thoughts of protecting homes against the enemy — who might be a close neighbor. The anticipated stampede over the Smoky Hill Road faded into oblivion; it had been built two years too late.

The work was not to be in vain. Some travelers did go up the Smoky Hill Road to the mines. But the greatest impact of the road was to come in the years ahead, when the Butterfield Overland Despatch sent its stagecoaches rumbling over the road to the mountains and the railroad laid its tracks just north of the Smoky Hill.

NOTES

1. Daniel Blue, *Thrilling Narrative of the Adventures, Sufferings and Starvation of Pike's Peak Gold Seekers on the Plains of the West in the Winter and Spring of 1859* (Chicago: Evening Journal Steam Print, 1860; reprint ed. Fairfield, Wash.: Ye Galleon Press, 1968), p. 6.
2. Calvin W. Gower, "The Pike's Peak Gold Rush and the Smoky Hill Route, 1859–1860," *Kansas Historical Quarterly* (Summer 1959), p. 161.
3. Blue, *Pike's Peak Gold Seekers*, p. 14. Although he was lost, he guessed that he was on Beaver Creek. This likely was Bijou Creek, which seems to have been called Beaver Creek by some travelers in 1859. In a letter to his father a few days before, hoping someone would find it and deliver it after his death, Charles said they were on the Big Sandy, which was probably right in light of later developments.
4. Margaret Long, *The Smoky Hill Trail* (Denver: W. H. Kistler Company, 1943), pp. 13–15. Daniel Blue was taken to Station 25 on the L&PP on Bijou Creek, just two stations from Denver. This section of the trail, where all the Blue party except Daniel died, later became known as the Starvation Trail.
5. Blue, *Pike's Peak Gold Seekers*. Daniel Blue's story was written after Daniel had returned to his Illinois home and was published originally in 1860. A very few copies remained a hundred years later and it was republished in 1968.
6. Gower, "Smoky Hill Route, 1859-1860," pp. 162–3.
7. *Rocky Mountain News* (Denver), 21 March 1860.
8. *Lawrence* (Kansas) *Republican*, 5 April 1860.
9. *Rocky Mountain News* (Denver), 23 May 1860.
10. Gower, "Smoky Hill Route, 1859-1860," pp. 168–9.
11. Ibid., p. 169.
12. *Topeka State Record*, 17 November 1860.

III.

TRAIL OF THE BUTTERFIELD OVERLAND DESPATCH

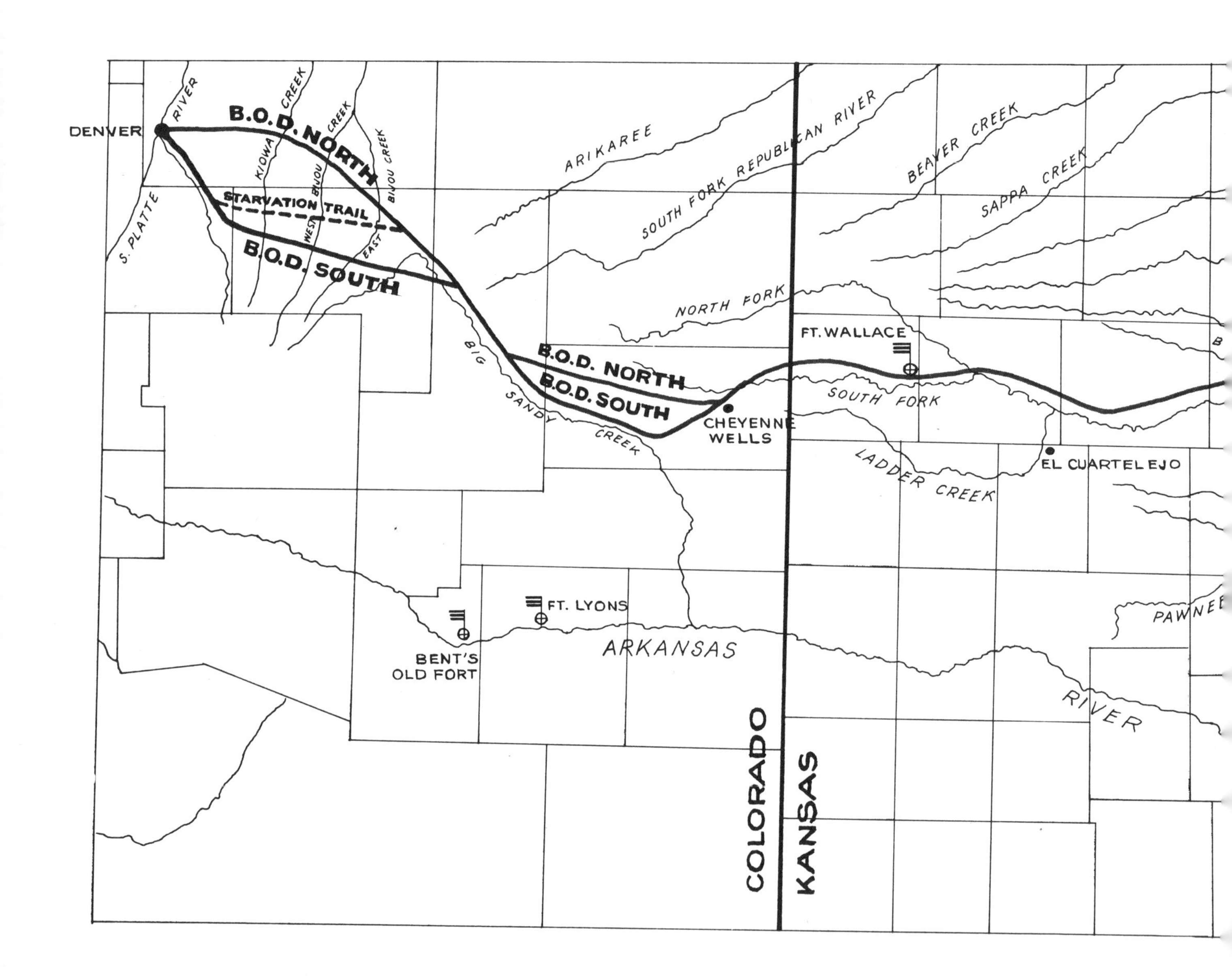

DENVER
S. PLATTE RIVER
B.O.D. NORTH
KIOWA CREEK
BIJOU CREEK
WEST BIJOU
EAST
BIJOU CREEK
STARVATION TRAIL
B.O.D. SOUTH
ARIKAREE
SOUTH FORK REPUBLICAN RIVER
BEAVER CREEK
SAPPA CREEK
NORTH FORK
FT. WALLACE
BIG SANDY CREEK
B.O.D. NORTH
B.O.D. SOUTH
CHEYENNE WELLS
SOUTH FORK
LADDER CREEK
EL CUARTELEJO
FT. LYONS
BENT'S OLD FORT
ARKANSAS
RIVER
PAWNEE
COLORADO
KANSAS

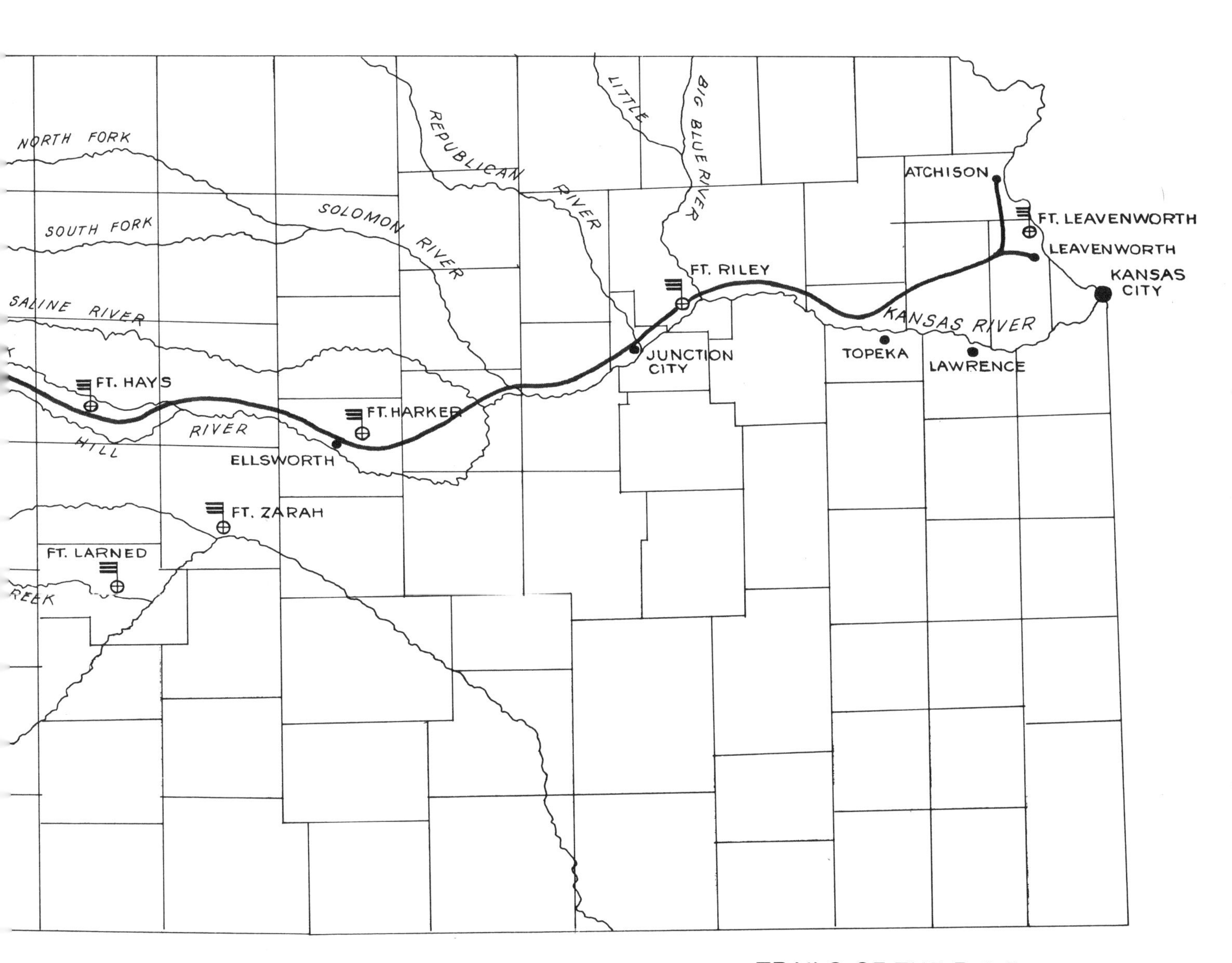

TRAILS OF THE B.O.D.

CHAPTER 6

ESTABLISHING THE B.O.D.

LIKE ALMOST EVERYTHING ELSE in both halves of the United States, the Smoky Hill Trail was virtually paralyzed during the four years of the Civil War. Travel over the trail became more difficult as the markers disappeared, and more travelers were afraid to trust it. This did not hinder the dreamers who had visions of better days ahead.

One of those dreamers was a man named David A. Butterfield. Born on January 17, 1834, in the little village of Jay in Franklin County, Maine, Butterfield grew up there. On March 25, 1855, when he was twenty-one, he married Mary M. Stephens of Portland, Maine.[1]

The West intrigued Butterfield, and in 1856 he took his family away from the East Coast and settled in Kansas. Then came the discovery of gold in the Colorado mountains. When war began between the states Butterfield felt the safest and most prosperous place for him and his family was Denver, and he moved there in 1862.

In Denver he operated a grocery and commission business, but he dreamed of a stage and freight line directly from the Missouri River to Denver across Kansas. As the trains of supplies coming in over the Platte River Road or up the Arkansas River then north to Denver took longer and longer to reach their destination, his dream began to grow. A direct route would be so much faster.

In 1864 Butterfield moved back to Kansas, settling in Atchison. There he set up another commission business and also became agent for a line of packet boats making semiweekly trips up the Missouri River from St. Louis. He saw the immense quantities of freight going overland to Denver and the mining districts, and he realized more than ever how profitable a freight line straight across the plains to

Courtesy Mrs. Harold DeBacker

David A. Butterfield

Denver would be. He had many acquaintances among mining and business men in and around Denver. With the assurance of their freighting business he was certain he could soon corner almost all the hauling from the Missouri River to the mountains because of the shorter route and the guaranteed faster delivery time. He had no illusions about securing the mail contract; Ben Holladay already had the contract to carry the mail over the Platte River route.

Butterfield studied the survey maps of the Smoky Hill Road as laid out in 1860 and decided that much of the same route could be used for his line, but his road had to be shorter, safer, and faster then the earlier Smoky Hill Road. Speed was the real key. The merchants in Denver wanted faster service on the goods they ordered, and Butterfield was convinced that he could deliver.

Butterfield was a hard worker and a shrewd dealer. He was very ambitious and had few equals as an organizer. From his base in Atchison he began to plan his stage and freight line to Denver. Realizing he had to have the backing of moneyed men in the East for such a gigantic project, he began his advertising in the East almost simultaneously with the work of surveying the actual route in Kansas. He spent a great deal of money advertising the new road and its advantages in the leading newspapers in New York, Chicago and St. Louis. He also got plenty of publicity in Denver and in his hometown paper in Atchison.

He established eastern headquarters in New York City, where he had gigantic signs put up, one very close to the famous Astor House, showing huge covered wagons pulled by mules or oxen. This attracted a lot of interest among the businessmen. When Butterfield felt interest was at its peak he made a trip to New York and Boston. There he laid his plan before the leading investors and succeeded in organizing the Butterfield Overland Despatch with a capitalization of $3 million. Offices of the new B.O.D. were opened in New York, Boston, Philadelphia, Cincinnati, St. Louis, Chicago, Denver, and Salt Lake City.

Harper's Weekly, January 27, 1866

Banking house, Denver City

The real work of opening the new route, however, was going on along the Smoky Hill River. Lt. Julian R. Fitch of the U.S. Signal Corps was detailed to go with the Butterfield Overland Despatch expedition as surveyor.[2] He made a lengthy and detailed report to Butterfield upon completion of the survey.

Lieutenant Fitch brought four men with him when he joined the expedition at Leavenworth — Daniel Clark, Charles Fitch, Abner Coleman and Joseph Cornell. Issac E. Eaton was in charge of the expedition. They left on June 13. At Fort Riley Major Pritchard joined them, along with two companies of the Third Wisconsin cavalry under command of Captain Pond.[3]

With this escort they followed the military trail to the southwest along the Smoky Hill River to Fort Ellsworth. Here the expedition planned to branch off the military trail which turned southwest to Fort Zarah and head directly for Denver and the goldfields beyond, surveying the route for the new road.

Having been with the surveying crew that laid out the Smoky Hill Trail in 1860, Lieutenant Fitch was quite familiar with the hazards that lay ahead, and he hoped to avoid some of the mistakes incorporated into the 1860 trail. He reported to Butterfield:

Our road from this point laid over a hard stretch of level bench land covered with a luxuriant growth of buffalo grass, intersected every three or four miles with fine streams of water. Our party at this time consisted of Colonel Eaton and his party of constructionists, twenty-six in number, eleven four-mule wagons loaded with tools, reapers, and everything necessary for putting the road in fine condition, Major Pritchard and 250 cavalry as escort, and the Engineer Corps. On the 14th of July with everything looking fair and all in good spirits, we started on our work.[4]

Finding fine springs as we traveled along, thirty-four miles west of Fort Ellsworth we found a fine coal bed on what we named Coal Creek. Twelve miles farther west we came to Big Creek, a large stream having a beautiful valley with heavy timber. Here we made a good rock ford and erected a large mound and stake for a home and cattle station.

Photo by Author

Butterfield Overland Despatch marker near rock corral at Death Hollow campground (Forks of the Smoky Hill).

On the morning of the 18th we left camp, bearing a little south of west over the same character of country, close to the Smoky and at a distance of twenty-eight miles came to a fine large spring — one of the largest in the West.[5] Fifteen miles farther west we bore away from the river, and kept on high level ground about three miles north of the river which here makes a southerly bend. On the south side of the river, opposite this point, we discovered high bluffs, covered with cedar.[6]

Twelve and a half miles west we camped at the head spring of a stream emptying south three miles into the Smoky Hill. The water and grass at this place we found unusually fine. We called this place Downer Station. Nine miles west we came to a splendid basin of springs, covering an area of one mile square — one of the finest spots on the route. We called it Ruthton. Nine and one fourth miles farther west we crossed Rock Castle Creek.[7]

Camped two days to rest. The scenery here is really grand. One mile south is a lofty calcareous limestone bluff, having the appearance of an old English castle with pillars and avenues traversing it in every direction. We named it Castle Rock.

At a distance of about fifty miles we found the largest springs on the route, situated on a pleasant valley, one half mile north of Smoky Hill.[8] Eight miles further on we crossed the north fork, keeping up the south fork. The great difficulty on what was known as the old Pike's Peak road lay in the fact that emigration kept up this [north] fork, then bore across a divide eighty-five miles without water.

Later in his report, Fitch gave his views on the advantage of the Smoky Hill route:

The advantages of the Smoky Hill route over the Platte or the Arkansas must be apparent to everybody. In the first place it is one hundred and sixteen miles shorter to Denver, and emigration, like a ray of light, will not go around unless there are insurmountable obstacles in the way. In this case, the obstructions are altogether on the Platte and Arkansas routes. Aside from the difference in the distance in favor of the new route, you will find no sand on it, whilst from Julesburg to Denver, a distance of two hundred miles, the emigrant or freighter has a dead pull of sand, without a stick of timber or a drop of living water, save for the Platte itself, which is from three to five miles from the road; and when it is taken into consideration that a loaded ox train makes but from twelve to fourteen miles a day, and never exceeds sixteen, it will not pay and will double the distance to drive to the Platte for the purpose of camping and all will admit that the Platte waters are so strongly impregnated with alkali as to render it dangerous to water stock in it.[9]

Lieutenant Fitch arrived in Denver on August 7.[10] His report was everything Butterfield had hoped it would be. If there had been any hesitation on the part of some doubters, this report was intended to dissipate it. Just in case there were doubters left, Colonel Eaton's report sent to the various newspapers for publication in September put the clincher on Fitch's report. With a dateline of September 12, 1865, Ellsworth, Kansas, he stated:

> I have returned from Denver via Smoky Hill River route to this point with ten men, without a military escort, without molestations from the Indians or any other sources. Two hundred and fifty mules belonging to Butterfield's Overland Despatch reached here a few days since, with which I returned and stocked the road to Denver. The road has been fully stocked for a daily line from here to Leavenworth, and with the stock I have with me, it will be complete to Denver in fifteen days.[11]

He proceeded to give the first listing of stations between Leavenworth and Denver. Many of the stations had name changes shortly after this, and some were abandoned in favor of more suitable station sites with new names. Since the road from Leavenworth to Junction City was through an area already settled and roads were maintained there, Colonel Eaton simply states that the distance between these two places was 116 miles. Then he lists the stations as he had laid them out:[12]

Herseys	16
Solomon River*	17
Salina*	16
Spring Creek	15
Ellsworth*	14
Buffalo Creek	14
Lost Creek*	15
Fossil Creek	14
Forks Big Creek*	14
Downer Station	14
Ruthton**	10
Blufton	11
Bridgens Raisin	18
Grannell Spring	12
Chalk Bluffs	13
Monuments*	14
Four Crossings	12
Eaton**	11
Henshaw's Springs	13
Pond's Creek*	11
Fitch's Meadows*	14
Blue Mound Creek	9
Cheyenne Wells*	13
Eureka Creek	21
Dubois*	13
Cornell Creek**	11
Coon Creek	12
Hedinger's Lake*	18
Big Bend Sandy	10
Reed's Springs*	17
Beaver Creek	10
Bijou Basin**	12
Box Elder	10
Parkhurst*	11
Cherry Valley	14
Denver	14
Total distance	588

The stations maked with one star (*) were home stations, where passengers on the stages could get meals. These were always run by a family. The other stations might be managed by a single man or two or three men, according to the amount of work to be done. The stations marked with two stars (**) were both home and cattle stations. Here passengers could get meals, and the freighters with oxteams could change their cattle for fresh ones, leaving their trail-weary animals to rest and be ready to exchange with the next weary animals to come through. The cattle stations were selected because of the great amount of fine grass in the vicinity and the amount of hay that could be stored for winter use.

Eaton was liberal in his praise of this new route:

> At fifteen of the stations named there are large springs of water, varying from five to twenty feet in depth, and these springs or pools formed from the springs are filled with bass and other pan fish, sufficient to supply all the demands of the stations. There is no alkali whatever on the route, and if all the sand was put together it would not reach five miles. The roadbed itself is the best natural one I have ever seen, and I fail to do the Smoky Hill

route justice when I say it is 100 per cent superior to either the Platte or Arkansas routes in every respect. I have no doubt of the verification of my prediction when I say that in twelve months from now there will not a wheel turn, destined for Colorado, New Mexico and Utah, from St. Joseph and points south of it, except by this route.[13]

Eaton was grandly overoptimistic in his predictions, but the road was destined to become not only a major thoroughfare to the West but also one of the bloodiest battlefields between the white and red men.

A later list of stations on the B.O.D. showed several changes. Some of these were made before a stage ever ran over the road; others were made shortly after the road became operational. A quick glance at the revised list of stations and distances between them compared with the names and distances put forth by Colonel Eaton before the first stagecoach headed west will show several changes both in names and distances. Again there is no listing of stations between Atchison and Fort Riley, which was a distance of 116 miles.[14]

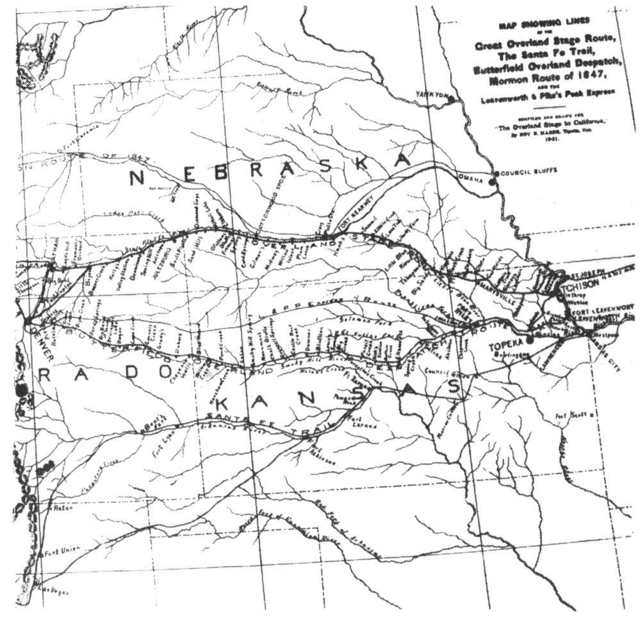

Courtesy the Kansas State Historical Society, Topeka

Map showing lines of the Great Overland Stage route, the Santa Fe Trail, Butterfield Overland Despatch, Mormon route of 1847, and the Leavenworth & Pike's Peak Express.

Station	Miles
Fort Riley	116
Junction City*	3
Chapman's Creek	12
Abilene*	12
Solomon River	10
Salina*	13
Spring Creek	15
Ellsworth*	14
Buffalo Creek	12
Hick's Station*	15
Fossil Creek	15
Forsythe's Creek	11
Big Creek*	11
Louisa Springs	12
Bluffton	14
Downer*	13
Castle Rock Creek	9
Grannell Spring	11
Chalk Bluffs	12
Monument*	13
Smoky Hill Spring	11
Eaton*	12
Henshaw Creek	13
Pond Creek*	11
Willow Creek	14
Blue Mound	9
Cheyenne Wells*	13
Dubois*	24
Grady's	11
Cornell Creek*	13
Coon Creek	12
Hogan	11
Hedinger's Lake	9
Big Bend of Sandy	13
Reed's Springs*	13
Bijou Creek	12
Kiowa Creek	9
Ruthton*	9
Cherry Valley	16
Denver*	14
Total distance	592

The stars (*) denote home stations; there were no cattle stations designated on this list. Many of the changes occurred in an effort to straighten the route; others took place to shorten or lengthen the distance between stations. Still others were made to give the stations better protection from the Indians.

The Indians made no pretense that they wanted to live at peace with the white men who were invading the Smoky Hill region. This was their best buffalo-hunting grounds, and they knew they had to make a stand here or forever give up their land. The white men were just as determined to use this short route to the mountains and the goldfields. A bloody clash was inevitable, in spite of all the talk that the Indians would not fight on the Smoky because it would squeeze them between the army's forces on the Platte and the Arkansas.

The first readjustment of stations took place early, when a more direct route was selected to run almost due west from Fossil Creek, establishing stations at Forsythe Creek, Big Creek, and Lookout, then connecting with the original survey at Louisa Springs. Bluffton, Downer, Ruthton, and Castle Rock were unchanged.

When the Indians began burning stations a new spacing was made. Forsythe Creek was replaced by Forks of Big Creek (Fort Fletcher) nearly five miles farther west. Louisa Springs was abandoned in favor of Stormy Hollow, between five and six miles farther on. Bluffton gave way to White Rock, about three miles beyond Bluffton, Ruthton was eliminated altogether. Ruthton's name was then given to a station about thirty miles from Denver. Goose Creek Station was established between Pond Creek and Willow Creek, dividing the rather long distance between those two stations and offering more protection to the travelers along the road.

The western half of the trail also underwent changes. Although the Smoky Hill River itself rises on the eastern plains of Colorado, the entire road into Denver was called the Smoky Hill Trail. The first big change came when travelers began to understand that the direct route was waterless. After the Blue brothers experienced their death march on that trail, it became known as Starvation Trail.

Lieutenant Fitch knew the story of the Blue brothers when he made his survey in 1865, and he swung up the south fork of the Smoky Hill in western Kansas and then went over the divide to Big Sandy Creek. This proved to be a good trail, with water and grass, and was used as long as Butterfield owned the Overland Despatch. Later the route was changed to run on what was called the north route, leaving the south route at Cheyenne Wells and heading west northwest, joining the old trail for a few miles near Hedinger's Lake, then heading northwest until it hit the Fort Morgan Cutoff from the Platte River Road and going into Denver from the east. This route change wasn't made until Wells Fargo bought out the B.O.D.

All the changes were made to make the trip over the B.O.D. faster and safer, but there was to be little safety on the Smoky Hill Trail until the railroad got its tracks laid. The Indians were not willing to give up their best hunting grounds without a struggle. It was a bitter struggle, painted red with the blood of warriors both red and white.

NOTES

1. Ella A. Butterfield, "Butterfield Overland Despatch," *The Trail* (December 1925).
2. Mrs. Frank C. Montgomery, "Fort Wallace and Its Relation to the Frontier," *Kansas Historical Collections, 1926–1928* 17 (1928), p. 190.
3. Ibid., p. 191.
4. Ibid.
5. This spring is the site of the Pawnee Indian Village that Fremont visited in 1844. It is on the northeast quarter of 21-15-19, surveyed and mapped in 1953 by Howard C. Raynesford.
6. Known now as Cedar Bluffs.
7. Hackberry Creek on today's maps.
8. This is Russell Springs, eight miles east of the forks of the Smoky Hill River.
9. Montgomery, "Fort Wallace," p. 193.
10. Ibid., p. 199.
11. Ibid., p. 194.
12. Ibid., p. 194.
13. Ibid., p. 195.
14. Ibid., p. 196.

CHAPTER 7

THE BEGINNING OF TRAVEL

THE FIRST REAL TRAVEL over the new Butterfield Overland Despatch began on June 24, 1865, almost in the shadow of the surveying party that started out on June 13.[1] It was considered a small train, carrying only one hundred and fifty thousand pounds of freight bound for Denver and other Colorado points.

Since this train carried just seventy-five tons it was about the size of the typical ox-team train that Alexander Majors, of Russell, Majors, and Waddell, described in his book, published in 1893:

> The organization of a full-fledged train for crossing the plains consisted of from twenty-five to twenty-six large wagons that would carry from three to three and a half tons each, the merchandise or contents of each wagon being protected by three sheets of thin ducking, such as is used for army tents. The number of cattle necessary to draw each wagon was twelve, making six yokes or pairs, and a prudent freighter would always have from twenty to thirty head of extra oxen, in case of accident to or lameness of some of the animals. In camping or stopping to allow the cattle to graze, a corral or pen of oblong shape is formed by the wagons, the tongues being turned out, and log chain extended from the hind wheel of each wagon to the fore wheel of the next behind, etc., thus making a solid pen except for a wide gap at each end, through which gaps the cattle are driven when they are to be yoked and made ready for travel, the gaps being filled by the wagonmaster, his assistant, and the extra men, to prevent the cattle from getting out. When the cattle are driven into this corral or pen, each driver yokes his oxen, drives them out to his wagon, and gets ready to start. The entire train of cattle, including extras, numbered from 320 to 330 head and usually four to five mules for riding and herding. The force of men for each train consisted of a wagonmaster, his assistant, and the teamsters, a man to look after the extra cattle, and two or three extra men as a reserve to take the places of any men who might be disabled or sick. The average distance traveled with loaded wagons was from twelve to fifteen miles per day.[2]

With no established stations on the trail at this time there could be no exchange of weary draft animals for fresh ones. The teams that started the trip had to finish it, making for a slower crossing of the plains.

That did not discourage others from starting over the trail almost before it was marked. On July 15 another train carrying seventeen steam boilers left for the mountains, followed by a big train carrying over six hundred thousand pounds of miscellaneous supplies.

Courtesy the Kansas State Historical Society, Topeka

D. and B. Powers, wagon train of Leavenworth, at Denver, June 20, 1868.

Steamboats began unloading great quantities of freight on the Atchison levee for shipment over the Despatch Line. A large amount of freight also came by rail through St. Joseph, bound for transport over the B.O.D. On one day in July nineteen carloads of freight consigned to the B.O.D. were unloaded at Atchison.

The cost of sending freight from Atchison to Denver was not cheap, but considering the danger and the cost to the operators it probably was not exorbitant either. It cost twenty-two and a half cents a pound to transport the freight when the first freight trains began moving slowly over the Smoky Hill Trail.[3]

The cost of the oxen alone will give an idea of how expensive it was to outfit a freight train to travel the trail west. Good oxen sold for $160 to $170 a yoke in Atchison that summer of 1865. In preference to oxen Butterfield bought twelve hundred mules to stock the stations. Most of these were to be used to pull the stagecoaches. They were bought in St. Louis.[4]

To stimulate freighting over the new road Butterfield placed a full-page advertisement in the *Business Mirror for 1865*. It emphasized the advantages of the Butterfield Overland Despatch. The advertisement was spread throughout the country.

> Rates as low as any other parties. Time as quick. Butterfield's Overland Despatch. To all points in Colorado, Utah, New Mexico, Arizona, Buffalo and Montana Territories and the State of Nevada. The company owns its own transportation and gives a thorough bill of lading which protects the shipper from the extreme east to the far west. Express department: August 1, 1865, the company will have a line of daily express coaches between Atchison, Kansas, and Denver, Colorado, and about the first of September, 1865, to Santa Fe, N. M., and as early in the spring as possible the line will be running tri-weekly between Denver and Salt Lake city. Time to Denver 8 days. Mark goods for cattle and mule trains: "Butterfield's Overland Despatch, Atchison, Kansas." Goods to be sent by fast line: "Butterfield's Overland Express, Atchison, Kansas."[5]

Courtesy the Kansas State Historical Society, Topeka
Copied from Harper's Weekly, January 27, 1866

Butterfield's mail coach starting out from Atchison, Kansas

Listed then are the names and addresses of agents in New York City, Boston, Philadelphia, Chicago, Cincinnati, St. Louis, Atchison, Leavenworth, Denver, and Salt Lake City. The officers of the company were listed at the end of the advertisement: "E. P. Bray, president, 66 Broadway, New York City; W. K. Kitchen, Esq., treasurer, Park Bank, New York City; D. A. Butterfield, Esq., General Superintendent, Atchison, Kansas."

The Indians, though alarmed, were not aroused to the point of all-out war against the new road through their hunting grounds by the time the first stagecoach was ready to roll over the new line. That first coach left Atchison on September 11, 1865.[6] One of its passengers was Butterfield himself.

The coach made the trip without any serious trouble, arriving in Denver early in the day on September 23. The trip was over well-traveled roads as far as Fort Ellsworth. The stage left there on the sixteenth and made the rest of the journey over the new road in seven days without a change of stock.[7] The stations were not yet equipped for such changes.

Denver turned out in force to greet the first stagecoach to come over the new road. The *Rocky Mountain News* headlined its report, "Ovation to Colonel Butterfield."

At eight o'clock this morning, word was brought to town that the first coach over "The New Smoky Hill Route" was approaching and a large number of our citizens turned out to meet Colonel D. A. Butterfield, to welcome him to the old home, and to show him and the capitalists connected with him in this monster enterprise, with what favor people of this country view their efforts to shorten up the great thoroughfare to the east. The procession was made up of carriages filled with the businessmen of our city and a cavalcade of horsemen preceded by the First Colorado Band. A banner was borne in one of the leading carriages with the following inscription, "Welcome home, Dave."

The coach was met about four miles up Cherry Creek, where Colonel Butterfield was taken into a carriage with his Honor, George T. Clark, the Mayor, and other distinguished citizens, and escorted to the Planters House, through several of the principle streets, the band playing lively and patriotic airs in its most inspiring manner. When Colonel Butterfield appeared upon the veranda he was received with such a salvo of cheers as must have told him that the people stood with their hearts in their hands.[8]

As the passenger service between the Missouri River and Denver got under way in earnest on the B.O.D., the fare for one passenger, not counting the meals, was $175. Generally the meals were good substantial food for the dust-covered, well-jostled travelers. Fried ham and bacon were the standard meats, with an ample supply of buffalo hump. At the eastern end of the line there were fresh eggs, chicken, and vegetables, along with butter, cream, and coffee. The farther west the traveler went, the less choice of food he had, and the cost of a meal went up from fifty cents to a dollar. Nor was it always clean. One passenger complained about the dirty food, and the station master calmly told him, "I was taught long ago that we must eat a peck of dirt in our lifetime." The traveler shot back, "I am aware of that, sir, but I don't like to eat mine all at once."

Courtesy the Kansas State Historical Society, Topeka
Harper's Weekly, January 27, 1866, T. R. Davis

"The Overland coach office, Denver City, Colorado"

The standard pastry was dried apple pie. The drivers had to share this fare with the passengers on every trip. While the passengers had to put up with the meals on only one trip, the drivers were subjected to it again and again. They reached the point where they could barely look at a dried apple pie. One driver was quoted as saying, "It's dried apple pies from Genesis to Revelations." Another put his feelings into verse that somehow was preserved and passed down for readers who never had to face the daily menu of dried apple pies:

> I loathe! Abhor! Detest! Despise!
> Abominate dried apple pies;
> I like good bread; I like good meat,
> Or anything that's good to eat;
> But of all poor grub beneath the skies
> The poorest is dried apple pies.
> Give me a toothache or sore eyes
> In preference to such kind of pies.
>
> The farmer takes the gnarliest fruit,
> 'Tis wormy, bitter, and hard, to boot;
> They leave the hulls to make us cough,
> And don't take half the peelings off;
> Then on a dirty cord they're strung,
> And from some chamber window hung;
> And there they serve a roost for flies
> Until they're ready to make pies.
> Tread on my corns, or tell me lies,
> But *don't* pass to *me* dried apple pies![9]

The drivers were plenty busy when they first pulled out of a swing station where a fresh team had been put on the coach. But after the sharp edge had been run off the horses by letting them have their heads for a half-mile (and jolting the passengers into a bruised blob of complaining or swearing cargo) he settled down to a monotonous trip to the next station. If no Indians or rain-filled gullies appeared to break that monotony, he often had to resort to singing to keep himself awake. One of the favorite ditties was a song written by Nathan Stein, a fellow employee. He called it simply, "Song of the Overland Stage Driver."[10]

I sing to everybody, in the country and the town,
A song upon a subject that's worthy of renown;
I haven't got a story of fairy land to broach,
But plead for a cause of sticking to the box seat of a coach.

Statesmen and warriors, traders and the rest,
May boast of their profession, and think it is the best;
Their state I'll never envy, I'll have you understand,
Long as I can be a driver on the jolly "Overland."

Travelers on the coachs of the B.O.D. found it a fairly easy journey until they reached Fort Ellsworth. Fort Ellsworth had been established in August 1864 where the military road crossed the Smoky Hill River on its way to Fort Zarah on the Arkansas. Fort Ellsworth was on the north bank of the river and was a one-company post. It was not enclosed by a stockade. The most imposing building was the commissary, a sod house about 25 by 40 feet in size, overlooking the river. The officers quarters and barracks were nothing but dugouts in the bank along the river front.[11]

Old Fort Ellsworth was small, but it straddled what later surveys showed to be the dividing line between two townships, being partly in Section 2, Township 16, Range 8 and partly in Section 35, Township 15, Range 8.[12]

The travelers left the estabished trail here and turned northwest, staying to the north of the Smoky Hill River. About twelve miles from Fort Ellsworth they came to Buffalo Creek Station.[13] Buffalo Creek was only a swing station where the team was changed. This was usually accomplished in three to five minutes, and the coach rumbled on.

Often the driver would let the team loaf along until he came in sight of a station and then would crack the whip and gallop into the station yard like a messenger of Mercury.[14] It added a bit of novelty and excitement to the monotony of the journeys for the passengers.

About fifteen miles beyond Buffalo Creek they came to a station first called Lost Creek, then Wilson Creek, and later Hick's Station.[15] This was a home station, where the passengers were allowed to disembark and get a meal. The trail now turned almost due west, keeping to the level benchland north of the twisting Smoky Hill River.

Another fifteen miles brought the coach to Fossil Creek Station.[16] From here the trail swung a little to the northwest, leaving the banks of the river. The next station, eleven miles from Fossil Creek, was Forsythe's Creek, sometimes called Walker Creek.[17] It was soon abandoned in favor of Fort Fletcher, about five miles farther west, when the fort was established October 11, 1865.[18]

Fort Fletcher was a home station with soldier protection. That was a rarity on the B.O.D. and was welcomed by both passengers and drivers. It was first called Forks of Big Creek, then Fort Fletcher, and finally Old Fort Hays.[19] The trail from Forsythe's Creek veared a little southwest to Fort Fletcher, but by now the trail was five or six miles north of the Smoky Hill.

About eight miles to the west was Big Creek Station.[20] In spite of its nearness to Fort Fletcher it became one of the more important stations on the route. It was almost exactly halfway between Old Fort Hays, or Fort Fletcher, and the new Fort Hays that was built in 1867. It was a home station, where meals were served and

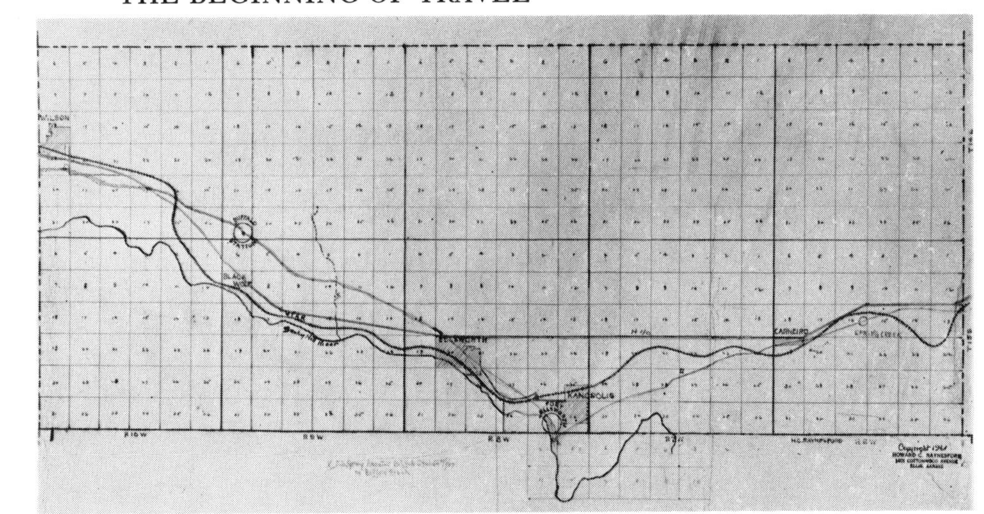

Butterfield Overland Despatch route through Ellsworth County, Kansas.

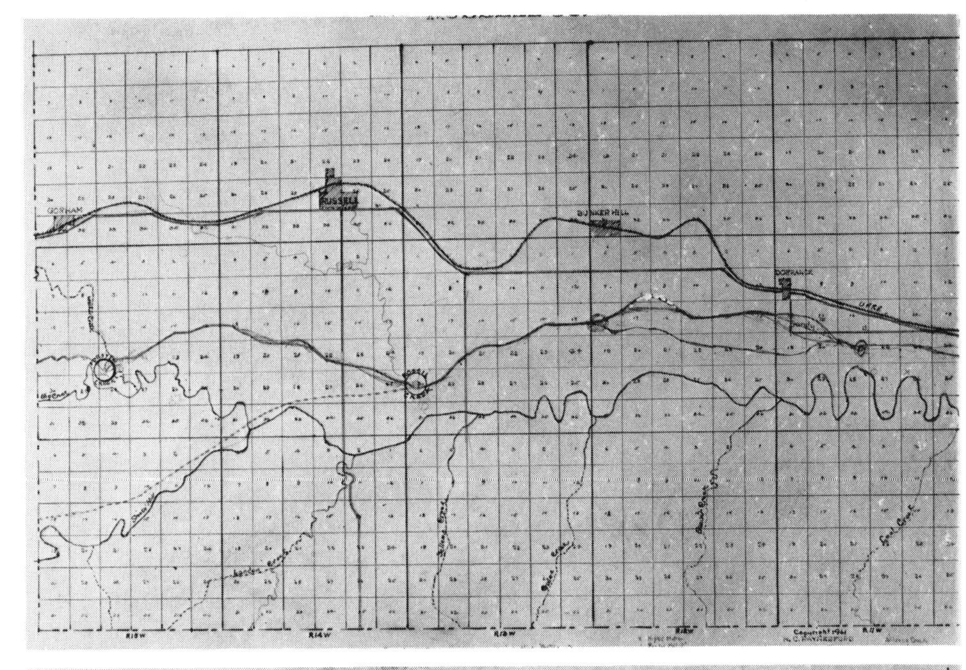

Butterfield Overland Despatch route through Russell County, Kansas.

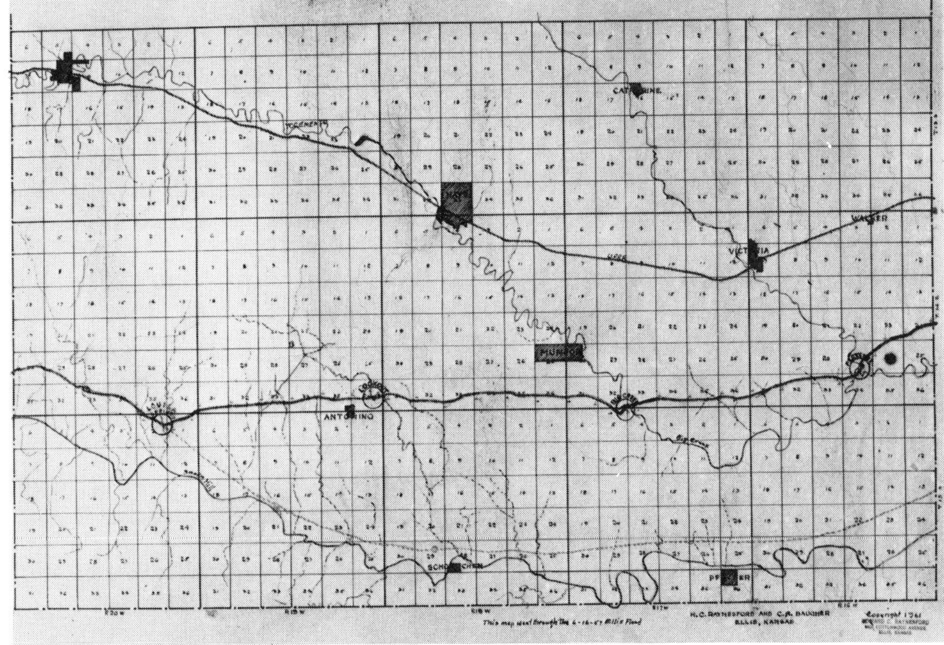

Butterfield Overland Despatch route through Ellis County, Kansas.

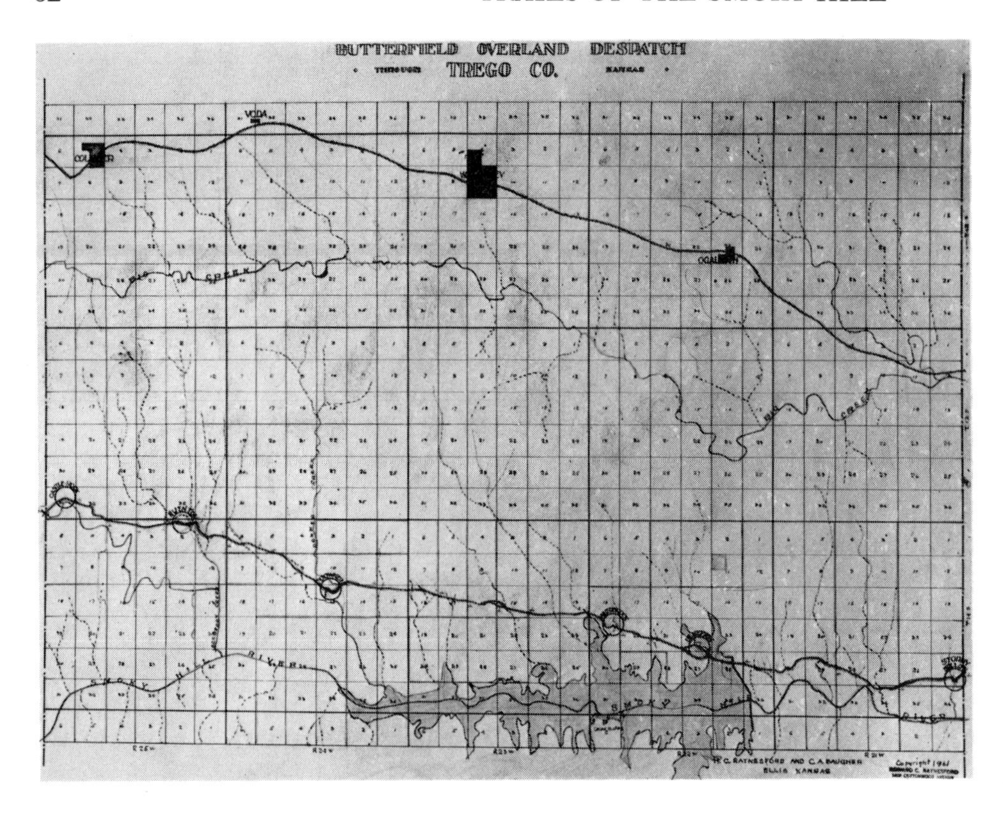

Butterfield Overland Despatch route through Trego County, Kansas.

stock was kept. The stables and pasture were on the north side of the creek.

Stage drivers changed here, so there were always drivers boarding at the station, waiting to take their turns driving the coaches. There were eight or ten tenders working here under the direction of Nate Swan. A. C. Pyle ran a blacksmith shop. Enoch Cummings was resident division agent of the B.O.D. from Big Creek Station west.

Eight miles to the west and still well north of the Smoky Hill River was Lookout Station.[21] The stables were some distance from the rest of the buildings and separated from them by a small ravine. It was one of the few stations where there were no tunnels joining the main station house with the stables. The stables opened out onto the creek to the north.

Another seven miles to the west was Louisa Springs.[22] This was soon abandoned in favor of Stormy Hollow, [23] another five miles to the west. Horses and mules were kept here for use on the coaches.

Eight or nine miles farther west was Blufton Station, often spelled Bluffton.[24] This station became a victim of the respacing of stations when Indian raids became unbearable. It was abandoned in favor of White Rock Station farther to the west.

As a B.O.D. station Blufton had a short life. The site is better remembered for a incident that took place there sometime after the station itself was moved to White Rock. It was a picturesque spot and became a favorite camping place, even though there was no station at the site. One stagecoach traveler described it in a letter after seeing it; "A picturesquely located station. What strange convulsion caused the strange crag-like mass? It rises from the plain like a vast castle, fashioned by the most ancient architects."

The bluff from which the station got its name stood about seventy-five feet high and was almost perpendicular. Some say it rivaled Independence Rock for the number of names per square foot craved into it. In many cases names were carved over earlier carvings. One of the earliest

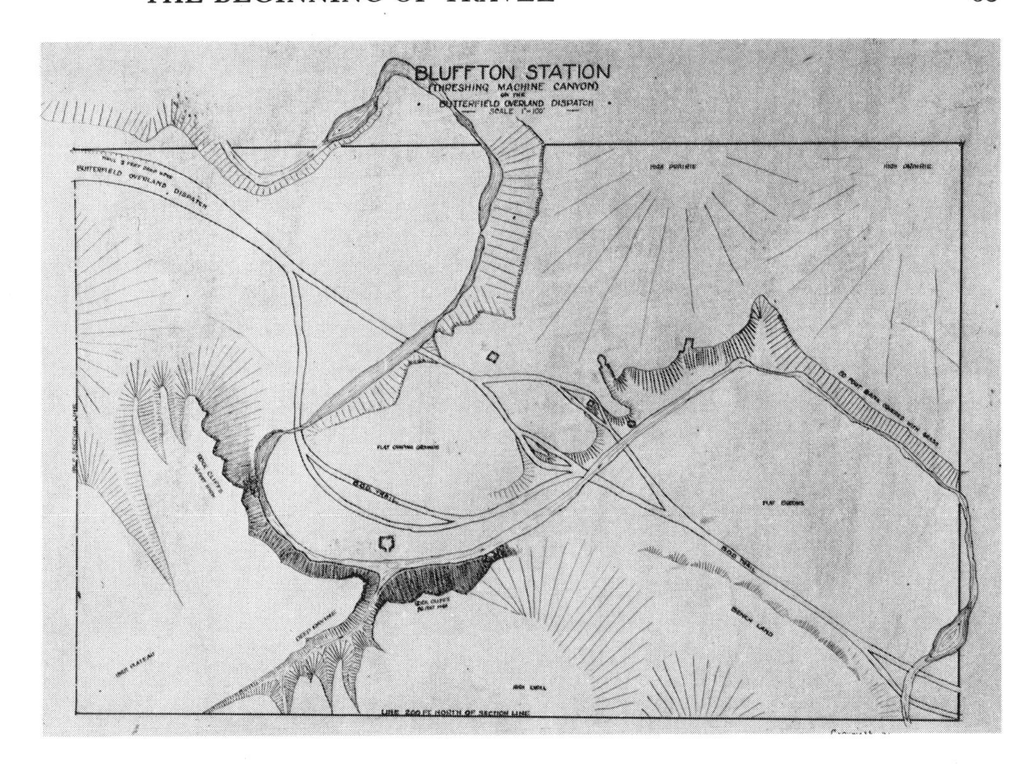

Blufton Station

names recorded on the rock was that of T. R. Hunt of New Jersey in 1849. He was probably a member of the government surveying party authorized by Congress, as a result of Fremont's report, to determine whether the Smoky Hill route would be practical for a government road to the West.

Two other deeply inscribed names were C. Kelley and W. W. Spencer in 1859. These names were accompanied by the outline of an antelope and a well-defined Masonic square and compass. These men were likely among those who took the short route, the Smoky Hill Trail, to the goldfields to "get rich quick."

The bulk of the early names, however, were carved into the rock in 1865. Many were members of the Third Wisconsin Cavalry, which accompanied the surveying party of Lieutenant Fitch in the summer of 1865.

Because it was such a favorite camping spot, it isn't hard to understand why the freighters who were transporting a horse-powered threshing machine to Utah for Brigham Young's farmers happened to camp here. Instead of stopping on the grassy flat where the station buildings had been, they camped close under the bluff and directly in front of a deep rocky gully which cut down through the bluff. This made it easy for the Indians, who undoubtly had been watching them on the trail, to crawl down the gully until they were close enough to pick off every one of the freighters at their campfire. The Indians then set everything on fire, including the threshing machine.

The metal parts of the machine were still around for the settlers to find when

Canyon From West Showing Trail

Photo by Howard Raynesford

Blufton Station (Threshing Machine Canyon)

they arrived, and they named the place Threshing Machine Canyon. Few people knew or remembered that it originally had been Blufton Station on the B.O.D.[25]

NOTES

1. Ruth Jackson, "Butterfield Overland Despatch Trail Markers," *Fort Wallace* (Kans.) *Bugle*, June 1965.
2. Robert W. Richmond and Robert W. Mardock, *A Nation Moving West* (Lincoln: University of Nebraska Press, 1966), p. 216.
3. Noel Loomis, *Wells Fargo* (New York: Clarkson N. Potter, 1968), p. 176.
4. Jackson, "B.O.D. Trail Markers."
5. *Atchison City Directory and Business Mirror for 1865*. The advertisement was distributed all over the country to attract business to the B.O.D.
6. Floyd Benjamin Streeter, *The Kaw* (New York: Farrar & Rinehart, 1941), p. 11.
7. Ibid., p. 12.
8. *Rocky Mountain News* (Denver), 23 September 1865.
9. Streeter, *The Kaw*, p. 20.
10. Ibid., p. 23.
11. George Jelinek, "The Ellsworth Story," *Ellsworth* (Kans.) *Reporter*, 3 August 1967.
12. All the station sites in western Kansas were located by Howard Raynesford over forty years of careful searching of the areas and meticulous research of every document relating to the trail and the surveys. The legal descriptions of these locations are included here for the history buff who wished to stand on the site of the old stations where so much history of the plains was made.
13. Buffalo Creek Station was on the SE quarter of Section 31-14-9.
14. Streeter, *The Kaw*, p. 22.
15. Hick's Station was on the east half of Section 21-14-11.
16. Fossil Creek Station was on Section 30-14-13.
17. Forsythe's Creek Station was on the SW quarter of Section 21-14-15.
18. Mrs. Frank C. Montgomery, "Fort Wallace and Its Relation to the Frontier," *Kansas Historical Collections, 1926–1928* 17 (1928), p. 196.
19. Fort Fletcher was on the SE quarter of Section 27-14-16.
20. Big Creek Station was on the NE quarter of Section 5-15-17.
21. Lookout Station was on the SE quarter of Section 36-14-19. This was the first B.O.D. station surveyed and mapped by Howard Raynesford and his son, Kirk, in 1930.
22. Montgomery, "Fort Wallace," p. 198. Louisa Springs Station was on the NE quarter of section 2-15-20. This section was probably named for Lieutenant Fitch's wife, Louisa, who accompanied her husband on his survey.
23. Stormy Hollow Station was on the SE quarter of Section 25-14-21.
24. Blufton Station was on the SE quarter of Section 22-14-22.
25. There is little resemblance to the site as it was in the 1860s. The dust storms of the 1930s covered the grass with dust. Weeds grew up where the grass had been so lush. A flash flood shortly after that filled some of the draw with debris. Great chunks of the cliff have crumbled away, including huge slabs that were carved full of names. Now the Cedar Bluff Dam, just a little over a mile to the east of the canyon, banks water up to the base of the bluff, covering a big portion of the B.O.D. trail between the campsite and the present dam.

CHAPTER 8

ON TO THE WEST

WHITE ROCK STATION, which took the place of abandoned Blufton Station, was only about three miles to the northwest of Blufton.[1]

Downer Station, the next in line, was about nine or ten miles to the west and a little north, being almost three miles north of the river.[2] Present-day WaKeeney is the nearest town of any size to this site, about fourteen or fifteen miles to the north.

Lieutenant Fitch made it a home station because of the fine grass and water. It was not situated well for defense and suffered heavily from Indian attacks before it was abandoned on May 28, 1868.

About seven miles to the northwest was the next station, Ruthton, which was used only a short time.[3] Castle Rock was next, about four miles west of Ruthton.[4] It was on the western edge of Trego County, perhaps six or seven miles as the crow flies southwest of the huge rock for which it was named. Castle Rock is in eastern Gove County.

The trail veered to the southwest here about eight or nine miles to Grannell

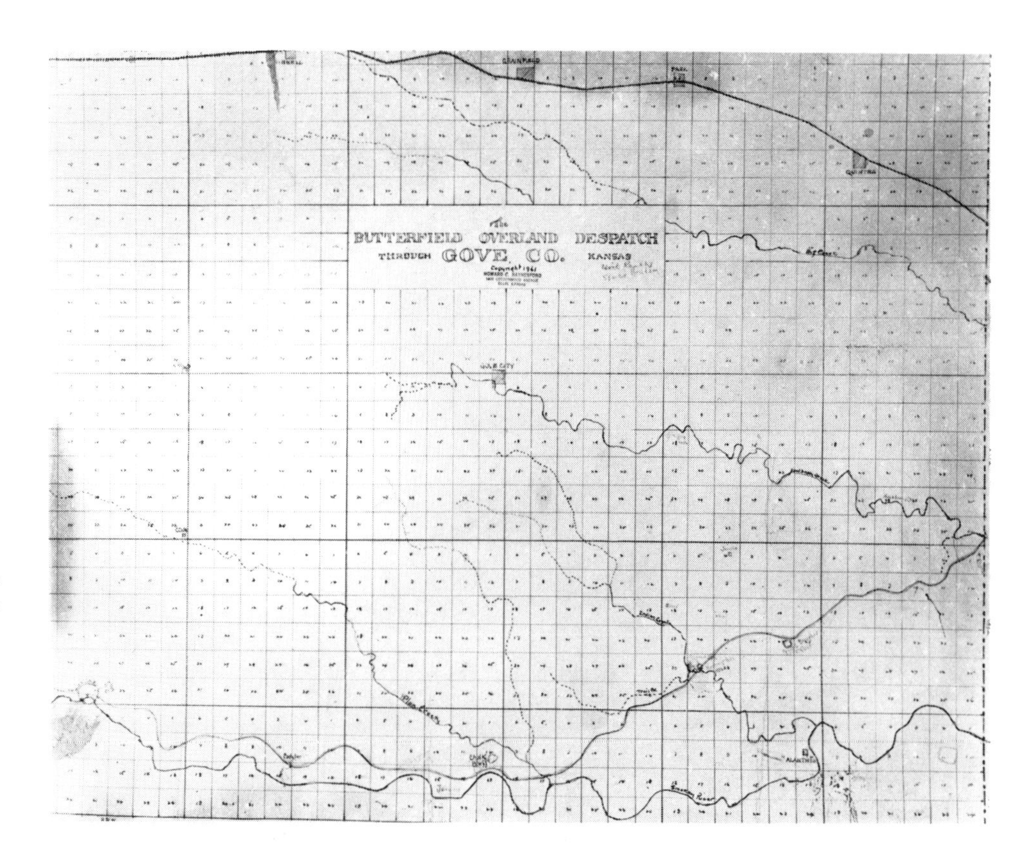

Butterfield Overland Despatch route through Gove County, Kansas.

Photo by Author

Old B.O.D. to White Rock Station as it appears today

Photo by Leslie Linville

Monument Rocks

Springs.[5] Chalk Bluffs was twelve to fourteen miles farther southwest, on the north banks of the Smoky Hill River.[6]

Then came Carlyle Station, sometimes called Bridgins Raisin, about seven or eight miles west of Chalk Bluffs, the trail running parallel to the river.[7]

Monument Station was next.[8] It was one of the most famous stations along the trail, not only for the unusual rock formations in the vicinity but for the Indian troubles that forced the army to station a detachment of soldiers here and designate it a fort.[9]

A mile to the northeast of the station were the Monuments, castle-like rocks that rose abruptly out of the level prairie. These rocks are sometimes called the Pyramids because of their proximity to Chief Smoky the Kansas Sphinx. This solitary rock stands to the north of the main cluster of towering monuments and does bear a remarkable resemblance to a human head. The monuments are just north of the Smoky Hill River near the western boundary of Gove County, about twenty-five to twenty-eight miles south of Oakley and three or four miles east of Highway 83.

The station was built very much like the others. The stable was a long dugout gouged into the north bank of the river, where it was well protected from the weather and within easy reach of the river itself.

About eleven or twelve miles to the northwest, in Logan County, was the

Harper's Weekly, April 21, 1866

Interior — Smoky Hill Station

Courtesy the Kansas State Historical Society, Topeka *KSHS Photo 1957*

Smoky Hill Trail ruts, Monument Rocks

Smoky Hill Springs Station, sometimes referred to as Four Crossings.[10]

Eaton Station was named for Colonel Eaton, who headed the construction crew of twenty-six men who built the stations along the B.O.D. There were some fine springs here. This was a home station and was also called Russell's Springs.[11]

The road held to the north of the river bottom here to avoid the twisting course of the river and the bluffs. Just a few miles west of Eaton Station the river forked, and here the trail crossed the forks to continue toward the west. There was no station here, but it was a favorite campground called the Forks of the Smoky. After several Indian raids the place earned the name of Death Hollow.

William A. Bell described this campground as it appeared in the 1860s: "We had crossed the Smoky Hill Fork for the last time and had pitched our tents on its banks, in a spot known as Death Hollow. The name was not a prepossessing one, but so many trains had been attacked there, and so much life had been taken on that piece of bottom-land, that it was, at all events, appropriate."[12]

The rumor circulated among all travelers that any train that camped there was almost certain to be attacked. However, the abundance of water, wood and grass overrode the apprehension of the travelers.

Bell's description continued: "On one side were the bluffs, which abruptly separated the depressed valley from the general level of the plain. On the other flowed the stream, its banks clothed with willow, cottonwood trees, and tall rank grass; beyond were the bluffs of the opposite side, lying pretty close to the river."[13]

It was at these forks that the early travelers in 1858 and 1859 made a serious mistake. The North Fork of the Smoky Hill River has more water in it at the confluence than does the South Fork. Travelers, not knowing what lay ahead, logically took the North Fork. This fork however, soon becomes dry. There are few creeks in

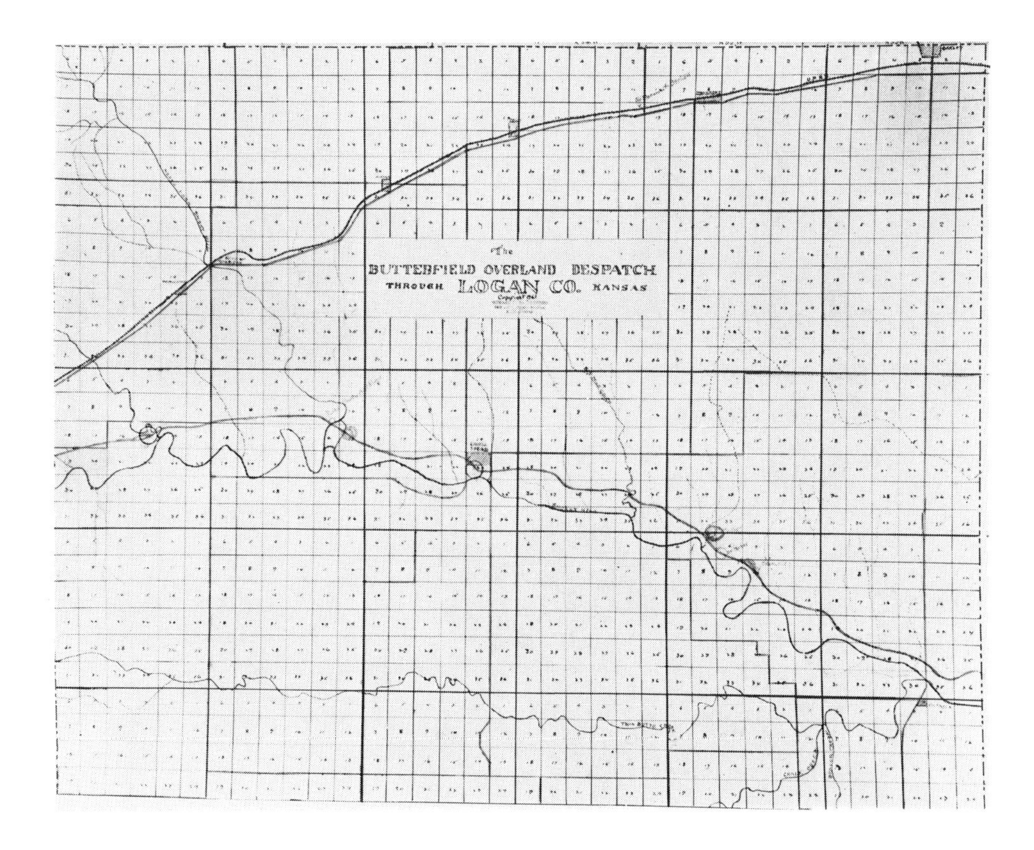

Butterfield Overland Despatch route through Logan County, Kansas.

that area that have water, especially in the dry season, so the travelers were faced with many long miles of parched prairie with not a drop of water for themselves or their stock.

By 1865, however, Lieutenant Fitch knew about the dry country up the North Fork of the Smoky, so he led his surveying party up the South Fork. This was a fortunate choice. Even in dry seasons there was usually water to be had by digging in the sand in the bed of the South Fork.

Fitch laid out the next station on the north bank of the South Fork of the Smoky Hill and named it Henshaw Springs. Some called it Henshaw Creek.[14]

The next station he laid out was Pond Creek station. It was set up for business on the B.O.D. in September 1865[15] and was destined to become one of the major points along the Butterfield Overland Despatch. Fort Wallace, which played such a heroic part in the battles on the western Kansas and eastern Colorado plains, was established only a short time later just to the east of Pond Creek Station.

Pond Creek was a home station. The station and the stable were built fairly close together for defense purposes. Beyond the barn was the corral, built of rocks. There was also an enclosure built of rocks that contained the hay stacked for winter use.

Like most of the stations on the B.O.D., Pond Creek had underground tunnels running from the house to the barn and from both buildings to rifle pits. These pits were big enough for two men to stand in them and maneuver comfortably. They were roofed by a huge slab of stone held off the ground by short pieces of wood. The defenders could fire at the raiders from under this roof of stone with deadly accuracy while enjoying almost complete protection from the rifle balls and arrows of the Indians.

There were three of these defense pits. One was at the end of the tunnel running out from the stable; one went from the house; and one, larger than the others, guarded the rear of the station. There were several Spencer repeating rifles and Henry breech-loading rifles at the station. Two men, armed with a couple of these rifles each, could hold a great number of attackers at bay. The Spencer rifles held seven cartridges, while the Henrys were eighteen-shot repeaters.

The defenders of the station put little black flags above each of the stone-covered rifle pits. After a few attempts to

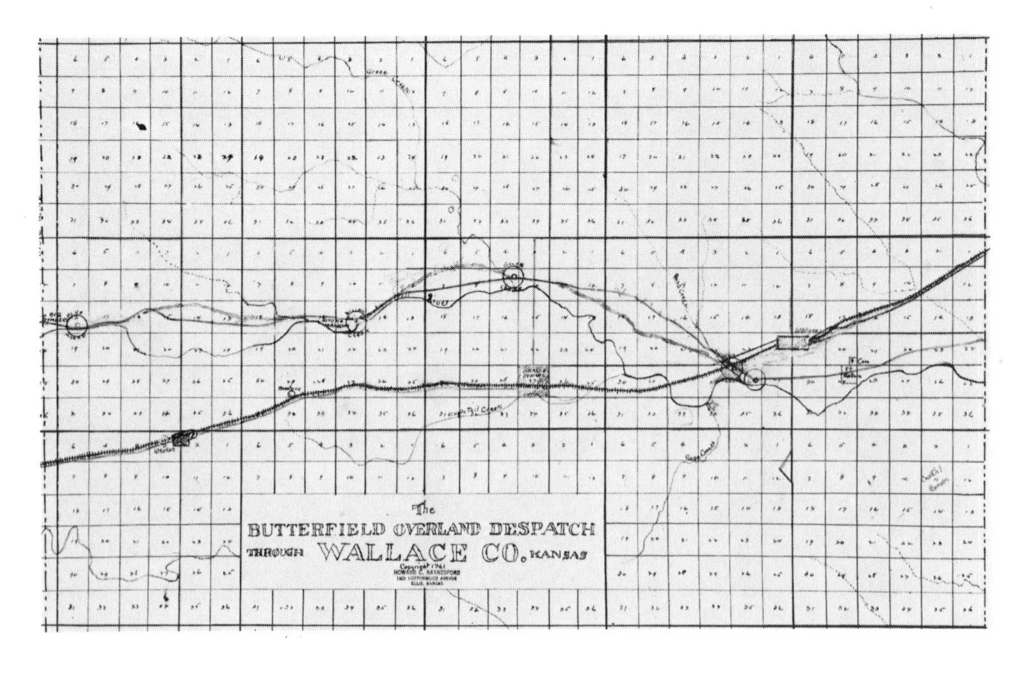

Butterfield Overland Despatch route through Wallace County, Kansas.

Courtesy the Kansas State Historical Society, Topeka

Pond City Stage Station, 1865 — Fort Wallace Museum, 1963

overrun the Pond Creek Station, the Indians learned that the little black flags meant there was no quarter asked and none given.[16]

The next station, Goose Creek, was not marked out by Fitch in his original survey. It was put in later because of the long distance between Pond Creek and Willow Creek. Goose Creek Station was at the mouth of Goose Creek.[17] The soil here is very sandy. Floods were a constant threat to the buildings and have long since washed out any trace of the old station.

The next station had two names. Since it was at the mouth of Willow Creek it was generally called Willow Creek Station, but it was also given the name of Fitch's Meadow, for Lieutenant Fitch who led the surveyors. [18] The grass was good in this area and Indians fought hard to keep possession of it, so both Willow Creek and Goose Creek stations had more than their share of trouble with the Indians.

Within about a mile of the Kansas-Colorado border was the last B.O.D. station in Kansas. It also shared two names: Blue Mound and Big Timbers.[19] There were several acres of big cottonwood trees here with no underbrush. Trees were very scarce in this area, and this was a favorite camping place for the Indians. Less than a year before the stages started running, the remnants of Black Kettle's band that escaped from Chivington at Sand Creek in November 1864 came to the big timbers to camp and recover from their wounds and their losses.

Blue Mound Station got its name because, from a distance, the tops of the huge cottonwood trees looked to the surveyors like a blue hill or mound on the horizon.[20] George Bird Grinnell states that these cottonwoods looked like blue smoke from a distance and that this gave rise to the name of Smoky Hill for the river.[21]

Barely out of sight of Blue Mound Station the trail crossed out of Kansas State into Colorado Territory. About fifteen miles west of the state line the road came to the next station, Cheyenne Wells.[22] Lieutenant Fitch had been here in 1860 on a survey and had dug the well just north of the south fork of the Smoky. In his report to David Butterfield, he said "Sixteen and a half miles west [from Blue Mound Station] we reached the Cheyenne Well, at the head of Smoky Hill. This well was built by our party in 1860 and is one of the finest of wells, yielding sufficient water to supply a heavy emigration."[23]

Fitch reported that he located the next station about eleven miles to the southwest of Cheyenne Wells. He erected a mound there to have a well dug, since the trail had left the Smoky Hill River and was cutting across toward the Big Sandy. This station was called Eureka.[24]

Another thirteen miles to the southwest the trail hit Big Sandy Creek. Here Lieutenant Fitch established Dubois Station.[25] At this point the travelers heading toward Bent's Fort on the Arkansas River left those going to Denver and headed mostly south, while B.O.D. travel-

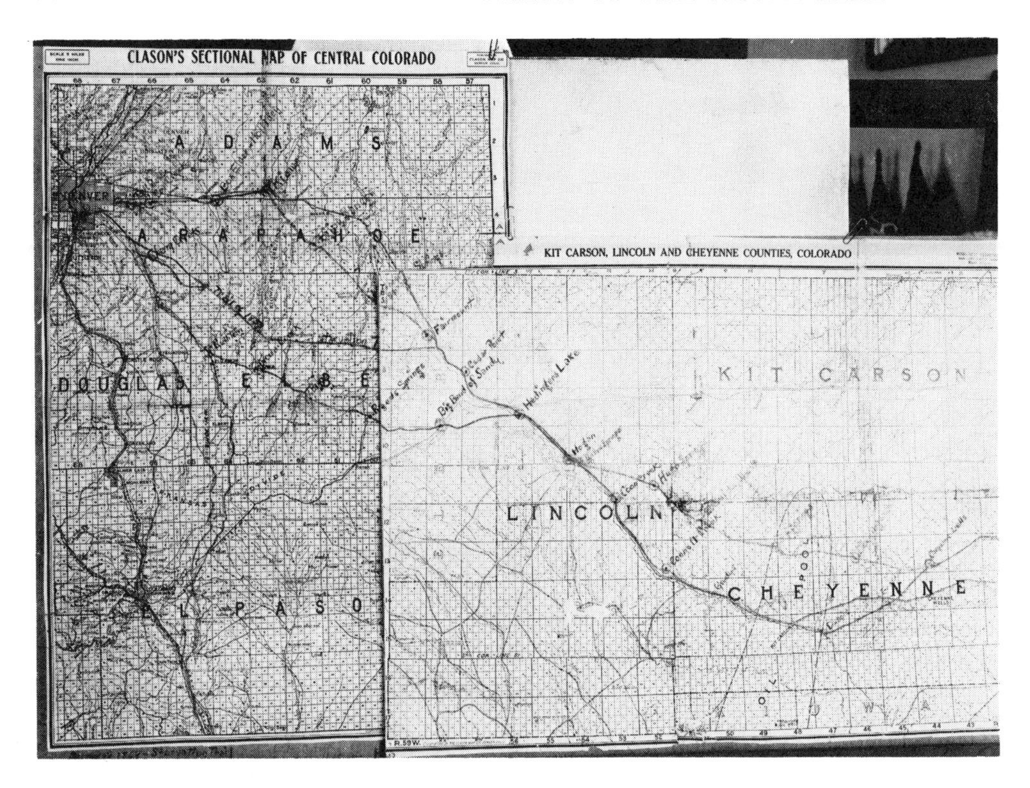

Smoky Hill Trail in Colorado

ers turned to the northwest along the banks of the Big Sandy.[26]

Grady's Station was on the north bank of the Big Sandy about eleven or twelve miles farther on.[27] Bayard Taylor mentions it briefly in his report. "At Grady's Station, there was but one man, a lonely troglodyte, burrowing in the bank like a cliff swallow."[28]

Connell Creek Station was thirteen miles farther up the Big Sandy.[29] Various descriptions of the trail list this as Cornell Creek or Cornett Creek. It was at the point where Connell Creek ran into the Big Sandy.

Coon Creek Station was on the north bank of Coon Creek where it ran into the Big Sandy.[30]

Hogan's Station was eleven miles northwest of Coon Creek Station.[31] There was a spring here called Cap Barron Spring on the north bank of the Big Sandy.

Hedinger's Lake Station, often shortened to Lake Station, was only nine miles farther to the northwest.[32] It was an important station; it was here that the Smoky Hill South and the Smoky Hill North trails separated in 1866. This station was a huge dugout with sod walls above the ground. Loopholes were in the sod walls for fighting Indians. The station was large enough to hold an entire stagecoach if the need arose. Not far from the house was the stable, also a dugout. The drivers called it a mule cellar. A tunnel connected the station and the mule cellar.[33]

The Smoky Hill South Trail of 1865 crossed the big Sandy here and headed due west until it crossed the Big Sandy again at Well's Ranch. This saved several miles for the travelers because it cut off the meandering northern loop of the Big Sandy. The station at Well's Ranch was called the Big Bend of the Sandy.[34] This station had a board stable covered with cottonwood poles for a roof.

Reed's Spring Station was another thirteen miles to the west.[35] The barn here was a huge dugout, with room between the stalls for a stagecoach to be driven in without unhitching the team — a factor worth a good deal to a driver coming in

Photo by Author

Smoky Hill marker — Denver

under pursuit from Indians. In the harness room at one end of the barn they stored flour and seed and even sold articles such as tobacco, red jacket bitters, and other luxuries.[36]

The trail here began turning to the northwest toward Denver. The next station was Bijou Creek,[37] about twelve miles from Reed's Springs. Another nine miles to the northwest was Kiowa Station.[38] This station had its full share of Indian troubles.[39]

Another seven miles west and two north was Ruthton Station, referred to at first as Running Creek.[40] It picked up its name of Ruthton after the Ruthton Station in Kansas was abandoned.

Another ten miles toward Denver was Sulphur Station, also called Parkhurst Station.[41] It was on the south bank of Sulphur Gulch and had a good well. This station was only a short distance from the spot where Twenty Mile House was established, and it may be that all the facilities were moved to Twenty Mile House.[42]

Only a few miles farther up Cherry Creek was Cherry Creek Station,[43] at the junction of Cherry Creek and Sampson Gulch. This was the point where Starvation Trail, or Middle Smoky Hill Trail, reached Cherry Creek. This trail was later moved to the ridge above Sampson Gulch. There is speculation that Cherry Creek Station was moved to Twelve Mile House.[44]

About fourteen miles down Cherry Creek the trail came to an end at Denver. A plaque was placed on the Broadway side of the Pioneer Monument at the three-street junction of Broadway, Colfax, and Fifteenth Streets in Denver. It reads:

> Here was the end of the famous Smoky Hill Trail emigrant and stage road extending from the Missouri River to Denver. Traveled by pioneers 1858. Surveyed by W. G. Russell 1860.[45] Route of Butterfield Overland Despatch and Wells Fargo Express. The trail took its human toll. Death by thirst and Indian raids. Placed by the State Historical Society of Colorado from the Mrs J. N. Hall Foundation and by the City and County of Denver. 1936.

There were several "mile houses" on Cherry Creek south of Denver. They were, for the most part, taverns which

Photo by Author

Smoky Hill Monument — Denver

served meals and rented beds to weary travelers. With travel from Denver to Santa Fe going up Cherry Creek, as well as travel over the Smoky Hill Trail, these houses did a thriving business.

Twenty Mile House was established in 1864 at the junction of Sulphur Gulch and Cherry Creek. When Lieutenant Fitch surveyed for the B.O.D. in 1865 he laid out a station very near Twenty Mile House. That was Sulphur Gulch or Parkhurst Station. Evidence seems to point toward the combining of these two places at Twenty Mile House later.

Seventeen Mile House was not a stage stop but did serve as a tavern and hotel. Twelve Mile House and Four Mile House were much like Twenty Mile House, giving meals and other accommodations to travelers.

Twelve Mile House was the largest hotel in the country. The ballroom was on the second floor, and great dances were held there. The band was brought out from Denver for $50. Tickets to the dance and the meal that went with it were $5 each. John and Jane Melvin were the proprietors in the late 1860s. Mrs. Melvin cooked and baked far into the night for three days before a dance. She roasted meat, churned butter, baked endless loaves of bread and thirty-six cakes for each dance.[46] These taverns remained a thriving business even after the railroad reached Denver, replacing the through stagecoaches. There was still travel down from Denver to the Santa Fe Trail and quite a bit of travel to the settlements south of Denver.

It was customary for stage drivers to change their teams from mules to horses at Twelve Mile House or perhaps closer to town in order to make a more dashing appearance on the streets of Denver.

Neither Nine Mile House nor Seven Mile House were stage stops, but they apparently did a good business. Four Mile House was a stage stop, and the coaches usually halted there to allow passengers to refresh themselves and wash off the dust of the road before riding into Denver. It was also a place where freighters often camped, making the trip into Denver the next day to transact their business. They would then come back to Four Mile House for the night before starting the long journey back over the monotonous trail. Four Mile House was built in 1858.

By late 1865 the Butterfield Overland Despatch had been marked out, the stations established, and travel begun. But the trouble had only started. Travel was not a pleasure. The road was dusty and rough, water was scarce in places, the food was not the best at many stops.

The worst, however, was the fury of the Indians. The Smoky Hill area was one of their best hunting grounds, and they were determined not to lose it. To the north a man named Bozeman had laid out a road to the goldfields of Montana, through another of the Indians' favorite hunting grounds. Although the Indians must have seen now hopeless their battle was, they had no choice but to fight if they hoped to survive as free men. Both in Wyoming and Kansas, the prairie would turn red with blood before the battles were over.

NOTES

1. White Rock Station was on the NE quarter of Section 19-14-22.
2. Downer Station was on the NE quarter of Section 15-14-24.
3. Mrs. Frank C. Montgomery, "Fort Wallace and Its Relation to the Frontier," *Kansas Historical Collections, 1926–1928* 17 (1928), p. 198. Ruthton Station was probably named for the wife of Captain West, who accompanied her husband on the surveying trip in 1865. It was located on the NE quarter of Section 2-14-25.
4. Castle Rock Station was on the Ne quarter of Section 31-13-25.
5. Grannell Springs Station was located by E. M. Bougher on the SE quarter of Section 23-14-27 in Gove County.
6. Chalk Bluffs Station was on the south half of Section 12-15-29.
7. Carlyle Station was on Section 15-15-30.
8. Monument Station was on the SW quarter of Section 33-14-31.
9. Charles R. Wetzel, "Monument Station, Gove County," *Kansas Historical Quarterly* (Autumn 1960).
10. The exact site of Smoky Hill Springs Station has never been determined to the complete satisfaction of historians. It is believed to be on the NW corner of Section 4 or the NE corner of Section 5-14-33.
11. Eaton Station, or Russell's Springs Station, was on the west half of Section 23-13-35. This is right in the southeast corner of the present town of Russell Springs. This town became the county seat of Logan County and held that position until the early 1960s, when the county seat was moved to Oakley in the northeastern corner of the country.
12. William A. Bell, *New Tracks in North America* (New York: Scribner, Welford & Company, 1870; reprint ed. Albuquerque: Horn & Wallace, 1965), p. 48.

13. Ibid.
14. Henshaw Springs Station was on the NW quarter of Section 13-13-37.
15. L. G. Delay, "Pond Creek Centennial" *Fort Wallace* (Kans.) *Bugle*, June 1965. Pond Creek Station was on the east half of Section 26-13-39.
16. Bell, *New Tracks*, p. 48.
17. Goose Creek Station was on the NE quarter of Section 9-13-40.
18. Montgomery, "Fort Wallace," p. 198. Willow Creek Station was on the east half of Section 15-13-41. Present-day Willow Creek cuts through to the Smoky Hill River about a mile and a half west of the old station site, but the long-abandoned bed of the creek can be traced to the site of the station. The creek has cut a new channel through the soft sand, probably during some flood.
19. Blue Mound or Big Timbers Station was on the SE quarter of Section 18-13-42.
20. The settlers who began coming into this area as early as 1886 cut down almost all the cottonwood trees for firewood and lumber to build houses and barns. Only the stumps remained, and later floods washed many of these stumps away. The riverbed, which evidently was of normal size when the B.O.D. ran along its banks, is now almost a quarter of a mile wide but with very little water in it. Floods have washed away the sandy banks and thrown up new ones.
21. Montgomery, "Fort Wallace," p. 198.
22. Cheyenne Wells Station was on the SE quarter of Section 28-13-44.
23. Montgomery, "Fort Wallace," p. 192. There is evidence that other wells were dug here, in addition to the one dug by Lieutenant Fitch's party in 1860. A. A. Pelton, who lives only about a mile from the wells, said there were three distinct depressions of wells when he came there about 1930. He said the wells were about sixteen to twenty feet square and were lined with timbers standing upright. The wells were necessary because the Smoky Hill was dry through much of the season here. However, the water level was only a few feet below the dry river bed, so the wells were shallow.
24. Eureka Station was on the SW quarter of Section 30-14-45.
25. Dubois Station was on the NE quarter of Section 20-15-47.
26. Margaret Long, *The Smoky Hill Trail* (Denver: W. H. Kistler Company, 1943), p. 68.
27. Grady's Station was on the SW quarter of Section 17-14-50.
28. Long, *Smoky Hill Trail*, p. 51.
29. Connell Creek Station was on the NW quarter of Section 26-13-52.
30. Coon Creek Station was in the center of Section 33-11-53.
31. Hogan's Station was on the NE quarter of Section 36-10-55.
32. Hedinger's Lake Station was on the NE quarter of Section 27-9-56.
33. Long, *Smoky Hill Trail*, p. 70.
34. Big Bend of the Sandy Station was on the south side of Section 33-9-58.
35. Reed's Spring Station was near the middle of Section 28-9-60.
36. Long, *Smoky Hill Trail*, p. 72.
37. Bijou Creek Station was on the SE quarter of Section 11-9-62.
38. Kiowa Station was on the SE quarter of Section 17-8-63.
39. The town of Kiowa, Colorado, is situated right on the site of the old Kiowa Creek Station. The old station was on the north side of what is now the main street. The Indian massacres that occurred in the vicinity are commemorated by a monument erected on the courthouse grounds.
40. Ruthton Station or Running Creek Station was on the NW quarter of Section 6-8-64.
41. Sulphur Station was in the middle of Section 26-6-66.
42. Long, *Smoky Hill Trail*, p. 76.
43. Cherry Creek Station was on the SW quarter of Section 18-5-66.
44. Long, *Smoky Hill Trail*, p. 76-7.
45. This was the W. Green Russell hired by the city of Leavenworth in the spring of 1860 for $3500 to survey a road up the Smoky Hill to Denver.
46. Long, *Smoky Hill Trail*, p. 44.

CHAPTER 9

THE BEGINNING OF TROUBLE

AS FREIGHT TRAINS AND STAGECOACHES began to travel over the Butterfield Overland Despatch, encounters with Indians erupted in a fury that the travelers and planners had not anticipated. Calls for help from the government rolled over the prairies to Washington. The big war between the states had barely ended, and it was difficult for those in the east to realize that a skirmish with the Indians could be worthy of notice after such battles as Shiloh and Gettysburg.

Reports of deaths on the trail continued to come in, however, and eventually the army decided to use some of the men who insisted on staying in uniform. The soldiers who were sent west included some battle veterans who thought they knew every tactic of war. But the Indian had tactics never seen in organized battle. The anticipated skirmish with the red man to put him forever on a reservation turned out to be a fifteen-year war that spread over all the western states. The soldiers soon learned that they couldn't whip an enemy they couldn't catch.

There was already a tiny fort on the Smoky Hill River in central Kansas. In August 1864 Lt. Allen Ellsworth had been sent to this isolated spot with one company of Iowa soldiers and instructions to build a fort. General Curtis decreed that the fort should be named Fort Ellsworth in honor of an uncle of Lieutenant Ellsworth, Col. E. E. Ellsworth, who had been killed at Alexandria, Virginia, May 24, 1861, the first Union officer killed on the Virginia front.

The lieutenant located the fort on the north bank of the river close to a wooden bridge that the army had built there about ten years before on the road to Fort Zarah on the Arkansas River. This one-company post was the only settlement between Salina and Fort Zarah.[1]

As freight trains and emigrants began pouring over the Butterfield Overland Despatch trail, Fort Ellsworth was the last touch with civilization the travelers could expect until they reached Denver. Indian raids on the emigrants and freighters reached a point where the army was forced to do something. The first post established along the Smoky west of Fort Ellsworth was at Pond Creek, near the western border of Kansas. Camp Pond Creek was established in September 1865 and was somewhere near the middle of the long trek from Fort Ellsworth to Denver.

Gen. Grenville M. Dodge, who had been commander of the Military Department of the Missouri in 1864, was sent to set up communication between the posts along the Arkansas and the Smoky Hill in the fall of 1865. He was responsible for establishing some of the posts along the Smoky Hill.[2]

Pond's Creek was named for Maj. Burton Pond of the Third Wisconsin Volunteers, who had traveled as escort to Lieutenant Fitch and Colonel Eaton in their survey and establishment of stations on the B.O.D. Camp Pond Creek was on Pond Creek near its confluence with the Smoky Hill River.

Although it was set up before the worst hostilities broke out, it had little effect in holding down the fighting and the slaughter that followed. Ben Halladay had the mail contract from the Missouri River to Denver and ran it on his stages along the Platte River across Nebraska Territory. With the mail contract went army protection. The B.O.D. never had that protection,[3] and the coaches that traveled over the trail ran a greater risk and suffered greater losses than the ones on the Platte.

When the Indians realized that the B.O.D. intended to establish itself permanently across their favorite hunting grounds they became desperate. Their fall buffalo hunt was diverted into hunting the white invader of their demain.

On October 2, 1865, about thirty Indians attacked a B.O.D. stagecoach near Monument Station. The passengers fought desperately but finally had to abandon the coach. They took the horses and made a run back to the east toward Carlyle Station.[4]

The Indians took what they wanted from the coach and then burned it. From there they went to Monument Station and plundered it, finally setting it on fire.[5]

This and other attacks prompted the army to establish Fort Fletcher on October 11, 1865. It was just west of the confluence of Big Creek and the North Fork, often called Victoria Creek.[6]

Capt. J. F. Bennett, adjutant to General Dodge, reported on October 18 that General Dodge had placed troops at Fort Fletcher, Monument Station, and Pond's Creek Station.[7] These troops were too few and too far apart to be much deterrent to the Indians. But the posts gave the travelers a sense of security, even though in most cases it was a false one.

The Indians increased their efforts to oust the white invaders. On November 19 they struck at Downer Station. This battle ended differently from the one the month before at Monument Station. Here the Indians killed three men, as well as burning the stagecoach that was at the station.[8]

Three days later the Indians attacked a stagecoach as it was leaving Chalk Bluff Station. This coach had an escort of soldiers and managed to continue its run to the west. According to reports of the coach passengers, the Indians were Cheyenne, under the leadership of a chief named Fast Bear. Fast Bear and his warriors had been raiding and murdering whites all along the Smoky Hill route.

A glimpse of what was taking place along the route can be had by reading part of an article written by Theodore Davis, an artist for *Harper's Weekly*, who made more than one trip across the plains on the B.O.D.

> Two hundred and fifty miles from Atchison we became aware that Indians were more plentiful than usual along the route. This gave us no uneasiness: but soon after the discovery of the bodies of murdered men — some of whom had been captured alive, and undergone the most awful torture, such as the cutting out of tongues and other parts of their persons, then burning them alive — caused us to be continually on our guard.
>
> Soon after this we discovered the bodies of two more men, from which we drove the wolves, and buried them. These men had fought and been killed; their bodies were covered with arrow-wounds. Brave men as they were, we could only cover them with so thin a blanket of prairie sod that would hide them from sight but not from the wolves.
>
> Still further on we buried three more bodies that the Indians had left most barbarously mutilated. These discoveries, following each other so rapidly, caused us to be ever on the alert for an attack.[9]

After these reports reached the papers General Dodge sent more troops to Big Creek,[10] Monument Station, and Pond's Creek.[11] The troops at Monument Station that December were under the command of Captain Stroud.[12]

These troops only irritated the Indians. The red warriors' ability to strike swiftly and then disappear before pursuit could be organized kept the soldiers in a state of frustration. Wherever the soldiers were, the Indians were not. If the soldiers rushed to the scene of a fight or massacre, the Indians would strike somewhere else, maybe right where the soldiers had been. Pursuing Indians was like trying to catch a shadow.

The Indians struck again in December at Big Creek Station. This evidently was the Forks of Big Creek or Fort Fletcher. The report said: "Big Creek Station, on the Butterfield route, was attacked by Indians a few days ago, since the massacre at Downer's Spring.[13] The marauders drove off the cattle at the fort, and chased a lieutenant about eight miles and wounded him severely."[14]

These and other troubles along the trail, plus the long rough ride and cramped conditions in the coaches to Denver prompted someone to write the Ten Commandments of the Butterfield Stage Route:

1. The best seat is the forward one, next to the driver. If you have tendencies toward stage sickness when riding backwards, you'll get over it quicker in this seat and receive less jolts and jostlings.

2. If the stage teams run away or are pursued by Indians, stay in the coach and take your chances. Don't jump out, for you will be either injured or scalped.

3. In cold weather abstain from liquor for you are subject to freezing quicker if under its influence than as though you were cold sober.

4. But if you are drinking from a bottle, pass it around. It is the only polite thing to do.

5. Don't smoke a strong cigar or pipe on the stage, especially when women or children are present. If chewing tobacco, spit to leaward side.

6. Don't swear or smoke or lop over on neighbors when sleeping. Let others share the buffalo robes provided in cold weather.

7. Don't shoot firearms for pleasure while enroute as it scares the horses.

8. Don't discuss politics or religion. Don't point out sites where Indian attacks took place.

9. While at stations, don't lag at wash basins or privies. Don't grease hair with bear grease or buffalo tallow as travel is very dusty.

10. Don't imagine you are going on a picnic, for stage travel is inconvenient. Expect annoyances, discomfort, hardships. Bear them with fortitude. Be friendly and helpful to other passengers and you will be a more pleasant one.[15]

Winter usually halted Indian troubles on the plains, but it did not stop the raids on the B.O.D The Indians were determined to drive the white man from their favorite hunting grounds, and winter could not stop them.

For those who had not experienced travel over the trail or had never encountered the Indian when he was in an angry mood the tales of torture and mutilation were hard to believe, but for those who had ridden over the Smoky Hill Trail and had run afoul of the Indians' fury it was no myth.

If the generals who made the decisions on how many troops to commit to the protection of the road had been forced to take a coach ride from Fort Ellsworth to Denver, there likely would have been many more soldiers along the road and not so many graves. The decisions were usually made by those who had no firsthand knowledge of the situation, and the travelers on the B.O.D. paid for this lack of knowledge with their lives.

NOTES

1. George Jelinek, "The Ellsworth Story," *Ellsworth* (Kans.) *Reporter*, 3 August 1967.
2. Mrs. Frank C. Montgomery, "Fort Wallace and Its Relation to the Frontier," *Kansas Historical Collections, 1926-1928* 17 (1928), p. 189.
3. Margaret Long, *The Smoky Hill Trail* (Denver: W. H. Kistler Company, 1943), p. 39.
4. Charles R. Wetzel, "Monument Station, Gove County," *Kansas Historical Quarterly* (Autumn 1960), p. 251.
5. Leslie Linville, *The Smoky Hill Valley and Butterfield Trail* (Colby, Kans.: Leroy's Printing, 1974), p. 72.
6. Montgomery, "Fort Wallace," p. 196.
7. Ibid., p. 189.
8. Ibid., p. 198.
9. *Harper's Weekly*, 21 April 1866, p. 249.
10. This in all probability was the Forks of Big Creek — Fort Fletcher, not the Big Creek Station, about eight miles farther up the creek from Fort Fletcher.
11. Montgomery, "Fort Wallace," p. 198.
12. Wetzel, "Monument Station," p. 251.
13. This refers to the killings at Downer Station on November 19, 1865.
14. *Atchison Free Press*, 18 December 1865.
15. Linville, *Smoky Hill Valley*, inside back cover.

CHAPTER 10

A TRIP OVER THE B.O.D. IN 1865

THERE ARE HUNDREDS of fact-laden, colorless reports of what it was like on a trip across the prairies when pleasures were few and troubles were plentiful. It took an artist, who was also a master at painting word pictures, to describe how travel really looked and felt. He had the misfortune to make his first trip over the Butterfield Overland Despatch during the Indians' concentrated drive to eliminate the stage stations in November 1865.

Theodore H. Davis was the artist for *Harper's Magazine* who came west to make sketches of life on the prairies. He also wrote of his experiences as he traveled. Although he made this trip in late 1865, his article did not appear in *Harper's Monthly* until July, 1867. He observed everything — the mode of travel, the country itself, the Indian raids — with the fresh eye of a newcomer, undimmed by repeated exposure as was the case of most stage drivers and travelers.

It is with a feeling of almost being there that the historian reads his report. The article is too long to repeat in its entirety but portions of it will give a picture of what travel on the Butterfield Overland Despatch was like and what a passenger was likely to see in November 1865.[1]

The Concord coach used for the convenience of passengers on the Overland Route is so arranged that nine persons may be crowded into it and seated. When so packed, and a journey of more than six hundred miles is to be undertaken, the passengers are said to be "accommodated."

A party of four persons entirely innocent of any knowledge of the plains, or the inhabitants thereof, left Atchison at sunrise on the 17th of November, 1865. Their "outfit" consisted of a Concord coach painted to a degree of redness that could not fail to attract the attentive consideration of the un-read men of the country into which four spanking steeds, driven by a Jehu who had never "upsot an outfit," were rapidly rattling us.

The "boot" or "shoe" of the coach contained a moderate quantity of necessary baggage and a comfortable supply of rations. One of the party had an assortment of beads, small mirrors, and a few books filled with brightly colored pictures. These he fondly hoped to exchange with Indians for many bows and arrows, a few tomahawks, and a scalping knife.

Another was prepared to pre-empt large tracts of land when he should discover a location entirely satisfactory to him. "A coal mine would be rather good," he remarked; "sell to the Pacific Railroad people when they get their road out there."

The price of hay, condition of stock (mules and horses, not Erie), and the progress made in the construction of stations, was the subject under consideration in the mind of the third, he being the Vice-President of the company over whose route we were traveling.

The remaining member of the party — the writer hereof — was located on top of the coach in quest of such information as the Jehu might be willing to impart with reference to Indians, buffalo, antelope and coyote.

"How far do you drive?" we inquired; to which he responded "The drives is forty miles from home-station to home-station. Thar we change drivers. Stock stations be some twelve miles, some fifteen. We'll get a hoss team next; then mules, till you get near Denver."

We had by this time arrived at the first station out, a comfortable frame house of one story. At a little distance from it was a good stable, near which were great stacks of prairie hay.

"Yip! Yip!" from the driver announced his readiness to proceed, fresh stock having replaced the team with which we left Atchison. Long trains of

Courtesy the Kansas State Historical Society, Topeka

Theodore R. Davis, a self portrait

Courtesy the Kansas State Historical Society, Topeka
Copied from Harper's Monthly, July 1867

Departure from Atchison by T. R. Davis

"Prairie Schooners" give a picturesqueness to the plains that greatly enhances the journey across.

The wagons are generally doubled up — that is, the tongue of one wagon is passed beneath the body of the wagon next preceeding it, and then securely lashed. Eight or ten yoke of oxen, under the lash of a "bullwhacker," is the motive power furnished each double. This arrangement enables the wagon-master to handle his train with a smaller number of men that would be possible if each wagon had its separate team.

Beside the first yoke of oxen trudges the character of the plains — a bullwhacker. His unclean appearance indicates a catlike aversion to water. He is more profane than the mate of a Mississippi River packet. Accompanying this assertion were seven of the most astounding oaths that ever fell on an ear used to the strong language with which the army teamster encourages his mules. The handle of the ordinary whip is not more than three feet in length; the lash of braided rawhide is seldom less than twenty feet long. A lazy ox occasionally receives a reminder in the shape of a whack in the flank, that causes him to double up as if seared with a red-hot iron. The blow is invariably accompanied by a volley of oaths that seems to startle the whole team into a more rapid pace.

The first night in a stage-coach is undoubtedly the most uncomfortable. As soon as night falls, passengers evince a desire to make a noise. Conversation quickly gives place to song. This night our songs were of home, and our wandering thoughts annihilated the long miles between our rumbling coach and the bright firesides on the Atlantic coast. The drowsy god soon spread his wings among us, knocking the pollen of the poppy into our eyes to an extent that caused a general remark of bedtime. What a misnomer under the circumstances!

Sleeping in a stage-coach is not the most desirable method of passing the night, although it is far preferable to the deep mud of the battleground in which we have slept soundly more than one night. The top presented a prospect for longitudination if an arrangement could be projected to prevent being rolled off. The writer slept on the top of the coach during the rest of the trip while traveling at night. The rest of the party disposed themselves as best they could inside, and complained of cramps.

The second day was almost without incident. We were traveling through a rolling country entirely destitute of wood. The grass, though snow had fallen and disappeared, was still high and in some places almost green. Droves of black-tail deer were seen occasionally.

At evening we passed Fort Ellsworth. By sunrise we were in Buffalo Country. The grass was no longer high but short and thick as closely shaven sod. "Buffalo chips" were scattered in all directions.

The "Yip! Yip!" of the driver sounded wilder as we came to the next station. We were in Indian country, and half fancied that a yell of such unearthliness could only have been learned from a native whose best garments consisted of the brightest paint. The station was yet to be built. At present a cave dug in the side of a hill, near the sinkhole from which water is obtained for stock, served for the two stock-herders who were content to abide therein for twelve dollars a month. The mules that were to be our next steeds grazed unpicketed at a short distance from the station.

While the stock was being driven up we set to work to prepare breakfast. One of us went to request a little wood from the stock-herder. The demand was met by a prolonged W-h-a-t! that conveyed extreme surprise. "Want to make a fire, eh? Get chips, then."

"Where are they?"

"Why, stranger, don't you see 'em all over the country?"

A glance at the fire smoulding near solved the mystery. Buffalo "chips" were the substitute for wood. So, comprehending the situation, our chip-gatherer, bag in hand, departed to secure the necessary material with which to build our fire.

There is no better broiling fuel than a perfectly dry "buffalo chip." That a doubt arose, as the smoke curled up from the newly lighted pile, as to the judiciousness of depositing a juicy steak on those coals, it is useless to deny. The appearance of a bright red coal with an ash of almost snowy whiteness soon became apparent. The steak was quickly deposited on the fire, notwithstanding the expostulations of the chip-gatherer.

The air of the plains is a wonderful appetizer. A cup of good coffee, steaming hot, is a good foundation. Venison steak, baked potatoes, and a hot corn-dodger composed the bill of fare.

The general accepted idea is that the plains, like the prairies, are perfectly flat, unbroken stretches of land. This is not the fact. They are rolling and broken by innumerable gullies or canyons through which the flood poured by the great rain-storms escapes to the creeks or, as they are dignified, rivers.

During the first day in Indian country we saw thousands of buffalo, and for days they were continually in sight. To estimate their number would be impossible. It is said that they are rapidly decreasing in number but that would seem impossible. The herds move in regular order, the cows and calves occupying the center, and the bulls ranging themselves on the outside. In this way the wolves are kept off.

As soon as a bull becomes old he is driven out by the younger males and not again permitted to join it. These old fellows may be seen wandering over the plains singly, though occasionally four or five will herd together, seemingly to protect themselves from the coyotes that are now persistent and familiar in their attentions. They are evidently in haste to attend a feast that will be certain to occur at the funeral of the aged bull.

The plains are dotted with circular cavities of ten or twelve feet in diameter, known as "wallows." To these the buffalo resorts to roll, covering himself with a coat of moist earth, that he seems perfectly aware will discommode the lively inhabitants of his shaggy coat.

During the afternoon we reached Fort Fletcher, a newly established government post, garrisoned by a force of three hundred men, under the command of Colonel Tamblyn. The fort is so in name alone, as the work is yet to be built. A cottonwood grove, a sort of an oasis in this treeless country, had been selected as a campground which was not only picturesque but comfortable.

From the Colonel we learned that the Indians were not troublesome — that is, they had not committed any outrages for a few days past. This was encouraging and we continued our journey,

Courtesy the Kansas State Historical Society, Topeka
Copied from Harper's Monthly, July 1867

Fort Fletcher by T. R. Davis

congratulating each other on the prospects of meeting "friendly" Indians. We were not then aware that fifty miles in advance of us these very "friendly" persons were at the moment engaged in the neighborly employment of roasting two poor fellows who had fallen into their hands. An Indian, like a rattlesnake, may be trusted only when his fangs are removed; otherwise, it is well to give him a wide berth or be prepared to kill him on sight.

At sunset we arrived at Ruthden Station,[2] twenty-two miles distant from Fort Fletcher, where a cave similar to the one previously described served as an abode for the stock-tenders and made the station. A small train was camped here, water being plenty and the grazing good. Much of the waters on the plains is so strongly impregnated with alkali that the grass and weeds on the brink of the sink-hole containing the water are covered with a frosting coat.

Sunset this evening was the most gorgeous that we ever witnessed. The western skies were gold, then crimson, with the brightest of golden ripples threading through. As they purpled with the twilight the crimson became fire. The splendor of color was dazzling. Not until that moment have you seen old Sol retire in his imperial robes.

At Ruthden a discovery was made by one of the party. The stock-tenders were using roots to wash with. The root of the soapweed, or amole, as it is commonly designated, is an excellent subsititute for soap. For washing woolens, it is particularly valuable, as it cleanses without shrinking them.

Our repast of buffalo steak and et ceteras disposed of, we started off on our journey. As the darkness settled above us a feeling prevaded the party that all was not right. Conversation turned upon Indians. We heartily wished that it was morning. Shortly after midnight, the coach stopped. "Turn out!" shouted the driver. "Indians!"

We were off the coach in a moment. A small body of men were visible advancing toward us through the darkness. Revolvers in hand, one of the party started toward the strangers, who were discovered to be white men. From them we learned that the coach preceding ours had been attacked by Indians, from whom, after a desperate struggle, these men had escaped. The men were perishing with cold and were out of ammunition. The Indians were in strong force and evidently intent on their work of murder and destruction. All things considered, it was determined to return to Ruthden and dispatch a messenger to Colonel Tamblyn asking for an escort. The coach was turned about, the newcomers having been made as comfortable in it as possible.

"More haste the less speed" was our fortune. In crossing a gully, the king bolt was displaced, making it necessary to unload the coach before it could be rearranged. The coach was repaired and we proceeded on our return, during which we learned the story of our new passengers.

The coach had arrived at Downer's Station about two o'clock in the afternoon, one passenger, the messenger, and the driver being the occupants. At the station they found two stock-tenders, the carpenters, and a Negro blacksmith. The mules were unharnessed and turned loose, when a band of mounted Indians charged, whooping among them; the men retreated to the cave, or " adobe," as they designate it. Indians came from all directions and completely surrounded the adobe, the occupants of which prepared to fight. An Indian will never fight until he has obtained every possible advantage, then he makes a rush. A half-breed son of Bill Bent,[3] the old mountain man, was one of the leaders of the Indians; being able to speak English, he managed to call to the occupants of the adobe that he wanted to talk. This was assented to. He came up and inquired whether the treaty had been signed. He was informed that it had, to which he replied, "All right!" They would have peace if the occupants of the adobe would come out and shake hands, leaving their arms behind, and the Indians would do likewise. The men came out, and a general hand shaking followed. The Indian is great at this; he will shake your hand all day and at nightfall will take your scalp. It is simply a way he has of expressing his brotherly sentiments toward the white man.

The Indians still further deceived the party by driving up the mules that had been stampeded by them, telling the messenger that the coach should proceed without molestation. Such evidence of friendship disarmed the party of any suspicion of hostility, though the Indians were in full paint and without squaws. In a moment all was changed. The Indians turned upon the party — bows, arrows, and revolvers were produced, and a desperate attack at once inaugurated. The messenger, Fred Merwin, a very gallant young man, was killed instantly; others of the party were wounded, and the two stocktenders captured. Mr. Perine, the passenger, the driver, carpenters, and blacksmith ran for the neighboring bluffs, which they succeeded in reaching. Taking possession of a buffalo wallow, they fought until nightfall, when the Indians withdrew, and they made good their escape.

Mr. Perine gives a very interesting account of the fight from the wallow:

"They formed a circle about us, riding dexterously and rapidly; occasionally one more bold than the rest would come within range of our revolvers, but he was careful to keep his body on the side of his pony away from us. Arrows came from all directions; a rifle or revolver bullet would whistle past us or strike the earth near. It was evidently their purpose to permit us to exhaust our ammunition, when they would be able to take us alive. Of this fact we were painfully aware and only fired at them when we were sure of a good shot. This kept them at a distance. The Negro blacksmith was armed with a Ballard rifle, with which he was a capital shot. He bravely exposed himself to obtain a shot, and came near losing his life by so doing. A bullet struck him in the head, when he fell, as we supposed, dead. I took his rifle, rolled the body up to the edge of the wallow to serve as a breastwork to shot from, and commenced to fire. I had made several shots in this way, and had the rifle across his neck with a dead aim on an Indian when the darkey came to and remarked, 'What you doin dar, white man?' thus discovering to us the fact that he was anything but a 'gone coon dis time.' He had been deprived of speech and power of motion by the shot, but was fully aware of what was going on about him. He was not disposed to regard the use of his body as a breastwork as altogether a pleasing performance.

"While we were fighting from the wallow, we could plainly see the Indians that still remained about the adobe, at work torturing the stock-herders that they had succeeded in capturing alive.

"One poor fellow they staked to the ground, cut out his tongue, substituting another portion of his body in its place. They then built a fire on his body. The agonized screams of the man were almost unendurable; about him were the Indians dancing and yelling like demons. The other stock-herder was shoved up to look at the barbarous scene, the victim of which he was soon to be, but they reserved him until nightfall, evidently hoping that we might be added to the number of their victims.

"There could not have been less than a hundred and fifty Indians in the entire party — that is, those who were about us and those near the adobe. Bent told us that Fast Bear, a Cheyenne chief, had command, but Bent is worse than any Indian, for he knows better. Had there been a possible chance to rescue the stock-herders, we should have attempted it. When darkness came the Indians withdrew, and as soon as we were convinced of the fact, we followed their example, going, it is unnecessary to remark, in the other direction. Chalk Bluffs[4] we found deserted and the station burning. Then we heard the coach coming and came to it. The Indians would have probably taken you in if we had not."

We had by this time reached Ruthden. Mr. Perine's narrative had made us particularly anxious to reach a point where we could have a chance of fighting without giving the Indians all the advantage. It was not yet daylight but we made all arrangements for a fight if we should be attacked at dawn, as we fully expected. A messenger was dispatched to Colonel Tamblyn. The stock was picketed sufficiently near the corral of wagons to enable us to drive them into the circle. Our party were disposed at points to give the alarm in case of danger, and we were ready to fight Indians.

This day, the 20th of November, passed without incident. Buffalo were in sight on all sides, but we considered the risk too great in hunting them. The quantity of buffalo skulls scattered about the plains near this place seems remarkable. The coyote and gray wolf abound near here in greater numbers than we have before seen. At midnight, we discovered a welcome sight — soldiers marching toward us from the direction of the fort.

On the morning of the 21st we left Ruthden but moved slowly to enable the troops to keep pace with us. Chalk Bluffs [Blufton], a picturesquely located station, we found desserted and burned. We found no trace of any fight at this place and concluded that the herders had escaped or been carried off by the Indians.

In the afternoon we reached Downer's. The devastation here had been complete. The coach, and everything about the station that would burn, had been destroyed. The ground was everywhere tracked over by the unshod hoofs of the Indian ponies. We could not find a trace of the bodies of Merwin or the stock-tenders; neither could we account for their disappearance. Mr. Perine, who had now become one of our party, was at a loss to know the reason as he was confident that Merwin was killed at the first fire and he very sagely concluded that men that underwent the torture inflicted on the stock-tenders were not likely to live but a very short time.

We broke camp at daylight. A few miles from Downer's, we found a body, or rather the remains of a man, evidently killed the night before. The wolves had stripped the bones of all flesh; face, hands and feet alone were unmarked. As we came near, the wolves withdrew. The scalp was gone, and a few arrows that still remained in the ribs marked the tribe to which the victim belonged — Cheyenne and Apache.

The stations thus far had been deserted. We were unable, however, to discover any signs of Indian visitations. Wolves were abundant. At noon the next day we reached a station where we found a Government train corraled. The Indians had attacked the train and driven off a number of the mules. One soldier had been killed, and another shot through the neck with an arrow and scalped, having feigned dead while the Indians were engaged in "lifting his hair." His wounds were not considered serious, but the doctor says that he will have a bald spot on the top of his head. A coach was here on its way east.

The mysterious disappearance of the bodies of Fred Merwin and the two stock-tenders was accounted for. The train corraled here, passed Downer's the morning following the massacre, and buried the bodies, beating down the grave to prevent resurrection by the wolves. Here Colonel Tamblyn left us, considering it safe for the coach to proceed with an escort of five cavalrymen.

"The Monuments" were reached this evening; near them is a camp of more than two hundred soldiers. A fort is to be built, also a station. These Monument rocks are considered the most remarkable on the plains; at a distance it is difficult to realize that they are not the handiwork of man, so perfectly do they resemble piles of masonry.

The wind that night was terrific. Two tents were blown away, and a wagon that was not brought into the corral overturned. The mules stood with their backs to the blast, that caused their hair to stand out like fur.

We left Monument early on the morning of the 25th, to continue our journey. An ambulance, containing a surgeon and four men, accompanied us as well as the escort of five cavalrymen. The next station was twenty-two miles distant.

By eleven o'clock the driver pointed out the station. "Thar's Smoky Hill Springs — purty place, ain't it?" When within half a mile the ambulance left us, taking a short cut to the road on the other side of the station, which was located for convenience to water at some distance from the direct route. The cavalry galloped on to the station, which they reached, while we were some distance from it.

When within two hundred yards of the adobe we glanced back to see the country over which we had passed, and discovered, within sixty yards of the coach, a band of nearly a hundred mounted Indians, charging directly toward us. The sight, frightful as it was, seemed grand. "Here they come!" and the crack of a rifle was responded to by a yell, followed by the singing whiz of arrows and the whistle of revolver bullets. The first shot dropped an Indian. Next a pony stopped, trembled, and fell. The driver crouched as the arrows passed

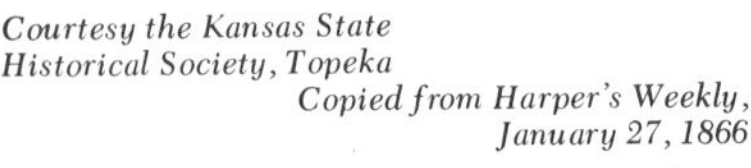

Courtesy the Kansas State Historical Society, Topeka
Copied from Harper's Weekly, January 27, 1866

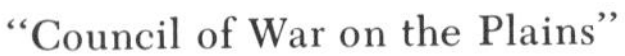

"Council of War on the Plains"

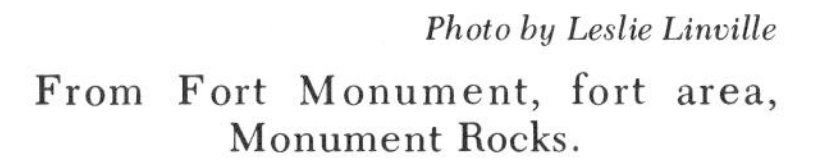

Photo by Leslie Linville

From Fort Monument, fort area, Monument Rocks.

over him, and drove his mules steadily toward the station. The deadly fire poured from the coach windows kept a majority of the Indians behind the coach. Some, however, braver than the rest, rushed past on their ponies, sending a perfect stream of arrows into the coach as they sped along. We were by this time in front of the station. The cavalrymen opened with their revolvers, and the Indians changed their tactics from close fighting to a circle. One, more daring than the rest, was intent on securing the scalp of a stock-herder whom he had wounded. He lost his own in so doing.

The first brush was over. A dash was made to secure the body of the fallen brave, but given up as soon as it was evident that he had lost the top of his head. Indians have strange ideas with reference to a scalp. The body of a scalped brave is neglected; he can not enter the happy hunting ground with a bare head, so no trouble is taken to bury him. The ravens and coyotes save the trouble. Plainsmen tell you that "coyote will not eat Indian." This we do not believe.

From the adobe we discovered a sight that was not to be looked at quietly. The four mules attached to the doctor's ambulance were flying across the plains at a dead run. Indians enveloped the ambulance like a swarm of angry hornets. The men in the ambulance were fighting bravely, but the Indians outnumbered them ten to one. If rescue was to be attempted there was not an instant to lose. The five cavalrymen were sent off at a gallop. Seeing them, the men in the ambulance jumped out and ran through the Indians towards them, rightly conjecturing that the Indians would secure the ambulance before turning to attack them.

Courtesy the Kansas State Historical Society, Topeka
Copied from Harper's Monthly, April 21, 1866

This artist's etching shows the B.O.D coach attacked while approaching Smoky Hill Station from the east.

It was a plucky thing to do, but the doctor determined that it was their only chance. The Indians caught the mules, then turned to look for scalps, which they supposed were to be had for the taking. The doctor and his men were giving them a lively fight when we came up. The value of a well-sighted and balanced rifle was soon evident. With every crack a pony or an Indian came to earth.[5] This fire was evidently unendurable, and the circle quickly increased in diameter, when, with the rescued men mounted behind, we slowly moved toward the station, before reaching which two more dashes were repulsed.

The strain on the nervous system of the rescued men must have been intense. As we reached the station one of them broke down completely and sobbed like a child. The doctor was one of the gamest of little men. "Ah," quoth he, as he gazed through the glass at the crowd of Indians about the ambulance, "I put the contents of the tartart emetic can into the flour before I left the ambulance, and if that does not disorder their stomachs I won't say anything — I wish that it had been strychnine!"

A redskin had mounted each of the mules, and as many Indians as the vehicle would contain had located themselves in the ambulance for a ride. The cover had been torn off, as it probably impeded their view. Becoming tired of this, they detached the mules, unloaded the ambulance, and drew it to a point which afforded us the best view of their performance; when, greatly to the indignation of the doctor, they crowned their disrespect for him and his carriage by setting fire to what he declared to be the best ambulance on the plains.

The Indians now engaged in a successful dance

Courtesy the Kansas State Historical Society, Topeka
Copied from Harper's Weekly, April 21, 1866

Adobe fortification at the Smoky Hill Station

about the burning ambulance, during the continuance of which a survey was made of our situation.

The station had been furnished with a garrison of ten soldiers. Five of these, with the best arms and most of the ammunition, had started early in the morning on a buffalo hunt. We had altogether twenty-one men, armed with seven rifles and thirteen revolvers. For four of the rifles and five of the revolvers we had an abundance of ammunition, which it was not possible to use in the other arms, for which there was but a scant supply. The adobe was well located for defense, and surrounded by a well-constructed rifle pit. To attack the Indians was not prudent, although all were anxious to do so. We could count in the circle about us one hundred and five, many more being visible on the bluffs near.

A new style of fighting was now inaugurated by the Indians. The bluff in which the adobe was located was covered with tall dry grass. This was in flames before we were aware of a fire other than that about the ambulance. Each man seized his blanket and started out to meet the fire, which was nearly subdued, when a sudden attack was made by the Indians on all sides. For a few moments it was a doubtful contest. The Indians were at last driven back and the fire extinquished. Several of our men were suffering with arrow wounds, none of them severe, fortunately; but all needed attention. If poisoned arrows had been used, our loss would have been serious. The arrows used were about three feet in length, and supplied with an iron head two inches long.

At nightfall the Indians withdrew. But this was not a subject for congratulations, for we expected them back during the night. The anticipation was not erroneous. Three hours of darkness had passed, when a rustling whiz cut the air over our heads. The sharp twang of the bowstring informed us that the Indians were very near. Arrows came in flights. The Indians were within close revolver range; but a shot from a pistol or rifle would have exposed the person firing, as the flash would reveal his precise location. So many arrows could not be fired among our small party without inflicting serious damage.

That something must be done to drive off the Indians was plain. One of the party, an old hunter, volunteered to stampede the Indians if he might be permitted to take four revolvers. If he failed, the revolvers would be lost, which loss would severely cripple the party. Still, it was the last resort. Divesting himself of garments, with the exception of underclothing, he crawled out into the darkness toward the spot from which the twang of bow strings came most frequently. In five minutes the repeated crack of the revolvers and the yells of the Indians told of the successful issue of the bold effort. The bows were still and in another moment our Indian fighter returned to the adobe to receive the heart-felt thanks of the garrison.

The remainder of the night was passed in quiet. Sleep was impossible, and dawn found the paty on the alert for another attack. Mid-day and dawn are the favorite times of Indians for an attack. It was well for us that we were ready; for the Indians had crawled up as closely as possible, evidently intending to rush upon us if there seemed any chance for success. A single rifle shot seemed to satisfy them, as they withdrew in haste, with the exception of one. His scalp locks were "saved."

Toward noon a body of men were seen approaching from the east. If they were Indians we were "gone." If white men, the danger might be said to be over. The Indians observed them as quickly as we, and a band of twenty or thirty started off to reconnoiter. We watched the result anxiously. The Indians wheeled about and returned to our vicinity. A moment more and the whole band were galloping off out of sight over the bluffs. Then we knew that the strangers were white men. They were a company of infantry in wagons, who, together with a small cavalry command, were coming to bury us. The Monuments had been attacked the day previous, and a number of stock driven off. We afterward learned that a general attack had been made along the entire line of two hundred and fifty miles. The stage company lost eight men and nearly two hundred mules; the Government lost several men and a hundred animals; the Indians committing the outrage being at the time on the way to Fort Zarah to secure the presents stipulated for in the late treaty.

We left the adobe at Smoky Hill Springs and proceeded with a strong escort, and camped at night at Henshaw Springs, which we found deserted. The following evening we arrived at Pond

Creek. During the day a great number of dog villages[6] were passed, the little villagers squeaking out a salute as we passed.

Pond Creek is the most picturesque station on the route. The creek comes out of the plains near a fine cottonwood grove, runs with a considerable current for five or six miles, and sinks into the plains. Among the branches of the cottonwood trees are swung the remains of Indians encased in a basket-work of twigs.

From Pond Creek the stage line had not been disturbed, and we traveled uninterruptedly to Denver, which place we reached on the 2nd of December, after a trip of fifteen days across the plains from the Missouri River to the base of the Rocky Mountains.

NOTES

1. Theodore H. Davis, "A Stage Ride to Colorado," *Harper's New Monthly Magazine* 35:206 (July 1867), pp. 137–150.
2. Ruthden Station was also called Louisa Station. Not to be confused with Ruthton Station farther west.
3. Mrs. Frank C. Montgomery, "Fort Wallace and Its Relation to the Frontier," *Kansas Historical Collections, 1926–1928* 17 (1928), p. 207. Charles Bent was the son of William Bent, the trader, and a Cheyenne woman. He was said to have been more bloodthirsty than any Indian. His father disowned him.
4. Chalk Bluffs Station, referred to here by Mr. Perine in his story and by T. H. Davis in his description of this section of the B.O.D., is actually Blufton Station, which was abandoned after it was burned in this raid in favor of White Rock Station a little farther to the west. The maps of the B.O.D. show that the real Chalk Bluffs Station was farther west, in what is now Gove County. Blufton Station was in Trego County between Fort Fletcher and Downer Station.
5. In a report given by another member of the party fighting that day at Smoky Hill Springs, T. H. Davis himself was identified as one of the men who went to the rescue of the doctor and the men at the ambulance. This man gave Davis credit for killing the first Indian during the rescue.
6. Prairie dog towns.

CHAPTER 11

YEAR OF CHANGE

AFTER THE BLOODBATH during the last two months of 1865, the new year began in comparative calm. The Indians hadn't given up their efforts to drive the white men from their hunting grounds, but they couldn't make themselves believe that cold weather was the time for fighting. Besides, they had their losses from the previous November's fighting to adjust to and preparations to make for new offensives as soon as the grass was high enough to support their ponies.

The white invaders of this hunting ground also knew the fighting was not over, even though the lull as 1866 began was most welcome. The soldiers and stage-line employees had learned that the Indians were not as aggressive when the temperatures were low. They used the cold months to complete their fortifications as best they could and to lay in a bigger supply of guns and ammunition.

The little fort at Monument Station was having trouble surviving. According to the Fort Fletcher records an officer was sent to Monument Station on January 12. On January 14 Lieutenant Bell of the Thirteenth Missouri Cavalry was sent to Fort Fletcher with two wagons for supplies for Pond Creek Station and Monument Station.[1]

There is no record that the supplies ever reached Monument Station. It is a good guess that they didn't, for the post apparently was abandoned. The record shows that Companies A, E, and I of the First Volunteer Infantry were sent to Monument Station on March 1 to "re-establish" the post.[2]

It seems quite apparent that all three companies did not stay at Monument Station, because it is called a one-company post. Even the army never designated it a fort, always referring to it as Monument Station. Living quarters at the post, once it was established, consisted of only three buildings. They were constructed mostly of native stone with a bare minimum of sawed lumber, which had to be hauled from great distances. The main building,

Drawn by J. Stadler

Monument Station

according to a drawing made by a soldier in the Fifth Infantry, was a story and a half high and served both as post headquarters for the soldiers and a home and eating station for the B.O.D. Capt. Hooper Straud[3] of Company A was relieved by Capt. Charles Norris of Company E of the Second Cavalry on March 20, 1866.[4]

In the meantime bigger changes were in the works for the Butterfield Overland Despatch. Due to the Indian raids during the last months of 1865, Butterfield's stage and freight lines were losing money on the Smoky Hill route. Too many horses and mules were lost. Stations, stagecoaches, wagons, and supplies were burned. Shippers and travelers were frightened off. The shorter route that promised faster delivery was too dangerous. Both freight and passengers used the longer route along the Platte.

Ben Holladay had the mail contract along the Platte River, and that also took away much of the income that could have helped the B.O.D. survive. Ben Holladay was a big man in the shipping and passenger business. In addition to his stage and freight lines he had steamship lines to Oregon, Panama, China, and Japan.[5]

Holladay was called the Stagecoach King. He was a successful businessman in 1862 when he bought the bankrupt firm of Russell, Majors, and Waddell. Within a few years he controlled more than three thousand miles of stage lines.

One very satisfied passenger wrote, "With such coaches, whips [drivers], teams and messengers as put us over the road last week, we think he must be a bold man who attempts to throw down the gauntlet or break a lance with Ben Holladay up and down these plains."[6]

Early in 1866 Holladay heard that Wells Fargo was planning to put in a stage line from the Missouri to Salt Lake City so they wouldn't have to connect with Holladay lines to carry freight, passengers, and mail over that route.

Holladay had no intention of losing his monopolistic grip on the business, so he looked for a way to counter Wells Fargo. He thought he saw it in the Butterfield Overland Despatch.

Holladay owned a mansion on Fifth Avenue in New York, a home in Washington, D.C., and another mansion near White Plains, New York. He sent a request to Edward Bray, president of the Park Bank in New York City to come and visit him. Bray was also president of the Butterfield Overland Despatch. Holladay made it very clear to Bray that he knew how much the B.O.D. was losing and that it stood to lose a lot more during the coming season. He offered to buy out the B.O.D. at a bargain rate.

Bray called a meeting of the board of the B.O.D to discuss the offer. Perhaps it was the accuracy of Ben Holladay's estimate of

Courtesy the Kansas State Historical Society, Topeka

Ben Holladay

the financial condition of the Butterfield line that caused the board to accept his offer. The line was sold to Holladay in March 1866, actually before all the stations had been completed.[7]

With the purchase of the B.O.D. line, Holladay sent word to Wells Fargo to go ahead and stock their line from the Missouri River west and see what they gained from it.

Included in Holladay's purchase of the Butterfield line were one hundred and fifty large six-ox wagons and fifty six-mule wagons. Now he controlled almost five thousand miles of stage lines. Altogether he hired seven hundred men and owned fifteen hundred horses, seven hundred mules, and eighty coaches and express wagons, not to mention oxen and freight wagons.[8]

Work on completing the stations along the Smoky Hill didn't even pause because of the transfer of ownership. The men at every station were keenly aware that prairie war was almost certain to return with the coming of the new grass, setting the Indian free to roam the plains again. As long as there was no grass for the Indians' ponies the warriors were confined to the reservations, where they declared themselves "heap good Indians" and drew rations for themselves and their ponies. New grass would release the warriors from their enforced dependence on the food and forage of the reservations.

According to army records the first regular soldiers assigned to Camp Pond Creek arrived shortly before April 1, 1866. Other units had manned the post before that. Capt. Edward Bell, Second Cavalry, was the commandant.[9] The chief duty of the soldiers at this post was to escort and protect travelers on the B.O.D. on either side of Pond's Creek Station. From the first it was a very active post.

Bayard Taylor, a correspondent for the *New York Tribune*, made a trip over the B.O.D. in June 1866.[10] His report gave readers a good look at the Smoky Hill route during a lull in the fighting with the Indians:

> At Big Creek Station, we took on board Mr. Scott, superintendent of the Middle Division of the road. There was still no moon and fortunately, no musketoes also. Half asleep and half awake, now lulled into slumber by the slowness of our progress, now bumped into angry wakefulness in crossing some deep gully, we dragged through the night, and in the morning found ourselves at Downer's, 44 miles farther.
>
> Our breakfast here was another "square meal" — pork fat and half-baked biscuits. At all the stations the people complained of lack of supplies; some were destitute of all but beans.
>
> From the first rise after leaving Downer's, we saw, far away to the right, a long range of chalk bluffs, shining against a background of dark blue cloud.
>
> Monument Station is so called from a collection of quadrangular chalk towers, which rise directly from the plain. At first sight, they resemble a deserted city, with huge bastioned walls; but on a nearer approach they separated into detached masses, some of which resemble colossal sitting statues. The station house is built of large blocks, cut out with a hatchet and cemented with raw clay.
>
> During this day's journey we kept more away from the Smoky Hill, but we still saw, from time to time, its line of timber and cedared bluffs in the distance. We now had shorter stations for some distance, and made the distance to Pond Creek in the morning. At this point there is a new military post called Fort Wallace. Fort Lyon on the Arkansas, is but 45 miles distant.[11]
>
> We reached Willow Springs, 18 miles, by sunrise. A forlorn place it was! The stationmen lived in holes cut out of a high clay bank, and their mules had similar half-subterranean lodging. I saw no provision, and they said they could give us no breakfast. The team was speedily changed, and we set out for Cheyenne Wells, 25 miles distant and through a country more nearly approaching barrenness than any we had yet seen. The timber almost entirely disappeared, and finally the Smoky Hill itself, now so near its source became a bed of waterless sand.[12]

Taylor had crossed the Kansas plains at a time when the Indians were doing little damage, but the hatred and fury was building up to explode in the near future. Although Taylor seemed unaware of this

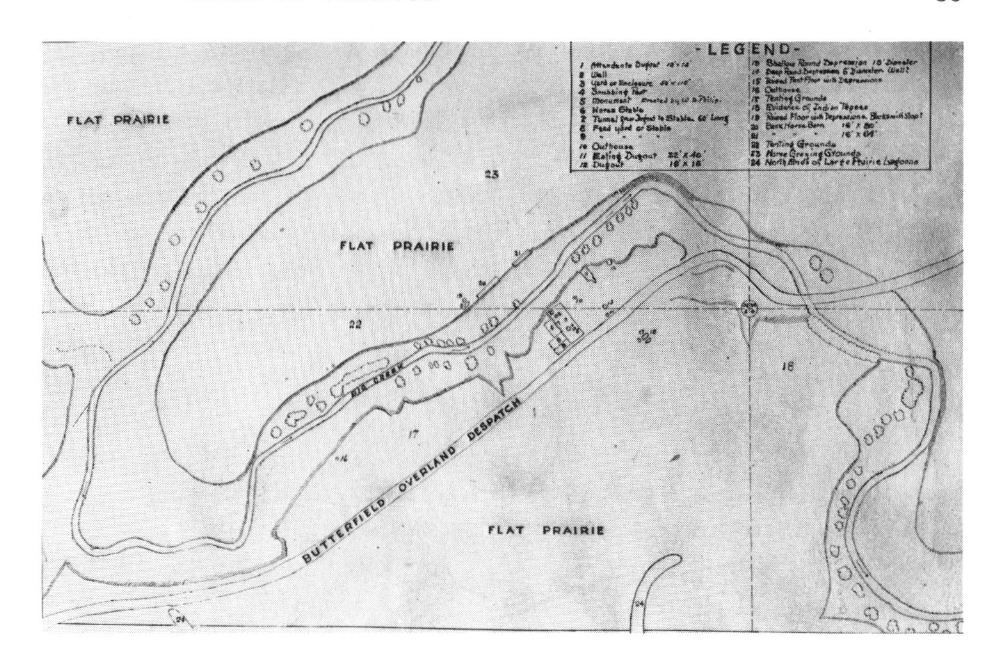

Big Creek Station, Butterfield Overland Despatch.

seething unrest, the people who lived and worked on the road were not. Bayard Taylor picks up the story of his trip at Cheyenne Wells:[13]

At Cheyenne Wells we found a large and handsome frame stable for mules, but no dwelling. The people lived in a natural cave, extending some thirty feet under the bluff. There was a woman, and when we saw her we argued good fortunes. Truly enough, under the roof of conglomerate limestone, in the cave's dim twilight, we sat down to antelope steak, tomatoes, bread, pickles, and potatoes — a royal meal after two days of detestable fare. Here we saw the last of Smoky Hill Fork. The road strikes across a broad plateau for twenty miles, and then descends to the Big Sandy, a branch of the Arkansas.

From the western edge of the watershed, we overlooked many a league of brown, monotonous, treeless country, through which meandered, not the water, but the dry, sandy bed of the Big Sandy. At the stage station,[14] we found two men living in a hole in the ground, with nothing but alkaline water to offer us. At Grady's Station, 18 miles farther, there was but one man, a lonely troglodyte, burrowing in the bank like a cliff-swallow.

What a night followed! The hard "hack" bumped and jolted over the rough roads; we were flung backward and forward, right and left, pummelled, pounded and bruised, not only out of sleep, but out of temper, and into pain and exasperation. At one o'clock we were at Hedinger's Lake, ninety-seven miles from Denver.

From Hedinger's Lake to Denver a new cut-off has recently been made, shortening the distance about twenty miles. Ours was the last coach which passed over the old road, the stations and stock being taken up behind us, and transferred across the country to their new positions.

At Reed's Springs we obtained our last "square meal," with the inevitable bacon, for a dollar and a half. Thenceforth our road led over the high divides between Beaver,[15] Bijou,[16] and Kiowa Creeks, all of which flow northward to the Platte.

Midday was intensely sultry. We took a hasty dinner at Running Creek,[17] and then made our slow way, with poor horses, across the ridges to Cheery Creek. At last, four miles from the town, we reached a neat little tavern, beside which grew some cottonwoods.[18] Here were two or three ranches in the process of establishment.

Our next sign of life was the evidence of death — the unfenced cemetery of Denver, on the top of the ridge. Presently we were rolling through gay, animated streets, down the vistas of which the snowy ranges in the west were shining fairly in the setting sun. The coach drew up at the Pacific Hotel, and in just four days and six hours from Ft. Riley I sat down, not to a "square meal," but to an excellent supper.

As Bayard Taylor said in his report, this was the last stagecoach to go by regular schedule over the southern route of the Colorado section of the B.O.D. The new cutoffs were in two sections. One started at the Cheyenne Wells Station and headed almost due west, hitting the southern route again just to the southeast of Hogan's Station. It traveled the same course to Hedinger's Lake, where the southern route turned almost straight west to the Big Bend of the Sandy Station on Well's Ranch. The new cutoff went on to the northwest, finally joining with the Fort Morgan cutoff from the Platte River Road into Denver. From here the two roads traveled together due west into Denver.

For those who would like to trace this new cutoff on a map or to find the sites of the stations, the route ran something like this:

About thirteen miles west of Cheyenne Wells was the first station, called Deering's Well Station.[19] It was almost exactly halfway between Cheyenne Wells Station and Big Springs Station, which was on the east side of Big Springs Creek where the creek curves around a hill.[20] On top of the hill were fortifications about forty feet in diameter surrounded by a trench.

The trail turned a little to the northwest from this station. About ten miles farther was David's Well.[21] It was surrounded by a trench for the protection of riflemen during an Indian attack.

Another ten miles to the northwest was Hugo Springs Station.[22] It was thirteen miles to the next station, Willow Springs, on the east bank of Willow Creek, close to its confluence with the Big Sandy.[23] Just three or four miles before reaching Willow Springs Station the new northern route of the B.O.D. joined with the old southern route. Apparently Hogan's Station, which was only a short distance northwest of Willow Springs, was abandoned in favor of the new station site, since Willow Springs divided the distance between Hugo Springs Station and Hedinger's Lake more evenly.

It was eleven miles northwest to Hedinger's Lake and what was called Lake Station. Here the new cutoff separated sharply from the old route. This is the only place between Cheyenne Wells and Denver that used the same station on both the southern and northern routes.

Cedar Point Station[24] was nine miles northwest of Lake Station. Three wells were dug here — the second after the first one turned too alkaline to use, and the third after the second became unusable. A half-mile south of this station was a small post called Cedar Point Fort, where soldiers were stationed to protect travelers. The fort was on a flat area on top of a hill.[25]

Only eight miles beyond Cedar Point was the next station, Fairmont,[26] sometimes called Godfrey Station. Benham Station was nine miles from Fairmont on the east side of Station Gulch, which had several springs that guaranteed good water the year around.[27]

It was eleven miles to the next station, Bijou Springs. It was on a tributary to West Bijou Creek and had several springs near the sandy bed of Station Gulch.[28]

A mile and a half before reaching the next station, Kiowa,[29] the B.O.D. joined the Fort Morgan Cutoff of the Platt River Road to Denver. At the junction both trails turned almost due west toward Denver.

Box Elder Station was twelve miles farther west.[30] The stage lines on both the Fort Morgan Cutoff and the B.O.D. were owned and operated that summer of 1866 by Holladay.

Coal Creek Station was seven or eight miles closer to Denver. The station here was a grout house, a mixture of clay and lime. The mule barn was a dugout, and a tunnel connected the house and the barn for defense against the Indians.[31]

Tollgate Station was five miles beyond Coal Creek.[32] It was sometimes called Eight Mile Creek on the Fort Morgan Cutoff log. Toll was collected on the east end of the bridge over the creek — ten cents per passenger and twenty-five cents per horse.

Ten miles from Tollgate Station the line ended in Denver. This route reduced by several miles the long journey from the Missouri River and had better water than was found in some spots on the first road traveled by the B.O.D.

There were several other changes made in 1866 on the Smoky Hill Road to Denver. In September of that year the military post was moved from Camp Pond Creek to the newly established Fort Wallace about two miles[33] to the east. The name of the post was officially changed to Fort Wallace on September 18, 1866.[34]

A new scout who was to be quite prominent in military operations along the Smoky Hill for the next couple of years appeared in the records that summer. A letter written in August shows the respect this young man already had in military circles:

> Aug. 23, 1866. Bvt. Capt. W. C. Harrison. Sir: I have the honor to request that the pay of William Comstock, guide of this post, be increased from $100 to $125 a month. Comstock has been offered better pay near his own place in Colorado and as I consider it of the greatest importance to keep as good and reliable guide as he is in the District, I have made this request so that his pay may remain equivalent to $100 per month and one ration. A. E. Bates, Comdg. Post.[35]

Comstock must have gotten the pay increase because he was still listed as scout when Indians struck at the new Fort Wallace on September 19 and drove away fourteen horses and two mules. No mention of Comstock is made in the pursuit that followed. Likely he had either gone on a scouting mission or was at his ranch on Rose Creek, about eight miles west of Fort Wallace. Bill Comstock was the first owner of this ranch, mentioned so frequently in connection with the history of Fort Wallace. It was from this ranch that hay was cut for the fort, about two to three hundred tons a year, selling for $20 to $25 a ton.[36]

Another change of ownership of the Butterfield Overland Despatch was due in late 1866. Ben Holladay, who had bought the B.O.D. in March, was having his own financial difficulties. He had spread himself too thin. In a effort to salvage his sprawling business he helped form a corporation in which he was only one of the directors.[37]

In October 1866 Holladay and Wells Fargo began negotiations to join forces. On paper Wells Fargo agreed to sell its stage company to the Holladay corporation for forty thousand shares of Holladay stock. There were two strange points about this transaction. First was the stipulation that, although Wells Fargo was selling to Holladay, the name of Wells Fargo would be used by the new company. Also not publicized was the fact that forty thousand shares of stock would give Wells Fargo control of the company. No matter how it sounded to the public, the truth was that Wells Fargo was buying out Ben Holladay. The merger included the Butterfield Overland Despatch, the Overland Mail Company, the United States Express Company, the American Express Company, and the Pioneer Stage Company.[38]

When the big deal was finally completed on November 1, 1866, Wells Fargo emerged as the company controlling all the stage lines of any consequence west of the Missouri River, including the B.O.D.

Another change to strike the Smoky Hill Road was at Fort Fletcher. The fort had been established in October 1865. On November 17, 1866, the name of the fort was officially changed to Fort Hays,[39] honoring Bvt. Maj. Gen. Alexander Hays, who was killed in the Battle of the Wilderness.[40]

In November 1866 Company I of the Seventh Cavalry under command of Capt. Myles W. Keogh was at Fort Wallace. In Keogh's report of December 20, 1866, he said that Capt. Michael Sheridan, guided by Scout William Comstock, was in pursuit of Indians who had driven off some stock from the post.

Captain Keogh's report included a brief resumé of trouble at other places along the B.O.D.

Dec. 20, 1866. In regard to the circumstances of the driving away from this post of Government stock by the Indians and the more serious circumstances attending the burning of Chalk Bluffs Station and the killing of the stock tenders. . . . The Indians were Cheyennes as horses or ponies lost by them were afterward claimed and turned over to a Cheyenne chief called Bull Bear. Some of the party were recognized by an escaped ranch man from Chalk Bluffs. They are the same Cheyennes to whom I saw issued rifles and ammunition at Zarah in November last. I would respectfully call the attention of the Major General to the fact that my horses are unsheltered except by bare walls. I have expected from day to day to receive nails so as to put a temporary roof on. The cold has been intense for the last 8 days with a severe snow storm, and the thermometer standing yesterday and today at Reveille [5 A.M.] at 6 below zero. M. W. Keogh, Captain, Commanding Post.[41]

So ended the year of change. The forts were better established and ready for battle if need be. The Indians were even better prepared, and the time of the next new grass was set for the all-out drive to rid the hunting grounds along the Smoky Hill River of the hated white men.

NOTES

1. Charles R. Wetzel, "Monument Station, Gove County," *Kansas Historical Quarterly* (Autumn 1960), p. 251.
2. Ibid., p. 252.
3. Captain Straud's man is sometimes spelled Straut. It is uncertain which is correct.
4. Mrs. Frank C. Montgomery, "Monument Station and Its Last Commander, Col. Conyngham," *Fort Wallace* (Kans.) *Bugle*, June 1971.
5. Noel Loomis, *Wells Fargo* (New York: Clarkston N. Potter, 1968), p. 178.
6. Robert W. Richmond and Robert W. Mardock, *A Nation Moving West* (Lincoln: Univ. of Nebraska Press, 1966), pp. 222–3.
7. Loomis, *Wells Fargo*, p. 178.
8. Ibid., pp. 178–9.
9. Mrs. Frank C. Montgomery "Fort Wallace and Its Relation to the Frontier," *Kansas Historical Collections, 1926–1928* 17 (1928), p. 204.
10. Margaret Long, *The Smoky Hill Trail* (Denver: W. H. Kistler Company, 1943), p. 97.
11. Bayard Taylor was badly misinformed about the location of Fort Lyon. From Fort Wallace it is sixty-five miles south to the Arkansas River and from that point another eighty miles west to Fort Lyons, up the river in Colorado.
12. *Junction City* (Kans.) *Union*, 4 August 1866; reprinted from the *New York Tribune*.
13. Long, *Smoky Hill Trail*, pp. 50–53. These excerpts were quoted from Baynard Taylor's book, *Colorado, A Summer Trip*.
14. Dubois Station.
15. What Taylor calls Beaver Creek is likely East Bijou Creek.
16. This would be West Bijou Creek, according to Margaret Long.
17. Also called Ruthton Station.
18. Four Mile House, one of the main taverns just outside Denver.
19. There is no trace of this station now, but it is believed to have been on the NW quarter of Section 20-13-46.
20. Big Springs Station was on the NE quarter of Section 12-13-49.
21. David's Wells Station was on the NE quarter of Section 24-12-51.
22. Hugo Springs Station was on the NE quarter of Section 31-11-52. There may have been springs here, but there is no trace of them now. It is a known fact that there was a dug well at this station.
23. This station was on the ground now enclosed by the Lincoln County Fair Grounds at Hugo, Colorado.
24. Cedar Point Station was on the north half of Section 19-8-57.
25. Long, *Smoky Hill Trail*, p. 101.
26. Fairmont Station was on the SW quarter of Section 24-7-59.
27. Benham Station was on the SE quarter of Section 21-6-60.
28. Bijou Springs Station was on the NE quarter of Section 12-5-62. Almost every creek and gully where water was found for the stage stations became known in later years as Station Gulch. Few were called that when the stage lines were active.
29. Kiowa Station was on the SW quarter of Section 28-3-63. The site of this station is almost within the town limits of Bennett. It was a busy station, as were all those from this point on to Denver, because it catered to traffic on both the B.O.D. and the Ft. Morgan Cut-off of the Platte River Road.
30. Box Elder Station was on the NW quarter of Section 5-4-64.
31. Long, *Smoky Hill Trail*, p. 189. Coal Creek Station was on the NE quarter of Section 12-4-66.
32. Tollgate Station was on the SE quarter of Section 7-4-66.
33. L. G. DeLay, "Pond Creek Centennial," *Fort Wallace* (Kans.) *Bugle*, June 1965. This locates the new Fort Wallace two miles southeast of Pond Creek. Some sources state that the move was almost three miles due east. Pond Creek remained as a station on the B.O.D. after the military post was moved.
34. Montgomery, "Fort Wallace," p. 199. There is little doubt about the date of moving the post from Pond Creek to the new fort, but there is doubt about the official date of the name change. Although the adjutant general of the U.S. sent a letter to the Kansas Historical Society in 1927 stating that the name was officially changed on Septemer 18, 1866, another report says that the name was changed on April 16, 1866, before the post was moved from Pond Creek. Bayard Taylor, as quoted earlier in this chapter, wrote in June 1866 when he passed Pond Creek Station that there was a new military station here called Fort Wallace, so it was obviously known then by the name of Fort Wallace whether the name had been officially changed or not.
35. *Fort Wallace* (Kans.) *Bugle*, June 1965.
36. Montgomery, "Fort Wallace," p. 226.
37. Loomis, *Wells Fargo*, p. 179.
38. Ibid., p. 180.
39. Montgomery, "Fort Wallace," p. 196.
40. Blaine Burkey, *Custer Come At Once* (Hays, Kans.: Thomas More Prep, 1976), p. 17.
41. *Fort Wallace* (Kans.) *Bugle*, June 1965.

CHAPTER 12

WAR RENEWED

WHILE WINTER KEPT MOST of the warriors and soldiers close to warm fires, plans were being forged on both sides to renew the struggle when grass greened up. The Indians made an occasional raid on a post or stage station to steal a few horses or mules and to let the white men know they had not been forgotten, but the sharp winds of winter ruled the battlefields.

In January 1867 Bvt. Maj. Gen. George A. Custer, stationed at Fort Riley, sent a message to Captain Keogh, commanding Fort Wallace, asking for the services of Bill Comstock the scout at Fort Wallace.

The Seventh Cavalry was headquartered at Fort Riley then. Captain Keogh was a member of the Seventh, temporarily stationed at Fort Wallace. He had little recourse but to send the scout to General Custer, his commander. There was no great need at the fort for a scout during the cold months, and Comstock was eager to make the trip. Not only did he consider it an honor to be called by the famous young general, but it meant he would get a chance to ride on a train — something he had never seen, much less ridden. Keogh sent a letter of recommendation to Custer with the scout.[1]

Comstock's background was an enigma, clouded by various stories he told on himself. At times he said he was part Indian and had been born near the Smoky Hill River. At other times he claimed Kentucky as his birthplace. One reporter got the idea he was from Wisconsin. It was years after his death before his true origin was uncovered.

He was born William Averill Comstock in Comstock, Michigan, on January 17, 1842.[2] His mother died when he was five, and he was farmed out to two uncles in New York. From there he went to his sister's family in Wisconsin and moved with them to Omaha in 1857. He next showed up as an Indian trader at Cottonwood Springs, near the forks of the Platte River, when he was eighteen years old. From then on he lived off the land in the West, quite often with the Indians themselves. He was known over the plains by the name of Medicine Bill. According to his own story he got that name from the Arapahoe tribe. While he was with them an Indian was bitten on the finger by a rattlesnake. Bill promptly cut off the man's finger and thus saved his life. From that time on the Arapahoes called him Medicine Bill.[3]

He came to Fort Wallace and was hired as a scout on December 23, 1865.[4] He was only twenty-three years old but possessing a knowledge of the plains and the Indians unequaled by most scouts employed by the army.

His visit with General Custer at Fort Riley was brief. He evidently returned immediately to Fort Wallace, because Captain Keogh made a request for a horse for him. He had nothing but a mule to ride while scouting. In a letter dated February 19, 1867, Keogh asked: "I beg respectfully

Courtesy the Nebraska State Historical Society, Lincoln
Fort Wallace, Kansas, 1879

to inquire if the guide and interpreter [Comstock] is authorized to have a Government horse. He is often so exposed to capture from frequent scouting where Indians abound that it would appear proper that he be furnished with better means of locomotion than a mule." It is signed by M. W. Keogh, Captain, Seventh U.S. Cavalry, Commanding Post.[5]

The War Department continued to insist there were no hostile Indians within the Department of the Missouri. Those who knew the facts simply suggested, "Wait till spring."

All through the winter of 1866–67, the chiefs and the warriors warned repeatedly that as soon as the grass was up in the spring they would make a combined attack along the entire frontier and drive the white men from their hunting grounds.

Not all the whites were complacent about the warning. Gen. Winfield Scott Hancock, who had assumed command of the Department of the Missouri in the summer of 1866, decided to stop the summer raids before they began in 1867.[6] General Hancock knew little about Indians and was certain that a show of strength in Indian territory would frighten them into submission. If they wanted to fight, however, the general would accommodate them.

He sent letters to the agents of the plains tribes, telling them he was bringing an expedition west to talk peace with the chiefs. He asked that the chiefs meet him when he arrived. He then made up an array of strength such as had never before been seen by the Indians.

On March 27, 1867, Hancock personally led his expedition of infantry and artillery from Fort Riley. Its destination was the big Cheyenne camp on the Pawnee Fork south of the Smoky Hill River, not far from Fort Larned.[7] To show strength and mobility to his expedition, General Hancock took along the Seventh U.S. Cavalry under Custer. He now had a force of almost two thousand men, by far the largest army ever to march against the Indians. Thus began what many referred to as Hancock's War.

On April 7 they reached Fort Larned, 160 miles from Fort Riley, passing through Fort Harker on the way. There the agents of the Comanches, Kiowas, Cheyennes,

Courtesy the Kansas State Historical Society, Topeka
Winfield S. Hancock

Courtesy the Kansas State Historical Society, Topeka

Bull train crossing the Smoky Hill River at Ellsworth, Kansas, 1867.

Arapahoes, and Apaches met the expedition and told General Hancock that the chiefs of the tribes would meet him near the fort on April 10.

A heavy snowstorm delayed the meeting, but some of the Indian chiefs came in to discuss it with Hancock. The general said that on the next day he would march his troops up the river to meet the chiefs. The Indians wanted to delay the parlay until they could bring the chiefs to the fort to see the general. Hancock refused to wait any longer.

Custer wrote of this campaign after it was over:

> The following morning, our entire force marched from Fort Larned up Pawnee Fork in the direction of the main village, encamping the first night about 21 miles from the fort. Several parties of Indians were seen in our advance during the day, watching our movements, while a heavy smoke, seen to rise in the direction of the Indian village, indicated that something more than usual was going on. We afterward learned that the Indians, thinking to prevent us camping in their vicinity, had burned all the grass for miles in the direction from which they expected us.

Pawnee Killer, a Sioux chief, and White Horse, a Cheyenne chief, came to Hancock's camp to say that the chiefs of all the tribes would come to Hancock's camp the next morning at nine for a conference.

Hancock prepared for the meeting. Nine o'clock came but the chiefs did not. Bull Bear, a Cheyenne chief, finally came in to say that the chiefs were coming but would be delayed. Hancock saw through the deception and told Bull Bear he would move closer to make it easier for the chiefs to reach his camp. Custer reports on the next move:

> At 11 A.M., we resumed our march, and had proceeded but a few miles when we witnessed one of the finest and most imposing military displays which it has ever been my lot to behold. An Indian line of battle was drawn directly across our line of march, as if to say, this far and no farther. Most of the Indians were mounted; all were bedecked in their brightest colors, their heads crowned with their brilliant war-bonnets, their lances bearing the crimson pennant, bows strung, and quivers full of barbed arrows. In addition, each warrior was supplied with either a breech loading rifle or revolver, sometimes with both — these latter obtained through the wise foresight and strong love of fair play which prevails in the Indian Department.
>
> For a few moments appearances seemed to foreshadow anything but a peaceful issue. General Hancock, coming in view of the wild fantastic battle array, which extended far to our right and left and not more than half a mile in our front, hastily sent orders to the infantry, artillery and cavalry to form a line of battle. . . . Bright blades flashed from their scabbards into the morning sunlight and the infantry brought their muskets to a carry. . . . After a few moments of painful suspense, General Hancock, accompanied by General A. J. Smith and other officers, rode forward and though an interpreter invited the chiefs to meet us midway for an interview. In response to this invitation, Roman Nose, bearing a white flag, accompanied by ten other chiefs, rode forward to the middle of the open space between the lines, where we all shook hands, most of them exhibiting unmistakable signs of gratification at this apparently peaceful termination of our encounter.

The Indians declared their peaceful intentions in spite of the two hundred and fifty lodges that made up the village, about half Cheyenne and half Sioux. All soldiers had strict orders to stay away from the village, and there were few soldiers who had any desire to disobey that order.

One of General Hancock's scouts, who

was also an interpreter, was sent to stay in the Indian village until the meeting with the chiefs the next morning. However, the scout was back in Hancock's camp by 9:30 P.M. to report that the Indians were packing up and leaving.

Hancock called Custer immediately and gave him orders to mount his cavalry and surround the Indian village to make sure none of them escaped until after the conference the next morning.

In Custer's own words, that was easier said than done. No bugle call was allowed, since Custer was to surround the village without noise. It took him some time to get his men roused and into the saddle. They moved swiftly but stealthily. The moon was almost full, but clouds kept it hidden most of the time. When it did peep out, the men could see the lodges of the Indians along the creek.

When they had the village surrounded, they waited. They had seen no sign of the reported exodus of the Indians. Most of the men felt that the Indians very likely had seen the cavalry leave the army camp and were now lying in ambush along the banks of the creek, waiting for the pony soldiers to get within range of their rifles and bows.

Just after they had completed the encirclement the moon broke through the clouds, lighting up the peaceful village. Custer had to know whether the Indians were sleeping in those lodges or waiting the advance of the troops so they could ambush them — or perhaps had already escaped.

Custer dismounted and, taking his half-breed guide and interpreter, Ed Gurrier,[8] whose wife was a Cheyenne living in this village, crept forward so the guide could hail the camp and announce their peaceful presence. Custer's problem was to get close enough to the village to talk but not to get too far from his horse to escape if need be.

Gurrier called to the camp but got no response. Custer was still not sure whether the warriors were lying in ambush, waiting for them to get closer. Their stealthy advance was not challenged, and they reached the conclusion that the Indians had escaped. Reaching the first of the lodges they found it empty but with the fire still smoldering and the household goods, such as door mats, paint bags, and rawhide ropes, left just as though the owners had stepped out for only a minute.

Examination of other lodges proved that the Indians had made a hasty departure, leaving behind most of their belongings. Perhaps they feared a fate such as had befallen Chivington's victims on Sand Creek two and a half years before.

Custer sent a messenger back to General Hancock to report what he had found. Hancock immediately sent an order to Custer to pursue the Indians with all eight troops of his Seventh Cavalry. Custer took some Delaware scouts and a group of white and half-white scouts. He also had Wild Bill Hickok and Will Comstock as guides.[9] They left at dawn, following the easily discernible trail left by the Indians.

General Hancock stayed at the site, placing guards over the empty Indian camp to prevent any Indians from sneaking back and taking some of the possessions left behind.

But the Indians did not return. Custer was sure he would catch up with them before nightfall of the first day, April 15. The trail led straight toward the Smoky Hill River. Obviously the Indians were depending on the speed of their ponies and the surprise of their departure to escape pursuit.

When it became apparent that their winter-weakened ponies could not outdistance the grain-fed cavalry horses, they used another strategy. They broke into many groups, fanning out in a semicircle to the east, north, and west. It was next to impossible to detect which was the main body of fleeing Indians.

Courtesy the Kansas State Historical Society, Topeka *From Hunnius Sketchbook*

Sketches of three stations, 1867

Custer had to depend on his Delaware scouts to pick the main trail. After nearly two days of riding they reached the Smoky Hill about thirteen miles west of Downer's Station on the B.O.D., arriving at Downer's on April 17.[10]

Here Custer got his first inkling of what the Indians were doing. Downer Station had not been attacked, but the frightened men there reported they had heard that the three stations to the east had been burned and the people either murdered or driven away.

Custer sent another report to General Hancock by courier.[11] He had his troops on the march the next morning before five o'clock. They passed White Rock Station, which was abandoned. At Stormy Hollow Station they found the attendants alive but frightened. They reported that eight hundred Indians had passed within five hundred yards of the station a couple of days before. Some of the Indians had tried to get into the station, but the men had held them off. Even allowing for the exaggeration of frightened men, there obviously had been a large number of Indians.

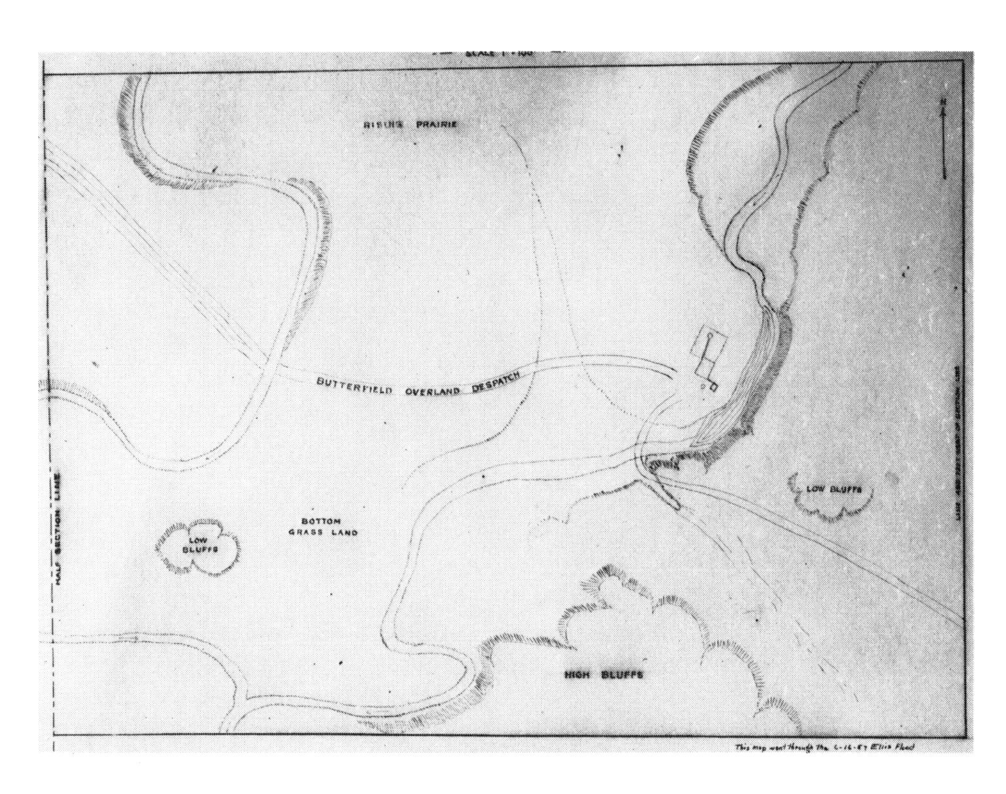

White Rock Station on the Butterfield Overland Despatch.

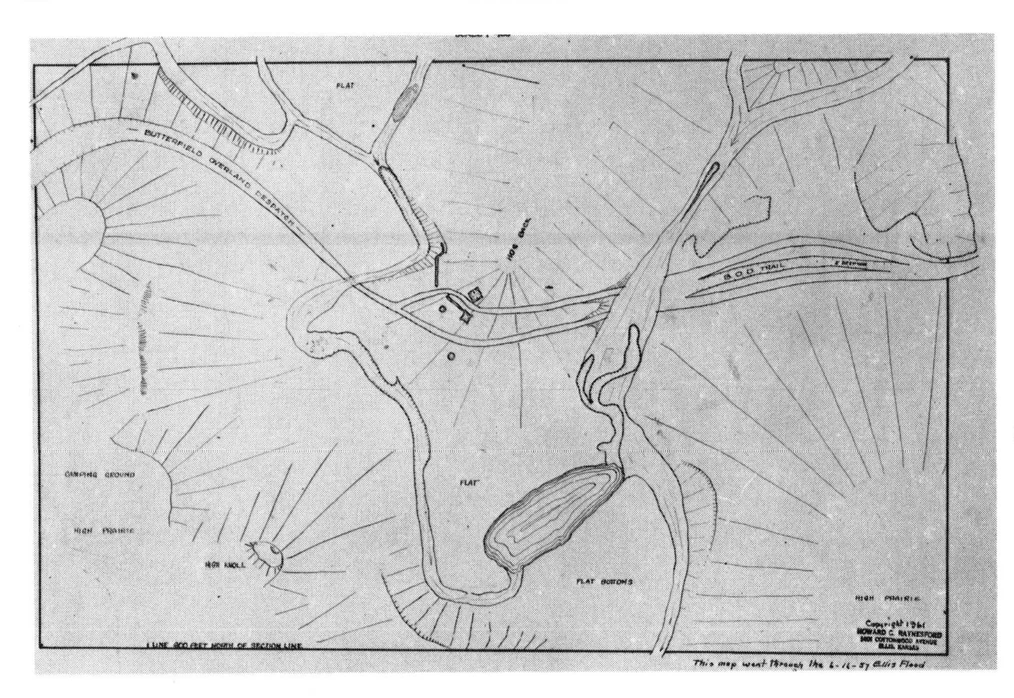

Stormy Hollow on the Butterfield Overland Despatch.

The Indians had taken four mules that were at the station.

Custer hurried on and arrived at Lookout Station at five o'clock that afternoon. Here he saw hard evidence of the intensity of the Indian's fury. The men at Big Creek Station, just to the east of Lookout, had seen the fire from the burning station on the evening of April 15, verifying the speed with which the Indians had come from their camp on Pawnee Fork the night of April 14.

Two men at Big Creek Station, John Betts, the trader, and Captain Barron, a driver, went up the trail to see if they could help the men there. They gave Custer their report. They found "the station had been burned, the stock tender and the cook nailed to the barn and the barn burned, and the bodies of the men badly burned and the stock driven off. The side of the barn where the boys had been nailed up was badly charred, but that portion was still standing; the remainder of the building was all burned."[12]

Custer sent his report to Hancock on the conditions at Lookout Station:

> I was the first of the command to reach the station and found the station house, stable, and haystack a pile of ashes, a few pieces of timber being still burning. The bodies of three murdered men were lying near the ruins. It appears a party of men had been to the station from the next station east and attempted to bury them, but from a lack of implements or through fear had merely covered them with some poles; the wolves had uncovered them and eaten a considerable portion of their flesh from their legs. I caused them to be buried near the station with as much care as the circumstances would permit. They were so badly burned . . . the hair singed from their heads . . . their intestines torn out (not by the wolves, however, as they could only reach their legs).[13]

Custer heard many reports of large bands of Indians crossing the Smoky Hill and going north. They seemed to be heading for the Solomon or possibly the Platte River. Custer was low on forage for his horses, so he had to abandon the pursuit and head for Fort Hays to get supplies for his horses and men.

At Fort Hays Custer found only enough forage for his animals for one day, certainly not enough to allow him to go after the Indians. He sent another message to General Hancock still down on the Arkansas.

General Hancock had received Custer's

report on conditions on the Smoky Hill River and reacted immediately. On April 19 he ordered Col. A. J. Smith to destroy totally the Cheyenne and Sioux village that had been vacated by the Indians on the Pawnee Fork.[14]

The Indians had obviously mistaken General Hancock's great show of strength as a prelude to their annihilation and had struck back before they were hurt. The stations along the Smoky Hill route suffered the heaviest blows. This, according to Lt. James Montgomery Bell in his report on the activities of the spring of 1867, was the start of "the war of 1867, 1868 and 1869."[15]

On April 22 a message came from General Hancock to Custer at Fort Hays. It gave Custer command of the Smoky Hill and the posts all the way to Denver. He could range as far to the north and south as he thought necessary. Realistically, he couldn't move because of the lack of feed for his horses. He spent most of the month of May fuming at the delay in getting forage delivered to Fort Hays so he could take up his pursuit of the Indians.

There was no lack of reports of murders and burnings by the Indians all up and down the B.O.D. Mr. Burnham, division agent of the B.O.D., asked Custer for a cavalry escort for the stages that had been held up at Big Creek Station because of Indians to the west. Custer was unable to give any escort because his horses were in no shape to travel without forage. Custer was sure that twenty well-armed men in coaches, if the coaches traveled together, would be enough to assure safe passage.[16]

The agents of the B.O.D. met with Custer shortly after he was put in command of the Smoky Hill region and demanded military escort for stages along the line. Custer agreed and sent five-man details to Stormy Hollow, White Rock, Downer's, and Castle Rock. He had already sent twelve men to Lookout Station, which had been burned a few days before. He also ordered five-man details from Fort Wallace sent to stations farther west on the trail.[17]

As soon as Custer was established as commander of the Smoky Hill region he sent word to Captain Keogh at Fort Wal-

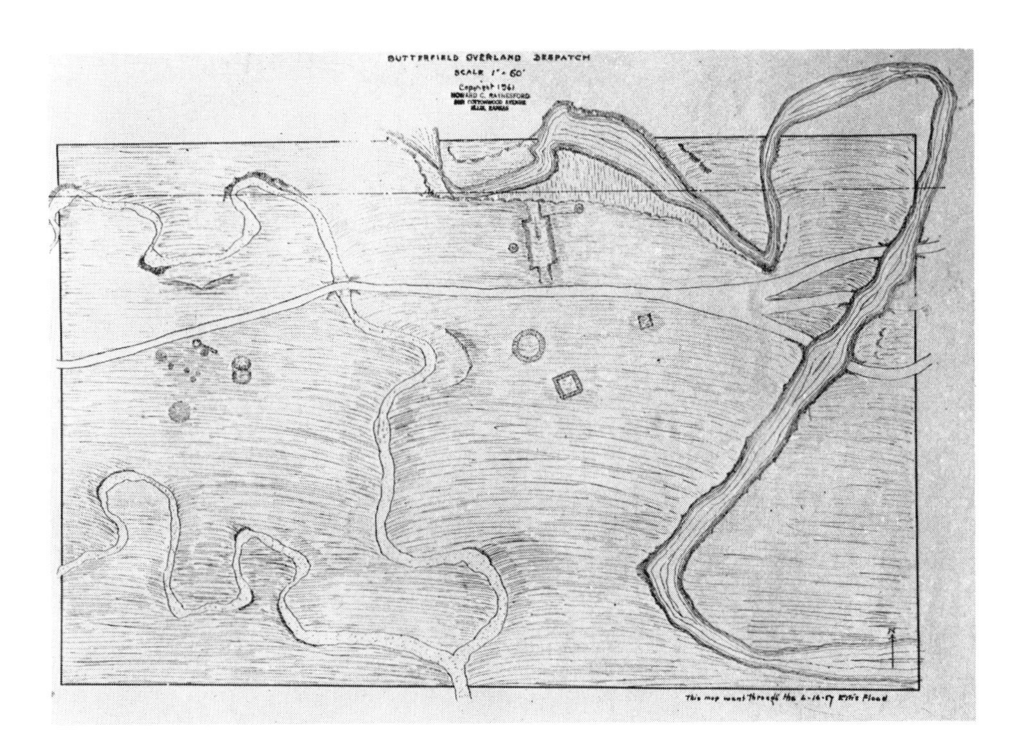

Lookout on the Butterfield Overland Despatch.

Courtesy the Kansas State Historical Society, Topeka
Copied from Harper's Weekly, June 8, 1867

Burning the Cheyenne village near Fort Larned, April 19, 1867

lace to send Will Comstock back to him. The scout returned to Custer but remained on the rolls at Fort Wallace, listed "on detached service with General Custer."[18]

After the heavy raids on the B.O.D. stations in their flight from General Hancock the Indians made hit-and-run raids all along the western Kansas and eastern Colorado sections of the stage road.

The April 30 raid on Goose Creek, just to the west of Fort Wallace, seemed to mark the beginning of these raids. The stock was run off, three mules were killed. This was followed by attacks in May on Monument and Chalk Bluffs, where the Indians tried to burn the station.[19]

At Big Timbers Station, twenty-five miles west of Fort Wallace on the Kansas-Colorado line, the Indians struck four times in May — on the sixth, eleventh, twenty-third, and twenty-fourth.[20]

Big Timbers was one of the favorite burial sites of the Indians, and they vigor-

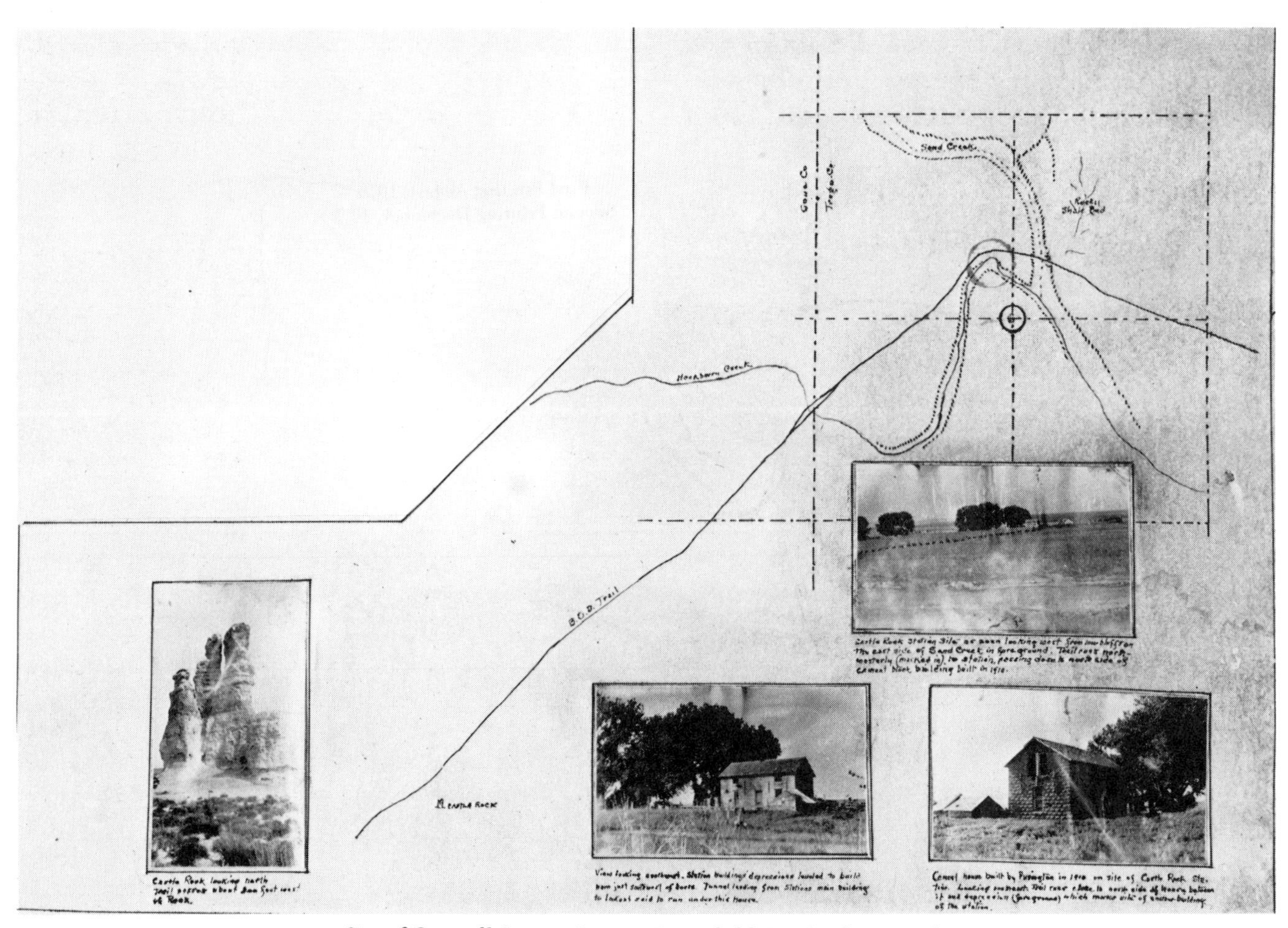

Site of Grannell Springs Station, Butterfield Overland Despatch

Courtesy the Kansas State Historical Society, Topeka

Fort Hays — evening parade, Seventh Cavalry camp, 1867.

ously resented the whites building a stage station hear those sacred grounds. This station was subjected to many severe attacks.[21]

Also in that frantic month of May, Indians struck at Pond Creek on the eleventh and tried to burn the station. On the eighteenth they struck at Smoky Hill Springs Station. They attacked Pond Creek again on the twenty-seventh, this time driving off most of the cattle.

May also brought Theodore R. Davis to Fort Hays. He had been with General Hancock, sketching scenes for *Harper's Weekly* and *Harpers New Monthly Magazine.* [22] He had reported on Hancock's fiasco that ended in the Indians' renewing the war with greater vigor than ever.

Davis made the trip to Lookout Station on the night of May 13. There had been a steady stream of reports of Indian raids on stations and wagon trains, but the soldiers could never find any evidence when they went out to investigate.

In his report Davis wrote: "A wagon proceeding toward Downer's Station, with an escort of five men, had barely escaped capture by them. [The messenger of the news] had gone out immediately to make sure of the number of the Indians, and, if possible, to determine to which tribe they

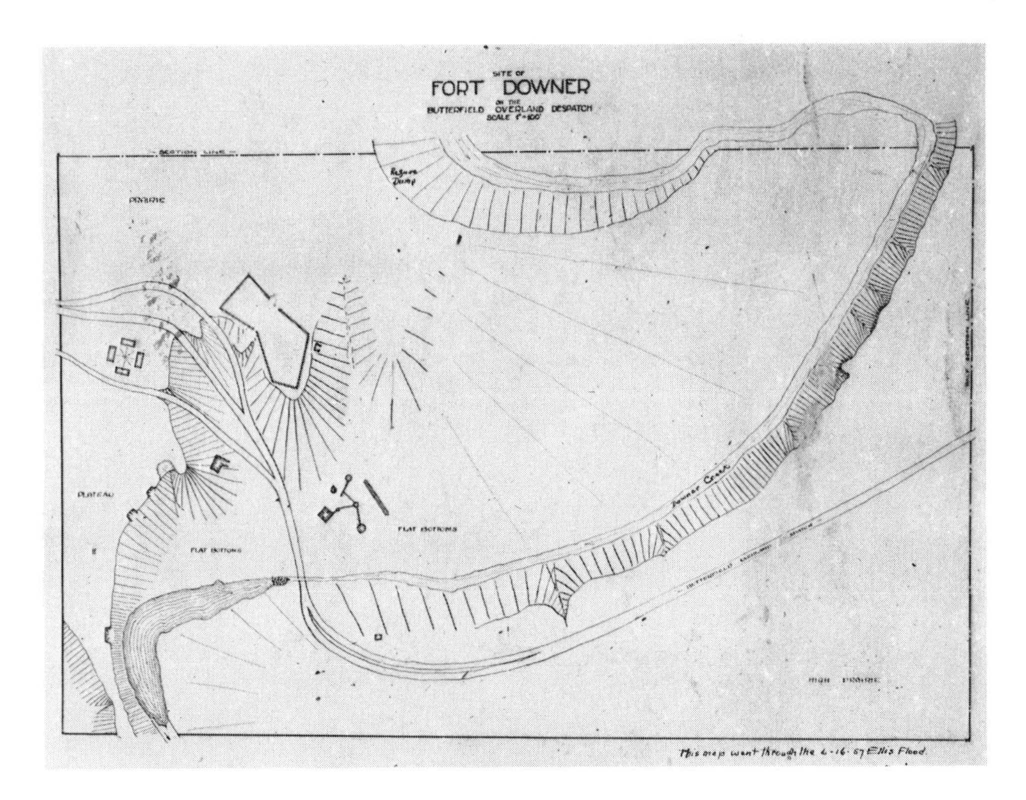

Fort Downer on the Butterfield Overland Despatch.

belonged. He was satisfied that they were Cheyennes, and numbered about four or five hundred. There could be no doubt of it, as he had been within sixty yards of the Indians, and had narrowly escaped being captured by them."[23]

Custer doubted this report because there had been so many false alarms. Nevertheless, he took all the troops that could be spared from Fort Hays and made a forced night march to Lookout Station. When he got there he found nothing wrong. The men, who were living in a cave until the new station could be built, were playing cards.

At daylight Custer found a man who had "seen" the Indians and who led them to the spot. The ground showed plain evidence that a herd of buffalo had passed there. In total disgust Custer took his men back to Fort Hays and issued an order that anyone making a false report of Indians being sighted would be punished severely.[24]

On May 30 more soldiers were sent to Downer's Station, and a fort was established. This post survived until May 28, 1868, lacking two days of being in existence one year.[25]

With the Indians striking someplace along the trail almost every day, drastic measures had to be taken or the stage route to Denver would be totally shut down. By the first of June these measures were being put into effect.

Lt. James M. Bell, stationed at Fort Wallace, was given the task of stationing a noncommissioned officer and three men at each post to the west of Fort Wallace and providing them with means of defense. "For this purpose circular pits were dug in the ground and about ten feet in diameter, just deep enough so that a man standing in them could comfortably aim over the top. Around the edge of this pit was built a heavy wall of sod, pierced at intervals with loop-holes. Across this was laid a frame of logs and brush, on top of which was placed a heavy covering of earth. These little underground forts were connected with the buildings with a subterranean passage, and were supplied with a barrel of water, ten days' ration, and a supply of ammunition, to serve in case of siege, or the destruction of the building by fire."[26]

Some posts, such as Pond Creek Station, made excellent use of these underground forts. The Indians came to respect them to such a degree that they usually bypassed them in favor of easier prey.

As May faded into June, the army was plagued as much by heavy rains and desertions as by Indian raids. Custer, at Fort Hays, was losing a big portion of his army by desertions. The Junction City paper reported, "The expedition of Hancock [Custer's troops] or the remains of it, is still at Fort Hays, and is considerably reduced by desertion. Over thirty left one night lately."[27]

Other reports said that over a third of the men had deserted. Theodore Davis reported to his paper that many of the men had enlisted under assumed names in order to get to a country where they could desert and begin a new life. Davis said that in less than one year the Seventh Cavalry lost by desertion nearly eight hundred men.

Custer blamed poor food for the desertions, saying they were being issued the old rations left over from the War between the States. He worked hard to bring back the deserters and punish them. His method of punishment was to have the deserter's head half shaved and then parade him before the other troops.[28]

It wasn't a well-disciplined army of high morals that Custer led in pursuit of Indians on the first of June.

NOTES

1. John S. Gray, "Will Comstock, Scout: The Natty Bumpo of Kansas," *Montana Western History* 20 (Summer 1970), p. 11.
2. Ibid., p. 6.
3. Ibid., p. 8.

4. Ibid., p. 9.
5. *Fort Wallace* (Kans.) *Bugle*, June 1965.
6. George Jelinek, "The Ellsworth Story," *Ellsworth* (Kans.) *Reporter*, 3 August 1967.
7. John S. Manion, "Indian Attack," *Fort Wallace* (Kans.) *Bugle*, March 1971.
8. Mrs. Frank C. Montgomery, "Fort Wallace and Its Relation to the Frontier," *Kansas Historical Collections, 1926–1928* 17 (1928), p. 214.
9. Gray, "Will Comstock," p. 12.
10. Montgomery, "Fort Wallace," p. 214.
11. Blaine Burkey, *Custer Come at Once* (Hays, Kans.: Thomas More Prep, 1976), p. 4. This message was sent by a corporal and five privates, guided by a Delaware scout. A previous message to Hancock had been sent by courier Thomas Kinkaid.
12. Ibid., p. 6.
13. Ibid.
14. Montgomery, "Fort Wallace," p. 213.
15. Manion, "Indian Attack."
16. Burkey, *Custer Come at Once*, p. 8.
17. Ibid., p. 9.
18. Ibid., p. 20.
19. William A. Bell, *New Tracks in North America* (New York: Scribner, Welford & Company, 1870; reprint ed. Albuquerque: Horn & Wallace, 1965), p. 35.
20. Montgomery, "Fort Wallace," p. 205.
21. Bell, *New Tracks*, p. 35.
22. Burkey, *Custer Come at Once*, p. 11.
23. Ibid., p. 14.
24. Ibid.
25. Montgomery, "Fort Wallace," p. 198.
26. Manion, "Indian Attack."
27. *Junction City* (Kans.) *Union*, 1 June 1867. Report was dated May 22.
28. Burkey, *Custer Come at Once*, p. 24.

CHAPTER 13

THE BLOODY MONTH

JUNE 1867 BEGAN AND ENDED in a sea of blood, as the Indians concentrated on a mighty effort to halt travel over the Smoky Hill Trail and to drive the hated white man from the hunting grounds along the river.

It began with Custer's long-delayed departure to the north, looking for the Indians that he had been chasing in April when he ran out of forage for his horses.

Before leaving Fort Hays, however, he made sure that his wife, Libbie, who had joined him during his wait at the fort, had a good campsite and was as comfortable as possible. He didn't expect to be gone too long.

Old Fort Hays, as a fort, was in its last days, although the event that was to hurry its move was entirely unforeseen at that time. In Custer's own words:

> In selecting the ground on which the tents intended for the ladies were to stand, I had chosen a little knoll, so small as to be scarcely perceptible, yet the only elevated ground to be found. It was within a few steps of the bank of the stream, while the main camp [of the Seventh] was located below and nearer the bluff. . . . The bank on which the little knoll was, by actual measurement, thirty-six feet above ordinary water mark. Surely this location might be considered well enough protected naturally against the rainy season. So I thought, as I saw the working party putting the finishing touches to the bright white canvas house, which to all intents and purposes was to be to me, even in my absence, my army home. I confidently expected to return to this camp at the termination of my march.[1]

While the Seventh Cavalry started its trek to the north on the morning of June 1, Custer himself did not leave Fort Hays until midnight that night. With two soldiers, four Delaware scouts, and Bill Comstock as guide, he rode up the North Fork of Big Creek, reaching the camp of his troops just in time to continue the march the next morning.

In his book *My Life on the Plains* Custer described the guide who made this campaign with him:

> Our guide was a young white man known on the plains as Will Comstock. No Indian knew the country more thoroughly than did Comstock. He was perfectly familiar with every divide, water course, and strip of timber for hundreds of miles in either direction. He knew the dress and peculiarities of every Indian tribe and spoke the languages of many of them. Perfect in horsemanship, fearless in manner, a splendid hunter, and a gentleman by instinct, as modest and unassuming as he was brave, he was an interesting as well as valuable companion on a march such as was then before us.[2]

Photo by Author

B.O.D. Trail out of Fort Fletcher (Fort Hays) looking west, as it looks today.

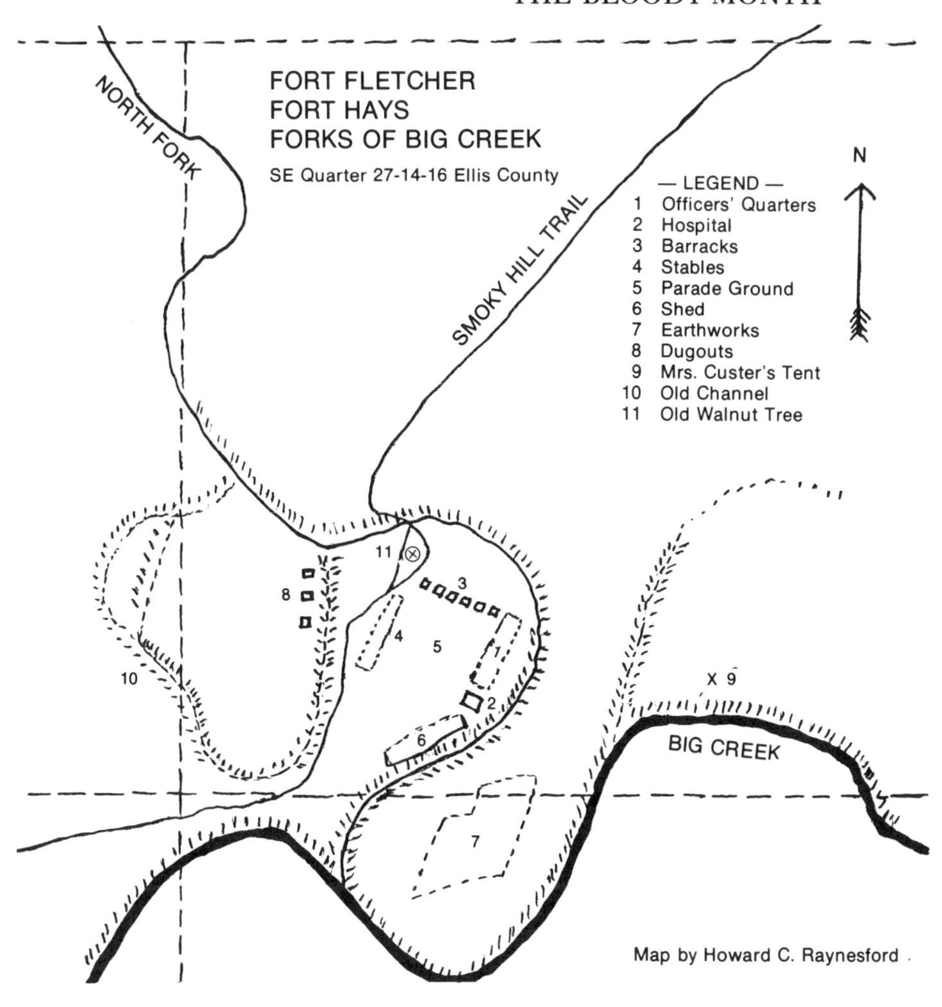

Map by Howard C. Raynesford

Fort Fletcher (Fort Hays) — Forks of Big Creek

Custer led his troops north to Fort McPherson on the Platte River, finding no Indians and unaware of what was going on back along the Smoky Hill River. This time, instead of moving into the action Custer had marched away from it. He would probably have turned around and returned in spite of his orders if he had known what was to happen in the next few days.

Raynesford Photo, 1931

Knoll where Libbie Custer's tent stood

Most of the trouble with the Indians was west of Fort Hays. Fort Wallace was the center of it, as usual. On June 3 two residents of Pond Creek named Favor and Thompson were killed and scalped by Indians between Pond Creek and Goose Creek Station. The next day Indians tried to steal the horses at Fort Wallace. On June 6 two men riding their horses east from Denver were killed at almost the exact spot where Favor and Thompson had met their end. Eight stage drivers refused to take their coaches west toward Denver;[3] few could blame them.

To the east of Fort Wallace a new threat struck the Smoky Hill River and its tributaries, completely unrelated to the

Raynesford Photo, 1931

"Mrs. Custer's tree"

Courtesy the Kansas State Historical Society, Topeka

Fort Hays — 1867, after the flood

Indian wars. Fort Hays bore the brunt of this, although the disaster covered a large territory.

On the night of June 5 a prairie thunderstorm came up out of the northwest, complete with thunder, lighting, and wind. The rain poured down in torrents, but it was no spring shower. The rain continued hour after hour. It was described by a writer who witnessed the flood and saw its aftermath:

At bed time, the streams had risen but little, but at midnight the heavy downpour still continuing, and the firm surface of the plains shedding water like a roof, the streams rose ten feet in an hour and the foaming currents roaring like cataracts, came down with the force of mighty waves. Fort Fletcher,[4] at the mouth of the North Fork and supposed to be above high water, was inundated, six or eight soldiers being swept away, while the remainder were obliged to seek safety on the roofs of the barracks and other buildings. Large numbers of mules picketed on the adjacent bottoms were drowned. Their picket pins fast in the earth, the animals were swept from their feet by the rising waters and towed under by the firmly held lariats.

Emigrants encamped on the bottoms heard the roar of the flood and with no time to harness, they seized the tongues of the wagons themselves. But the rising tide gained on them too rapidly and they were glad to save life at the expense of oxen and goods.

The horrors of the night are indescribable, and to crown it all, they took place amid a darkness that

Courtesy the Kansas State Historical Society, Topeka
Copied from Harpers Weekly, June 29, 1867

The Indian War — General Custer's scouts

Courtesy the Kansas State Historical Society, Topeka

Remains of Fort Fletcher

Approaching on trail from west

was total. Above the roar of water descending — below the answering roar of the floods, as they rolled madly onward, carrying in their embrace the wreckage and corpses by the score.[5]

Another witness to the flood was Libbie Custer, who had been left behind by her husband when he went north to look for Indians. She lists seven soldiers drowned in the flood.

She first realized the magnitude of the situation when officers from the post hurried over to her tent to help her. The ground where the post stood was already under water. When the officers attempted to go back to their men they couldn't get through the water. Mrs. Custer reported that whenever a horse was sent into the water to swim to safety it was swept away by the flood.

The water continued to rise until it almost reached Mrs. Custer's tent. The little knoll where General Custer and put her tent was an island, and there was no escaping from it in any direction. Libbie Custer, in her book *Tenting on the Plains*, described the situation in the fort:

> The flood came so unexpectedly that the first known of it was the breaking in of the doors of the quarters. The poorly built, leaky, insecure adobe houses had been heretofore a protection, but the freshet filled them almost instantly with water. The quarters of the laundresses were especially endangered, being on an even lower ground than the officers' houses. The women were hurried out in their night-dresses, clasping their little children while they ran to places pointed out by officers, to await orders. . . . The Government property had to be temporarily abandoned, and a great deal was destroyed or swept away by the water.

Of her own plight on the little island, she wrote:

> Our little strip of land narrowed and narrowed, until we all appeared to be doomed. The officers decided that if the water continued to rise with the same rapidity, we would be washed away, as we could not swim nor had we strength to cling to anything. This determined them to resort to a plan that, happily we knew nothing of until the danger was past. We were to be strapped to the Gatling guns as a anchorage. They are, perhaps, the lightest of all artillery, but might have been heavy enough to resist the action of what current rose over the island. There would have been one chance in ten thousand of rescue under such circumstances, but I doubt if being pinioned there, watching the waves closing around us, would have been as merciful as permitting us to float off into a quicker death.

This flood necessitated immediate implimentation of the plan to move Fort Hays to the vicinity of the railroad several miles to the northwest of the present post, still on Big Creek. No attempt was made to restore the old post. The soldiers salvaged what could be saved after the flood.

Shortly after the heavy rains that brought the flood to Big Creek and subsequently to the Smoky Hill River, Indians struck at Big Creek Station, just to the west of old Fort Hays. When the herder of the station's horses came in for a drink on a hot afternoon, Indians charged out of nowhere. They drove off fifty-six stagecoach horses and six government mules. Although pursuit was swift, none of the animals was recovered.[6]

Still farther west, at Fort Wallace, the troops were kept busy escorting coaches. Even then not all coaches made their runs, and those that did usually encountered trouble.

Lt. James Montgomery Bell, who had been given the assignment of protecting the stations west of Fort Wallace to Denver, reviewed the situation in June:

The Indians were so active and persistent that nearly all the stations were destroyed, horses stolen and keepers killed for a distance of 150 miles east and west of Wallace, so that it became necessary for a time to haul the stages over this part of the route with government mules. Two coaches were run together, one carrying the passengers and mail, the other an escort of soldiers.[7]

After putting soldiers at each station west of Fort Wallace, Lieutenant Bell went on to Denver. When he was ready to come back he could not find a stage driver willing to make the trip. When he did find a coach going east, there was a scarcity of passengers. As Bell reported:[8]

Passengers could not be induced to take the chances of the trip, so the driver, one man employed as mail guard, and myself, started on our journey, uncertain as to what the outcome would be. The country was full of Indians and it would be an extraordinary piece of good luck if we succeeded in getting through without encountering them. Thus we traveled 140 miles, when to my delight, I found three men of my troop at one of the stations, who had been sent out as guard for a west bound coach.[9] At the next station[10] I found one of the guards there sick with fever. I placed him on a bed spread for him on the top of the coach."

Courtesy the Kansas State Historical Society, Topeka

James Montgomery Bell

A short time later in the trip (June 11) Bell reported:

We reached Cheyenne Wells a short while before noon, and stopped to get dinner and rest our tired team.

The buildings here had not been burned, although several attempts to do so had been made. The wife of the station keeper had been with him through the trying experience of the summer and, being anxious to get out of the country, begged me to let her go with us. I told her she could go if she was willing to take the chances, which she decided to do. All went well till we reached a point midway between Cheyenne Wells and the next station, Big Timbers.

At this point the trail crossed a dry fork of the Smoky Hill River. The animals were tired, and while they were slowly dragging the stage through the deep sand of the creek bed, we were startled by a heavy volley fired into us by a band of twenty-five Indians, concealed under a steep bank seventy-five yards away. The stage was riddled with bullets, the glass lamps at the driver's feet were broken into a hundred pieces, and it was as if by a miracle that any of the party escaped instant death. A number of the shots passed through the top of the stage, scattering splinters about the woman and me. The three men of my troop were sitting on the top of the stage where the sick man was lying. We seized our Spencer rifles and returned a rapid fire. As we reached the opposite bank of the creek I called to the men to jump to the ground, and seizing the woman, forced her to the floor of the stage, telling her not to move, knowing that if the Indians saw her they would have an additional motive in capturing the stage, and also that the heavy frame work would be a protection to her.

I hastily opened the door to get out and while doing so the sick man swung himself from the top of the stage, down through the opening of the door, and as he did so said, I am killed, and began to deliver to me his dying message to his mother; but there was no time even to listen to such a sad message, for the lives of the entire party were trembling in the balance.

We had now reached ground high enough to see that our fire had been effective, and observed the Indians placing the bodies of two dead warriors on their ponies. Those of their party not thus occupied had left their place of concealment and were rapidly riding around our flanks to cut off our line of march. The country was much broken and traversed by ravines. In these they concealed themselves and opened fire upon us as we approached. Fortunately, a third Indian was killed who had ventured too close to our trail, but, nevertheless, they kept up the fight for two hours over a distance of more than five miles. Several of our animals were badly wounded, but were fortunately able to keep going till we reached Big Timbers.

Bell goes on to explain that when he helped the woman out of the coach to go inside the station she had two complaints. One, she hadn't gotten to see a single Indian; the other, the trouble she had rolling the dead body of the soldier back on the seat each time a lurch of the coach rolled him off on top of her. The sick man had been shot on top of the coach and had died shortly after getting inside.[11]

Not all the coaches were as lucky as the one in which Lieutenant Bell traveled. The Indians were determined to halt travel, and they almost succeeded.

Fort Wallace, the center of all the hostilities, had few dull moments. On June 18 the coach coming in from the west reported that the coaches that had left Fort Wallace the previous Saturday (June 15) had been attacked by Indians. The soldiers had been unable to recover the bodies of their comrades and the citizens who were killed.

This prompted General Hancock to take forty men and Capt. Myles Keogh and start west. They would bury the dead beside the road when they reached them. That left Lt. James Hale of the Third Infantry in command of Fort Wallace.[12]

Shortly after Custer led his Seventh Cavalry north to Fort McPherson on the Platte River in Nebraska, the Indians struck in force all along the Smoky Hill. Custer had chased in vain after so many rumors of Indian atrocities before leaving Kansas that he had decided most of the reports were false — or else the Indians did not want to fight. He couldn't have been more wrong on both counts. The "Indian telegraph" got word to all warriors that Custer had gone north and pony soldiers were scarce along the Smoky Hill. They made good use of the knowledge.

A report reached Fort Hays that five men had been killed and scalped within five miles of Fort Wallace.[13] Indians struck at most B.O.D. stations and the surveying and construction crews of the railroad. It appeared they might overrun the entire frontier, and the officers at Fort Hays sent Mrs. George Custer and the ladies with her back to Fort Riley.[14]

Custer's trip to Fort McPherson was uneventful and likely would have been almost unnoted except for his conference with the Sioux chief, Pawnee Killer. Custer was so impresssed with the peaceful declarations of the chief that he gave him some rations. It later became evident that he was likely the one who had led some of the most vicious raids on the Smoky Hill a month and a half previously. He definitely was identified as the one responsible for later attacks on Custer's men.[15]

Custer returned to the southwest from Fort McPherson and camped at the forks of the Republican River near the Kansas line. From here he sent supply trains to Fort Wallace for food and ammunition for the soldiers and forage for the animals.[16] He was impatient to get to Fort Wallace, for he expected Libbie to be there waiting for him.[17]

The Indians were not only aware of Custer's location, they kept pecking away at his forces whenever a small detachment left the main camp. Meanwhile, warriors terrorized the Smoky Hill route, knowing that most of the pony soldiers were bottled up on the Republican.

When Hancock left for Denver, taking with him Captain Keogh and forty men, he left the post with less than fifty soldiers, although it was established to accommodate five hundred. This apparently was noted by the Indians; they struck the post the next day, June 22.

There were several civilians at the post, men who worked at various jobs. Also Colonel Greenwood with twenty-five colored troops had just arrived. Greenwood was surveying for the railroad, which it was hoped would be coming past the fort before too long. (It would actually be two years before it reached there.)

Cheyenne dog soldiers under Roman Nose had struck at Pond Creek Station the day before and managed to run off some stock. On the morning of the twenty-second they were back with heavy reinforcements, led by Charles Bent, the half-breed son of William Bent, the trader. These forces made a token strike at Pond Creek Station and then directed their full attention to the army post. Capt. Alfred Barnitz, Lt. Fred Beecher, and James M. Bell were the commissioned officers involved in the fight. Sergeant Dummell took a prominent roll as well.[18]

William A. Bell, with Colonel Greenwood's advance surveying party, got a firsthand view of the battle. Since he wanted to see how "the noble red men" fought, he rushed up into the front line. What he saw did little to endear the half-naked warriors to him.

Shortly after he joined the battle, fifty more Indians rode toward the battlefield. At the same time Sergeant Dummell came from the fort with ten men. He ordered a charge, but only three men went with him. They rushed into the fifty Indians, and a battle erupted some distance from the scene of the main engagement. As William Bell described it:

> For a few minutes the yells of the savages, the rattle of Spencers, and the encouraging shout of the young sergeant, could be heard. Before assistance could reach them, the Indians were reinforced, and the little band were trampled under the feet of the Indian horses. After the soldiers had fallen, the Indians fired on them and speared them. They were about scalping them, when the remainder of our little force rushed to the rescue, and the red-men fell back.[19]

Bell leaves the impression that all four soldiers were killed, but records show that two soldiers were killed and two wounded in this battle.[20] There were several small battles raging all around the fort, wherever the Indians could isolate a few soldiers.

One of these was out at the rock quarry, about three miles from the fort but in plain sight of it. Thirty men were quarrying stone, while other soldiers were hauling it to the fort for building barracks, officers quarters, and other necessary buildings. Six teams were being used to haul the stone. When the Indians struck at the men in the quarry they surprised two teams close to the quarry. Those teams and men made a dash back to the quarry. One driver made it; the other one, Pat McCarty, was killed, his team stolen, and the wagon upset.

The men in the quarry decided their only chance for survival was to get to the fort. They started, using their rifles to hold the Indians at bay. The mounted soldiers from the fort who had been fighting Indians elsewhere now turned to the aid of the men at the quarry and helped them reach the fort. The quarry had scarcely been evacuated when the Indians burned the tents and huts that the workers had been living in.[21]

The final toll of the day's fighting was four soldiers dead and four seriously wounded. The fort considered itself in a virtual siege. The Indians, however, did not appear the next day, Sunday. On that day the four soldiers who had died were buried in the cemetery just to the north of the new post.

On Monday General Wright's[22] surveying party arrived at the post, along with two stagecoaches traveling together for protection. There was some optimism that the Indians had given up their efforts to overrun the fort.

Courtesy the Nebraska State Historical Society, Lincoln

This monument erected in cemetery at Fort Wallace, Kansas, in 1867 in memory of those of I Troop, Seventh Cavalry, killed by Indians.

At dawn on Wednesday, June 26, the Indians struck again. They had fresh reinforcements, and the men at the post were sure the warriors had visions of a battle that would end like Fetterman's fight near Fort Phil Kearny the December before. They obviously were not aware of the reinforcements at the post in the form of the military escort of Wright's surveying crew.

The Indians struck at Pond Creek Station first, but the underground forts were too much for them. They succeeded in stampeding four stage horses, and it was these horses running pell-mell past the fort (two abreast as they would go while pulling a coach) that warned the soldiers of approaching trouble. The Indians were not far behind the four horses, trying to catch them.[23]

Perhaps the best account of the battle that followed can be found in the *Harper's Weekly* of July 1867:

> The war on the Smoky Hill Route through Kansas continues with great fury. On the 26th of June last a band of three hundred Cheyennes under a chief called "Roman Nose," attacked a station two miles from Fort Wallace and ran off the Overland Stage Company's stock. They then advanced toward the fort, when Company G of the Seventh United States Cavalry, under command of Captain Barnitz, went out to meet them. The Indians fell back to the brow of a hill two miles from the fort, then turned and awaited the attack. The cavalry charged at a gallop, and were met by a counter charge. The Indians, with lances poised and arrows on the string, rode at them with great speed, and a hand-to-hand fight followed, in which the savages displayed unlooked-for daring. With their overwhelming numbers they succeeded in driving the cavalry back to the fort, with a loss of seven men killed, several wounded, and half the horses captured or killed. "Roman Nose" was very conspicious in the fight, dashing into the midst of the fray on his powerful gray horse. He carried a spear, with which he unhorsed a soldier, and was about to spear him as he lay on the ground, when Corporal Harris struck the savage with his sword, which he had in his left hand. "Roman Nose" turned upon him, but as he did so Harris placed the muzzle of the Spencer rifle which he carried in his right hand at the breast of the savage and fired. With the blood spouting from his wound, the Indian fell forward on his horse.[24]
>
> The Indians committed unheard-of atrocities. A powerful warrior was seen to pick up the bugler, Charles Clark, who had been pierced by three arrows, and strip him as he rode along; after taking off all his clothing he mashed the head to a jelly, with his tomahawk, and then threw the body under his horse's feet. The body of Sergeant Frederick Wyllyams was also fearfully mutilated. His scalp was taken, two balls pierced his brain, and his right brow was cut open with a hatchet. His nose was severed and his throat gashed. His body was opened and the heart laid bare. The legs were cut to the bone, and the arms hacked with knives.

. . . We received from Major A. R. Calhoun the following list of the soldiers killed in the battle near Fort Wallace on June 16: Sergeant Frederick Wyllyams; Bugler Charles Clark: Corporals James Douglass and James K. Ludlow; and Privates Nathan Trail, Frank Rahme, all of Company G. and Welsh, Company E.[25]

Sergeant Wyllyams was mutilated the worst of any soldier killed. Such mutilations seemed the work of demented demons but William A. Bell points out that many of the gashes were the "signs" of the tribes involved. For instance, the sign of the Cheyenne Indians, or "cut-arm" Indians, was the slashed arm. The Arapahoe Indian sign was grabbing the nose or "smeller" tribe. The Sioux sign was a finger drawn across the throat or "cut-throat" tribe. So it was obvious that Sioux, Cheyenne, and Arapahoe Indians each put their mark on Sergeant Wyllyams.[26]

Harper's Weekly also states: "Major Calhoun describes Fort Wallace as being beautifully located on the north fork of the Smoky Hill River.[27] Buildings are being erected of a beautiful pink-colored magnesian limestone[28] which can be cut with a saw and plane, and hardens on exposure."

Courtesy the Kansas State Historical Society, Topeka

Fort Wallace — monument erected in 1867

While Fort Wallace licked its wounds and braced itself for further attacks, the Indians were counting their dead and preparing to strike at other places where the enemy was not concentrated in such great numbers. Their war against the white invader was far from finished.

NOTES

1. Blaine Burkey, *Custer Come at Once* (Hays, Kans.: Thomas More Prep, 1976), p. 25.
2. John S. Gray, "Will Comstock, Scout: The Natty Bumpo of Kansas," *Montana Western History* 20 (Summer 1970), p. 12.
3. Mrs. Frank C. Montgomery, "Fort Wallace and Its Relation to the Frontier," *Kansas Historical Collections, 1926–1928* 17 (1928), p. 206.
4. This was the old name for the fort. Fort Fletcher's name had been changed to Fort Hays a few months before the flood.
5. *Hays* (Kans.) *Sentinel* (reprinted), 18 January 1878.
6. Montgomery, "Fort Wallace," p. 197.
7. J. M. Bell, "Reminiscences," *Cavalry Journal* 10 (1897).
8. John S. Manion, "Indian Attack," *Fort Wallace* (Kans.) *Bugle*, March 1971. Manion has quoted Bell's report of his trip to Big Timbers, parts of which have been requoted here.
9. Army records show only two men of Company I were with Lieutenant Bell on the latter part of this run.
10. Likely Deering's Wells Station.
11. Manion, "Indian Attack."
12. "Smoky Trail Aflame," *Fort Wallace* (Kans.) *Bugle*, June 1965.
13. Ibid.
14. Burkey, *Custer Come at Once*, p. 26.
15. Ibid., p. 26, p. 29.
16. Montgomery, "Fort Wallace," p. 217.
17. Burkey, *Custer Come at Once*, p. 32.
18. Montgomery, "Fort Wallace," p. 207.
19. William A. Bell, *New Tracks in North America* (New York; Scribner, Welford & Company, 1870; reprint ed. Albuquerque: Horn & Wallace, (1965), pp. 53–54.
20. Montgomery, "Fort Wallace," p. 207.
21. Bell, *New Tracks*, pp. 55–56.
22. This is W. W. Wright, listed as general superintendent of the Union Pacific, Eastern Division, by Mrs. Montgomery and as chief engineer of the surveying crew by William A. Bell, who was the physician of that same crew.
23. Bell, *New Tracks*, p. 58.
24. Almost every report describes the death of Roman Nose in this battle. Although the leader of the dog soldiers was certainly shot at close range and "fell forward on his horse" he was not killed. He survived to lead the famous charge against Forsythe's scouts at Beecher Island on the Arickaree River in September of the following year. Roman Nose was a huge warrior, easily identified, so it isn't likely that it was a case of mistaken identity. He was in perfect physical condition and likely this helped him to survive and recuperate. His "medicine" was good that day. Warriors often tied themselves on their ponies so that, if they were killed in battle, the ponies would take them back to their comrades. The Indians believed that if they lost their scalps they could not enter the Happy Hunting Ground. While it is common belief that Indians scalped their fallen enemies for trophies to display, it is more likely that they scalped their enemies to keep them from going to the Happy Hunting Ground.
25. *Harper's Weekly*, 27 July 1867.
26. Bell, *New Tracks*, p. 63. Bell also describes the sign of the Comanche or "Snake" Indian as waving the arm like a snake crawling, the Crow Indian as waving the arms like a bird flying, the Pawnee or "Wolf" Indian as placing two fingers erect on each side of the head like pointed ears, the Blackfoot Indian as touching the heel and toe of the foot.
27. Actually Pond Creek instead of the north fork of the Smoky Hill. The north fork of the Smoky joins the south fork about fourteen miles east of Fort Wallace.
28. The "stone posts" erected from Fort Harker to the Colorado line in the 1960s by Howard Raynesford to mark the course of the B.O.D. were cut from this same pink limestone.

CHAPTER 14

SUMMER OF WAR

GENERAL CUSTER MISSED some of the bloodiest fighting along the Smoky Hill Trail when he was sent to chase Indians toward the Platte River in Nebraska. The Indians had been waiting for the pony soldiers to leave the Smoky Hill, and they lost no time in taking advantage of it.

Custer was unaware of what was going on along the Smoky Hill. The flood that destroyed Old Fort Hays forced an immediate move of the fort to the proximity of the new railroad. Fort Hays spent much of June making the move up Big Creek and had little time to communicate with Custer.

Custer, assuming all was well along the Smoky Hill, wrote Libbie to meet him at Fort Wallace as soon as he returned from the Platte. However, his orders were changed; he was commanded to proceed to the forks of the Republican River. He was to camp there to let the Indians know there was a strong fighting force ready to counter any move they made against travelers or settlers anywhere.

The Indians knew that as long as the soldiers stayed at the forks of the Republican they didn't have to worry about them. They continued their raids along the Smoky Hill River.

Custer did not know that Libbie had already been sent to Fort Riley, far to the east, to be safe. He sent Colonel Cooke from the camp to Fort Wallace with a wagon train to bring back supplies and Libbie. After the train had left, a number of Indians showed up around camp — enough to make Custer realize the danger Libbie would be in if she left Fort Wallace to come to him.

He dispatched Capt. Edward Myers with a full squadron to overtake other troops in the field under Capt. Robert West. Custer's written orders were for both commands to turn south to meet the wagon train from Fort Wallace and give it escort. With that kind of protection Custer was sure Libbie would be safe.[1]

Will Comstock had been sent ahead of Colonel Cooke to make contact with Libbie. In case she hadn't arrived at Fort Wallace, Will was to go to Fort Hayes and get her reply as to when she would reach Fort Wallace.

When Comstock got to Fort Wallace he found Captain Barnitz, who had just arrived from Fort Hays. Barnitz told Will that Libbie had left for Fort Riley. Comstock did not go farther; he headed back to Custer's Camp on the Republican with the wagon train of supplies Colonel Cooke had gathered.[2]

The Indians struck at the wagons about two days out of Fort Wallace. It was June 27, the day after the Indian's failure to overrun Fort Wallace.[3] They had apparently hurried north after the battle, overtaking the wagon train. It was a running battle that lasted several hours, but the Indians were unable to overpower the soldiers guarding the train. The number of

Indians who attacked this train was estimated at between four and five hundred.[4]

Custer remained at his camp on the Republican Forks until June 19. Then he moved southwest along the South Fork of the Republican.[5] There were hundreds of Indians around him now, harrassing the fringes of his march whenever they thought it safe. Custer, with only three hundred soldiers, deemed it wise not to try to engage them in battle. The Indians had a way of striking and then fading into the distant prairie. It was like fighting a ghost, trying to bring them to bay for a decisive battle.

So it was that Custer was miles from the camp where he was expected to be when Lt. Lyman S. Kidder reached the site about the 30th of June with a message for him from General Sherman. Lieutenant Kidder had arrived at Fort Sedgwick in the northeastern corner of Colorado Territory in the middle of June 1867. He was assigned to Company M of the Second Cavalry, and his first detail was to take ten men and an Indian guide and carry a message from General Sherman to General Custer camped at the forks of the Republican River. It was not thought to be a dangerous mission, since only a few Indians had been sighted along the Platte recently, and they were not belligerent.[6]

The ten men assigned to Lieutenant Kidder's detail were all from Company M. They were Oscar Close, Charles H. Haynes, Rodger Curry, Michael Connell, William Floyed, Michael Groman, William J. Humphries, Michael Haley, Michael Lawler, and Charles Teltow.[7] The guide was a Sioux Indian,[8] Red Bead, who lived near Fort Sedgwick. His loyalty was unquestioned.[9]

Custer turned north about the first of July and went directly to Riverside Station on the South Platte, southwest of Fort Sedgwick. There was a telegraph station here, and he learned then that Lieutenant Kidder had been sent with a message for him. Not having seen the lieutenant, Custer was immediately alarmed.

He started south again without reporting to Fort Sedgwick. His march retraced his trail until he reached the North Fork of the Republican River; there he turned downstream. He branched off this stream to the trail between his previous camp at the forks and Fort Wallace. Here he discovered the trail of Lieutenant Kidder and followed it toward Fort Wallace.

The next day they found evidence of a battle, and scouting parties soon discovered the final battlefield of Lieutenant Kidder and his men. All were dead, congregated in a small area. There were twelve bodies, including the Indian guide, Red Bead. The number of arrows and empty rifle cartridge casings gave strong evidence that a terrific battle had been fought there. Custer reported there was every indication that the attacking Indians were Roman Nose and his Cheyenne dog soldiers.[10]

Custer buried the remains in a common grave. There was no way of identifying any of the bodies except Red Bead.[11]The Indians had stripped off the clothing and mutilated the bodies as always. The Cheyenne mark was on them.

Custer reported to Fort Wallace on July 12. He was quartered outside the post in a sod house with walls three feet thick.[12] His men, as usual, were in tents.

Cholera was rampant in Fort Wallace when Custer arrived. Deaths were recorded almost every day. There was no hospital, no nurses, and few medical supplies.

The food was bad, according to reports, consisting of rancid, moldy bacon and hard bread. The commissary was nothing but an open spot on the prairie enclosed with a wall of gunnysacks filled with sand and covered with a tarpaulin. Rats, mice, and dust were all through the supplies.[13]

Things were at a standstill at the fort. The mail stages had stopped coming, due

Courtesy the Kansas State Historical Society, Topeka

Custer finds the remains of Lieutenant Kidder and his men.

to the increased Indian raids, and the telegraph had not yet reached the fort. The men working at the hay camps had been forced to come into the fort for protection, so forage for the horses was running low.

Custer had hoped that his wife would be at Fort Wallace when he got there. Instead, he learned that the cholera rampaging at Fort Wallace was also running wild at Fort Hays and Fort Harker. He feared for Libbie's safety.

Determined to find out about Libbie, and also to secure much-needed supplies for Fort Wallace, he started east on the evening of July 15[14] with one hundred of his best mounted men under command of Captain Hamilton and two lieutenants.[15]

Courtesy the Kansas State Historical Society, Topeka *From Gardner Collection*

Fort Riley

On July 17 some of his men ran into trouble five miles west of Downer Station. Custer's pace was such that all his men could not keep up. The Indians struck at

Courtesy the Nebraska State Historical Society, Lincoln

Capt. Samuel B. Lauffer, about 1870. He was a quartermaster at Fort Hays, Kansas, 1867, at Fort Wallace, Kansas, 1868, at Fort Wingate, New Mexico, 1870, and discharged, disabled in 1879. He was a postmaster at Greensburg, Pennsylvania, following his service.

these stragglers and killed two of them. They were buried at Downer Station.[16] Custer did not go back to look for the Indians.

Custer only paused at Fort Harker when he found that Libbie was not there. There are reports that supplies were sent to Fort Wallace from Fort Harker. It is a definite fact that Custer went by train to Fort Riley where he was reunited with his wife.

It was from Fort Riley that he was recalled and charged with deserting his command without permission when he was supposed to be actively pursuing Indians. There were additional charges such as abusing both men and horses in traveling too rapidly from Fort Wallace to Fort Harker. Another charge stemmed from the fact that he did not pursue the Indians who killed two of his men west of Downer Station.[17] The arrest was made on July 28 by Gen. A. J. Smith on orders from General Hancock.[18]

Custer was removed from active participation, but the war went on. In midafternoon of August 1 approximately thirty Indians attacked railroad construction workers about ten miles east of the new Fort Hays.[19]

When Capt. George A. Armes, a brevet major, arrived with troops from Fort Hays, he found six men dead and one wounded. The six dead were the foreman of the crew, P. S. Ashley from Wisconsin, and laborers Thomas Carney from Iowa, Charles Watson from Canada, John Harrington and Pat Rafferty both from Kansas City, and Hugh McDonough from Denver. William Gould from Illinois was badly wounded and was taken to the post hospital at Fort Hays, where he died.[20]

At almost the same time, at Big Creek Station about six or seven miles to the southwest more Indians stampeded the station herd and ran off about thirty head of horses. In the fight with the soldiers at Big Creek Station two Indians were killed. Here, as at the construction crew's camp, the men had grown a little careless. There were no herders with the horses when the Indians struck. The contruction crew, while possessing plenty of good rifles, had left them at camp while they worked a short distance away.

Captain Armes realized he didn't have nearly enough men to go after a large band of Indians, so he sent to the fort for reinforcements. When those reinforcements didn't come by dawn the next morning he started after the Indians anyway, chasing them to the north of Fort Hays.

Somewhere on the Saline River north of Fort Hays, Armes and his thirty-five men came up against three hundred and fifty to four hundred warriors. Armes dismounted his men and began slowly retreating toward Fort Hays, fighting as he went. It was thirty hours after they left the fort before they returned. Armes was wounded in the hip, one sergeant was killed, and three men were wounded. Six of his men had come down with cholera during that time and had to be strapped on their horses to get back to the fort.[21]

The war against the Indians went on

Photo by Author

Marker of six railroad workers killed by Indians in 1867 east of Fort Hays. Marker at Victoria, Kansas.

without letup. Monument Station had two changes of command during the hot months of the summer. Capt. John Conyngham was sent to Monument Station (sometimes called Fort Monument) in August to relieve Lt. David Ezekiel, who had assumed command on July 14. Lieutenant Ezekiel stayed at the post under the orders of Captain Conyngham.[22]

A concentrated effort was made to drive the Indians out of the country. Major Armes played a big part. Major Moore and his Eighteenth Volunteer Cavalry also were in on the campaign. It was Armes who found the Indians August 21 on Prairie Dog Creek. Major Moore found no Indians on his entire expedition.[23]

Armes' men, divided into three scouting groups, were attacked simultaneously by large bands of warriors under such leaders as Sa-tan-ta, Charlie Bent, and Roman Nose.[24] The battle lasted three days, as Major Armes and the troops reunited and retreated toward Fort Hays. Armes lost two men killed and twenty-four wounded.[25]

August also saw the trial date set for Custer's court-martial. The *Leavenworth Conservative* published the report:

> Brevet Major General Custer has been ordered to Fort Leavenworth for trial. . . . The charge against him is for leaving his command at Wallace, and going to Harker without leave. We presume he will not be dealt with very severely if this is all the government has against him. The court-martial assembles at Fort Leavenworth September 15.[26]

Before Custer's trial another plague hit the Smoky Hill Valley. On September 9, 1867, Lt. D. W. Wallingford wrote to Governor Crawford from Fort Wallace:

> The grasshoppers here might be measured by the cart load. The heavens are filled with them and the earth covered with them. In fact, we have them to eat for dinner and supper. At breakfast, they are

Courtesy the Kansas State Historical Society, Topeka

Fort Leavenworth Post Headquarters, 1872

too stiff to get into our food, for we have breakfast very early, so it is one meal that is not flavored with them. Lucky they came late, or they would have eaten up every green sprig of grass. They are so numerous, some places one inch thick on the ground.[27]

In late October the U.S. Peace Commission met with leaders of the Indian tribes at Medicine Lodge and signed a peace treaty in which the Kiowas, Cheyennes, Comanches, and Apaches agreed to stop all opposition to the building of the railroad.[28] It is doubtful that any but the most optimistic really believed the Indians would remember the treaty when the grass greened in the spring.

In November the court-martial decision was reached. The *Leavenworth Conservative* stated: "The late Brevet Major General G. A. Custer, Lieutenant Colonel commanding the Seventh Regiment, United States cavalry, has been deprived of his rank with pay for one year, by sentence of a court-martial. He is to leave Fort Leavenworth today."[29]

The year 1867 was a bloody one on the Smoky Hill River, and many a soldier wished he had been stationed anywhere but there. Lt. James Montgomery Bell, who was at Fort Wallace during some of the worst fighting, was transferred to Fort Leavenworth in November as quartermaster of his regiment, the Seventh Cavalry. He had some words for the war-torn country as he left:

> Oh, Smoky Hill, my Smoky Hill,
> The day has come when we must part,
> And candor bids me freely own.
> How few regrets oppress my heart.[30]

NOTES

1. Blaine Burkey, *Custer Come at Once* (Hays, Kans.: Thomas More Prep, 1976), p. 32.
2. Ibid.
3. John S. Gray, "Will Comstock, Scout: The Natty Bumpo of Kansas," *Montana Western History* 20 (Summer 1970), p. 12.
4. Barton R. Voigt, "The Death of Lyman S. Kidder," *South Dakota History* (Winter 1975), p. 9.
5. Burkey, *Custer Come at Once*, p. 24. In Custer's letter to Judge J. P. Kidder, Lyman Kidder's father, dated August 23, 1867, he states that he broke camp on the forks of the Republican on June 29, which agrees with the maps showing locations and dates of his camps.
6. Voigt, "Death of Lyman Kidder," p. 8. The letter of Dr. H. Latham, post surgeon at Fort Sedgwich, to Judge Kidder, dated August 10, 1867, states that there had been no Indians seen recently between the Platte and the Republican. The explanation is obvious. The Indians were south of the Republican, raiding travelers and forts along the B.O.D.
7. Ibid., p. 14.
8. Ibid., p. 14. Custer erroneously lists Red Bead as Pawnee. Records show that he was Sioux.
9. Ibid., p. 11. Dr. Latham described Red Bead as an Indian loyal to the whites. Indians had stolen Red Bead's stock earlier that summer. He left his family and all his possessions at Fort Sedgwick when he went with Lieutenant Kidder on that fatal detail. His body was found with Kidder and his men on Beaver Creek in northwestern Kansas.
10. Ibid., p. 15. Custer's letter to Judge Kidder, dated August 23, 1867. The attack could very likely have been made by the Cheyenne dog soldiers, but it is highly unlikely that Roman Nose was present. He had been shot by Corporal Harris just five days before this in the battle at Fort Wallace. All who saw it were certain that Roman Nose had been killed, but his appearance at Beecher Island the following year proved them wrong. However, he could hardly have recovered quickly enough to be present at the massacre of Kidder's men.
11. Mrs. Frank C. Montgomery, "Fort Wallace and Its Relation to the Frontier," *Kansas Historical Collections, 1926–1928* 17 (1928), p. 218.
12. Ibid., p. 219.
13. Ibid.
14. Burkey, *Custer Come at Once*, p. 32. Richard Blake, who worked at the sutler's store at Fort Wallace, wrote a letter to his mother on July 14 then added a hasty postscript dated July 15: "General Custer is going down to Fort Hays after his wife this evening — so will send this by him."
15. Montgomery, "Fort Wallace," pp. 219–20. There is sharp controversy among historians as to the reason Custer made his dash from Fort Wallace to Fort Riley. Some say he did it to go to his wife; if so, there was just cause for the court-martial that followed. Others insist that he went for supplies for Fort Wallace. But it seems strange that he would go himself if supplies were all that he wanted or that he would take an escort of one hundred of his best mounted men.
16. Ibid., p. 220.
17. Ibid., p. 220.
18. Burkey, *Custer Come at Once*, p. 32.
19. This is just west of the present town of Victoria, Kansas.
20. Burkey, *Custer Come at Once*, p. 35. A monument and markers have been erected at the west edge of Victoria, commemorating the event and marking the graves of the six men killed in the raid. The marker reads: "This stone marks the burial place of six track laborers who were in the employ of the Union Pacific Railway, Eastern Division, and while on duty about one mile west of here were massacred by a band of Cheyenne Indians, October, 1867." This date is hard to understand, since the massacre occurred on August 1, 1867. See *Leavenworth Times*, August 6, 1867; *Leavenworth Conservative*, August 4, 6, 11, 1867; *Kansas City Tribune*, August 6, 1867. Gould, who died at Fort Hays, was not buried with the others.
21. Ibid., p. 35.
22. Charles R. Wetzel, "Monument Station, Gove County," *Kansas Historical Quarterly* (Autumn 1960), pp. 252–3.
23. Burkey, *Custer Come at Once*, p. 36.
24. Again, there is doubt whether Roman Nose himself was one of the leaders. It seems unlikely that he could have been recovered from his June 26 wound. However, he was a "splendid specimen of a man," and he might have been fit for battle again by mid-August.
25. Burkey, *Custer Come at Once*, p. 36.
26. *Leavenworth* (Kans.) *Conservative*, 31 August 1867.
27. Montgomery, "Fort Wallace," p. 224.
28. Ibid., p. 225.
29. *Leavenworth Conservative*, 27 November 1867.
30. John S. Manion, "Indian Attack," *Fort Wallace* (Kans.) *Bugle*, March 1971.

CHAPTER 15

COUNTERATTACK

AFTER THE BLOODY SUMMER OF 1867 the Indians went into their winter camps as usual, putting up their lodges on the reservations, claiming to be good Indians and receiving their rations from the commissary. In return for the food and clothing they needed to survive the winter they reiterated their pledges never to lift rifle or bow against the white man again.

The advance of white civilization had driven the buffalo farther away from the good hunting grounds, and the Indians were hard pressed for food and clothing. They had spent the past summer at war instead of hunting and were destitute when snow covered the ground.

The soldiers, too, seemed satisfied to enjoy peace through the cold months. Will Comstock, the scout, stayed on his Rose Creek ranch about eight miles west of Fort Wallace.[1]

Wood was hard to find in western Kansas. Aside from the giant cottonwoods at Big Timber Station near the Kansas-Colorado line, there was very little to be had. A man named Wyatt had the contract to furnish wood for Fort Wallace, and he made a deal with Comstock. Comstock knew where wood was to be found and, for a share of Wyatt's profits, he showed him where it was. This worked fine until it came time to divide the profits.

The altercation came in Val Todd's sutler store at Fort Wallace. Wyatt was not a well-liked man; some called him obnoxious. Nobody knew his past, but it was rumored that he had ridden with Quantrill[2] and later with "Bloody Bill" Anderson, the famous post-Civil War outlaw.

Comstock asked Wyatt for his cut in the profits, and Wyatt refused to pay. A hot argument followed, but Wyatt showed no intention of paying Comstock as agreed. When Wyatt turned his back on Comstock and stalked out of the store, Comstock pulled his gun and shot him twice. Wyatt stumbled out of the store and fell dead.[3]

Comstock was promptly arrested and hauled off to Hays City for trial. Val Todd, the sutler store owner, was taken as the chief witness.

The trial was held in the court of the famous Judge Marcellus E. Joyce. The judge formed quick opinions. In this case he apparently decided that Comstock's

Courtesy the Kansas State Historical Society, Topeka *From Gardner Collection*

U.S. Express Overland Stage starting for Denver from Hays City, Kansas.

killing of Wyatt was justified or at worst, excusable. When Val Todd testified that he saw Comstock shoot Wyatt in the back, the judge asked if the shooting had been done with felonious intent. Todd admitted he had no idea what the intent had been. Judge Joyce immediately made his decision: Since there was no proof of felonious intent, the case was dismissed for lack of evidence.

Comstock, knowing that some people were not going to agree with the judge's verdict, hurried back to Fort Wallace and out to his Rose Creek ranch. Apparently he stayed close to the ranch during the following weeks.[4]

On March 2, 1868, Gen. Phil Sheridan took command of the Department of the Missouri.[5] Shortly after he became commander he relieved Lt. Fred Beecher as commander of Fort Wallace and assigned him as coordinator of Indian intelligance and mediation. Beecher was to hire dependable men to act as scouts and diplomats.[6]

Courtesy the Kansas State Historical Society, Topeka

Philip Sheridan

On May 12 Lieutenant Beecher hired his first scouts, Dick Parr, and Frank Espey. Four days later he hired Will Comstock. Since his trial at Hays City nothing had been heard of Comstock except that he was at his Rose Creek ranch. Now he was brought out of retirement at the highest salary of any scout, $125 a month. This was considered almost a fortune in that day, when $20 to $30 a month was good wages. It was over a month before Beecher hired the fourth and last of his scouts, Abner ("Sharp") Grover.[7]

The winter had been very quiet, and General Sheridan had hopes that the treaty at Medicine Lodge was going to be obeyed. However, on May 8 the first blow fell to shatter this treaty.

The Union Pacific Railroad was at that time laying its track west of Coyote,[8] which was the end of the passenger service. About seventeen miles west of this end-of-track town, a dozen Indians attacked the construction crew and drove the men away. They burned three railroad cars loaded with building material, tore down the telegraph poles and wire, and stretched the wire across the tracks to catch the engine when it arrived.[9]

The Indians struck at Fort Wallace at almost the same time, killing one man there.[10]

The track-laying north of the Smoky Hill continued to the west, and the rails reached Carlyle[11] that spring. A short time later they stretched to Antelope Station. This station became the end of passenger service. It also became the new eastern terminal of the B.O.D. stagecoaches and freight wagons, where they picked up passengers and freight to carry them west to Denver on the Smoky Hill Trail. Antelope Station soon had its name changed to Monument.[12]

That spring brought many changes

along the Smoky Hill Trail. Pond Creek Station became Pond Creek City — or just Pond Creek. There were enough people to feel they should bear the name of a city rather than a station.[13]

On June 24 the soldiers at the fort at Monument Station were ordered to the new end-of-track town of Monument to guard supplies and protect the railroad workers.[14] Since both stages and freighters were meeting the train at Monument there seemed little need of a fort down on the river. The town of Monument was thirty-five miles northwest of the Monument Station of the B.O.D.

Custer's loss of command was supposed to be for one year, but that time was abbreviated by orders of General Sheridan, and Custer was restored to rank and duty on August 1, 1868.[15]

At the same time Superintendent of Indians Affairs Murphy was at Fort Larned conferring with Indian Agent E. W. Wyncoop about giving guns and ammunition to the Cheyennes, Arapahoes, and Apaches, according to the treaty signed the fall before at Medicine Lodge. Fort Larned was on the Arkansas River, but what took place there had a crushing impact on Smoky Hill Valley.

The Indians demanded arms and ammunition and threatened to take them by force if they were not forthcoming. Agent Wyncoop was given permission to issue the arms. On August 9, he gave the Indians 100 rifles, 140 pistols, and 20,000 rounds of ammunition for the weapons. Then he reported: "I am perfectly satisfied that there will be no trouble with them this season."[16]

Black Kettle and his Cheyenne warriors showed up at Fort Hays, smoking the peace pipe with the officers. Black Kettle made a long speech, pledging lasting peace with his white brothers. He declared that even though the Sioux went on the warpath the Cheyennes would not follow. He was rewarded with ten sides of bacon, ten sacks of flour, and a large quantity of beans, salt, and coffee. Within two or three days Cheyenne warriors were raiding the settlements on Spillman Creek and on the Solomon, killing men and stealing women, children, and horses.[17]

Word of these atrocities reached Lieutenant Beecher on Walnut Creek west of Fort Zarah. Scouts Will Comstock and Sharp Grover were with Beecher. The lieutenant sent the two scouts to Turkey Leg's camp on the Solomon River to see if they could convince the Cheyenne chief to help bring in the raiders for a peace talk. Both Comstock and Grover knew Turkey Leg. They realized the risk they were taking, but they had hired out to do jobs like this.[18]

At Fort Hays, on their way to Turkey Leg's camp, they heard more details of the raids. Apparently about two hundred

Courtesy the Oklahoma Historical Society

Black Kettle

Cheyennes, plus a few Sioux and Arapahoes, had struck at the settlements on the Solomon River and on the Saline River in Lincoln County. The two scouts went northwest to Turkey Leg's camp on the headwaters of the Solomon River,[19] not sure they could persuade their old hunting and fishing friend to help put a stop to the raids.

While they were on their way the Cheyennes under Black Kettle[20] went on a rampage on the Solomon. After stirring up a hornet's nest there by killing several men[21] and stealing two little girls, they fled back to the Saline River in Lincoln County.

Brevet Colonel Benteen was sent on a forced march to Saline County, to the relief of the settlers. He arrived just as the Indians were raiding a farm. The settler, a man named Schermerhorn, was barricaded inside his house and was fighting back. Colonel Benteen heard the firing and rushed to the scene. In the running fight, three Indians were killed and the two captive girls were abandoned. Benteen picked them up.[22]

Benteen had no way of knowing that his battle on the Saline would bring tragedy to the scouts farther west. Comstock and Grover reached Turkey Leg's camp on Sunday morning, August 16. Late that afternoon a messenger came into camp with news that soldiers had killed some Indians on the Saline River.

Comstock and Grover knew they had to get out of camp quickly. In time of war all white men looked alike to Indians; their friendship with Turkey Leg would not save them.

A short distance from camp they were overtaken by seven Indians who appeared friendly, as though they were an escort sent by Turkey Leg. Although the scouts were suspicious they were taken by surprise by the suddenness of the attack when it came.

There were Indians beside them and behind them. Those behind suddenly brought up their guns and started shooting. Comstock was struck fatally and knocked from his horse. Grover was also shot from his horse, but his wound was not fatal.

The Indians apparently had enough respect for the bravery of the scouts not to scalp them. After looking at their work they rode off. Grover moved into some tall grass and hid through Sunday night and all day Monday. Monday night he made his way to the railroad, where he flagged down a train and rode it to Monument. From there he was sent to Fort Wallace. Captain Bankhead reported the next day from Fort Wallace to Fort Harker:

Headquarters
Fort Wallace, Kansas
Aug. 19, 1868

Acting Asst. Adj. General
Hdqs. District of Upper Arkansas
Fort Harker, Kansas

Sir:

I have the honor to report that Grover, alias Sharp, the scout who was wounded Sunday night [August 16th], rumors state 30 miles north of Monument, by Indians, was brought into this post yesterday. The surgeon reports him severely wounded. He left William Comstock's body at the place where he was shot. Grover has been too feverish to be disturbed by questioning, so I only

Courtesy the Kansas State Historical Society, Topeka
Copied from Custer's "My Life on the Plains"

"Will Comstock and his companion pursued by Indians"

learn from others that Comstock and himself had gone to this Cheyenne village; on Sunday night while there, an Indian runner came in with the news that some Indians had been killed and wounded in a fight with the soldiers on the Saline.[23] The Indians then drove Comstock and Grover out of camp, when about two miles away were overtaken by a party of seven, who at first appeared friendly, and after riding along with them, fired into their backs, killing William Comstock instantly. Grover remained hid in the grass during Monday — Monday night walked to the railroad, which he struck about seven miles east of Monument, and sent on to this post.

H. C. Bankhead
Capt. 5th Inf. Ba.,
Col. U.S.A.
Commdg. Post. [24]

The Indian raids continued all along the Kansas frontier. On August 23 the troops that had been transferred from Monument Station on the B.O.D. to the new town of Monument on the Union Pacific Railroad were ordered to march to Fort Wallace. Thus ended the short life of "Fort" Monument.[25]

The rails ran only as far as Sheridan. Thc railroad company had run out of money, and things were at a standstill until more could be raised. The stages were running from the end of the track at Sheridan to Denver, but they were having more trouble than they could overcome. Drastic action had to be taken immediately, or all travel to Denver would stop.

General Sheridan had 2,600 men under his control, but 1,800 of them were occupied protecting forts, railroads, and stage lines. The 800 left were not enough to launch a major offensive against the elusive plains warriors. General Sherman was not in favor of accepting help from state troops, so General Sheridan was left with one choice — volunteers.[26]

He turned to a junior officer, Maj. George Forsythe. Forsythe had asked General Sheridan for a command to go after the Indians. Being a junior officer there was no way Sheridan could promote him over his senior fellow officers, but he could give him command over a group of volunteers. He called him in and explained the situation. Forsythe quickly accepted.

He was given a brevet colonel rank and told to gather fifty good fighting men who would be called scouts, since they could not be designated as soldiers. Each man was to get a dollar a day, plus thirty-five cents a day for the use of his horse.[27]

Forsythe began his search for men at Fort Harker. Many of the men who came to volunteer were men whose families had suffered in the raids in Lincoln County and along the Solomon River. Most were Civil War veterans, from both the North and the South.

At Fort Harker Forsythe signed on thirty men. Moving to Fort Hays he signed up the other twenty men that he was allowed.

Courtesy the Kansas State Historical Society, Topeka

George A. Forsythe

Courtesy the Kansas State Historical Society, Topeka

Fort Harker

He was sure he had fifty of the best fighting men in Kansas, and many of them had personal grudges against the Indians.[28] Besides equipment for camping, cooking, and caring for his horse, each man was issued a Spencer rifle and a revolver, with 140 rounds of ammunition for the rifle and thirty for the revolver.[29] The Spencer held six cartridges in the magazine besides the one that could be pumped into the barrel.

On August 29 Forsythe was ordered to move to Fort Wallace from Fort Hays. At Fort Wallace he was to be joined by Lieutenant Beecher, who was to be his second in command. Forsythe and his scouts arrived at Fort Wallace on September 5.

Here he picked up his chief scout, Sharp Grover, who had just recovered from the wound he received when leaving Turkey Leg's camp. Grover had married a Sioux woman and had lived with the Indians for years. After the Indian uprising against white invasion he had to leave the Indians to save his own life. He could speak the language well and knew most of the Indians' habits. It was said he could tell by looking at horse tracks whether they were Indian ponies and how many had been ridden and how many driven. At an old campsite he could tell how many Indians had stayed there, how many of them were women, and which tribe they belonged to by the shape of the moccasins and the bits of things left at camp.[30]

On September 8 word reached Fort Wallace that a Mexican train of freight wagons leaving the end-of-track town of Sheridan on its way to Santa Fe had been attacked a short distance from Sheridan and two Mexican drivers had been killed. Forsythe and his scouts were sent to pick up the Indians' trail and go after them.[31]

Two of Forsythe's men were sick and had to be left in the Fort Wallace hospital, but, with Lieutenant Beecher and Surgeon Mooers, Forsythe had fifty men besides himself. The trail led north from the scene of the raid on the Mexican wagon train, and Forsythe's men followed it. The Indians were aware they were being followed. Not wanting to fight a force the size of Forsythe's they began splitting off the main group until there was no trail.

Courtesy the Kansas State Historical Society, Topeka *From Gardner Collection*

Fort Hays, Kansas

Courtesy the Kansas State Historical Society, Topeka

Lt. Fred Beecher

Grover led the scouts to the Republican River, where they again found a trail. As they followed it west, the trail grew broader and deeper. Grover pointed out each new group that joined the Indians going west.

The trail passed the forks where the south branch of the Republican came in. At the next confluence of streams the trail turned southwest up the smaller fork. Forsythe called it the Delaware Fork of the Republican and didn't learn until later that it was really the Arickaree Fork.

They were following entirely too many Indians to fight if they should catch up with them. Some of the scouts pointed this out to Forsythe, he reminded them that they had come to fight Indians and they would do just that if they could catch them.[32]

The trail deepened and widened as more Indians joined the retreat up the Arickaree. Forsythe's scouts, had they known about the raids and battles still going on to the south along the Smoky Hill, would not have believed it possible. It seemed to them that all the Indians on the plains were congregating ahead of them. Sharp Grover didn't have to tell the others they were in deep trouble. They were already entirely too far from any white settlement or fort; they were in Indian country now. Still they moved grimly ahead.

Forsythe's men camped that night on the south bank of the Arickaree Fork, which had only a little water in it that time of year. Its wide sandy bed was proof that if often ran high in the spring. Forsythe's camp was even with an island in the mid-

Courtesy the Kansas State Historical Society, Topeka

Attack of Indians on a bull train near Sheridan, Kansas.

dle of the stream, surrounded by an almost dry sandy stream bed seventy yards wide on either side of it.

NOTES

1. This ranch would have been just south of present-day Sharon Springs.
2. There was a man named Cave Wyatt listed as one of Quantrill's guerrillas.
3. John S. Gray, "Will Comstock, Scout: The Natty Bumpo of Kansas," *Montana Western History* 20 (Summer 1970), p. 13.
4. Ibid.
5. Mrs. Frank C. Montgomery, "Fort Wallace and Its Relation to the Frontier," *Kansas Historical Collections, 1926–1928* 17 (1928), p. 225.
6. Gray, "Will Comstock," p. 13.
7. Ibid.
8. Coyote was just west of the present town of Collyer.
9. Montgomery, "Fort Wallace," p. 225.
10. Blaine Burkey, *Custer Come at Once* (Hays, Kans.: Thomas More Prep, 1976), p. 38.
11. Carlyle became the present town of Oakley.
12. Charles R. Wetzel, "Monument Station, Gove County," *Kansas Historical Quarterly* (Autumn 1960), p. 253.
13. Montgomery, "Fort Wallace," p. 200.
14. Wetzel, "Monument Station," p. 253.
15. Montgomery, "Fort Wallace," p. 223.
16. Burkey, *Custer Come at Once*, p. 39.
17. George Jelinek, "The Ellsworth Story," *Ellsworth (Kans.) Reporter*, 3 August 1967.
18. Gray, "Will Comstock," p. 14.
19. Ibid., p. 14. There is a great deal of controversy concerning the location of Turkey Leg's camp and the place where Comstock was killed. One historian has placed the site south of the Smoky Hill River, and another says it was on the Smoky Hill. Neither seems likely in view of the official reports concerning the incident made right at the time. Captain Bankhead, in his official report, says it was about thirty miles north of Monument. Monument, whether referring to the stage station on the B.O.D. or the new town on the railroad, is north of the Smoky Hill. Thirty miles north from either of these places would put the location of the camp some distance north of the river. Most historians think Turkey Leg's camp was on a fork of the Solomon River. This would put it almost exactly fifty miles from Fort Wallace, which all reports seem to agree is correct. It also is about thirty or thirty-five miles north of old Monument Station on the B.O.D. All things considered, this seems the most plausible location of Turkey Leg's camp and the site of Comstock's death.
20. There is some disagreement as to whether Black Kettle was really the leader of the war party that raided the settlers on the Saline and Solomon rivers. He had been at Fort Hays about three days before the raids began.
21. Burkey, *Custer Come at Once*, p. 40. General Sheridan said there were thirteen men killed. The names of seven victims are known: B. Bell, Mrs. B. Bell, D. Bogardus, two brothers named Marshall, and two other men named Hewitt and Thompson.
22. Ibid., p. 39. The two girls, Maggie Bell and her sister, Esther, were the daughters of Aaron Bell, likely some relation of Mr. and Mrs. B. Bell who were killed in the raids.
23. Four Indians were killed and ten wounded.
24. Captain Bankhead's official report, a copy of which is in the Fort Wallace museum.
25. Wetzel, "Monument Station," p. 253.
26. Burkey, *Custer Come at Once*, p. 41.
27. General George A. Forsythe, "A Frontier Fight," *Beecher Island Annual* (St. Francis, Kans., 1960), p. 6.
28. Montgomery, "Fort Wallace," p. 230.
29. Forsythe, "A Frontier Fight," p. 6.
30. Cyrus Townsend Brady, *Indian Fights and Fighters* (McClure, Philips & Co., reprint ed. Lincoln: Univ. of Nebraska Press, 1971), p. 126.
31. Montgomery, "Fort Wallace," p. 230.
32. Forsythe, "A Frontier Fight," p. 12.

CHAPTER 16

THE BATTLES

AT DAWN on September 17 Indians tried to stampede the scouts' horses. Orders the night before had been for each man to hobble his horse and be doubly sure the picket pin was well anchored. In case of an attack each man was to grab his rifle and the lariat on his horse. The result was that the Indians' initial attack stampeded only two pack mules and two horses whose picket pins were pulled.

Daylight revealed hundreds of Indians to the north and west and south of them. They seemed to grow right out of the ground. Many were on foot, but there were also many mounted. Only to the east, the way the scouts had come the day before, were there no Indians. Forsythe and his men recognized this for the trap it was. Bluffs fenced the stream to the east. Seasoned Indian fighters in the group were willing to bet their lives that those bluffs hid the main fighting force of the Indians, waiting for the soldiers to try to escape between the bluffs.

Forsythe ordered his men onto the island in the middle of the river. Somehow the Indians had failed to occupy the island, apparently being too intent on driving the scouts into their trap. The soldiers reached it without harm, although they lost all their medical supplies in the process. They did get their ammunition across with them. The Indians seemed to be furious over their failure to prevent the whites from taking the island. They poured a heavy fire onto the island, killing the horses one by one.[1]

The men used the dead horses for breastworks, while they dug pits in the soft sand. Snipers lined both banks of the river and kept up a steady fire that made digging a dangerous but absolutely essential task. Some of the soldiers were wounded, including Colonel Forsythe. One bullet lodged in his thigh, another broke the opposite leg between the knee and ankle. Propped up in his hole in the sand, he directed the battle from there.

Few directions were needed for the battle-seasoned scouts, however, and the mounted Indians soon withdrew to the bluffs to the east. The scouts on the island guessed what was going on beyond their view around the bend of the river, but they couldn't know the magnitude or precision with which the coming assault would be carried out.

Meanwhile the snipers kept the island hot. At one time a few mounted Indians rode close enough to fire into the pits then quickly withdrew, leaving at least one of their number dead. The most serious casualty for the scouts from this assault was Dr. Mooers, the only medical man in the group.[2] He had been shot through the head, though he lingered for almost three days, he was never rational after being wounded.

The Indians were well armed. Many had Springfield breechloaders, which the scouts were sure they had taken from

Fetterman's men at Fort Phil Kearny a year and a half before. They also had Remington, Henry, and Spencer rifles.[3]

Then came the charge that no survivor would ever forget. It would go down in the history of Indian warfare as one of their most magnificent and concentrated charges.

It almost failed to happen, according to the legend that has lived through the years about the leader, the giant Cheyenne dog soldier, Roman Nose. After his wounding at the Fort Wallace battle a year before, no soldier ever expected to see him again. But there was no question about his presence that day on the Arickaree River.

The legend is told in *The American Heritage Book of Indians:*

There were many men of valor among the valorous Cheyennes but surely none more famous at the time to ordinary public both Cheyenne and American than a hook-nosed, 6 foot, 3-inch warrior named Bat. The Americans called him Roman Nose. Roman Nose was famous because he was invulnerable in battle. He had a magic head-dress and while he wore it, bullets and arrows could not touch him. He proved this time after time, riding at a leisurely lope up and down in front of the enemy, while the enemy shot at him and missed. This always inspired other Cheyenne warriors. There was only one catch. Roman Nose could never eat anything taken from the pot with an iron instrument; fork or knife. If he broke this taboo he broke the war bonnet's medicine, and long rites of purification would be necessary to restore it.

It happened in the summer of 1868 a company of experienced plainsmen, enlisted in the army as scouts, were trapped by a large number of Cheyenne, Sioux and Arapahoe warriors, possibly as many as 600. On the night before this battle started, Roman Nose was a guest in a Sioux lodge and the hostess, unaware of his taboo, took the fried bread from the skillet with a fork. Roman Nose did not notice this until he had already eaten some of the bread. The next day when the fight started, he did not go into it. But the chiefs came to him and told him he was needed to inspire the warriors. Roman Nose explained about his broken taboo. . . . "I know I shall be killed today." Then he painted himself, shook out his war bonnet, put it on, and rode very fast at the enemy.[4]

Courtesy the Kansas State Historical Society, Topeka

Three Cheyenne chiefs — White Antelope, Man on a Cloud, Roman Nose.

Of the charge itself, perhaps no better description could be given than by a man who watched every moment of it, Col. George Forsythe, who wrote:

Mounted on a large, clean-limbed chestnut horse, he [Roman Nose] sat well forward on his bare-backed charger, his knees passing under a horsehair lariat that twice loosely encirled the animal's body, his horse's bridle grasped in his left hand which was also closely wound in its flowing mane, and at the same time his rifle at the guard, the butt lay partially across the animal's neck, while its barrel . . . rested slightly against the hollow of his left arm, leaving his right free to direct the course of his men. He was a man of over six feet and three inches in height, beautifully formed, and, save for a crimson silk sash knotted around his waist, and his moccasins on his feet, perfectly naked. His face was hideously painted in alternate lines of red and black, and his head crowned with a magnificant war bonnet, from which, just above his temples and curving slightly forward, stood up two short black buffalo horns, while its ample length of eagle feathers and herons' plumes, trailed wildly on the wind behind him; and as he came swiftly on at the head of his charging warriors, in all his barbaric strength and grandeur, he proudly rode that day the most perfect type of a savage warrior it has been my lot to see. . . . Facing squarely toward where we lay, he drew his body to its full height and shook his clenched fist defiantly at us; then throwing back his head and glancing skyward, he suddenly struck the palm of his hand across his mouth and gave tongue to a war cry that I have never yet heard equalled in power and intensity.

Scarcely had its echoes reached the river's bank when it was caught up by each and every one of the charging warriors with an energy that baffles description. . . . On they came at a swinging gallop, rending the air with their wild war whoops, each individual warrior in all his bravery of war paint and long braided scalp-lock tipped with eagles' feathers, and all stark naked but for cartridge belts and moccasins, keeping their line almost perfectly, with a front of the sixty men, all riding bareback, with only loose lariats about their horses' bodies about a yard apart, and with a depth of six or seven ranks.

Riding about five paces in front of the center of the line, and twirling his heavy Springfield rifle around his head as if it were a wisp of straw, Roman Nose recklessly led the charge with a bravery that could only be equalled but not excelled. . . . It was far and away beyond anything I had heard of, read about, or even imagined regarding Indian warfare.[5]

As soon as it had become obvious to Forsythe that the mounted Indians intended to launch a charge he ordered every man to cease firing at the snipers, who seldom exposed enough of their bodies to present a target anyway. Each man was to load his Spencer rifle to the full limit of six cartridges in the magazine and one in the barrel and check his revolver to make sure it was loaded to capacity.

When Roman Nose launched his charge, the snipers sent a smothering fire into the island, apparently to keep the scouts down and unable to fire at the oncoming charge.

Courtesy the Kansas State Historical Society, Topeka *By Frederic Remington*

Beecher Island Battle painting

Forsythe's orders were to stay down until he gave the order. When the mounted Indians approached the island, the snipers suddenly went silent. Forsythe shouted the order, "Now!" Lieutenant Beecher and Scout Grover echoed the call.

All the able scouts came to their knees, their seven-shot Spencer rifles at their shoulders. After their third volley, great gaps appeared in the ranks of the Indian warriors. Roman Nose still rode at the head, and his yells of encouragement and his great courage kept the wave coming.

At the far left of the charge was Medicine Man,[6] second only to Roman Nose in importance in leadership. He went down at the fourth volley. Still Roman Nose came on, until he was at the edge of the island. In another five seconds the Indians would be swarming over the defenders of the little strip of sand.

On the fifth volley[7] both Roman Nose and his horse went down. The medicine of Roman Nose's war bonnet had lost its power. Two more volleys, the last in the Spencer rifles, broke the charge. The remaining Indians split as though the island were a cleaver, half sweeping past on one side, half on the other. The scouts leaped out of their pits and fired their revolvers at the Indians. A roaring order from Forsythe and Beecher sent them back into their pits before the snipers on the river banks dared begin firing again.

It seems uncertain whether a sniper or a shot from the departing Indians hit Lieutenant Beecher. A few minutes after the charge Beecher crawled over to Forsythe's pit and told him he had been fatally shot. He became delirious and died at sundown.

The Indians tried two more charges, but both were half-hearted affairs that broke before they got within effective range. The snipers continued to make it a risky venture to expose even a hand above the pits.

After darkness had enveloped the valley

and the Indians had withdrawn, Forsythe called for volunteers to try to slip past the Indians and go to Fort Wallace, about ninety miles away, for help.[8] One of the older men, well experienced on the plains, Pierre Trudeau, and a nineteen-year-old who had shown exceptional knowledge of the plains, Jack Stillwell, were chosen from those who volunteered.

They left the island about midnight, taking every precaution. They hung their boots around their necks and walked backward down the river bed in their stocking feet. If an Indian chanced to see the tracks by daylight he might mistake them for moccasin prints. Even if he questioned this he would see that they led toward the island, not away.

Once away from the island they put on their boots, but Indians were everywhere and they dared not stand up where their silhouettes might be seen. They crawled along the ground for the remaining hours of darkness and were only about two miles from the island when dawn made it manditory to seek a hiding place.

They spent the day in a dry ravine within sight and sound of a big Indian camp. Discovery meant death by torture, but the two agreed they would fight as long as possible and save their last bullets to end their own lives.

The second night they made better progress, but they had to avoid several Indian patrols. They spent the second day hidden under the banks of a river. They made much better time the third night, when patrols were not so numerous.

Daylight found them on an open prairie. The only protection they could find was a buffalo wallow. This was sufficient until a band of Indians halted only a few yards from the wallow. Shortly after the Indians slid off their ponies a rattlesnake slithered over the bank of the wallow into the bottom with the two scouts.

The scouts did not dare move or make any noise. They feared that even the rattle of the snake before he struck would attract the attention of the Indians. Stillwell met the crisis with instant action. He was chewing tobacco. As the snake coiled, preparing to rattle and strike, Stillwell squirted a huge stream of tobacco juice directly onto its head. The snake couldn't tolerate that and crawled out of the wallow faster than it had come in.[9]

The men pushed on with nothing to eat, the constant strain of extreme vigilance wearing them down. When they reached Fort Wallace two days later, Trudeau was a physical wreck. Stillwell, however, was ready to lead a rescue party back to his comrades on the island.

Meanwhile, back on the island, Forsythe had sent Chauncey Whitney and A. J. Pliley out the second night, fearing Trudeau and Stillwell had not gotten past the Indians.[10] They had gone only a short distance when they discovered that the Indians had completely surrounded the island. There was no possibility of getting through, so they returned to the island.

The third day of the battle Forsythe wrote a letter to Colonel Bankhead at Fort Wallace describing the desperate situation. That night he sent two more scouts out in an attempt to get through. A. J. Pliley was chosen again, but this time John Donovan went with him.[11]

The Indians were beginning to tire of the battle, and their patrols were not as numerous or as alert. Donovan and Pliley had less trouble getting through than Stillwell and Trudeau had.

The fighting slackened to just a few sniper bullets now and then to remind the scouts that the Indians had not completely forgotten them. The waiting was torture. Four men were dead, including Lieutenant Beecher and the doctor who could have helped the wounded. Scouts G. W. Culver and William Wilson had also been killed the first day of the battle.

The only food on the island was the horse and mule meat. The days were hot, and the meat soon became rotten. The odor was almost unbearable. The scouts mixed gunpowder with the meat and boiled it, hoping to take away the stench so they could eat it. They no longer feared that the Indians would overrun them, but starvation and festering wounds threatened to do what the Indians had been unable to accomplish.

Colonel Carpenter was at Cheyenne Wells with his Negro troops, all without battle experience, when Stillwell and Trudeau reported to Fort Wallace. A messenger was sent with all speed to tell Carpenter to turn north to the rescue of Forsythe. Colonel Bankhead took all the troops that could possibly be spared from the fort and headed for Forsythe, with Stillwell as guide.

When Donovan and Pliley arrived at Fort Wallace, Lt. Hugo Johnson was in charge of the post in the absence of Colonel Bankhead. He promptly sent Donovan to overtake Colonel Carpenter and guide him to the site of the battle. He offered Donovan an extra $100 to undertake the mission. There were only seven enlisted men at the post and no horses, Colonel Bankhead having taken all the available ones. Lieutenant Hughes found five men at Pond Creek who agreed to go with Donovan for $100 each.[12]

Donovan caught up with Colonel Carpenter while he and his troops were scouting up and down the South Fork of the Republican River, looking for the island. Donovan guided them over the divide to the Middle, or Arickaree, Fork. The scouts were almost hysterical at sight of the relief column, doing a "lunatic's dance" as the soldiers raced toward them.[13]

The doctor did all he could. He had to

Courtesy the Nebraska State Historical Society, Lincoln

Forsythe Scouts, Arickaree survivors. Taken at Battle Station in the early 1900s. Beecher Island Battle. Left to right: George Green, J. J. Peate, Hudson L. Farley, Howard Marton, Chalmer Smith.

amputate Louis Farley's leg because gangrene had set in. Farley did not survive. The next day Colonel Bankhead arrived with his troops and two howitzers, but the Indians were gone.

They buried their dead, made their wounded as comfortable as possible in the ambulances, and started back for Fort Wallace on September 27, arriving there on the thirtieth.[14]

Forsythe's scouts lost five dead; the Indians later admitted losing seventy-five killed and "heaps" wounded.[15]

The battle had to be considered a victory for Forsythe and his fifty scouts. However, General Sheridan saw only that the Indians had not been completely defeated. He believed they must be punished enough to make them go to the reservations. Since he felt there was no equal to George Armstrong Custer as an Indian fighter, he succeeded in getting the remission of the last of Custer's court-martial sentence and sent word to Monroe, Michigan, where Custer was then living, asking him to come at once to lead his troops against the Indians in a fall and winter campaign. The letter was dated September 24, less than twenty-four hours after Sheridan heard the news of Forsythe's predicament on the little island in the Arickaree. The campaign was scheduled to begin on October 1.[16]

Custer arrived at Fort Hays on September 30, but it would still be some time before he again assumed command of the Seventh Cavalry. Gen. Eugene Carr arrived shortly after this to be sent out to assume command of the Fifth Cavalry.[17]

Carr went by rail and stagecoach to Fort Wallace, where Colonel Carpenter was assigned as his escort to take him down Beaver Creek to meet the Fifth Cavalry. It was on this mission that Colonel Carpenter ran into an Indian battle that later merited him more promotions and honors.

Colonel Carpenter was still in command of his Negro troops, and he took Sharp

Courtesy the Kansas State Historical Society, Topeka

Gen. Eugene Carr

Grover along as scout. Since he had no mules for pack animals, Carpenter took eleven wagons with supplies. They reached Beaver Creek October 15. Three days later, on the morning of October 18, the Indians struck.

Carpenter's scouts had seen the trail of Indians for two days but no sign of the Fifth Cavalry, so Carpenter decided to return to Fort Wallace. Captain Graham had ridden out to scout in advance, when about twenty-five Indians charged out of the bluffs to cut him off from the rest of the soldiers. Graham had two men with him. They dashed to the river. Carpenter immediately sent out a detachment to chase the Indians off and rescue Graham and his two men.

This mission was successful, and the troops moved out, cautious now. Carpenter placed his wagons in double columns, six on one side, five on the other. They moved out onto the flat area on the north side of the river and advanced slowly.

Carpenter kept his men deployed just outside the wagons, as Indians appeared on all sides. The wagons moved on under Indian attack until Carpenter ordered them to turn toward a small knoll and to corral there. With only eleven wagons it was not a tight corral, but the teams were turned inside. The troops rode inside and dismounted. While a few soldiers watched the horses, the rest ran to places near the wagons.

By now an estimated six hundred Indians were in the attacking party. They charged but were met by a withering fire from the soldiers' Spencer rifles. Several Indians were killed, and the others withdrew. The medicine man rode back to within two hundred yards of the wagon corral and dashed back and forth to show the warriors that his medicine was good and the soldiers could not hurt him. Carpenter ordered some of his best marksmen to aim carefully and all fire at once. The medicine man was knocked off his horse, and the Indians howled like banshees.

Although Carpenter had his men build breastworks to resist the next attack, the Indians did not try again. The death of their medicine man apparently convinced them this was not their day to overrun the soldiers. As the heat of the day increased, Carpenter ordered the wagons to move on to the river for water. Some Indians followed but did not attack.[18]

For his leadership in handling the battle against six-to-one odds without serious loss. Carpenter received a brevet to full colonel.

General Carr, using Grover as an interpreter, talked to a wounded Indian who had been captured and learned where the main village was.[19] As soon as the troops arrived at Fort Wallace they discovered that the Fifth Cavalry had never reached Beaver Creek but had returned to the railroad. General Carr, went there and took command of the unit. He then returned to Beaver, Creek, found the main village of the Cheyennes, and drove them out of Kansas into Nebraska.[20]

Nothing had taken place to change the mind of General Sheridan that a winter campaign must be launched to put a stop to Indian raids on the settlements, the railroad construction crews, and the stage crews and passengers on the Butterfield Overland Despatch.

Statistics for the latter half of 1868 on the western Kansas plains show that Indians killed one hundred and fifty-seven people. Many were railroad construction men and employees of the B.O.D., but many were impatient homesteaders who settled too far beyond the safe borderland. Among those killed were fourteen women. Four women and twenty-four children were stolen by the raiders. Sixteen hundred horses were stolen, twenty-four ranches and small settlements destroyed eleven stagecoaches attacked on the B.O.D., and four wagon trains wiped out.[21]

So the winter campaign was put into motion. Nearly three thousand soldiers began to move toward Indian territory.[22] General Sheridan intended to lead the campaign, but before he was ready to start he sent General Custer and his regiment of the Seventh Cavalry ahead on a scouting mission.

Custer left Camp Supply at dawn on November 22 in zero weather and a blinding blizzard. A couple of cold dawns later he surprised Black Kettle's village on the Washita, killing more that one hundred Indians and capturing more than fifty squaws and children and nearly nine hundred horses.

It was not an easy victory, however. There were approximately two thousand warriors in winter camps nearby, and Custer was fortunate to retreat successfully to Camp Supply, leaving behind Major Elliott and fourteen men dead.

Elliott had given chase to some Indians

who broke out of the circle around the village, and he had come up against the warriors moving up from the camps below. Custer wasn't able to go to Elliott's rescue.

Custer went back on another campaign later in the winter. On this expedition he managed to rescue two white women prisoners, Sarah White and Anna Morgan, by capturing some of the chiefs of the Indians and threatening to kill them if the women were not released.[23] The women had been kidnapped from Kansas homesteads on the Solomon River.[24]

The campaigns in the south were intended to destroy the Indians' ability to wage war on the settlers and stage passengers in western Kansas. The next year, 1869, would prove that the campaigns had not been very successful.

NOTES

1. General George A. Forsythe, "A Frontier Fight," *Beecher Island Annual* (St. Francis, Kans. 1960), p. 14.
2. Ibid., pp. 17–18.
3. Ibid., p. 16. Shell casings found after the battle testified to the presence of all these rifles among the Indians.
4. *The American Heritage Book of Indians*. Reprinted in the *Fort Wallace* (Kans.) *Bugle*, March 1971.
5. Forsythe, "A Frontier Fight," pp. 18–19.
6. Some accounts say that Medicine Man was the name of a chief involved in the battle; others say he was the medicine man of the tribe.
7. In the various accounts of this battle, most say that Roman Nose fell on the fifth volley from the scouts; others say he didn't go down until the sixth volley.
8. Accounts written by many men shortly after the fight list Fort Wallace at a distance ranging from sixty to one hundred and ten miles from the scene of the battle. By a straight route it was actually between sixty-five and seventy miles.
9. Cyrus Townsend Brady, *Indian Fights and Fighters* (McClure Philips & Co.; reprint ed. Lincoln: Univ. of Nebraska Press, 1971), pp. 97–100.
10. Chauncey B. Whitney, "Diary of Chauncey B. Whitney," *Beecher Island Annual* (St. Francis, Kansas, 1960), p. 92.
11. Forysthe, "A Frontier Fight," p. 23.
12. Brady, "Indian Fights," p. 112.
13. Ibid., p. 119. Scout Sigmund Schlesinger, the Jewish boy, youngest of the scouts, used the words, "lunatic dance" to describe the antics of the rescued men when they saw Colonel Carpenter's troops coming.
14. Whitney, "Diary," pp. 92–93.
15. Forsythe, "A Frontier Fight," p. 26. Four years later, when General Forsythe was on a buffalo hunt in southwestern Nebraska with Grand Duke Alexis of Russia, he met and talked with a Sioux warrior who had been in the Beecher Island battle, and the warrior admitted the number of their casualties.
16. Blaine Burkey, *Custer Come at Once* (Hays, Kans.: Thomas More Prep, 1976), p. 42. Custer didn't wait for special orders but left immediately for Kansas. The orders caught up with him there.
17. Ibid., p. 45.
18. Brady, "Indian Fights," pp. 123–135.
19. Ibid., p. 140.
20. Burkey, *Custer Come at Once*, p. 45.
21. Brady, "Indian Fights," p. 148.
22. Burkey, *Custer Come at Once*, p. 45.
23. Ibid., p. 45.
24. George Jelinek, "The Ellsworth Story," *Ellsworth* (Kans.) *Reporter*, 3 August 1967.

CHAPTER 17

THE COACH'S LAST RUN

MANY CLAIMS WERE MADE that there would be no more Indian trouble on the frontier, due to Custer's smashing victory at Black Kettle's camp on the Washita. It was not to be.

On January 8, before the year of 1869 had really gotten under way, the Indians struck at Big Timbers Station on the Kansas-Colorado border. The next day they struck at Lake Station well over in Colorado and killed two station tenders.[1]

It was not the way of Indians to attack during winter, but apparently they had learned from Custer's strike on the Washita that winter was no longer a time of peace. Their strikes in cold weather, however, were few.

Since the summer of 1868 the Butterfield Overland Despatch had its eastern terminal at the end of passenger service on the railroad at Sheridan, about fifteen miles northeast of Fort Wallace. The railroad had stopped there because it ran out of money.

General Custer completed his winter campaign, having spent five months south of the Kansas border. He returned to the Washita after delivering his prisoners from Black Kettle's camp to Camp Supply. From there he went to Fort Cobb and Fort Sill, made a scouting foray up the North Fork of the Red River and back, then circled down near the Red River and up and across the Sweetwater to the Washita again. He then went north to Camp Supply and on to Fort Hays, arriving at Fort Hays on April 7.[2]

The regiment went into camp about two miles east of the fort on Big Creek. As soon as the camp was firmly established Custer took a leave of absence and went to Fort Leavenworth to see his wife, Libbie. He returned on April 28, and the camp settled in for the summer.

While some newspaper correspondents reported that General Custer was the idol of his men, facts throw a shadow on this statement. There were many desertions from the camp that spring and summer, and the deserters usually took their horses, which belonged to the government. Custer made a point of trying to return both deserters and horses. The horses received good care but the deserters did not fare so well.

If the deserter was also a troublemaker,

Courtesy the Kansas State Historical Society, Topeka

Fort Hays — Indian captives

Courtesy the Kansas State Historical Society, Topeka

Fort Hays — Officers' quarters and band of the Fifth Infantry, 1869.

he quite often received the "bucking" punishment. The man was set on the ground with his wrists tied together and his ankles tied together. His arms were forced down over his knees and a stick shoved under his knees and over his elbows. He was then unable to move without falling over. The regular guardhouse for the camp was a hole dug on the top of a knoll, twenty feet deep and twenty feet square. It was covered with brush and had a ladder for the men to climb in and out. The prisoners were kept in this hole during the night and allowed out to stay in specially guarded tents during the day.[4]

Courtesy the Denver Public Library

Cheyenne — Dull Knife, Big Head, Fat Bear

Custer had brought in three chiefs as prisoners when he returned from his winter campaign, captured at an Indian camp on Sweetwater River in the eastern panhandle of Texas. He used the threat of death to these chiefs to secure the release of the two white women prisoners. When he arrived at Fort Hays the three chiefs were put in the stockade with the Indian women and children who had been captured on the Washita the November before.

Bvt. Maj. Gen. Nelson Miles of the Fifth Infantry was named commander of Fort Hayes on April 21, and he set about trying to make things a bit better for the Indian prisoners in the stockade. The Indians, however, were intent on escape. The soldiers guarding them suspected the three chiefs of planning some mischief, so they decided to move them to the guardhouse.

Waiting their chance, the Indians leaped on the guards with table knives that had been honed to razor sharpness. One Indian named Fat Bear stabbed a sergeant. Several shots were fired, and one chief and a squaw were killed outright. Another of the three chiefs was mortally wounded and died later. The soldiers knew the two chiefs as Bighead and Dull Knife.[6] Dull Knife was killed with a bayonet.

Although Custer had been certain that he could guarantee peace with the Indians by holding the prisoners in the stockade at Fort Hays, the result was exactly the opposite. Beginning shortly after the two chiefs and the squaw were killed at the stockade, war parties began making raids all over western Kansas. For almost a month, from late May till late June, the attacks continued. The raiders would strike swiftly and then disappear before the army could arrive.

The raids were not confined to the Fort Hays area, although that part of Kansas got its share. One battle occurred near the end of May in the vicinity of Fort Wallace.

Gen. Eugene A. Carr brought his Fifth Cavalry into camp near Fort Wallace around the first of May 1869. Carr had taken both Wild Bill Hickok and Buffalo Bill Cody as scouts on his winter campaign, but when he got back to Fort Wallace he discharged Wild Bill Hickok. Hickok had been wounded three times by Indians while carrying dispatches on Sand Creek in Colorado during the winter. Fully recovered, he stayed a while at Fort Wallace then moved on to Fort Hays.[7]

On May 10, 1869, General Carr took his cavalry to the northeast along Beaver Creek in pursuit of a large band of Indians. He caught up with them at Elephant Rock on the Beaver. In the battle that ensued, twenty-five Indians and three soldiers were killed.[8]

Sheridan, approximately fifteen miles east of Fort Wallace, was a center of attraction for the Indians. It was the western end of rail service and the eastern end of stage and mule freight traffic. The Indians found this transition area a good target for raids.

They struck at a train of freight wagons just after it had left Sheridan on May 26, wounding two teamsters and driving off three hundred mules. A few days later they attacked another train just west of Fort Wallace on Rose Creek. This was a government train with a soldier escort. Two soldiers and five Indians were wounded.[9]

Before the month was out, Indians struck at a railroad section crew on Fossil Creek, about twenty-five miles east of Fort Hays, killing two and wounding four of the remaining five, including the foreman of the crew. These were obviously the dog soldiers led by Tall Bull.[10] The warriors cut the telegraph lines and derailed trains by tying logs on the rails. On the same day Indians struck on the Solomon River, killing John Wilson, and Dr. L. Rose.

Courtesy the Kansas State Historical Society, Topeka

Fort Hays — Indian prison, 1869

The dog soldiers went northeast from the railroad and two days later, on the afternoon of May 30, made a raid down Spillman Creek, which empties into the Saline River. It was a warm Sunday afternoon, and many of the residents along Spillman Creek had walked from their homes to visit neighbors.

Most of those killed were out in the open and unarmed. The raiders killed four men, one woman, and four children, including two boys fifteen and thirteen years old. They abducted two young women and a baby girl.[11]

One of the women taken was Susanna Alderdice, wife of Thomas Alderdice, one of Forsythe's scouts who fought at Beecher Island. Alderdice had gone to Salina for supplies, and his wife had gone to visit a neighbor that afternoon, taking her two sons by a previous marriage aged seven and four, and the two-year-old son and baby daughter of her current marriage. When the Indians caught up with the little family, they killed the oldest boy, shot the second one with an arrow, and drove a lance into his side.[12] Then they bashed out the brains of the two-year-old. They took Susanna Alderdice and her tiny daughter captive. They also caught George and Maria Weichell out on the prairie, murdered George, and took Maria captive.[13] After their raid they moved out of the valley before soldiers could locate them.

General Carr had gone to Fort McPherson on the Platte after his battle at Elephant Rock. Here orders reached him to make an expedition to the Republican to try to find the Indians responsible for the murders and abductions.

He left Fort McPherson on June 9 with eight companies of the Fifth Cavalry and three companies of Pawnee scouts under Maj. Frank North. Buffalo Bill Cody was Carr's chief scout. There were a few skirmishes but nothing of importance until the Indians tried to run off the army's horses and mules in an unusual night raid July 8.

When the soldiers located the camp where the Indians had been, they also learned from tracks left at the campsite that there were white women prisoners in the party. They knew at last they were on the trail of at least some of the Indians they had been sent to find. They had two goals now. The first was to prevent the Indians from getting across the Platte into the great empty land of Wyoming and Montana where they could disappear. The second was to rescue the prisoners.

The Indians' trail led northwest. In Colorado Territory they could slip across the South Platte, head into Wyoming, and be lost.

The cavalry horses set a fast pace and closed the gap. The Indians' trail divided. One trail, plainly marked by the travois poles, went north. The other trail, very faint, went northwest. Cody was not fooled by the division. After a conference with his scouts, General Carr sent two companies on the plainly marked trail. The rest of the soldiers and scouts found a sheltered spot and stayed out of sight.[14]

After hiding for a while Carr led his troops on the faint trail to the northwest. Soon the first two companies joined them; the plain trail had faded into a dozen separate trails. But the Indian ruse to fool the soldiers had backfired. The Indians had been deceived in turn by the sight of soldiers following the false trail, and now they were not moving rapidly. Carr and his men were.

Carr left the wagons behind, along with the soldiers and scouts whose horses could not stand any more forced marches. His striking force was down to less than two hundred and fifty men of the original eight companies and only fifty of the three companies of scouts. But they moved fast.

About noon on July 11 Cody reported that he had located the Indians in camp by a spring south of the South Platte River. If they were looking for an attack, it would be from the south or east. Carr swung his troops around to the north and moved in. This approach would also have the effect of cutting off the Indians' retreat to the north across the South Platte.

A heavy wind came in from the west, bringing a rainstorm. It was howling when Carr's men struck. The attack was a surprise and a total victory for the soldiers. Only one soldier was wounded, and that wound was not serious. The two white women prisoners were found. One, Maria Weichell, was seriously wounded but alive. Susanna Alderdice had been murdered by Tall Bull's squaw with a blow on the head from a tomahawk.[15]

Susanna Alderdice was buried at the scene of the battle; Maria Weichell was taken to Fort Sedgwick, where she recovered. Fifty dead Indians were counted. No one could tell how many wounded had crawled some distance away to die. Many squaws and children were taken prisoner. Everything in the eighty-four lodges was destroyed. Tall Bull, the leader, was killed in the battle.[16]

This battle, which killed the dog soldiers' leader and destroyed so much of their potential for fighting, did a great deal to bring the bloody war on the Smoky Hill to a halt.

While the fighting was going on in other sections, General Custer was having a fairly quiet summer in his camp a couple of miles from Fort Hays. The town of Hays City, now generally known as Hays, was anything but quiet. Ten or more men were killed in Hays in 1869. The graveyard where they were buried became known as Boot Hill, the first town to label its cemetery with that name.[17] Wild Bill Hickok, as marshall, did little to hold the total down. In fact he was responsible for two of the deaths.

Years later Libbie Custer described Hays that summer as she vividly remembered it:

There was hardly a building worthy of the name, except the stationhouse. A considerable part of the place was built from rude frames covered with canvas; the shanties were made up of slabs, bits of driftwood, and logs, and sometimes the roofs were covered with tin that had once been fruit or vegetable cans, now flattened out. A smoke rising from the surface of the street might arrest your attention, but it indicated only an underground addition to some small "shack," built on the surface of the earth.[18]

Courtesy the Kansas State Historical Society, Topeka

George A. Custer with Mrs. Custer and servant Eliza

The railroad, which had been stalled since May 1868 at Sheridan, now began to creep slowly forward as funds became available. It finally reached Fort Wallace. About the middle of November the rails reached Pond City, approximately seventeen miles from Sheridan.[19] However, the end of passenger service was still at Sheridan, and the stagecoaches still ran between Sheridan and Denver as they had done for over a year.

Fort Wallace was still the most active post on the plains. The War Department issued a description of the fort as it appeared about this time:

Two of the barracks are constructed of adobe, or rather of a marl, which can be easily worked with carpenter's tools, and in a recent state is of a light pink color. It grows harder and darker on exposure, owing to the presence of magnesium and iron. These buildings measure 118 by 25 feet. The walls are two feet in thickness.

The barracks are warmed with stoves provided with drums, the pipe extending the length of the room. Each dormitory contains forty double bunks in two tiers, intended for eighty men.

The remaining barracks of wood are a little wider. . . . The temporary structures used for kitchen and mess-room purposes are of rough boards, battened, roofs with tenting, and only in part floored.

A row of officers' quarters forms the limit of the parade to the north, while to the south the guardhouse and magazine are all that interfere with the view south of the river. The storehouses, occuying the southwestern portion of the camp, are durable buildings of stone, 128 feet in length, 24 feet in width, and 10 feet to the eaves. The grain house is constructed of wood, and has a capacity of 15,000 bushels.

The post guardhouse is a durable structure of stone, 34 feet front by 31 deep in depth, with a veranda in front, 8 feet in width. The economy, so rigidly enforced during the latter part of 1867, resulted in the roofing of the hospital before the

Courtesy the Kansas State Historical Society, Topeka

Fort Wallace — Officers' quarters

wards had reached to within three feet of the height contemplated in the original design. The building is well built of stone referred to, and is well adapted for its use. It consists of a control building and two wings as wards, with a back building to the central part, 40 by 20 feet, the wings are 48 feet in length and 24 in width.

The post is supplied with a well, located near the foot of the bluff, which does not extend below the bed of the stream, and furnishes only the surface drainage. The water is highly impregnated with minerals. An attempt had been made to secure water for the garrison by means of a well, located within the limits of the post proper. After penetrating . . . to a depth of thirty-six feet . . . the excavation proceeded for fifty additional feet, when the effort was abandoned. The appearance of petroleum in the underlying stratum was an interesting feature observed.

The fort being constructed on a gradual slope inclining to the river, no artificial drainage, is considered necessary.[20]

The battles of 1869 brought a more peaceful atmosphere in 1870 for the progress of the railroad and the settlement of western Kansas. The Indians didn't give up the fight, but their ferocity had been diluted. The overwhelming flood of whites coming from the east made the task of driving them all back appear hopeless.

The railroad builders didn't even stop for winter. In January 1870 the rails reached Eagle Tail Station.[21] The stage line moved its eastern terminal to Eagle Tail, and the stages ran from there to Denver.[22]

In late May 1870 the railroad equipment was taken from Sheridan, where it had been for almost two years, and moved to Kit Carson in Colorado Territory.[23]

Sheridan's heyday ended when the railroad equipment moved out. It had become one of the bloodiest and most notorious end-of-track towns in U.S. history. At its peak Sheridan had nearly two thousand residents, and at times the surrounding camps were jammed with almost a thousand wagons used by buffalo hunters and the freighters going to and from New Mexico or hauling army supplies to Fort Wallace.[24] In the spring of 1870 the Indians made their last try at stopping the railroad, which they recognized now as a greater enemy than the stagecoaches rumbling over the roads to Denver. On March 21 they attacked Eagle Tail Station, but soldiers, stationed all along the line, drove them off. In May they tackled Hugo, Lake Station, and even Kit Carson, the new end-of-track town. A report reached Fort Wallace that Major Dudley, a roadmaster, and ten of his workers had been killed west of Kit Carson. Soldiers were sent in pursuit, but they found no Indians.

As the rails moved west the towns behind them shrank to a size that could survive without the freighters and railroad construction workers to swell the coffers. In early July Pond Creek had forty people. Monument had only twelve. Other stations had even fewer.[25] The B.O.D. stations along the river were either completely abandoned or taken over by settlers. Progress was westward, and it moved rapidly, in spite of the last efforts of the Indians to stop it.

The end of the stage line moved west with the progress of the railroad. After Kit Carson, the eastern terminal of the Butterfield Overland Despatch became Lake. Stages operated between Denver and Lake until the rails reached Denver and passenger service was extended to that point. On that day the stagecoaches stopped running.[26] The last stage ran on August 18, 1870.

This article, titled "Swan Song of the Stage Coaches," was dated August 19, 1870:

Staging between Denver and the east ended when the Kansas Pacific was completed last Monday. The coach has given way to the palace car and staging for the overland traveler is a thing of the past.

We wish to bear witness to the amount of capital required and the pluck, energy and enterprise displayed in the running and management of those lines of travel which the railroads now unceremoniously shove off the theater of the present into the dead past. For eleven years these coaches have been running with a regularity unparalleled. They were our only means of public transportation.

While we yield full praise to the companies, there is another group of men to whom greater credit is due, still higher respect for services performed: the stage coach employees who took the risks of heat, cold and Indians — road agents who, by the power of their endurance, made the overland stage a success.

As the traveler glides over the iron rails in the luxurious palace car he sees where many a brave fellow met his fate from the bullet or arrow of a foe and fell true to duty with a death-grip on his reins. It was he who braved and dared so much on the lonely plains of Kansas and Colorado in pioneering the way for the trains in which we now ride.

Their occupation is gone. The bright stages will soon be dusty, the shining harness rusty, the handsome, prancing four-in-hands descended to the position of farm horses and draft horses. The overland boys will be scattered.

The honor of driving the last overland coach into Denver last night fell to Steve Harmon. With the Kansas Pacific completed, there will be no more staging between Denver and the East.[27]

The Butterfield Overland Despatch was history. The building of the railroad which took its place is a story in itself.

Courtesy the Nebraska State Historical Society, Lincoln

Pond Creek Stage Station built in 1865 near an area later designated Fort Wallace, Kansas — replica of stagecoaches which traveled on the Smoky Hill Trail. In the picture are Frank and Mayme, children of Tom Madigan who bought the building after it fell into disuse. Picture taken 1963.

NOTES

1. Mrs. Frank C. Montgomery, "Fort Wallace and Its Relation to the Frontier," *Kansas Historical Collections, 1926–1928* 17 (1928), p. 240.
2. Blaine Burkey, *Custer Come at Once* (Hays, Kans.: Thomas More Prep, 1976), pp. 46–7.
3. Ibid., p. 50.
4. Ibid., p. 51.
5. Ibid., footnote, p. 47.
6. Ibid., p. 68. George Bent later identified the chief called Bighead as Curly Head. He also said the one called Dull Knife was an eighty-year-old man named Slim Face. He certainly wasn't the famous Cheyenne chief, Dull Knife, who led the great breakout from Fort Reno in Oklahoma in 1878 and took his party north until captured at Fort Robinson in northern Nebraska.
7. Montgomery, "Fort Wallace," pp. 240–241. Hickok was soon to become marshal of Hays and enhance his reputation there.
8. Elephant Rock is in northern Decatur County, not far from the Nebraska-Kansas state line, west of Highway 83 between McCook, Nebraska, and Oberlin, Kansas.
9. Montgomery, "Fort Wallace," p. 241.
10. Col. Ray G. Sparks, *Reckoning at Summit Springs* (Kansas City, Mo.: Lowell Press, 1969), pp. 17–25. This gives a complete account of the fight as told by one of the wounded survivors.
11. Burkey, *Custer Come at Once*, p. 76.
12. This boy, Willis Daily, the younger of Thomas Alderdice's two stepsons, was badly wounded and left for dead. The arrow was broken off in his back. Alderdice, using a bullet mold as pincers, got the arrowhead out, and the boy survived.
13. According to the woman who survived the capture, Maria Weichell, the baby cried too much and the Indians "wrung its neck" the third day after its capture.

14. Cyrus Townsend Brady. *Indian Fights and Fighters* (McClure, Philips & Co.; reprint ed. Lincoln: Univ. of Nebraska Press, 1971), p. 173.
15. Sparks, *Reckoning at Summit Springs*, p. 49.
16. Ibid.
17. Joseph G. Rosa, *The Gunfighter: Man or Myth* (Norman: Univ. of Oklahoma Press, 1969), 1. 113.
18. Burkey, *Custer Come at Once*, p. 60.
19. Montgomery, "Fort Wallace," p. 242.
20. Ibid. This description includes only excerpts from the report. For a complete description of the post, see pp. 242–245.
21. Eagle Tail is now the town of Sharon Springs, county seat of Wallace County.
22. There are reports that the stage line continued to run from Sheridan until May 1, 1870, but Butterfield Overland Despatch records show that the eastern terminal of the line was moved to Eagle Tail as soon as rail passenger service was extended to that point.
23. Montgomery, "Fort Wallace," p. 246.
24. Ibid., p. 246.
25. Ibid., p. 248.
26. Margarent Long, *The Smoky Hill Trail* (Denver: W. H. Kistler Company, 1943), p. 68.
27. E. O. Davis, *The First Five Years of the Railroad Era in Colorado*, pp. 111–12.

IV.

TRAIL OF THE IRON HORSE

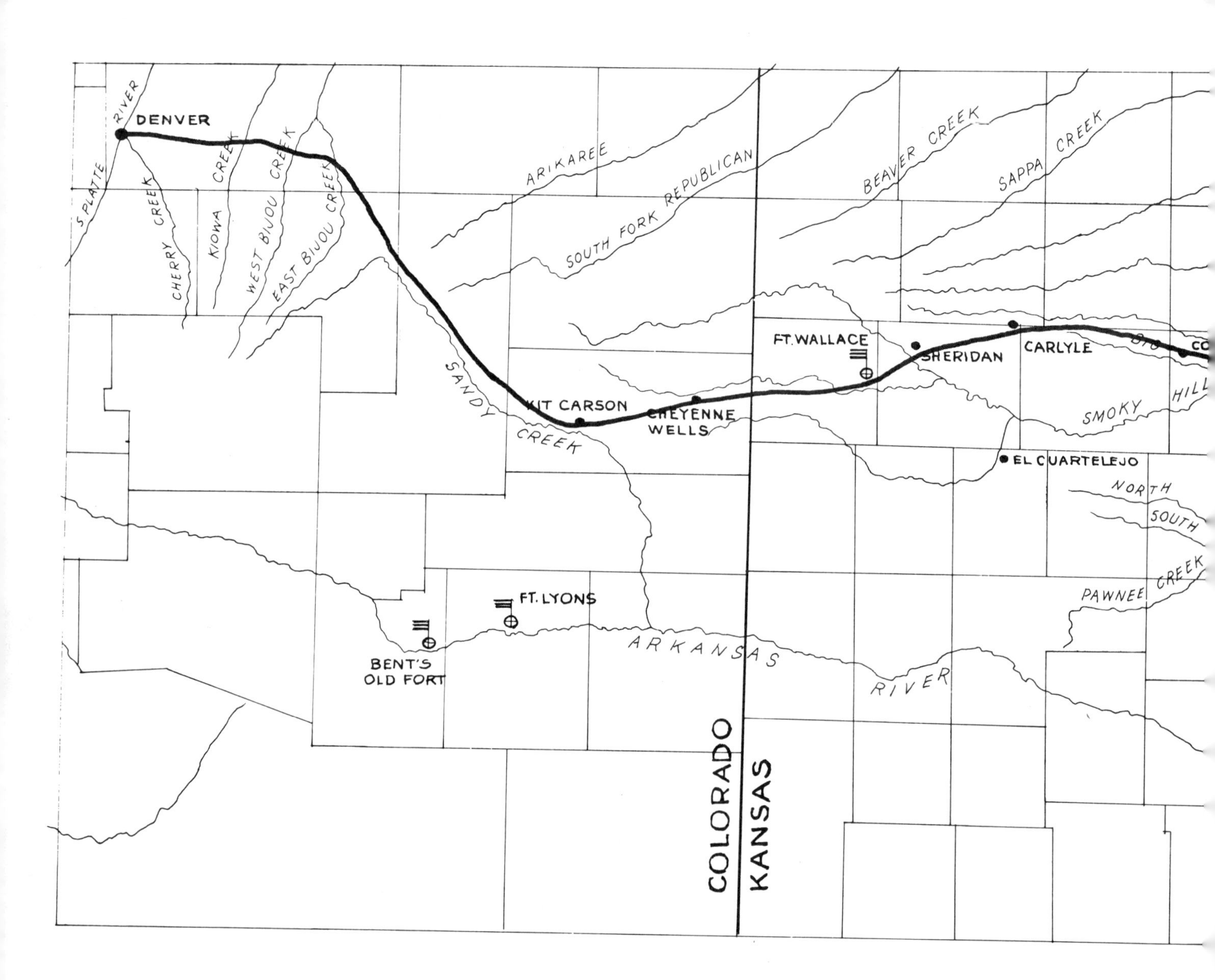

DENVER
S. PLATTE RIVER
CHERRY CREEK
KIOWA CREEK
WEST BIJOU CREEK
EAST BIJOU CREEK
ARIKAREE
SOUTH FORK REPUBLICAN
BEAVER CREEK
SAPPA CREEK
FT. WALLACE
SHERIDAN
CARLYLE
SANDY CREEK
KIT CARSON
CHEYENNE WELLS
SMOKY HILL
EL CUARTELEJO
NORTH
SOUTH
PAWNEE CREEK
FT. LYONS
BENT'S OLD FORT
ARKANSAS RIVER
COLORADO
KANSAS

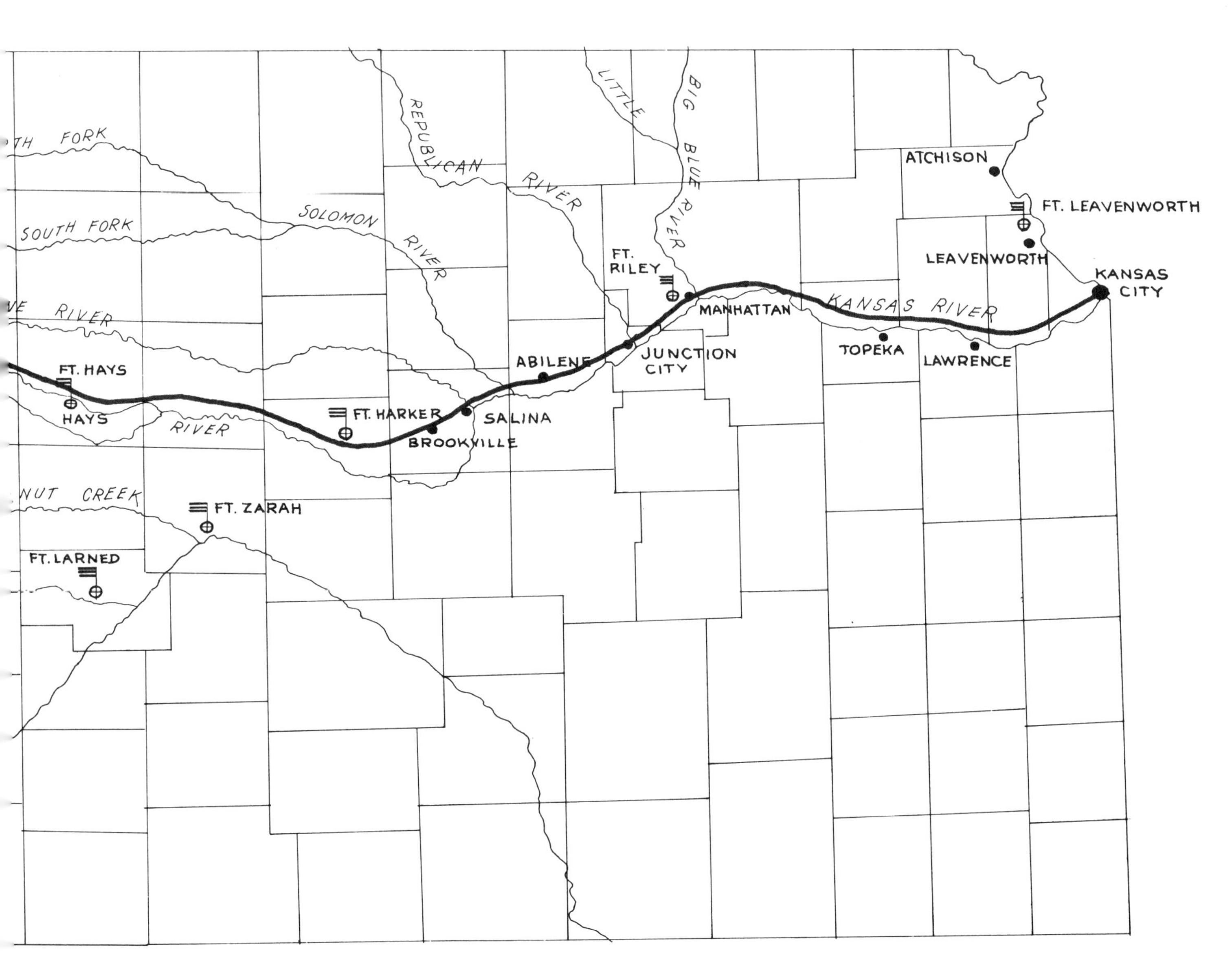

TRAIL OF THE IRON HORSE

CHAPTER 18

RACE OF THE IRON RAILS

AS THE IRON HORSE HUFFED AND PUFFED in its stable on the Missouri River, impatient to race across the plains of Kansas, people on the frontier dreamed of the luxuries it would bring. A train would mean swift travel and the bringing of needed freight — good things that were only memories out on the plains. The most optimistic pioneer expected the trains tomorrow. But between today and tomorrow was a Civil War and unbelievable troubles and delays.

As early as 1861 the Territorial Legislature of Kansas had chartered no fewer than fifty-one railroads.[1] Practically all of them were just that — charters, nothing more. There was no sign of rails or even grades in most instances.

On July 1, 1862, the Union Pacific and the Central Pacific railroads were authorized, and expectations of rail travel began to reach a high pitch.[2] Still, nothing really was accomplished toward that end until two men, Samuel Hallett and John C. Fremont, acquired controlling stock in the Leavenworth, Pawnee and Western Railroad Company at the end of May 1863.

Hallett was a young banker with offices in New York City; he had helped build the Atlantic and Great Western Railroad in the East. His name put solid backing behind the move to get the railroad built. Fremont was the big name in exploration in early Kansas and had made a great deal of money from the sale of his ranch in California. When Fremont was elected president of the new company and Hallett the general superintendent, the prospects of success soared to the pinnacle. The name of the company was changed to the Union Pacific Railway Company, Eastern Division.[3]

Although it may not have been intended to create competition between lines, the

Courtesy the Kansas State Historical Society, Topeka

Samuel Hallett

law of July 1862 accomplished just that. This law, which established the Union Pacific and the Central Pacific railroads, provided that the Union Pacific build from the 100th meridian westward and the Central Pacific from the Pacific Coast eastward. They were to meet at the California-Nevada line. If either got there ahead of the other, it was to build on until union was accomplished.

That left the strip from the 100th meridian eastward to the Missouri River without specific authorization. It was generally accepted that the first railroad to reach that 100th meridian on the Platte River would get the contract to build on to meet the Central Pacific.

One section was scheduled to build west from Omaha, but Fremont and Hallett envisioned their new company as the one to reach the 100th meridian first. Even the name they gave their company, the Union Pacific Railway Company, Eastern Division, proclaimed their intentions. They were to build west from the Missiouri along the Kansas River, then turn up the Republican River, continuing northwest to Fort Kearny on the Platte River in Nebraska, then westward to the 100th meridian. They were better organized than the railroad company at Omaha, and the people of Kansas saw no reason why they shouldn't win the race. Their railroad would cut right through the inhabitated part of Kansas, and no one objected then to its turning north into Nebraska.[4]

Hallett was one who believed in organization and cooperative effort. His timing was not good, however, in soliciting the subscription of $100,000 for stock in the railroad from the people of Leavenworth. The week before he made his appeal to the town council, Quantrill made his famous raid on Lawrence, and the people of Leavenworth were concentrating on sending aid to the stricken city on the Kaw River. They reacted to Hallett's suggestion coolly. Hallett immediately moved his headquarters to Wyandotte, farther downstream.[5] From then on the railroad pushed west from that point.

Hallett moved into Wyandotte early in September and ran an ad in the *Wyandotte Gazette* calling for a thousand workers to begin clearing land and grading. The work was to begin on Monday, September 7. The wages were to be $1.50 a day, with payment being made every Saturday night. Foreman were to receive from $50 to $100 a month, and each foreman was to furnish twenty-five men to work on the road.[6]

The government subsidy was to be paid upon completion of each section of road, and the time limit for the first hundred miles was November 1864. Hallett was confident it could be done.

The subsidy consisted of a grant of land, alternate sections in a strip ten miles on either side of the right-of-way, and government bonds to the extent of $16,000 a mile — plus the privilege of issuing railroad bonds in an equal amount.[7]

Used to hearing vague promises about work to begin soon, the people of Wyan-

Courtesy the Kansas State Historical Society, Topeka
Copy of painting by L. L. F. Fisk

Lawrence — Quantrill's raid

Courtesy the Kansas State Historical Society, Topeka
Sketches by Merrick from Harper's Weekly, January 27, 1866

Sketches by Merrick

dotte and the neighboring community were not only surprised but greatly excited when Hallett arrived on the appointed morning with a hundred men ready to work. The starting point of the railroad was on the Missouri-Kansas state line, three-fourths of a mile west of the Missouri River on the north bank of the Kaw (Kansas) River. Hallett's brother John L. Hallett, was there and directed the first moves. The *Wyandotte Gazette* of the following Saturday, September 12, reported the scene:

> Last Monday at 10½ A.M. work on the Union Pacific R. Road was commenced in a manner quiet and unassuming. . . . Immediately on the arrival of Mr. Hallett he gave directions to his superindendent to clear a space of 50 feet on each side of the line. Mr. Silas Armstrong and A. B. Bartlett, Esq., each claimed the privilege of cutting the first tree. Each held his ax, standing by trees of about the same size. Mr. Hallett gave the order to cut and both trees fell about the same instant. A single cheer resounded through the woods and was lost in the quiet waters of the river, and the great Pacificator of the Nation had sprung into life.[8]

The railroad missed Wyandotte by less than two miles, but this didn't stop Samuel Hallett from getting the town to vote an issue of $100,000 in bonds to be traded to Hallett for stock in the railroad. A spur line would be run into town from the main track, Wyandotte was going to become a city.

According to a report published in the *Congregational Record* in Lawence in October of the previous year, Wyandotte had failed to reach its potential. "The Indian Reserve on one side, and Rebeldom on the other, have prevented Wyandotte from reaching its early expectations. Loose clapboards, broken windows, and faded paint indicate a place where early growth surpassed its subsequent importance."[9]

That was changed now. The great railroad had begun its push west to the distant coast. The grading of the roadway was progressing rapidly. By January it had reached a point even with Lawrence.

By contrast, the Union Pacific starting out from Omaha had just broken the first ground for its grade in December. Some Kansans called it the "branch line."[10] Hallett was far ahead of the Nebraska work, and everyone was certain he would reach Fort Kearny first and get the contract to meet the Central Pacific coming from California.

There was trouble behind the scenes, however, on the Kansas line. General Fremont, the president, and Hallett, the superintendent, had a sharp disagreement. When election time for officers came up in April, there were two stockholder meetings held in Leavenworth. At the meeting in the railroad company's office. John D. Perry, president of the Exchange Bank in St. Louis, was elected president of the Union Pacific Railway Company, Eastern Division. At another meeting at another site in town, General Fremont was elected to another term as president of the company.

The conflict was resolved when Hallett pointed out some facts that most stockholders had ignored. Fremont and the new board of directors elected that day based their eligibility to hold office on the strength of the shares of stock they held in the company. Four months earlier, however, the company had assessed a ten percent payment on all stock, and none of those at Fremont's meeting had paid their assessment. The rules of the company declared that the holders of stock on which the payment had not been made were ineligible to vote. To make sure that he won his argument with Fremont, Hallett had bought most of the stock from one man, J. C. Stone, and then made the payment to the company himself. So Hallett became the principle owner of the entire railroad and invalidated any action made by the group meeting with Fremont.[11]

The grading moved ahead very rapidly, but the boats and barges bringing the iron rails to Wyandotte were frozen into the river by an early fall freeze, and the laying of rails had been suspended through much of the winter. With spring, work began again in earnest and by the first of July was progressing so well that Hallett sent invitations to people in the East to come and help celebrate the completion of the first forty miles of railroad to Lawrence. The celebration was set for August 18. Hallett was sure the rails would be at Lawrence by that time.

On July 2 Congress passed an amendment to the railroad law granting the builders 12,800 acres of land on either side of the roadway for each mile of road built. This amendment also practically assured that the first railroad to get its rails to the 100th meridian would get the right-of-way to build to meet the Central Pacific.[12] No one in eastern Kansas had any doubts that Hallett would win the race easily. He was far ahead of the line starting from Omaha.

Every day Lawence citizens scanned newspaper reports on the progress of the railroad. They began preparations for the August 18th fling. Committees were set up to oversee the rounding up of chickens and pigs for the big barbecue, while dozens of other work assignments were handed out.[13]

Then all their plans received a paralyzing jolt. On July 27 Hallett was in Wyandotte. He had just finished his noon meal at the Garno House and was heading for the railroad's offices on Third Street. He spoke to some men in front of the drugstore as he passed. Among them was Orlando Talcott.

Courtesy the Kansas State Historical Society, Topeka *From Gardner Collection*

Wyandotte — railroad yards

Talcott had been brought to the railroad construction work by Fremont. When Fremont lost out in the spring election, Talcott lost his job. Some said it was because he had sent in an unfavorable report of the quality of the work on the railroad, hoping government subsidies would be held back. Hallett retaliated by giving orders that Talcott was no longer to be allowed on railroad property.

That day, after Hallett passed the men sitting in front of the drugstore, Talcott raised his big repeating rifle and shot him in the back. Witnesses rushed out to pick him up and carry him back to the Garno House, but he died before they could get him to the hotel.

In the meantime Talcott got on his horse and rode to Quindaro, where he lived. Pausing only briefly there, he rode on. A huge reward was put up for his arrest, but no one in eastern Kansas ever saw him again.[14]

Samuel Hallett was not an old man. He was just past his thirty-sixth birthday when he was killed.[15] His brother, John, who had worked with him, stepped into the gap and assured everyone, including the newspapers, that he would carry on and the railroad would progress without interruption.

The celebration scheduled for August 18 at Lawrence to welcome the arrival of the rails was postponed, however, because it quickly became obvious that the track would not reach Lawrence by mid-August. Delay after delay held up work. Most of the work was being done on the bridge over the Kansas River and on the line that would reach from the Pacific Railroad of Missouri to the Union Pacific, Eastern Division, in Kansas.

There were many reasons given for the delays. The war was absorbing both men and materials, so John Hallett couldn't get the rails or the men to lay them. One of the rich men backing the project, Thomas Durant, had heavy interests in the Union Pacific Railroad running out of Omaha and was diverting most of the available material to that line. When Durant's man, Silas Seymour, was dismissed from the work in Kansas, the newspapers cheered.[16]

Whatever the reason for the delay, the rails didn't reach Lawrence until November 26. Most people in eastern Kansas felt that the original schedule of August 18 would have been met if Samuel Hallett had lived.

Courtesy the Kansas State Historical Society, Topeka *From Gardner Collection*
View looking across Kansas River at Lawrence, Kansas

Since Samuel Hallett owned most of the shares in the railroad, lawsuits arose over the settlement of his estate. This had a crushing effect on the progress of the rails westward. John D. Perry, the new president of the railroad, sued Hallett's estate for the shares of stock that he had been promised by Hallett for accepting the president's job.

It was some time after the rails and the work train arrived at Lawrence before passenger service was established. The

Courtesy the Kansas State Historical Society, Topeka *From Gardner Collection*
Lawrence, Kansas — view of Wakarusa Valley

Courtesy the Kansas State Historical Society, Topeka *From Gardner Collection*
Leavenworth, Lawrence & Galveston Railroad bridge across the Kansas River, Lawrence, 1867

Courtesy the Kansas State Historical Society, Topeka *From Gardner Collection*

Lawrence — depot

celebration that had been planned for August 18 was finally held on December 19, four months late. It was an enthusiastic celebration, nevertheless.[17]

To the sharp observer, however, it was becoming obvious that the Kansas branch of the Union Pacific was not going to get to Fort Kearny ahead of the Omaha branch. While the line in Kansas was held up for half a dozen different reasons, the line in Nebraska was slowly pushing westward.

Perry, president of the Kansas branch, saw what was happening and proposed to make the best of a bad situation.[18] Before the year was out he had asked Congress for permission to build his railroad up the Smoky Hill River to Denver, rather than up the Republican River to meet the Nebraska line at Fort Kearney. In his request he pointed out that the route up the Smoky Hill was 134 miles closer to Denver than the Republican route would be and was over land more suitable for railroad construction. It would go up a fertile valley that no other line came near.[19]

The work progressed very slowly west of Lawrence. The first forty miles from the river to Lawrence had not yet been accepted by the government. A new contract to go west from Lawrence was not let until July 1, 1865.[20] R. M. Shoemaker and Company got the contract and began to survey in early September.

Even the survey was delayed from its intended beginning by vicious storms that swept over the prairies from July through September. Heavy downpours of rain held up work and washed out grades and bridges on tracks that were already in use. In places the floods cut gullies through high grades, leaving the rails stretched across the gullies and the ties clinging to the rails like toothpicks ready to fall at the slightest breeze. Before any forward progress could be made, damage to the established road had to be repaired in order to bring material from the Missouri River.[21]

About the middle of September Shoemaker sent surveying crews out to map the possible route of the railroad. Since the contract still called for the rails to go up the Republican and on to Fort Kearny, one crew, led by P. Goloy, was sent up the Republican. Another crew, under George T. Wickes, went up the Smoky Hill River — Shoemaker's choice if he could get permission from Congress to switch the route.

In his report Shoemaker showed why he favored the Smoky Hill route. In the first place, the route to Denver was 134 miles shorter. The grades were easier, and most of the way there was good timber and fine coal. He admitted that the one drawback was the scarcity of water west of Pond Creek.[22]

Progress continued to drag until President Andrew Johnson finally accepted the first forty miles of the road on October 30, 1865.[23] This approval put new life into the project, and the road began reaching out at a faster pace.

In November the papers began to proclaim that the railroad would reach Topeka the following week. They insisted the track was going down at the rate of a mile a day. It was December 29, however, before the rails reached Topeka.[24]

The *Topeka Record* reported that construction trains were running between Topeka and Lawrence every day and that passenger service would begin January 1, 1866.

Exactly at the time set, 11:30 A.M. on Monday, January 1, the first passenger train pulled into Topeka. A big celebration followed. The band met the train and played for the crowd. Senator Lane, one of sixty guests on the train, gave a speech. Carriages took all the guests to either the Capital House or the Munro House, where dinner was served.

Then they were hurried back to the waiting train to leave for Lawrence at the departing time of 1:30. The report concluded: "After the public entertainment was over, the celebration was continued by a number of prominent gentlemen on their own account. We regret to hear that, during the festivities, a terrific melee occurred, in which several necks were broken.

"P.S. We have since been informed that they were the necks of champagne bottles."[25]

As the rails pushed west from Topeka, the Butterfield Overland Despatch moved its headquarters from Atchison to Topeka and ran its stagecoaches west up the Smoky Hill Trail from there. The first coaches started from Topeka on April 28.

The road moved slowly west. Most of the building crew was moved back to finish the short line connecting Leavenworth to the main line west of Wyandotte. The direction the road would go from the Republican River crossing at Junction City was still a question. Shoemaker still had his eyes set to the west up the Smoky Hill River Valley. There was no longer any point in going north to Fort Kearny. The Union Pacific out of Omaha already had 240 miles built, while the road out of Wyandotte had less than 120. A turn up the Republican to Fort Kearny would only divert traffic and freight out of Kansas to the Nebraska railroad.

Courtesy the Kansas State Historical Society, Topeka *From Gardner Collection*

Leavenworth — Fifth Street, 1867

It wasn't until July, however, that President Johnson signed the bill authorizing the railroad to proceed up the Smoky Hill Valley and on to Denver. All those involved celebrated that as a great day for the future of Kansas.[26]

NOTES

1. Joseph W. Snell and Robert W. Richmond, "When the Union and Kansas Pacific Built through Kansas," *Kansas Historical Quarterly* (Summer 1966), p. 161.
2. Alan W. Farley, "Samuel Hallett and the Union Pacific Railway Company in Kansas," *Kansas Historical Quarterly* (Spring 1959), p. 2.
3. Ibid., pp. 3–4.
4. Snell and Richmond, "Union and Kansas Pacific," pp. 161–2.
5. Farley, "Samuel Hallett," p. 5.
6. Snell and Richmond, "Union and Kansas Pacific," p. 164.
7. George L. Anderson, *Kansas West* (San Marino, Ca.: Golden West Books, 1963), p. 13.
8. *Wyandotte* (Kans.) *Gazette*, 12 September 1863.
9. *The Congregational Record* (Lawrence, Kans.), October 1862.
10. Farley, "Samuel Hallett," p. 6.
11. Ibid., p. 8.
12. Ibid., p. 9.
13. Snell and Richmond, "Union and Kansas Pacific," p. 174.
14. Farley, "Samuel Hallett," pp. 11–12. From the report of John D. Cruise, an eyewitness to the murder.
15. Ibid., p. 12.
16. (Lawrence) *Kansas Daily Tribune*, 17 November 1864.
17. Snell and Richmond, "Union and Kansas Pacific," p. 178.
18. O. P. Byers, "When Railroading Outdid the Wild West Stories," *Kansas Historical Collections, 1926–1928* 17 (1928), p. 341.
19. Anderson, *Kansas West*, p. 27.
20. Snell and Richmond, "Union and Kansas Pacific," p. 179.
21. Farley, "Samuel Hallett," pp. 14–15.
22. Anderson, *Kansas West*, p. 27.
23. Snell and Richmond, "Union and Kansas Pacific," p. 179.
24. Ibid., p. 180.
25. *Topeka Weekly Leader*, 4 January 1866.
26. Snell and Richmond, "Union and Kansas Pacific," p. 183.

CHAPTER 19

THE ENEMIES — INDIANS AND WEATHER

THE APPROVAL OF THE PLAN to send the railroad up the Smoky Hill Valley was greeted with great enthusiasm all along the eastern section of the railroad. Those towns would have been on the railroad whether the road went up the Republican or the Smoky Hill, but they saw great benefit in having the rails run the length of Kansas.

"This measure is now a law, and its importance to the State cannot be overestimated. This road will now run length-wise through the entire State, instead of deflecting to the northward for the benefit of Nebraska and Eastern interests, and will thus add millions to our taxable property, materially lessen the labor of the Company, and develop with unprecedented rapidity the beautiful country through which it will pass."[1]

Building proceeded at a much faster pace. Manhattan could barely wait for the rails to reach town. The bridge across the Blue River was not complete when the newspapers announced the arrival of the rails on the far side of the river.

> Hear! Here! We hear the whistle! The cars at last are here. Just over the river the iron horse is snorting. When he crosses the Blue River he will get some good clear water to drink. Workmen are engaged upon the R.R. Bridge, and in a short time trains will run over to the depot on this side. Farewell grief![2]

On August 20 the trains crossed the new bridge over the Blue for the first time. Even the Topeka papers took up the cheers for the advancement of the rails. "Since the 20th inst., passenger trains have been running through to Manhattan. Our neighbors of the 'Blue' are now within civilization."[3]

The rails pushed westward toward the Republican River crossing. Surveyors and graders were already far to the west, following the valley of the Smoky Hill.

The rails reached the Republican River at Junction City about the first of November. On November 6 a special excursion train ran from Leavenworth to Junction City. At the stop at Fort Riley, just outside Junction City, Bvt. Maj. Gen. George A. Custer and Bvt. Maj. Gen. John W. Davidson greeted those on the tour.[4]

After the decision was made to go up the Smoky Hill Valley, the rails pushed west from Junction City. By the end of November they were at Chapman Creek, near the spot where it empties into the Smoky Hill.

Courtesy the Kansas State Historical Society, Topeka *From Gardner Collection*

Manhattan, Kansas

Courtesy the Kansas State Historical Society, Topeka *From Gardner Collection*

Junction City, Kansas

Robert M. Shoemaker headed the company of Shoemaker, Miller and Co. that held the contract to build the railroad west to Fort Wallace. He traveled in a railroad car equipped with all the conveniences of a city hotel. The car was divided into four apartments — sitting room, dining room, bedroom, and kitchen. Every room was furnished with the most comfortable furniture, and the traveler could be at ease even in the roughest of surroundings.[5]

The cost of construction of the first 140 miles of the railroad averaged $65,203 a mile. The cost would go down to an average of $53,734 a mile for the next 265 miles. From there to Denver the cost would drop to $26,521 a mile.[6]

Railroad building had to stop for the winter with the grading crew just west of Fort Hays. Track-laying also stopped a few miles short of Abilene. Abilene, the county seat of Dickinson County, was looking forward to being a railroad town, but a letter written to the *Leavenworth Daily Conservative* in January 1867 describes the writer's trip to the end of the rails and then by stage to Fort Ellsworth. He predicted a dismal future for Abilene:

> Abilene has won a cheap immortality, from the fact that here our distinguished traveler [Bayard] got his first "square meal". It is to be a station on the Union Pacific Railway, and boasts of two hotels, a blacksmith shop, three or four saloons and two or three small stores. Yet I cannot say that I think its future, as a town, is very promising, as much of the land in its immediate vicinity is held by non-residents, as is nearly the whole area of Dickinson County; hence, population is sparse.[7]

A prairie blizzard on the last day of January halted all railroad travel. Two trains were stuck in the snow near Manhattan. Luckily both were freight trains. The passenger train that started on its eastward run from Junction City gave up and returned before it got stuck. The telegraph lines went down, and no one was sure which trains were stuck or where they were. The stagecoaches, now running out of Junction City, did not venture forth

Courtesy the Kansas State Historical Society, Topeka *From Gardner Collection*

Manhattan — water tank

Courtesy the Kansas State Historical Society, Topeka *From Gardner Collection*

Muddy Creek trestle near Abilene, Kansas

Courtesy the Kansas State Historical Society, Topeka *From Gardner Collection*

Salina — hotel and depot

Courtesy the Kansas State Historical Society, Topeka *From Gardner Collection*

Railroad bridge across the Republican River, Kansas

in the storm. The coach due in from the west did not arrive.[8]

When the weather warmed up the snow began to thaw, and rivers rose with the runoff. Floods rushed down the streams. The railroad bridge across the Republican River was washed out, and traffic to Junction City was halted. A temporary bridge was built as soon as the waters receded, and track-building resumed in March in spite of high water in the creeks.

Courtesy the Kansas State Historical Society, Topeka

"Mother" Bickerdyke

By March 23 the rails had reached Mud Creek at Abilene and went on toward the crossings of the Solomon and Saline rivers. The bridge at the Republican River was not considered completely safe, and locomotives did not cross it. Freight and passenger cars were pushed across one at a time, and locomotives on the other side hooked onto the cars.[9] April was another wet month, with floods along creeks and rivers. Traffic had great difficulty getting through. Junction City, sitting between the established route to the east and the newly opened road to the west, reported on conditions each week.

> Freight, mails and passengers have had a terrific time in attempting to go west by train, during the past two or three days. Some days the trains don't come or go. When they do, there is no knowing at what time of the day or night the occurrence will take place. One of the consequences is a great deal of heavy waiting at the depot. The old reliable Kansas Stage Company[10] is the only sure means of transit to the west at present.[11]

As the weather cleared and the land dried out, track was laid at the rate of a mile and a half a day. The rails reached Salina on April 16, but passenger service west of Junction City didn't begin until May 6.

A hotel was being built in Salina by Mother Bickerdyke that was to become the pride of the area. Mrs. Bickerdyke was a widow who served four years as a nurse in the Civil War and became known as Mother Bickerdyke. During the winter of 1866–67 she make a trip west by rail and stagecoach, looking for a place to build her hotel. She decided on Salina. She returned in the spring and began work. The railroad helped her. Mrs. Bickerdyke was a member of Edward Beecher's church, and she resolved that her hotel would be dedicated to temperance — a rarity on the Kansas plains. The building had thirty-two sleeping rooms and a large kitchen, and dining room.[12]

By the end of May the rails were approaching Ellsworth. Track-laying had speeded up considerably, the work being refined to an exact system. The Junction City paper described the work this way:

> A small car having been loaded in the same manner and with the same precision as the large ones had been, was run forward to the end of the track by horse-power. A couple of feet from the end of the rails already laid down checks were placed under the wheels, stopping the car at once. Before it was well stopped, a dozen men grasped a rail on each side, ran it beyond the car, laid it down in its chairs, gauged it, and ere its clank in falling ceased to reverberate, the car was run over it and another pair of rails drawn out. This process was continued as rapidly as a man would walk. Behind the car followed a man dropping spikes, another setting the ties well under the heads of the rails, and thirty or forty others driving in the spikes and stamping the earth under the ties. The moment that one car was emptied of its iron, a number of men seized it and threw it off the track into the ditch and the second followed on with its load.[13]

Farther west, where the surveying and grading crews were working, things were not running so smoothly. Indians began harrassing the workers shortly after they started work in the spring. Lt. Col. George Custer and the Seventh Cavalry were sent from Fort Riley up the Smoky Hill River, but they could be in only one place at a time, and the Indians seemed to be everywhere. They struck at places far from the spots the soldiers were guarding.

It was not entirely unexpected. The failure of the peace conference held at Fort Harker the year before had given warning that trouble could erupt as soon as the builders pushed into Indian territory.

The peace conference at Fort Harker had lasted three days. The Indians were represented by the leading chiefs and warriors of most of the Great Plains tribes. Besides top railroad officials, there were dozens of frontiersmen and interpreters, backed up a regiment of cavalry.

The Indians were not cowed by the display of force. They had an army of warriors within calling distance. There were many speeches made by Indian chiefs, army officers, and railroad officials. The railroad men first offered rewards for allowing the iron horse to go through the Indians' hunting ground. When that failed, they made threats. This had no more effect than the offer of rewards.

Still, it seemed there would be some accord reached as they neared the end of the third day of bargaining. Toward evening of the third day a huge Cheyenne, Roman Nose, stood up to make a speech. He was a chief of the dog soldiers of the Cheyennes, a big man with few adornments but a powerful physique. His speech was short but bitter and was against the railroad and its iron horses snorting through the Indians' hunting grounds, frightening the game away. The iron horse would also bring the white man to kill the buffalo and the Indian himself.

Within a few minutes Roman Nose had destroyed all the progress that had been made in the three days of talking. The Indians got up and stormed away from the conference. The white men, bitterly disappointed and apprehensive, went back to the fort.[14] The railroad men were determined to push into Indian territory. Once they passed Fort Harker they knew they would be inviting trouble.

In January 1867 the town of Ellsworth was laid out. It was four miles from the new Fort Harker but very close to the original Fort Ellsworth. Fort Ellsworth's name was changed to Fort Harker on November 11, 1866, and was moved a few miles to a new site in January 1867.[15]

Fort Ellsworth had been established in August 1864 on the banks of the Smoky Hill River as a protection for the military road between Fort Riley and Fort Zarah on the Arkansas River. Soldiers manning the post lived in dugouts along the river banks. It was a home station for the Butterfield Overland Despatch and became end-of-track as the railroad built west.

In the spring of 1867 General Hancock launched his campaign from Fort Harker to drive the Indians from the country. Instead of eliminating the Indian threat he instigated open warfare between Indians and railroad builders.

The plat of the town of Ellsworth was officially filed on May 8, 1867. It was already a good-sized town, as towns were then rated on the prairies.[16]

The Indians' craze to avenge Hancock's destruction of their village in April, plus their determination to stop the white man's encroachment into their hunting grounds, erupted in an attack on a railroad surveying crew near the newly designated station of Monument, in what is now Logan County.

The Indians hit the surveying crew about midmorning on Saturday, May 18. They drove off thirteen mules and fought the white men for four and a half hours. They were unable to overrun them, however, because the surveyors were well armed. The surveyors killed two or three Indians. When the Indians finally gave up the fight, the surveyors retreated to their main camp to the east, resolving to stay there until the army sent soldiers to protect them while they worked.[17]

Courtesy the Kansas State Historical Society, Topeka *From Gardner Collection*

Fort Harker — parade ground

Lt. Gen. William Sherman was commander of the Division of the Missouri. He wasn't convinced there was any need of army protection for the railroad men, and he refused to send any soldiers.

Late in May the *Junction City Weekly Union* criticized Sherman for his attitude, listing some of the reasons why the army should think that an Indian war was imminent. The *Union* stated that since April 15 the Indians had stolen sixty head of stock along the Smoky Hill River and had burned two stage stations, the stables at two others, and a great amount of hay. They killed two white men in the process. The *Union* felt there was just cause for alarm among the men who had to work along the western reaches of the Smoky Hill.[18]

On Saturday and Sunday, June 8 and 9, rain fell in torrents on Kansas. Rivers broke out of their banks and flooded entire valleys. The Smoky Hill and Republican rivers spread over thousands of acres of bottomland. No one had ever seen anything like it before. The last time the rivers had swelled to such proportions white men had not been there to record it.

Railroad bridges went out and grades were washed away, leaving track suspended on floating ties. Trains were stopped. Stagecoaches were also halted; they couldn't ford streams that had suddenly gone berserk. What had been wide grassy meadows were now covered with the waves of a moving ocean.

The rainy weather continued, and the runoff from the grassy hills kept the rivers churning like the digestive system of a tormented giant. On Saturday, June 15, a week after the rains began, some trains tried to run. One got through to Junction City from the west. Two others, one passenger train and one freight, failed. The passenger train reached a point four miles from town and slid off a washed-out grade, the locomotive and one passenger car dipping into four feet of muddy water. The freight train was derailed in a washout three miles farther west.[19]

The flood brought havoc to the new towns and forts along the river. Ellsworth suddenly found itself standing in four feet of water. Houses were washed off their foundations, and all business was brought to a drowning halt.[20] Fort Hays was inundated and had to move farther up Big Creek to a spot near the railroad grade.

John D. Perry, president of the Union Pacific Railway, Eastern Division, made a trip west through Kansas, riding the train as far as Junction City then taking the stagecoach to Fort Wallace. He returned near the end of June, alarmed by what he had found. He sent a telegram to Governor Crawford expressing his concern and asking for immediate protection for the railroad workers.

Courtesy the Kansas State Historical Society, Topeka

Gov. Samuel J. Crawford

He reported that three men had been killed and scalped by Indians within twenty miles of Fort Harker on June 22 and that a thousand workers had been driven from seventy-five miles of surveying and grading work west of Wilson's Creek, eighteen miles beyond Fort Harker.

Courtesy the Kansas State Historical Society, Topeka *From Gardner Collection*

Trestle bridge near Fort Harker, Kansas

R. M. Shoemaker reported two more men killed on June 24. Three days later another man was killed and one seriously wounded in a skirmish at Wilson's Creek. A few Indians were also killed in that encounter.

Governor Crawford, bombarded by these telegrams, got permission from General Sherman to organize a volunteer cavalry battalion to protect the railroad workers and the stage stations. Sherman was still reluctant to admit there was any real Indian trouble. He blamed the lack of train travel and especially stagecoach travel on the recent rains and floods and on people with contracts trying to get compensation and damage without working.[21]

Governor Crawford organized the Eighteenth Cavalry Battalion and sent it west to help subdue the Indians. While this was of some help, it was not enough. Shoemaker asked for arms and ammunition to give to his workers so they could protect themselves. The *Junction City Weekly Union* reported that four wagonloads of guns and ammunition left that town in late June, bound for the end of track and the stage stations to the west.

In spite of Indian harrassment the tracks reached Fort Harker. The first train arrived on July 1, 1867, to complete another link in the chain that would reach from the Missouri River to the Rocky Mountains.

At almost exactly the same time that the railroad reached Fort Harker, cholera arrived, too. It struck at many other places up and down the Smoky Hill Valley. The plague lasted about three weeks. Almost three hundred people died at Fort Harker. Another fifty died in nearby Ellsworth, a town of one thousand population that suddenly dwindled to almost nothing. People, fearing for their lives, packed up and fled. When the plague ended, only forty people were left in Ellsworth. Those forty, however, were of sturdy stock and had no intention of giving up.

Courtesy the Kansas State Historical Society, Topeka *From Gardner Collection*

Ellsworth — depot

The railroad continued to move west slowly, reaching Ellsworth on July 17. The following day the town company of Ellsworth approved the first additon to the town. This addition was not intended to expand the town; it was aimed at moving the whole town to higher ground, away from future floods.

In the new addition, lots corresponding to lots in the old town were set aside. So people could move their home and business to the new town on high ground. Within a short time all the buildings of old Ellsworth were in new Ellsworth except for what was known as the Stockade, and it was burned. Old Ellsworth was no more.[22]

As each twenty miles of track were completed the work had to be inspected before the government would approve payment. The inspections were often anything but thorough, as reported in the *Junction City Weekly Union*. They reprinted the report of a *Missouri Republican* correspondent who went on one of the inspection tours of a newly finished twenty-mile section of track.

> On reaching the beginning of the division or section to be examined the Commissioners, together with Mr. Shoemaker, the contractor, and myself rested ourselves comfortably in arm chairs on the rear platform, having a full review of the track. The train started, taking a speed of twenty-five miles per hour, and mile after mile passed under review of our gazing eyes, rails, ties, spikes, grade receded

Courtesy the Kansas State Historical Society, Topeka
Copied from Harper's Weekly, September 7, 1867

Cheyenne Indians attacking a working party on the Union Pacific Railroad, August 4, 1867.

from us, or we speeding away from them, as fast as a bird flies through the air. Fragrant Havanas were distributed, and through the clouds of smoke we inspected the track. Next we looked at it through a bottle of Concord wine, and all looked rosy and good.

The medium examination was greatly improved by a bottle of the best of Bourbon from Nickleson's and through its amber or golden hues the prospect was charming, and all of the kinks and crooks of the track straightened out — the line was straight and smooth. The finishing touch was put on, when glasses of claret punch, excellently compounded, were placed in our hands by a colored gentleman, and through the rosy shades of this conciliating and charming medium, the three commissioners and myself took our final view of the well-built track, and the inspection was over, for by this time we had traversed the twenty-four miles — spending an hour in the arduous work, and viewed the road through media which clarified the vision, sharpened the judgment, inspired good nature and prepared us to make a most satisfactory report.[23]

Governor Crawford made a trip to Hays in September to see how work was progressing on the railroad and to get a personal look at the Indian trouble that General Sherman didn't believe existed. Crawford returned convinced. He reported there were Indians everywhere along the Smoky Hill River west of Fort Harker. They fired their rifles into a construction train while Governor Crawford was there. They captured parts of three trains and made attacks on working crews all along the line. They killed one contractor and eight workmen and wounded many more. Crawford was quite indignant about the lack of military protection for workers on the road.[24]

The governor sent a telegram to Sherman at Omaha, outlining what he had seen. The general didn't even bother to reply, apparently still not convinced there was real trouble on the railroad in western Kansas.

The war between the Indians and the iron horse went on.

NOTES

1. *Junction City* (Kans.) *Weekly Union*, 14 July 1866.
2. (Manhattan) *Kansas Radical*, 4 August 1866.
3. *Topeka Weekly Leader*, 23 August 1866.
4. Joseph W. Snell and Robert W. Richmond, "When the Union and Kansas Pacific Built through Kansas," *Kansas Historical Quarterly* (Summer 1966), p. 186.
5. *Junction City Weekly Union*, 8 December 1866.
6. George L. Anderson, *Kansas West* (San Marino, Ca.: Golden West Books, 1963), p. 21.
7. *Leavenworth Daily Conservative*, 24 January 1867.
8. Snell and Richmond, "Union and Kansas Pacific," p. 336.
9. Ibid. Although great stockpiles of material were at the end of track, new material was needed constantly. Communications with the head offices in the east were poor.
10. This stage line was the B.O.D. Since it sold to Ben Holladay in March 1866 and to Wells Fargo in the fall of 1866, it was now, in the spring of 1867, operated by Wells Fargo.
11. *Junction City Weekly Union*, 20 April 1867.
12. Snell and Richmond, "Union and Kansas Pacific," p. 337.
13. *Junction City Weekly Union*, 15 June 1867.
14. Floyd Benjamin Streeter, *The Kaw* (New York: Farrar & Rinehart, 1941), pp. 83–4.
15. George Jelinek, "The Ellsworth Story," *Ellsworth* (Kans.) *Reporter*, 3 August 1967.
16. Ibid.
17. Snell and Richmond, "Union and Kansas Pacific," p. 338.
18. Ibid., p. 338.
19. Ibid., pp. 338–9.
20. Jelinek, "Ellsworth Story."
21. Snell and Richmond, "Union and Kansas Pacific," p. 341.
22. Jelinek, "Ellsworth Story."
23. *Junction City Weekly Union*, 17 August 1867; reprinted from the *Missouri Republican*.
24. Snell and Richmond, "Union and Kansas Pacific," p. 343.

CHAPTER 20

WEST FROM FORT HARKER

IN SPITE OF SOLDIERS AS GUARDS, crews continued to have trouble as they built the railroad west from Fort Harker. Even the trains were attacked when they ventured out on the new rails. The Indians were convinced that this iron horse snorting across their hunting grounds would mean the end of their normal existence, and they fought to turn the metal monster back.

Nor was all the trouble west of Fort Harker. The Indians apparently decided to destroy one of the iron horse's stables to the east and thus prevent it from coming any farther into their hunting grounds. If it had not been for the warning given the little town of Brookville by a train coming from the west, the Indians might have succeeded in wiping out the town and destroying the roundhouse.

Brookville was about twenty miles east of Fort Harker and sixteen miles southwest of Salina. There was a big roundhouse there, with a turntable where engines could be serviced and repaired.

The train coming in from Fort Harker stopped to warn the citizens of the little town that they had seen a large war party of Indians to the west coming toward Brookville.

Living on the edge of civilization, the townspeople needed only one warning. An alarm was sounded, and everyone in town gathered quickly. It was decided to make a stand in the roundhouse, which was almost in the center of town.

There were several engines in the roundhouse, and everyone got inside among the engines. The doors were barricaded. They didn't have long to wait. There were a great many Indians, enough to have wiped out the town if the people had not been warned.

Their objective was obvious — to destroy the stable of iron horses and kill all the people. They surrounded the roundhouse, shooting and yelling. The people inside, snuggled among the engines, were in little danger of being hit.

Then someone watching at a window shouted that the Indians were piling railroad ties against the building. Everyone knew what that meant. Fire!

An immediate conference settled on a desperate solution. An engine which had been steamed up out on the track had been run into the roundhouse when the warning of the raid was given. It was still steamed up. They turned the engine toward the door leading to Salina, the closest town. Under full power the engine crashed through the unopened door and dashed up the track toward Salina, whistle blasting as it broke free of the roundhouse.

It not only got a messenger through for help, but it also had a devastating effect on the Indians. They were in awe of the big iron horses, anyway. To see one burst through barricaded doors, whistle screaming, was more than their nerves could stand. They broke for the open prairies to the northwest and disappeared, allowing

Courtesy the Kansas State Historical Society, Topeka

Brookville — view in 1870s

the citizens of Brookville to go to their homes and resume their precarious lives on the edge of constant trouble.[1]

Ellsworth was just a budding town when it had a visitor whose name would soon become a familiar sound on the frontier, William F. Cody. Here Cody met a man named Rose who had a contract to grade the roadbed for the railroad far to the west of Ellsworth. Rose owned some land up Big Creek from Fort Hays. It was on the right-of-way for the railroad and would make a fine site for a town. He needed a partner, and he found an eager listener in Bill Cody.

Cody and Rose surveyed their townsite and staked out lots. They built a cabin and stocked it with supplies to sell, then gave their new town the name of Rome. Cody and Rose reserved the corner lots on the blocks and offered other lots free to anyone who would build on the land. In less than sixty days there were two hundred cabins in Rome.

Photo by Author

Brookville Hotel, 1870, on B.O.D., Brookville, Kansas

Courtesy the Kansas State Historical Society, Topeka

William F. Cody

Courtesy the Kansas State Historical Society, Topeka

Fort Hays — trader's store

Courtesy the Kansas State Historical Society, Topeka *From Gardner Collection*

Hays City, Kansas

The town had been started early in May, and by the end of June it was a bustling city. Neither Cody nor Rose had any doubts whatsoever that this was going to be one of the biggest cities in Kansas.[2]

One day in June they had a visitor at their store, a man who called himself Dr. W. E. Webb, a well-dressed prosperous-looking man. He seemed friendly enough, but before he ended his visit he suggested that the two men needed another partner in their town.

If there was one thing Rose and Cody didn't want, it was another partner. They were becoming rich dividing the income from their brainchild two ways. They didn't want to share the fortune with another man who had done nothing to make the new town prosper. They politely turned down the offer.

It was then that Webb explained who he was. He was locating towns for the Union Pacific as it moved west. He thought Rome was an ideal site for a town and wanted to place the depot and railroad shop here. To do that the Union Pacific would demand a partnership in the town. Rose and Cody knew they had a good thing in Rome, and they didn't intend to share it. Besides, they were certain that they had the only site within miles where water could be found by drilling. They again refused Webb's offer.

Webb didn't insist. He left, and within a day or two Cody and Rose saw him staking out a town within sight of Rome. Residents of Rome went over to the new site and watched, making remarks about the foolishness of anyone laying out a town without first finding water.

Webb said the town would have water. He persuaded a well driller to set up his rig in the newly platted town of Hays City.

Courtesy the Kansas State Historical Society, Topeka

Fort Hays — officers' quarters about 1880.

Courtesy the Kansas State Historical Society, Topeka
Copied from Harper's Weekly, December 14, 1867
Shooting buffalo from Kansas Pacific

Courtesy the Kansas State Historical Society, Topeka *From Gardner Collection*
Abilene — prairie dog at prairie dog town

Each day every idle person in Rome went to Hays City to watch the well driller and hoot at him. The ground was extremely hard, and the driller soon pounded his mallet to bits trying to sink the drill into the ground.

The driller became discouraged and the residents of Rome triumphant. Still the driller worked, pounding several pieces of cordwood to splinters on the drill. Finally it sent back a sound that he recognized, and his features brightened.

"There she is!" he shouted.

Hays City had water.[3]

That was only the first blow to hit Rome. Webb quickly announced that the railroad shops and the depot would be in Hays City. Almost overnight Rose and Cody saw their people swarm over to Hays City, dragging with them the shacks they had built on the free lots.[4]

Courtesy the Kansas State Historical Society, Topeka
Ellis — Kansas Pacific roundhouse — 1870s; Ellis is the first station west of Hays.

Then came July and the cholera plague. Cholera did to Rome what it was doing to every other community along the Smoky Hill River where it got a foothold: Rome was decimated. But when the plague was gone there were still people in Rome, hanging on and trying to make it the town they had dreamed it would be.

The flood that swept the area in June had not hurt Rome a great deal. Fort Hays, down toward the Smoky Hill, had been inundated and had moved, establishing itself near Hays City. It was also near Rome, but that was going to do little for the fading town now. The Eternal City, as some derisively called it, showed few signs of being eternal.

In spite of the blows that had befallen it Rome was still alive in the fall of 1867 when George Martin, editor of the *Junction City Weekly Union*, took a trip to the end of track, just to the east of Hays City, and rode on to Hays City to inspect it and its neighbor, Rome. He reported in his paper:

> Big Creek flows from the north between the two places. Rome, we understand, is not so far advanced as is Hays City, but if the people of the latter place are not actuated by local envy, Rome must then be the Mecca to which rushes all the males and females of loose virtue and bad morals. Indeed, the question as to which is THE town had been determined, and the excitement had centered

on the stupendous one as to which side of the track the depot would be built. We found a tolerable fair hotel, but the next morning, before starting homeward, we endeavored to find some crackers for lunch, but whiskey was the only commodity to be found.[5]

The tracks reached Hays City at last, and passenger trains began making regular runs between Ellsworth and Hays City on October 15, 1867. Hays City was well within the range of the buffalo herds roaming the prairies then, and it was no uncommon sight to see great herds passing the town.

Nor was its uncommon for people on the trains to see buffalo. Often it was a inconvenience. The buffalo had a peculiar habit (some called it instinct) which seemed to force it to cross in front of any moving object.

The speed of the trains on the prairies was slow. The maximum speed allowed passenger trains was eighteen miles an hour. A buffalo could run faster than that, at least for a short distance. The maximum speed allowed freight trains was only nine miles an hour. Likely those who ruled the railroads had misgivings about the safety of their new grades and tracks.[6]

In the spring and fall the buffalo migrated across the plains, wintering in the south where the snow would not cover the grass and moving back to the north in the spring when the new grass was abundant. During these migrations anything moving across the prairies was liable to be stopped while an entire herd of buffalo crossed in front of it.

Often buffalo a mile from the railroad tracks would be alarmed by the snorting iron monster and would charge, usually toward it, apparently determined to cross in front of it. The herd often underestimated the speed of the train and would be cut off by the cars. Then they would turn up the track in the direction of the train, as if determined to get ahead and cross its path. Many buffalo were killed or wounded by men on the train who delightedly jerked open a window and shot the animals running parallel to their line of travel. If they scored a hit, it meant that that animal would be totally wasted, meat, hide, and all.[7]

Sometimes some of the aroused herd would be far enough ahead of the train that their charge toward the tracks would get them there ahead of the engine. Then they would lumber across the tracks in an unending stream, and the iron horse would have to admit defeat and stop. Stories of such happenings often appeared in the papers to the east of the land of the buffalo.

The train was intercepted by whole herds of buffaloes and compelled to halt until they had crossed the track!

For three miles the buffaloes pushed along parallel with the train, heedless of many shots fired among them, and finally swept across the track, ahead of the locomotive, fairly worsing the iron horse by bringing him to a halt.[8]

Many Indians seemed to have a terrible fear of the rails. They would ride miles parallel to the tracks rather than cross them. Only when they found a bridge where they could ride under the tracks would they cross to the other side.[9]

Work on the railroad stopped during the coldest part of the winter. With the spring of 1868 work moved into full swing again, and the Indians renewed their war against the iron horse. They captured a train west of Coyote as it was moving material toward the end of track. They burned the train, but reports didn't list any casualties.

This caused renewed concern about protection of the workers, and Company A of the Thirty-eighth Infantry was assigned to the area west of Coyote.[10]

The track finally reached the station of Monument, well north and west of Monument Station on the B.O.D. The track was opened to traffic on June 1, 1868. From this station west to Denver by stagecoach would take only forty-two hours, according to the *Junction City Weekly Union*. The big worry among the builders now was the government subsidy. The contract called for the subsidy only to Mile 411 — a few miles east of Fort Wallace and about two hundred and forty miles from Denver. The builders were going to reach this milepost soon.

Monument was at Mile 386. Like all other end-of-track towns along the Union Pacific, it exploded into existence with no planning and very few controls. It was expected to be wild; it wouldn't fit the pattern if it were not. A reporter gave this summary of it.

> Monument, the new town started last week on the U.P. Railway, already contains a population of five hundred souls, and up to 12 o'clock last night not a man had been shot or hung in that city, which speaks volumes for the moral worth of its citizens.[11]

Another correspondent for an eastern Kansas newspaper was in Monument a few days later and described the ninety-five miles to Hays as a land where "not a tree or shrub relieved the monotonous landscape of level, parched prairie."

Hays drew the reporter's greatest attention, perhaps because it was still alive, while most bypassed end-of-track towns had died and disappeared:

> This city is the western frontier town of Kansas. From the few observations we have made while here, we judge Hays is probably not quite as moral or virtuous as Beecher's town of Norwood. Of its hundred or more places of business, there are very few places where liquor is not sold, and a drunken man does not excite any surprise. It is certainly a paradise for local editors, and a poor place for lawyers, the men generally preferring to do their own lawing, and in their own way.[12]

During the summer many excursion trips were made from eastern Kansas to the end of the track, giving easterners their first view of the vast treeless plains they claimed as part of their state. Many comments were made by the travelers. Probably none included more details than a letter written by one who made the journey from Topeka to Monument that summer.

It was a two-day trip, beginning in the early dawn of a Thursday morning and ending at "two and a half o'clock" on Saturday morning. The writer of the letter was a young man named John Putnam. He remarks at the end of this letter that they traveled almost seven hundred miles in less than forty-five hours. Too fast, too fast! Too fast for pleasure.[13]

The excursion was made up of a group of young men and young ladies who apparently felt it was going to be the trip of a lifetime. From Putnam's letter it is obvious that none of them had ever been west of Topeka before.

Putnam describes the "Great American Desert," the prairie dogs and buffalo, and the attempts of the passengers to shoot both. They made it to Hays City in the evening, where they met Wild Bill Hickok and got their first look at a wild town.

At Hays the ladies received an invitation to sleep in beds "in a nice house in town" instead of trying to sleep in the railroad car. It was eleven o'clock before the decision was made by some of the young ladies to accept the invitation. Sleeping in the seats in the car didn't promise to be very comfortable. A party of young men gallantly offered to escort the girls to the place where they were to have the nice beds. They didn't know where the house was. The name of the man who had issued the invitation was Joyce, so they began asking for the residence of Mr. Joyce.

They were told that it was next to Pat Murphy's saloon or right opposite the Prairie Flower Dance House. That didn't sound like the nice quiet residence they had been led to believe was waiting for them.

With misgivings they went on, but they had to get the help of Wild Bill Hickok to find the "quiet residence" of Mr. Joyce. What they found was a wooden shanty in the noisiest part of town. The shack was locked, with one candle buring inside. There was no key, so they peeked through the window. They saw the "nice clean beds" they had been promised — three blankets spread on the floor between spatterings of tobacco juice. The ladies suddenly decided that the chairs on the train compared favorably with the "nice clean beds in a nice quiet residence" and headed back with their escorts to the train. They were told that the owner of the shanty was probably out on a spree and would be back in a short time to greet his guests, but the guests were reluctant to wait.[14] In all probability this was Judge Marcellus E. Joyce, who was presiding in Hays City at that time. He was rapidly building a reputation for twisting the legal statutes to fit any situation as he saw it.

Joyce was a small red-haired Irishman who enjoyed his "cup of joy" as much as any cowboy and more than a solemn judge should. His office was a dilapidated shack on main street in Hays City, with one door and high windows with wide sills.

In one instance he fined a man $40 and then discovered he was penniless. Joyce wanted the money. By chance he asked the identity of a stranger in the room and learned he was the brother of the convicted man and that he had money. The judge quickly changed his sentence. "The fine is on you, then," he shouted — and collected his fine.

When a sharp young lawyer threatened to appeal Judge Joyce's verdict the judge quickly informed him there was no higher court so there could be no "appale." He said he would fine the lawyer for contempt if he disagreed. The lawyer backed down.

According to one story $500 was appropriately placed to assure the acquittal of a man accused of murder. When the man stepped in front of Judge Joyce and was asked now he pled, he said, "Guilty." The judge exploded. "Guilty! Well, yees are a big fool to plade that way, and I discharge yees for want of ividence." The ruling stuck.[15]

A minor case came before him late one afternoon concerning the ownership of a heifer. Both judge and jurors were a little under the weather from too many trips to the adjacent saloons during breaks. The judge decided the jury must see the brand on the heifer, so he sent the sheriff to bring the animal. By the time the sheriff had the heifer at the door of the courtroom the jury had decided not a man of them was going outside to look at a heifer; if the judge wanted them to see it the sheriff could just bring it inside. The judge, as inebriated as the jury by now, ordered the sheriff to bring the "baste" inside.

All acceded to the judge's order except the heifer — she balked at the door. Tempers flared as the sheriff and his helpers tried to get the animal inside the courtroom. Finally the sheriff gave the heifer's tail a terrific twist when she had her head pointed toward the door. This account tells the rest of the story:

> The now enraged beast, with horns lowered and bawling with pain, incontinently rushed into the presence of the "coort" regardless of the sanctity of the place. It did not take a moment for the spectators at the trial to make good their escape by the door as the infuriated creature made a break for the little redheaded judge, who, the moment he saw the state affairs had assumed, got down prone upon the floor close to the wall, where the table under which he had crept shielded him from the horns of the heifer, who made several attempts to "get at his fat little person." The jury, suddenly sobered at the apparition of the maddened beast, took refuge on the broad sills of the windows, where they remained while the heifer tore around and demolished everything loose within her reach, after which she rushed out and down the prairie, which ended the proceedings of that trial for all time.[16]

A high wind came up that night, and the young men of the party who had slept in blankets outside the railroad cars, were buffeted around until they were fearful of their lives. None of them had ever encountered a prairie gale before. According to John Putnam's words, "It sweeps over a smooth level surface for hundreds of miles without the least obstacle, and it gets down to the ground like a race horse and gets up a rate of speed fearful to feel."

The group survived the night, and the train moved on to Monument the next day. Everyone was then ready to return. The train went back without an overnight stop, reaching Topeka before the dawn of a new day, the party of sightseers weary, bedraggled, and much, much wiser.[17]

NOTES

1. O. P. Byers, "When Railroading Outdid the Wild West Stories," *Kansas Historical Collections, 1926–1928* 17 (1928), p. 343.
2. Helen Cody Wetmore, *Buffalo Bill, Last of the Great Scouts* (Chicago: Duluth Press, 1899), p. 146.
3. Floyd Benjamin Streeter, *The Kaw* (New York: Farrar & Rinehart, 1941), p. 84–85.
4. Wetmore, *Buffalo Bill*, p. 147.
5. *Junction City* (Kans.) *Weekly Union*, 12 October 1867.
6. Byers, "Railroading," p. 345. One of the strictest rules trainmen had to follow was to make sure a train had enough brakes to hold it going downgrade. This was to be checked before each trip. Good brakes and low speeds were essential to safety on trips over the new road.
7. Robert W. Richmond and Robert W. Mardock, *A Nation Moving West* (Lincoln: Univ. of Nebraska Press, 1966), pp. 275–6.
8. *Junction City Weekly Union*, 2 November 1867. This particular incident occurred just west of Ellsworth.
9. Byers, "Railroading," p. 346.
10. Joseph W. Snell and Robert W. Richmond, "When the Union and Kansas Pacific Built through Kansas," *Kansas Historical Quarterly* (Autumn 1966), p. 345.
11. *Junction City Weekly Union*, 13 June 1868.
12. (Lawrence) *Kansas Weekly Tribune*, 18 June 1868.
13. John H. Putnam, "A Trip to the End of the Union Pacific in 1868," *Kansas Historical Quarterly* (August 1944), p. 201. Actually, the rail distance between Topeka and Monument was 318 miles, so the round trip was only 636 miles.
14. Ibid., pp. 196–200.
15. This may have been the trial of the scout, William Comstock, for killing the wood contractor, Wyatt, at Fort Wallace.
16. *Topeka State Journal*, 20 June 1890. Article written by Henry Inman.
17. Putnam, "A Trip," p. 202–3.

CHAPTER 21

THE LAST MILE TO DENVER

AFTER BILL CODY ESCAPED from his disastrous experience in town building (losing the battle of Rome versus Hays City) he continued with his grading contract for the railroad. An incident happened one day close to Fort Hays that led to Cody's future job after his contract had been completed.

Cody had bought a horse from a Ute Indian from Utah. The animal was fleet-footed and had a complete knowledge of hunting buffalo. Cody aptly called him Brigham.[1] He had also acquired a rifle that he swore by. It was a needle gun, a .50 calibre Springfield rifle converted to breechloading. It got its name from the needlelike firing pin. Cody had picked a name for his rifle, too. He called it Lucretia Borgia, apparently for a character in a play he had seen.[2] With the well-trained horse and the good rifle he felt he was able to kill more buffalo than any other man.

Brigham had to be used on a scraper at times, to keep the grading work going. It was on one of these occasions that someone spotted a small herd of buffalo on a hill ahead. The camp was low on meat, and Cody quickly unhitched the horse from the scraper and mounted him bareback, since the saddle was back at camp. Grabbing his rifle, he took out for the buffalo herd.

This was close to Fort Hays. Before Cody caught up with the herd he overtook some soldiers from the fort who had also sighted the buffalo. There were five of them, all officers. Seeing Cody on the bareback horse they took pity on him and

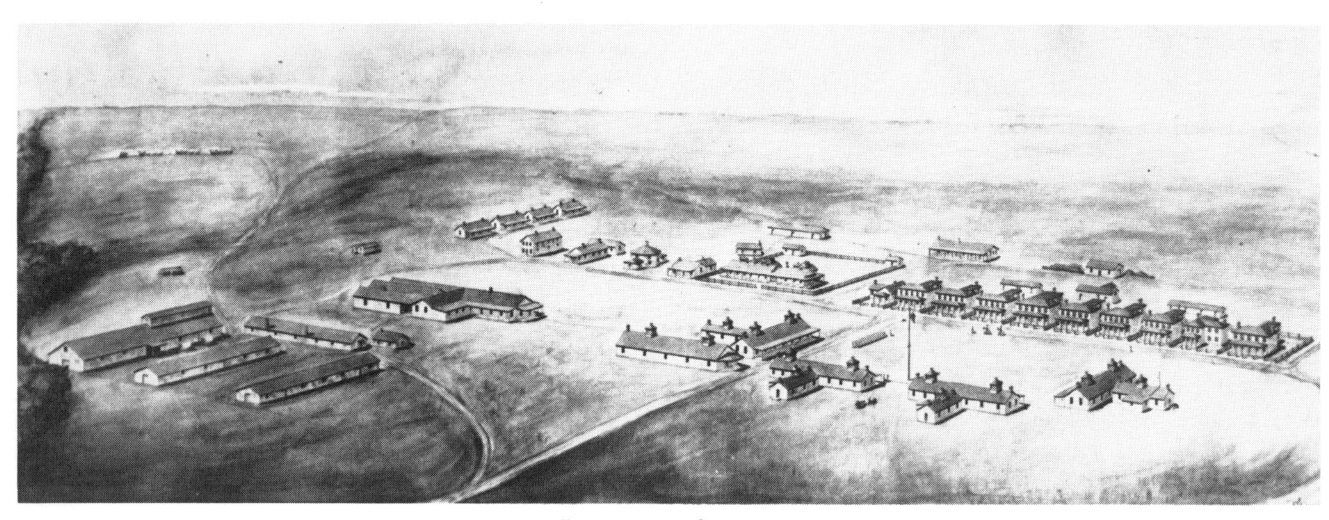

Bird's-eye view of Fort Hays

suggested he might follow them and learn how to kill buffalo. Cody agreed.

When the officers started charging the herd Cody made a quick survey and decided the buffalo were heading for the river. Nothing — certainly not a few soldiers poorly armed for buffalo hunting — was going to change their course. Cody reined Brigham toward the creek, coming up on the flank of the herd while the officers were hundreds of yards in the rear.

With his needle gun Cody brought down the first buffalo, Brigham quickly took him alongside another animal. Before the herd was gone Cody had brought down eleven buffalo, while the army officers were still far to the rear. They never got close enough for even one shot. They were very disappointed and disgusted at their failure; they were also very impressed by what they had seen of the bareback rider killing buffalo.[3]

Some sources refer to this incident as the beginning of Bill Cody's nickname of Buffalo Bill. Shortly after this Cody's job of supplying meat for the railroad added to the aptness of the name, and there were few who challenged his right to it after that.

Cody's contract was with Goddard Brothers, who had taken the job of feeding the workers. It called for twelve buffalo a day; there were more than twelve hundred men to feed.[4] His pay was $500 a month.

Most agree that the name, Buffalo Bill, was stamped indeliby on Cody during his buffalo-hunting days for the railroad crews. There were other Buffalo Bills in the western plains country, but none achieved the publicity given Buffalo Bill Cody.

Some historians attribute the final winning of the name by Cody to his buffalo-killing contest with Bill Comstock, the famous scout who was then stationed at Fort Wallace.

Comstock was a colorful character in his own right. Many claimed he was called Buffalo Bill and that the contest between him and Cody resulted from a challenge to prove which had the right to bear the name. However, most men who knew Comstock said he was known as Medicine Bill, not Buffalo Bill. He got his name from the Indians, with whom he lived off and on for some time.[5]

Comstock was a grandnephew of James Fenimore Cooper. His father was a state senator in Michigan and a wealthy man. Young William had every opportunity to get a good education and live in style if not in ease.

But Comstock had a yearning for adventure and the western frontiers. He was only sixteen when news of the gold strike in the Pike's Pike area swept the country and he answered the lure of the yellow metal.

He covered a great deal of the West, living as much with the Indians as with the white men. He was fresh from a job as scout for Fort Halleck in Wyoming when he arrived at Fort Wallace.[6]

It was probably in June 1868 that the contest between Comstock and Cody was staged. Exactly why it was staged is still clouded in the smoke screens of legend. Some said it was to prove the right to bear the name of Buffalo Bill; others said it was a contest between the rival forts, Fort Hays and Fort Wallace, each putting up its best buffalo hunter.

The contest was staged near the end of track and apparently drew a great deal of interest. Some reports say a special excursion train brought people all the way from St. Louis, including Mrs. Cody. Railroad men, plainsmen, and even soldiers took the day off to witness the hunt.[7]

No one recorded the exact day of the contest, but it can be generalized with some accuracy. Since the train brought the excursion group from St. Louis to witness the hunt and it has been definitely established that the hunt took place just a short

Courtesy the Kansas State Historical Society, Topeka *From Gardner Collection*

"Westward, the Course of Empire Takes its Way." Laying track six hundred miles west of St. Louis, Missouri.

distance west of Monument (Cody's own account said twenty miles east of Sheridan, which would put it almost exactly two miles west of Monument), it had to be some time after the trains made their first run to Monument on June 1. Comstock was killed August 16 of that year, so the hunt had to take place between those two dates.

At the site, a referee was assigned to each hunter to keep exact score of the number of kills made. Comstock was armed with a Henry repeating rifle, lighter than Cody's rifle. Cody was using Lucretia, his .50 caliber Springfield needle gun. He was mounted on his buffalo horse, Brigham.

A herd was in sight. The signal was given, and the two hunters rode together until the buffalo started running. Then they separated, each going after a segment of the herd. Comstock rode directly after his, firing his repeating Henry and bringing down the animals at the rear of the running herd. Cody circled his herd, shooting the leaders if they tried to break away. The others, confused, continued to run in a circle. When the first half of the hunt was over, Cody had thirty-eight, all in a small area. Comstock had killed twenty-three, but they were strung out over a distance of three miles.[8]

Champagne was served then, according to the reports. Archaeologists have found enough hand-blown beer and champagne bottles to feel certain they can pinpoint the exact location.

While they were enjoying their refreshments, another buffalo herd made the mistake of showing up. The two hunters once again mounted their horses and went after more trophies. In this run Cody killed eighteen and Comstock fourteen.

Moving on to another spot where they found more buffalo, the two hunters made a third and final run. Here Cody killed fourteen, making his final score for the day sixty-nine. Comstock killed nine more, giving him a total of forty-six.[9]

The best buffalo heads were mounted by the railroad and distributed throughout the east to advertise the country where the railroad could take its passengers.[10]

Cody's contract for supplying buffalo meat for the railroad crews didn't end until the railroad reached Sheridan. During that time, almost a year and a half, he killed 4,280 buffalo for the railroad.[11]

The rails were rapidly reaching the end of the section for which the contract had been signed. At the end of that section a town erupted out of the prairie. Sheridan was like all the other end-of-track towns, except that it promised to last longer. The rails had moved swiftly past other end-of-track towns, but here the contract and the money ran out.

One correspondent reported: "The

Courtesy the Kansas State Historical Society, Topeka

Fort Hays — buffalo hunt near Fort Hays, 1869

Union Pacific, E. D., will be finished to Sheridan by the middle of the month, where I understand the intention is to stop the work until additional subsidy is obtained, and as this cannot be done until the next meeting of Congress, it will probably be some time ere work will be resumed."[12]

A few weeks later this report appeared: "All of Shoemaker, Miller & Co.'s men, at the end of the track, have been paid off and discharged."[13]

Sheridan was to be the end of track for more than a year, and it earned the reputation of being one of the toughest towns in the West. It boasted of several things that helped make it boom. Besides being the western end of track and the eastern terminal of the Butterfield Overland Despatch, it was the rail headquarters for the Santa Fe trade. The freight wagons came to the end of track with produce from the Spanish settlement at Santa Fe and took back supplies for the town. Sheridan was the eastern terminal of the Santa Fe trade for a longer time than any other end-of-track town.[14]

To give an idea of the magnitude of the trade to the southwest, Richmond and Mardock reports: "In a single day five carloads of freight bound for Santa Fe were unloaded."[15]

Sheridan was established in June 1868 when it became the headquarters of the grading crews working on the roadbed. The town was located on the North Fork of the Smoky Hill River, approximately 395 miles west of Kansas City, and was named for Gen. Phil Sheridan, who was then stationed at Fort Hays.

Law and order were words without meaning in Sheridan, as they had been in the other end-of-track towns. The counties in this unsettled country were enormous in size and usually meant little more than

Courtesy the Kansas State Historical Society, Topeka

Sheridan — buffalo hunter's home, 1870s.

a name designation for a vast tract of land. For instance, for some time Wallace County in western Kansas stretched from the west side of Ellis County, of which Hays was the county seat, to the Kansas-Colorado border. Kit Carson County extended from that same Kansas-Colorado border all the way to Denver, a distance of about two hundred miles.[16]

It was little wonder that Sheridan earned its wicked reputation. During that road-building layoff, many railroad workers stayed around Sheridan to be close in case work began again. On hand were the usual segments of camp followers, gamblers, prostitutes, and card sharks. Also, Sheridan was only about fifteen miles from Fort Wallace, and the army stationed a company of soldiers at Sheridan to handle the freight coming in for the fort. Many Mexican freighters from Santa Fe were in town most of the time. The buffalo hunters, who were following General Sheridan's advice to get rid of the buffalo so the Indians would starve and move peaceably to the reservations, were bringing their hides to the nearest railroad — which was Sheridan.

This was a motley mixture that fostered a variety of violence. With neither law nor newspapers to curb the most vicious violence, it was little wonder that vigilantes took over.

Just east of town was a railroad trestle over a dry wash that served as a perfect gallows. Many a misguided soul who thought he had found a place where nothing could prevent him from working his mischief to his own profit discovered his mistake when he was suddenly rousted from his sleep in the wee hours of the night by an angry citizenry. After a very brief and most informal trial he was led to the trestle and there dropped almost to the sand below. The rope had been measured to exactness so that his boots failed by a few inches to reach the sand.

There were two buttes across the creek southwest of town which were called by a variety of names. History records they were named Hurlbut and Lawrence. They were popularly called Twin Buttes or Mexican Buttes.

One of the first additions to the town was the graveyard. Before a single street had been surveyed a grave was placed on the high ridge north of town. This ridge quickly became the town's cemetery. Three men went to their final bed on the hill during the first week of Sheridan's existence. Before the winter was over, there were twenty-six graves, and none was filled as a result of natural causes. The common threat that circulated around Sheridan was, "I'll give you a high lot," which everyone understood to be six feet of sand up on Boot Hill.[17]

Life in the town was loose and easy and often fatal. It led one historian to say: "Morals in this mushroom town were among the articles of commerce. No one tried to possess any, unless money was to be made by it. From motives of courtesy, occasional women were called wives, but it was well to avoid inquisitiveness on the subject."[18]

On March 2, 1869, the name of the Union Pacific Railway, Eastern Division, was changed to Kansas Pacific Railway Company. Money from the government was sought to continue the line to Denver, where it could connect with lines running north to the transcontinental Union Pacific Railroad.[19]

Although Congress had passed the bill changing the name of the line to Kansas Pacific, it wasn't until April that the name was formally accepted by the stockholders of the Union Pacific, Eastern Division, who met in Lawrence, Kansas, on April 5, 1869.[20]

It was fall before construction of the railroad beyond Sheridan actually got under way in full swing. By October the grading was progressing at full speed once again. There was delay in getting the track laid because of some culvert and bridge work just west of Sheridan. Until that was finished the train couldn't bring the iron to the grade.[21]

This was soon completed, however, and by November 20 the *Junction City Weekly Union* could report that the rails were laid to a spot within twelve miles of the Colorado border. Fort Wallace was at last connected by rail to Fort Hays and Harker to the east without the fifteen-mile gap that had existed for well over a year between the end of the rails and the fort.

By the middle of January Eagle Tail (present-day Sharon Springs) was the destination of trains going west, and it became the eastern terminal of the stage line to Denver.[22] The rails were reaching west, but winter had slowed their progress.

Spring speeded up the work again and also brought back the Indians. Graders were killed in eastern Colorado, but the work went on — as it had in Kansas. By the end of July the Denver papers could report there was only a fifty-four mile gap between the end of the rails and Denver.

The contractors had set August 15 as the day to finish laying the track. However, when the day came there were still ten-and-a-quarter miles of track to be laid on the ties. The crews working from the east had run out of iron, and the rails had been hauled to them in wagons from Denver just the day before.

At dawn on August 15 the crews began work at top speed, determined to meet the self-imposed deadline. Skeptics were amazed at the rate the rails were put down. The *Rocky Mountain News* was lavish in its praise the next day:

> Every arrangement was complete, and the two forces under Eicholtz had Weed proceeded to make the word of the company good and join the rails of the Kansas Pacific, making it continuous from the mountains to the father of waters. . . . The gap was filled up, the last rail laid and the last spike driven at three o'clock, making ten and one-fourth miles in ten hours. This surpasses anything in the history of railway laying ever known in the country. The fastest time made was by Col. Weed, who laid the first mile in 55 minutes.[23]

A huge dinner was set up for the workers in Denver, including ice cream, champagne, and cigars. It was a great day for all.

But the trip across the plains, even though the rails now were continuous from the mountains to the Missouri, was not as safe as it would seem. Trains often had a military escort, and they were run across the hostile plains only in daylight. Yet they were frequently attacked by the Indians.[24] One reason for the attacks was very likely the slow speed of the trains.

Completion of the railroad to Denver had brought great changes during the few years since the iron horse had first appeared on the prairie. Those who had watched its growth looked back:

> Five years ago, trains that went through this country to Denver and the Pacific, consisted of mules, prairie schooners, rugged pioneer settlers, and split-bottom chairs. The curious who hung around to see the trains pass, were Indians in war paint. Five years, however, in the nineteenth century, bring about a wonderful change. . . . How rapidly these wonderful improvements of the hour take the place of the old canvas-covered wagons of "ye olden time." Now these retired servants of the emigrant stand on the shores of the Pacific with dry spindles and rusty tires — mementoes of the past. Pullman's palaces usurp their place on the great paths of travel.[25]

Courtesy the Kansas State Historical Society, Topeka

Fort Wallace — panorama about 1870

NOTES

1. Don Russell, *The Lives and Legends of Buffalo Bill* (Norman: Univ. of Oklahoma Press, 1960), p. 85.
2. Ibid., p. 86.
3. Helen Cody Wetmore, *Buffalo Bill: Last of the Great Scouts* (Chicago: Duluth Press, 1899), pp. 150–2.
4. Russell, *Buffalo Bill*, p. 88.
5. John S. Gray, "Will Comstock, Scout: The Natty Bumpo of Kansas," *Montana Western History* 20 (Summer 1970), p. 8.
6. Ibid., p. 9.
7. Wetmore, *Buffalo Bill*, p. 153.
8. Russell, *Buffalo Bill*, pp. 93–94.
9. Ibid., p. 95.
10. Wetmore, *Buffalo Bill*, p. 154.
11. Ibid.
12. *Leavenworth Daily Conservative*, 4 August 1868.
13. *Junction City* (Kans.) *Weekly Union*, 5 September 1868.
14. George L. Anderson, *Kansas West* (San Marino, Ca.: Golden West Books, 1963), p. 67.
15. Ibid.
16. O. P. Byers, "When Railroading Outdid the Wild West Stories," *Kansas Historical Collections, 1926–1928* 17 (1928), p. 344.
17. W. E. Webb, "Air Towns and Their Inhabitants," *Harper's New Monthly Magazine* (November 1875).
18. Robert W. Richmond and Robert W. Mardock, *A Nation Moving West* (Lincoln: Univ. of Nebraska, 1966), p. 274.
19. Joseph W. Snell and Robert W. Richmond, "When the Union and Kansas Pacific Built through Kansas," *Kansas Historical Quarterly* (Autumn 1966), p. 348.
20. Anderson, *Kansas West*, p. 25.
21. Snell and Richmond, "Union and Kansas Pacific," p. 349.
22. Ibid.
23. *The Rocky Mountain News* (Denver), 16 August 1870.
24. Byers, "Railroading," p. 342.
25. *Junction City Weekly Union*, 3 September 1870.

V.

END OF THE TRAILS

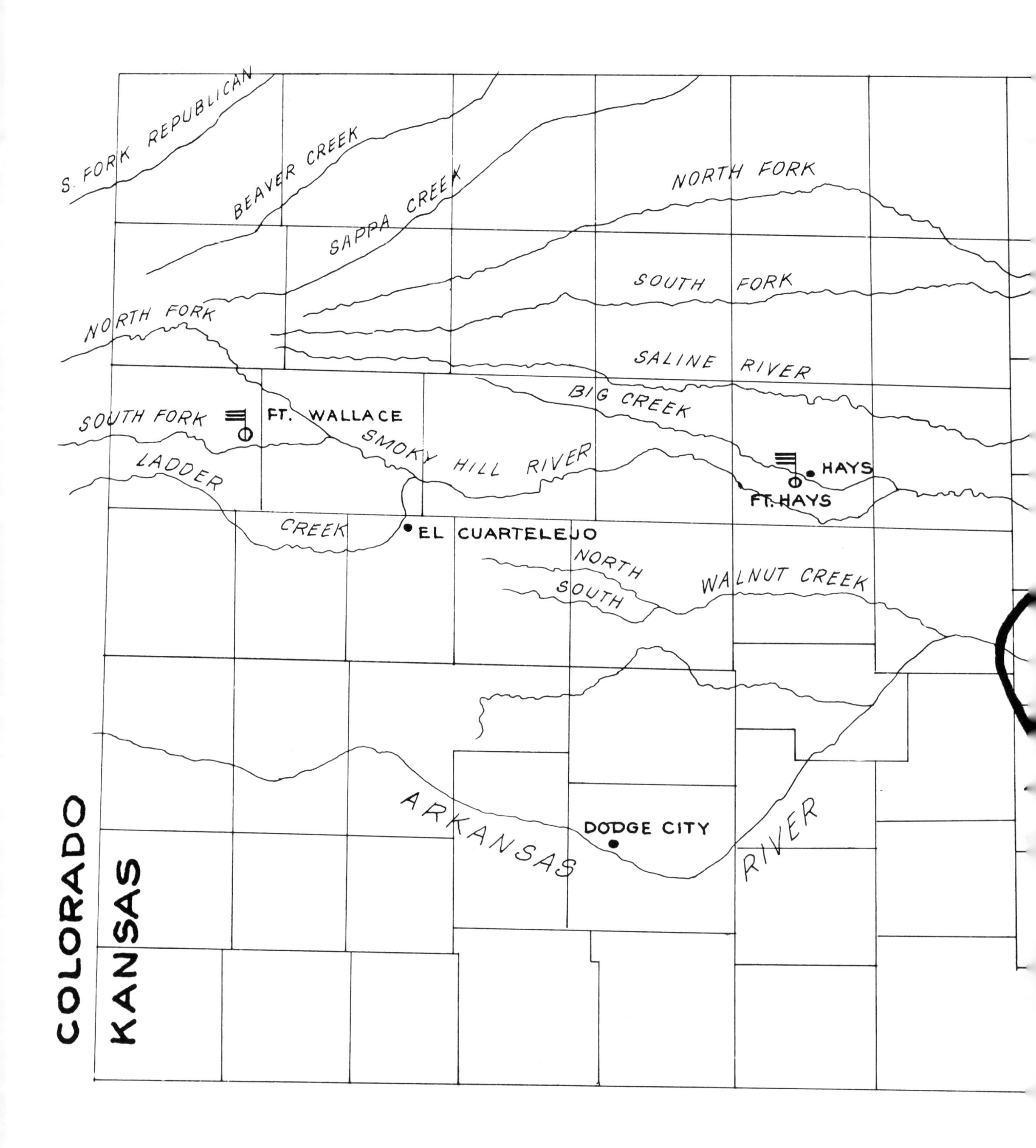
S. FORK REPUBLICAN
BEAVER CREEK
SAPPA CREEK
NORTH FORK
SOUTH FORK
NORTH FORK
SALINE RIVER
BIG CREEK
SOUTH FORK
FT. WALLACE
SMOKY HILL RIVER
LADDER
CREEK
HAYS
FT. HAYS
EL CUARTELEJO
NORTH
SOUTH
WALNUT CREEK
ARKANSAS
RIVER
DODGE CITY
COLORADO
KANSAS

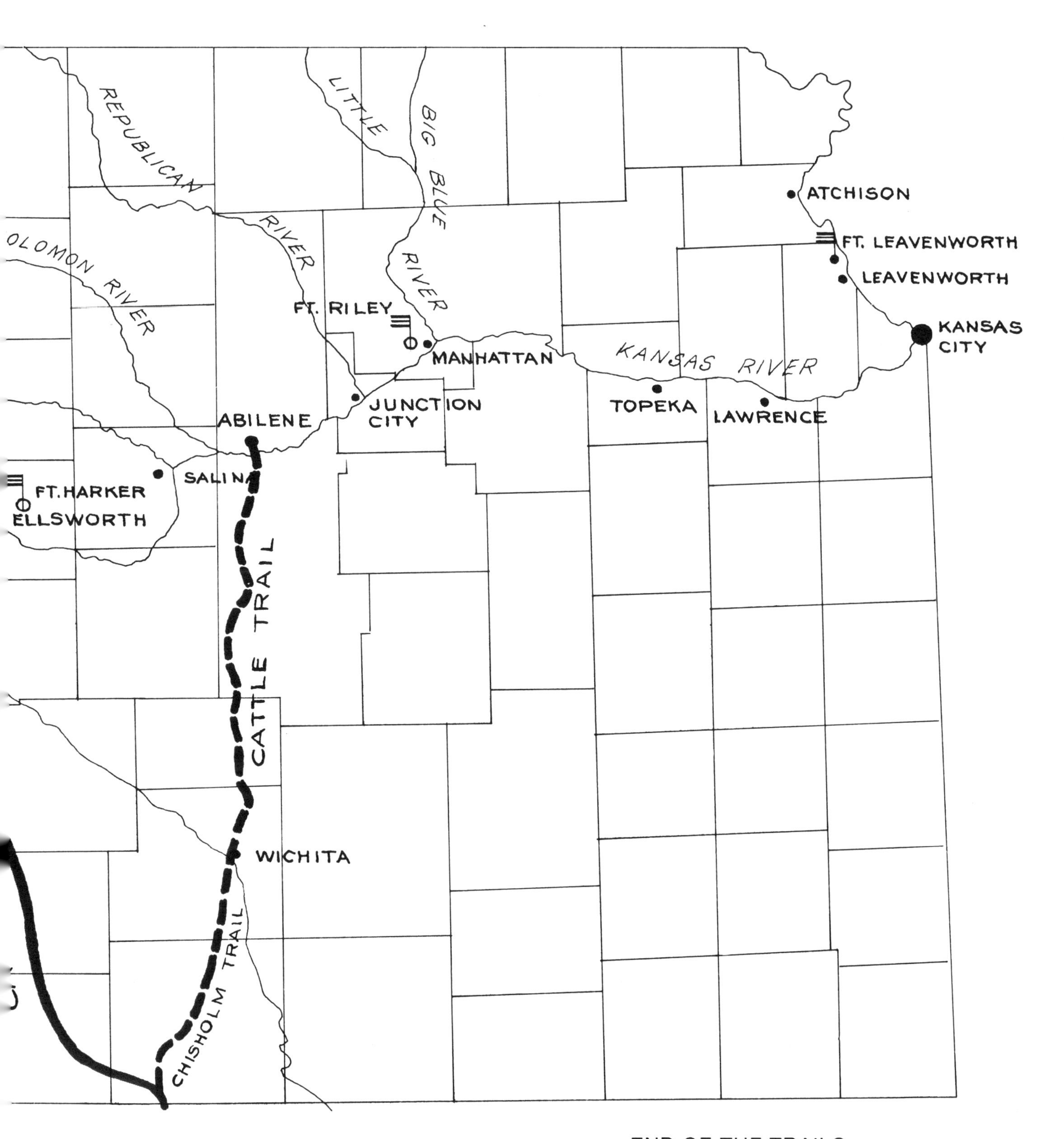

END OF THE TRAILS

CHAPTER 22

FIRST OF THE COW TOWNS

AS THE CIVIL WAR LOST ITS MOMENTUM, Kansas picked it up. The railroad built west with renewed vigor. The Butterfield Overland Despatch began the treacherous prairie crossings from Atchison to Denver. As the railroad moved west it brought farmers to break the sod and till the soil and build towns to supply their needs. It attracted another customer that brought an even greater change. Cattle! Cattle seeking a way to get to the hungry market in the East.

It took a visionary to point the cattle toward those shining rails. It found him in a young Illinois man who was engaged in a huge livestock business with his two older brothers. Joseph G. McCoy was the youngest child in a family of nine. In the summer of 1866 he was twenty-eight and a partner in the McCoy Brothers of Springfield, Illinois, a livestock shipping business. Often they shipped a thousand head a week, the cattle averaging from $80 to $140 a head.[1]

Joseph McCoy was pictured by those who knew him as ambitious, energetic, and quick to spot a promising opportunity.[2] One such opportunity appeared just a short distance from Springfield, in Christian County, in the fall of 1866. W. W. Suggs brought a herd of Texas cattle through Missouri to Christian County, where he wintered them. McCoy bought the herd early in the spring of 1867. He asked Suggs about the cattle business in Texas. What Suggs told him changed not only McCoy's life but the life of Kansas.

Suggs said that in Texas a man's "poverty was estimated by the number of cattle he possessed."[3] He told how he had run into irate farmers all the way through Missouri who were certain that his cattle were sick with fever that would kill all the domestic cattle.[4] Bandits and thieves waited along the way to rob the man trying to drive his cattle to market.

Courtesy the Kansas State Historical Society, Topeka

Joseph G. McCoy

McCoy sensed an opportunity but didn't see how to take advantage of it. Cattle were a good price here in Illinois; they were dirt cheap in Texas. How could he get those cheap cattle in Texas to the high-priced market in Chicago? There had to be a way.

Driving across Missouri was definitely not the way, McCoy decided. Missouri had a law, passed in 1861, that prohibited the trespassing of diseased cattle.[5] That law would be enforced now.

McCoy studied maps and rivers. There were too many settlements between the Texas plains and the big rivers like the Mississippi. However, there was nothing but uninhabited prairie and small rivers between Texas and the Kansas plains where the Union Pacific Eastern Division, was building west toward Denver.

In 1865 Kansas passed a law prohibiting Texas cattle from entering the farming area of Kansas. The law drew a straight north-and-south line about sixty miles west of Topeka, marking the limits of the agricultural area. West of there no restrictions were made. McCoy saw that Junction City lay outside the restricted area, and the rails had already reached that town. Texas cattle would have a straight, unopposed road to the Kansas railroad, where they could be shipped to the eastern markets without trouble.

Bouyed by his dream, McCoy went to Kansas to see for himself. It was already June. If he intended to ship cattle from Kansas that season, he had to work fast. At Kansas City he took the Union Pacific to the end of passenger service at Junction City. There he got a room at the Hale House, where he met a Texas cattleman, Colonel J. J. Myers. Myers had gone west with Fremont in the forties and had thousands of head of cattle around Lockhart.[6] He confidently promised McCoy that a million cattle would come up the trails to the Kansas railroad if a decent market could be promised.[7]

McCoy decided to locate a market somewhere along the Union Pacific on the Smoky Hill River. He tried to buy land near Junction City and build a stockyard and loading pens, but Junction City wanted no part of such an enterprise. The land was priced so high that a flat no would not have been any plainer to McCoy.[8]

He was not discouraged. He decided he should first make arrangements to ship the cattle. He went east to talk to the railroad companies. The Union Pacific, E. D., offered him encouragement but nothing else. The Missouri Pacific threw him out of the office, saying he must be a speculator and they wanted nothing to do with him. But the Hannibal and St. Joseph Railroad liked the idea, and McCoy signed a contract with that company.[9]

Riding the train back to the end of passenger service, McCoy rented a horse and rode down the new grade. The rails had passed the point where Mud Creek ran toward the Smoky Hill River, a mile away. At Solomon City, where the Solomon River ran into the Smoky Hill, McCoy spotted an ideal place for a stockyards, but the citizens there regarded an invasion of Texas cattle and cowboys with horror. The same was true of Salina, a little farther down the grade. He couldn't go farther west because the rails might not get that far this summer. He turned back.

He stopped at Abilene the little town on Mud Creek. It had no objection to the Texas cattle trade. In fact, "Abilene would stand for anything."[10]

In McCoy's own words, "Abilene in 1867 was a very small, dead place, consisting of about one dozen log huts, low, small rude affairs, four-fifths of which were covered with dirt for roofing, indeed, but one shingle roof could be seen in the whole city. The business of the burg was conducted in two small rooms, mere log huts, and, of course, the inevitable saloon also in a log hut."[11]

McCoy bought the land he needed and hired a civil engineer in Abilene, Tim Hersey, to help him lay out his stockyards and loading pens. Hersey's wife is credited by some as having named Abilene, taking the name from the first verse of the third chapter of Luke.[12] The house with the shingle roof that McCoy mentioned belonged to the Herseys. Just west of them was the old stone stable belonging to the first relay station west of Fort Riley on the Butterfield Overland Despatch, already abandoned because the railroad had taken over passenger service.

In spite of having to ship his lumber long distances, most of the work of building a barn, an office, and stockyards for three thousand cattle and installing some large scales was done in sixty days.[13] McCoy was ready for business by the first of September. He had also begun building a three-story hotel for the cattle buyers when they arrived.

McCoy had sent W. W. Suggs south to locate Texas herds on their way north and direct them to Abilene, guaranteeing them no trouble with farmers or with the law and promising a good market.[14] McCoy's only chance for business that fall was to intercept herds already coming north and pull them over to Abilene.

Suggs did his job well. Some reports say that two other men, Colonel Hitt and Charles Gross, went with Suggs, but it was Suggs who got credit for turning the herd of a man named Thompson to the north. Thompson sold his herd to Smith, McCord, and Chandler. These three continued to Abilene and were the first to drive their cattle to the new shipping point.[15]

Courtesy the Kansas State Historical Society, Topeka *From Gardner Collection*
McCoy's Drover's Cottage in Abilene. Train and trestle bridge near Abilene, Kansas.

McCoy had anticipated the arrival of the first cattle and had brought in dealers and buyers from his old home in Springfield, Illinois, to see the first cattle arrive. The Drover's Cottage, the hotel McCoy was building, was not ready for occupancy, but he managed to entertain his guests royally anyway.[16]

A Texas cattleman, Col. O. W. Wheeler, and his partners, Wilson and Hicks, were the first to bring their own cattle all the way from Texas to Abilene. They were heading for California with two thousand head when they heard of the Abilene market.[17]

On September 5 the first shipment of cattle out of Abilene was made. It marked the beginning of a new era in the history of the cattle business and also of Smoky Hill Valley.

All was not so rosy on the eastern end of the line, however. The cattle found a poor market in Chicago. The second shipment was sent on to Albany, New York, and the shipper took a loss on them. Easterners had been fed a heavy diet of propaganda that Texas beef was not fit to eat. It made the Texas cattle almost as unsalable in the East as "a shipment of prairie wolves."[18] However, in spite of the detractors, people soon learned that fattened Texas beef was as good as any — and much cheaper.

It had not been a good year for the trail drivers. It was a very wet season, the grass was coarse and washy, the thunderstorms had caused numberless stampedes. To climax it all, the cholera that had been plaguing the plains (particularly at Hays City and the neighboring town of Rome, as well as most army posts) hit the cowboys, too. Many were sick; some died.[19]

When the shipping season ended, thirty-five thousand head of cattle had been shipped from Abilene. All but seventeen cars had gone over the Hannibal and St. Joseph Railroad. An agent of the Missouri Pacific came to Abilene to see McCoy about shipping on the Missouri Pacific the next year. McCoy remembered how he had been thrown out of the main office by the president and told not to come back. He got sweet revenge for his humiliation by reversing the thrust: "It just occurs to me that I have no cattle for your road, never have had, and there is no evidence that I ever will have, and will you please say so to your president."[20]

Over half a million dollars passed into the hands of Texas cattlemen in Abilene that fall, and they took the money and news of the great market home with them. Plans were made all over Texas to hit the trail to Abilene early the next year. The cowboys were disappointed in Abilene itself. No games of chance, no girls, no dancing, poor whiskey. But news of Abilene had reached into the east, where all the things the cowboys had missed were preparing to move in.

McCoy rushed work on Drover's Cottage. It was to be the finest hotel west of the Mississippi, with the best cook and only the choicest wines and bourbons. The hotel was completed and furnished before spring, but it didn't open until the beginning of the next shipping season.[21]

Winter put a stop to all but dreams, however dreams and plans were never more active. Spring couldn't come soon enough to please McCoy. Early in the spring he hired engineers and laborers and sent them south under the direction of Tim Hersey to mark the trail clearly from the Arkansas River to Abilene. The summer before, herds had wandered all over central Kansas trying to find Abilene. McCoy's men blazed a trail directly from the Arkansas River to Abilene, cutting trees or notching the bark of trees at river crossings and building mounds of dirt on the prairies to mark the way.[22]

McCoy's dreams of spring did not include the nightmares awaiting Abilene. In early April trains from the east began dumping out passengers, the likes of which McCoy and other residents of Abilene had seldom seen and never associated with — gamblers, saloonkeepers, gunmen, pimps, and brothel keepers. Piles of building materials were dumped out, too, and the carpenters began working. Day and night they worked, until Abilene took on a veneer that completely hid the quiet respectable town of the year before.[23]

The newcomers built in a cluster, on one side of the tracks. The better residents on the other side would have tried to ignore the Texas Abilene if possible, but the post office was across the tracks and they had to go there for their mail.

The cattle came north from Texas to the Red River Crossing. It was the best-known crossing of this dangerous stream, and every trail driver aimed directly for it. From there the herds moved north to the Washita. At that point they hit a wagon road blazed by Jesse Chisholm. It ran to the confluence of the Arkansas and Little Arkansas rivers in southern Kansas.[24]

Chisholm was half Cherokee Indian and traded with the various Indian tribes. When the Wichita Indians settled at the mouth of the Little Arkansas River he moved there with them and set up a ranch, driving his wagons south to trade with the Ponca and Osage Indians on the Washita River. He plied his trade through 1866 and 1867, but he called his trail a wagon road.[25]

When the herds reached the Washita River and found this road they followed it to the Arkansas. In 1867 most herds going to Abilene followed the Arkansas River to the northwest, then cut back northeast toward Abilene. McCoy's marked trail led them directly from the mouth of the Little Arkansas to Abilene.

Texas cattlemen, returning to Texas from Abilene in the fall of 1867, talked about the easy trail from the Washita to the Arkansas on Chisholm's Road. Soon the name of Chisholm was applied to the entire trail from Texas to the Smoky Hill River. Chisholm died on March 4, 1868, at one of his ranches on the North Fork of the Canadian River from eating bear's grease melted in a brass kettle. Modern doctors would have called it acute ptomaine poisoning.[26]

Some trail drivers called McCoy's route from the Arkansas River the Abilene Trail. In 1868 those drivers were looking for the fastest means of getting to Abilene. There were an estimated ten million longhorn cattle in Texas that spring of 1868,[27] and as many as a million of them might come north to market. The earliest herds stood the best chance of finding buyers and getting the best price.

Abilene needed a bank. The Texas cattlemen were suspicious of Yankee paper money. They had boxes of worthless Confederate paper money at home. They wanted hard cash for their cattle. Two wealthy men, one a banker, came to Abilene at McCoy's invitation. They saw the opportunity and built a bank.

Abilene was really two towns. One belonged to the "God-fearing pioneers who established it," and the other to the "Texans who overran" it.[28] McCoy belonged to the former, although it was his business enterprise that had brought in the latter.

By July the herds were at Abilene, the cattle fattening up on the grass near town, and the gamblers, saloon keepers, and "painted ladies" fattening up their bankrolls on the cowboys' wages. An item appeared that month in the *Topeka Commonwealth* which said: "At this writing, Hell is now in session in Abilene."

Drunken cowboys, afoot and on horseback, roamed the streets; quarrels were settled with guns. Texas cowboys seemed to consider fists beneath their dignity when it came to settling a disagreement. The loser of a Texas argument, whether dead, or wounded, was picked up and carried back to his herd by his buddies and there nursed back to health or buried.

A correspondent sent this evaluation to his paper, the *New York Tribune*: "Gathered together in Abilene and its environs is the greatest collection of Texas cowboys, rascals, desperados and adventuresses the United States has ever known. There is no law, no restraint in this seething cauldron of vice and depravity."

July and August were the wildest months. The herds came early but were not sold immediately. The cattle needed a couple of months on grass to fatten up. The first herds to Abilene got the choice spots to graze.[29] Only a skeleton crew was needed to hold them on the grazing grounds, so the remainder of the crew went to town. With the wages they had earned driving up the trail they were ripe for plucking by the experts who waited for them.

Abilene was almost ruined by something over which it had no control. A Chicago firm had contracted for forty thousand head of Texas cattle to be driven to the Mississippi River and shipped by steamboat to Illinois. But no provision was made for feeding and watering the cattle on the boat, and they arrived in Illinois in horrible shape. They were loaded on a train and shipped to Tolono, about ten miles south of Champaign, where they were turned out to regain their strength and weight on the rich grass. They shared the grass with native cattle. Less than a month later the domestic cattle began to die. Local owners panicked and shipped their live cattle east to market. In so doing, they spread the disease to that area. The entire northeastern part of the country was horrified, and the cattle market collapsed so far as Texas cattle were concerned.[30]

It was July, and suddenly there was no market anywhere for Longhorn beef. Legislatures in the midwest and eastern states proposed laws prohibiting Texas cattle from entering their states. Abilene was desperate.

To make things worse for McCoy, local cattle were getting sick and dying. To keep down an uproar, McCoy and his brothers paid the settlers for their losses.

In desperation McCoy and others decided to hold an auction at Abilene. They printed handbills and sent men over eastern Kansas and Nebraska and into western Iowa and Missouri to distribute them.

The sale was a definite success. Most of the cattle sold were cows for breeding stock and big steers that could be used for work oxen. There was little demand for the thirty thousand head of fat beef ready for market.[31]

The cattle dealers decided on a wild scheme to advertise their beef — sure, after the success of the auction, that advertising was the key. They began by organizing a buffalo hunt. With a reinforced cattle car and another car for horses and equipment, they headed west to Fossil Creek siding, just north of the old B.O.D. Fossil Creek Station. There six men rode out to rope some buffalo. In two days they managed to capture ten. Four of the animals died from heat and anger. Three more balked too far from the car to get them aboard, so they ended up with only three healthy animals on board the cattle car.

Over the car they draped a huge canvas on which was painted their advertisement, showing the herds of cattle near Abilene. They sent the car to Chicago by way of St. Louis. In Chicago they roped the buffalo again at the fairgrounds to show the audience how it was done. They then gave the animals to Prof. John Gamgee, a veterinarian. Newspapers made a big thing of it, which was the purpose of the entire stunt.

McCoy then initiated an excursion for Illinois cattlemen to Abilene. The result was that the cattle market was booming again in Abilene.[32]

Seventy-five thousand cattle came up the trail from Texas to Abilene that summer. Two-thirds of the cattle ready for butchering were shipped by rail to the east; the rest went to contractors for military posts and Indian agencies. At its peak that summer Abilene loaded three thousand head a day to be shipped east.[33]

With the departure of the last of the cattle and the cowboys, Texas Abilene closed down for the winter like a frightened clam. The saloons were padlocked, the gamblers and ladies of the night packed their bags and followed the cattle cars east. Abilene became a respectable city once more. The salt in the wound they had made in respectable Abliene was the knowledge that, with the spring, they would all come back in greater numbers and create a wilder, more immoral town — if that were possible.

NOTES

1. Floyd Benjamin Streeter, *The Kaw* (New York: Farrar & Rinehart, 1941). p. 98.
2. Harry Sinclair Drago, *Wild Woolly and Wicked* (New York: Bramhall House, 1960), p. 10.
3. Streeter, *The Kaw*, p. 99.
4. No one had ever heard of tick fever then, but the farmers were right in suspecting the Texas cattle of carrying the sickness. They appointed men to examine every Texas critter that came in for signs of sickness. Since the Texas cattle were immune to the fever, few Texas cattle were found sick. But the ticks dropped off the Longhorns and crawled onto the farm-fed Shorthorn cattle. They were not immune, and they took sick and died. It was little wonder the farmers were so intent on keeping Texas cattle away from their livestock.
5. Drago, *Wild Woolly and Wicked*, p. 14.
6. Streeter, *The Kaw*, p. 100.
7. Mari Sandoz, *The Cattlemen* (New York: Hastings House, 1958), p. 58.
8. Streeter, *The Kaw*, p. 101.
9. Ibid., p. 102.
10. Drago, *Wild Woolly and Wicked*, p. 18.
11. Ibid., p. 102.
12. Ibid., p. 19. Not all authorities agree that Abilene got its name this way, but the story still persists.
13. Robert W. Richmond and Robert W. Mardock, *A Nation Moving West* (Lincoln: Univ. of Nebraska Press, 1966), p. 285. Some reports say there was room for only a thousand head of cattle in the pens.
14. Ibid., p. 285.
15. Ibid.; Streeter, *The Kaw*, p. 104.
16. Drago, *Wild Woolly and Wicked*, p. 28.
17. Ibid., p. 29.
18. Richmond and Mardock, *Nation Moving West*, p. 286.
19. Sandoz, *Cattlemen*, p. 58.

20. Drago, *Wild Wooly and Wicked,* p. 29.
21. Ibid., p. 30–31.
22. Streeter, *The Kaw*, p. 106. Drago says they put little Lone Star flags of Texas on each mound.
23. Drago, *Wild Woolly and Wicked,* p. 31.
24. This is the site of present day Wichita, named for the Wichita Indians who camped here in the mid-1860s, until they were relocated on the Washita River by the government in 1867.
25. Drago, *Wild Woolly and Wicked,* pp. 37–38.
26. Ibid., p. 40.
27. Ibid., p. 12–13.
28. Ibid., p. 19.
29. Streeter, *The Kaw*, p. 117.
30. Ibid., p. 180.
31. Ibid., p. 181.
32. Ibid., p. 182–3.
33. Drago, *Wild Woolly and Wicked,* p. 53.

CHAPTER 23

GODLESS ABILENE

SO FAR AS THE PIONEERS on the upper reaches of the Smoky Hill River were concerned, anything east of Fort Hays was civilized country. They couldn't know of the war being waged between two segments of the white man's own civilization in the cattle town of Abilene. "Godless Abilene," the newspapers in the holier-than-thou cities to the east called the cow town. At times Joseph McCoy, raised a reverent man, must have wondered how he could have opened such a Pandora's box when he had only intended to help both the cattle-poor Texas ranchers and the meat-hungry people in the eastern cities.

Before the opening of the 1869 season McCoy sold the Drover's Cottage so he would have more financial backing in his ventures. Maj. M. B. George bought it.[1]

The opening session of the Illinois Legislature brought a crisis that shook Abilene. A new legislator from Champaign County, where most of the domestic cattle had died the previous summer from the Texas fever, introduced a bill to prohibit all Texas cattle from setting foot in Illinois or even passing through the state by train.

Since almost every train from Kansas to the East Coast passed through Illinois, this would effectively end the market in Abilene. McCoy knew he had to do something immediately to save his dream. He went to Springfield, the Illinois capital, and fought the panic that had fostered the bill. But the odds were against him.

McCoy kept up his fight and finally managed to get an amendment tacked onto the bill that would allow Texas cattle to come into Illinois if they had been wintered in the north. The belief was that the ticks that were causing the fever would be killed by the cold weather.[2]

Back in Abilene a flash flood got in the next lick of the season. A cloudburst upstream sent little Mud Creek raging wildly through the town, practically wiping out Texas Abilene. There were those on the other side of the tracks who felt that a higher power had surely dealt the blow.[3]

The mud had scarcely dried when the washed-out part of the town north of the tracks began to rebuild. Where the cribs had been, a new hotel called the Abilene House went up. But the cribs were rebuilt a little farther away — more of them and fancier than the slapped-up shanties that had washed away in the flood.

The first herds reached Abilene on the first of June, much earlier than the year before. Texas Abilene was ready. The first killing in town was a surprise, even in a town where such things were commonplace. A cowboy shot a man through the big window of a saloon, then rode out of town before anyone could recognize him. Neither the killer nor his reason for shooting the man was ever discovered.

There was no police force to keep the law or tally the murders by gun and knife. Estimates by those who lived there through the summer ran around twenty deaths. Many a wounded cowboy clung to his horse to get back to his camp. There he died and was buried, his grave unmarked, his death unrecorded.

Respectable Abilene saw that its worst fears had been realized and magnified. Texas Abilene was surely the devil's playground. Even two women in the cribs were murdered that summer. The number of cowboys who were rolled before they had a chance to spend a cent of their wages was beyond count.

Some of the citizens of respectable Abilene met to consider ways of curbing Beelzebub across the tracks. They knew they couldn't do it without help, and it was too late in the season to get the right kind of help. But they could begin now to build the kind of town they hoped to have — once the denizens of Texas Abilene had been put to rout. They planned a church and a school. Unbelievably, they built both next to Texas Street.[4]

By the first of August twenty-eight hundred carloads of cattle had been shipped out of Abilene, and the town was still surrounded by a sea of Longhorns. Prices were high, and there had been no new outbreak of Texas fever.

McCoy in contrast to his usual nature, began speculating, buying cattle himself to sell later. The eastern market, absorbing the greatest flow of cattle ever seen from the West, suddenly had its fill; the market collapsed. McCoy, like many others, was left with cattle and no place to sell them. Even his extensive fortune was strained, and finally it gave way. McCoy's dream had become a nightmare. He was broke.[5]

Courtesy the Kansas State Historical Society, Topeka

Loading cattle at McCoy's stockyard, Abilene, Kansas

The Smoky Hill was still seething that summer of 1869. General Carr had eliminated Tall Bull and destroyed his village at Summit Springs, rescuing one of the white woman captives. This put an effective damper on the activities of the dog soldiers.

Hays City got one of the wounded scouts from an earlier Carr campaign in eastern Colorado. Wild Bill Hickok had come to Hays in the spring after recovering from his wounds and being discharged as scout by General Carr. Hays City had been having trouble keeping a sheriff and didn't have a peace officer when Hickok arrived. A short item in the Leavenworth paper, datelined Hays City, told the story succinctly: "Hays City, Aug. 31, 1869. At the election held here a few days ago . . .J. B. Hickok, familiarly known as 'Wild Bill,' elected Sheriff of the county."[6]

Less than a month later Hickok was involved in his first clash with the lawless element that ended in a killing. A man named Sam Strawhim[7] and some of his cronies were making a general nuisance of themselves and finally got out of hand. Hickok was called in. The newspaper report put it simply: "In the melee that followed, Stranghan (Strawhim) was killed. The coroner's verdict this morning was justifiable homicide. Stranghan was buried this afternoon."[8]

Back in Abilene, September saw the beginning of change. The past summer had been too much for respectable Abilene, which now numbered nearly three hundred permanent residents. By October Texas Abilene was almost deserted. The last of the cattle had got east, and the summer residents had followed.

Fearing that the mayhem in Texas Abilene would spill across the tracks next summer, Abilene decided to organize itself into a third-class city, and a petition was circulated. The necessary number of signatures was obtained, and the petition was presented to the court. Judge Cyrus Kilgore granted it. Abilene was now in a position to lay down laws. The question was whether Abilene was in a position to enforce them.[9]

More than one hundred and fifty thousand head of cattle were shipped from Abilene in 1869, more than twice as many as the year before.[10] Abilene was ready to withdraw for the winter, lick its wounds, and pass laws to prevent a repeat of the mayhem of 1869.

The new year dawned with the promise of being bigger than ever for Abilene. But what was "big" in the eyes of Texas Abilene was the thing that respectable Abilene intended to squelch.

There were four hotels, ten boardinghouses, five clothing and dry goods stores, and at least ten saloons in town as the 1870 season got under way.[11] Perhaps the most famous saloon was the Alamo on Cedar Street. It bragged that it was the fanciest saloon between Kansas City and Denver, and likely could have successfully defended that claim.

The newly organized city of Abilene elected a board of trustees early in the spring. The board's first act was to make it a crime to carry firearms within the city limits of Abilene. This was done, of course, before the residents of Texas Abilene returned. Since the board realized it could not do away with the gambling, saloons, and other vices, it decided the town coffers might as well profit from them. An ordinance was passed requiring a licence for each of the undesirable businesses across the tracks.

A new courthouse was begun and a jail built in the heart of Texas Abilene where it would be most convenient. Then the trustees began to look for a marshal to enforce the new laws.[12]

Takers were not plentiful. Those who had seen Abilene in 1869 wanted no part of trying to enforce the laws, and anyone who was new to the area was hardly qualified for the job.

Still there seemed no desire on the part of the summer residents to curtail their endeavors. Two old buildings were torn down to make room for the Novelty Theater on Texas Street (First Street). Almost opposite the school a fancy two-story house was built for employees and patrons of the newest and most elegant sporting house. It was painted a brilliant yellow, and Mattie Silks came out to run it. At twenty-one she was probably the youngest madam in Texas Abilene.[13]

The sheriff of Dickinson County was persuaded to take the job of marshal of Abilene, too. When the cowboys arrived from Texas, they seemed to go out of their way to defy every rule that he was called on to enforce. He quit, and his deputy took over. He proved to be a coward where Texas cowboys were concerned; he lasted an even shorter time than the sheriff.

The first Texas cattle arrived by May first, a month earlier than 1869 and two months earlier than 1868. The market was good again, and Abilene was braced for the biggest year ever. The town board decided to send to St. Louis for two competent men to handle the job of policing the town. Two former soldiers were sent. The day they stepped off the train the cowboys sensed why they had come. The men of Texas Abilene put on a show that promised no good for the two new marshals — who climbed on the next train back to St. Louis.[14]

While the town board debated what to do next, a man rode in from Kit Carson and applied for the job. The board hired him on the spot at $150 a month. He was Tom Smith, and he had earned a reputation in taming the tough end-of-track

Courtesy the Kansas State Historical Society, Topeka

Thomas J. Smith, Abilene

towns on the Union Pacific through Wyoming.[15]

Most marshals walked down the street and settled any argument with guns. Smith rode his horse down the street, his guns safely tucked in shoulder holsters out of sight. When challenged, he settled the issue with fists. This amazed the cowboys. As one Texas cowboy said, "We don't know no more about fistfighting than a hog knows about a sidesaddle."[16]

It was inevitable that Smith would be challenged on the new order to check all guns in town. The first to try it was a huge driver named Big Hank, who had bragged that nobody could disarm him. Finding the marshal, he asked what he intended to do about the law. Smith said quietly he intended to enforce it. He then asked for Hank's gun. Hank swore at him, increasing his oaths when Smith repeated the request. Then, before Hank was aware of what the marshal intended. Smith hit him on the jaw and knocked him flat. Grabbing the man's gun, he ordered Big Hank to leave town in a hurry. The braggart lost no time in obeying the order.[17]

This humiliation to cowboys in general was too much for a hulk of a man by the name of Wyoming Frank. He rode into town to uphold the honor of the cowboys. He deliberately challenged Smith by brazenly wearing his gun. Before Frank could work up a hot argument (and he really tried with curses and insults) Smith had dismounted and was close to him. Frank began to retreat so he would have room to grab his gun out of its hoster. Smith never gave him a chance. When Frank refused to hand over his gun, Smith floored him with his fists. He gave Wyoming Frank five minutes to get out of town and stay out. Frank accepted the invitation.[18]

Wild Bill Hickok has often been given credit for taming Abilene. Perhaps he retamed it, but Tom Smith tamed it first. The change in the town was remarkable. The town board voted early in August to raise his salary to $225 a month, dating back to July 4, just one month after he was hired.[19]

Theodore Henry and Joseph McCoy had worked together to build Abilene, but their ways were parting. Henry was a farmer; he saw great potential in farming the prairie around Abilene., McCoy saw cattle and nothing else. Their different views could only end in bitter rivalry.

To mark the settling down of the town, the *Abilene Chronicle* began publication late that summer.[20] The *Chronicle* took the side of the farmers in claiming their right to fence their land. The cattlemen and Texas drivers were strictly opposed. Trouble was brewing. The *Chronicle* demanded a herd law that would put the burden of keeping cattle out of fields on the cattle owner rather than on the farmer, as it stood under the fence law passed two years before.[21]

The season wound down to a close, and the final count showed that over two hundred thousand cattle went through the market at Abilene, the biggest year yet for the town.[22]

With the end of the season, Texas Abilene abdicated to more profitable areas for the winter. But trouble did not leave Abilene with the transients. Two neighbors northeast of town got into an argument over the trespassing of one man's cattle on the other's fields. The result was that a Scotsman, Andrew McConnell, shot and killed his neighbor, Irishman John Shea, while Shea was trying to drive his cattle off McConnell's land.

McConnell was arrested, but his close friend and neighbor, Moses Miles, testified it was self-defense; McConnell was released. Other neighbors brought in proof that Shea did not start the argument and that he had been killed deliberately. A new order went out for McConnell's arrest.

The sheriff, however, was run off McConnell's place when he tried to arrest the man. He called for help, and Marshal Tom Smith agreed to make the arrest. Deputy Sheriff McDonald went with him, but the deputy backed off in the face of a threat from Miles. Smith went into the dugout to arrest McConnell.

In the various versions of what followed, it is difficult to be sure just what did occur. There were shots in the dugout. McConnell was wounded in the hand, Tom Smith in the chest. Still, Smith brought McConnell outside. Deputy McDonald had already been run off by Miles, and it is obvious that it was Moses Miles who used an ax to smash Smith's head. Reports said that his head was almost severed from his body. The two fugitives rode away in haste.[23]

A posse was organized as soon as Deputy Sheriff McDonald reported in Abilene that Smith had been killed. Among those in the posse were Police Magistrate C. C. Kuney and an Abilene butcher, James Gainsford. While the rest of the posse went back to Abilene with Smith's body, these two took up the trail of the murderers.

Three days after the killing, on November 5, Kuney and Gainsford caught up with McConnell and Miles fifteen miles northwest of Clay Center, Kansas.[24] They apparently were on their way to the Rocky Mountains, where they had reportedly once lived. They were brought back to Abilene, where crowds were ready to lynch them. Guards protected them until they could be brought to trial. They were sentenced to long prison terms.

Tom Smith's funeral in Abilene[25] brought out all the citizens in a show of grief and as a tribute to the man who had made the town fit for respectable citizens.[26]

After the railroad reached Denver and the Indians finally conceded they were not able to drive the white man back to his eastern cities, there was much less trouble to the west of Abilene.

In late 1870 Othniel Charles Marsh, professor of paleontology at Yale College (University), brought a party to Fort Wallace to explore along the Smoky Hill River. A military escort from the fort accompanied the professor's party on its geological explorations.

After exploring the twin buttes where fossils had been discovered, near the rapidly disappearing end-of-track town of Sheridan, they moved southeast down the North Fork of the Smoky Hill River to the confluence of North and South forks and set up camp there.

They had killed some buffalo for fresh meat, and each night coyotes surrounded the camp, serenading the campers and trying to get close enough to steal the meat. On the night before Thanksgiving one overly brave coyote roamed the cliffs just above the camp and, finally letting his hunger overrule his judgment, leaped off the bluff to get to the meat.

He landed in the center of the staked-out mules. The terrified animals broke their ropes and stampeded away, knocking over many of the campers' tents as they went.

At daylight the damage was assessed. One lazy mule called Crazy Kate was discovered only a short distance away; she had refused to run any farther from a cowardly coyote. A soldier was sent on Crazy Kate to bring back the other mules, since the party could not move without them.

The soldier soon discovered that the mules, after their first stampede, had banded together and headed for home at Fort Wallace, fourteen or fifteen miles away. The soldier followed, taking his time since he knew where they were going.

When he arrived at the fort he found the place in an uproar. The mules had come into the fort with broken halters and ropes, and the commanding officer concluded immediately that the party had been attacked by Indians. He had sent a company of soldiers to the rescue, including a burial detail if needed.

Photo by Author

Natural Corral — Death Hollow — 12-73 — Forks of the Smoky Hill.

Colonel Bankhead's first question when he saw the soldier on the mule was to inquire about the soldier's rifle. The soldier, in his haste to go after the mules, had neglected to take his rifle. He was amazed that the colonel would be more interested in his rifle than in his message. The colonel ordered the officer of the day to arrest the soldier and put him in the guardhouse. "Even if you're fool enough to risk your own life in this country, you shouldn't risk a government mule," the colonel roared.

The rescue party arrived at the camp just before sundown. Professor Marsh and his men were preparing their Thanksgiving dinner of buffalo and antelope meat and stewed rabbit with canned fruit. They invited the soldiers to dinner. Like the pilgrims two hundred and fifty years before, they had guests for their Thanksgiving meal.

Before the expedition returned to the East, Professor Marsh found some bones in the area to prove there had been a flying dragon in prehistoric days that dwarfed all previously discovered pterodactyl skeletons.[26]

NOTES

1. Harry Sinclair Drago, *Wild Woolly and Wicked* (New York: Bramhall House, 1960), p. 55.
2. Floyd Benjamin Streeter, *The Kaw* (New York: Farrar & Rinehart, 1941), pp. 183–4.
3. Drago, *Wild Woolly and Wicked*, p. 58.
4. Ibid., p. 61.
5. Ibid., pp. 62–63.
6. (Leavenworth) *Times* and *Conservative*, 2 September 1879.
7. The name Strawhim is spelled in various ways in different reports. He was in Hays that summer, but if he was in other towns before he apparently failed to make the news. Earlier that summer he and another undesirable named Joe Weiss had been ordered out of town by the vigilantes. When they confronted one of the vigilantes Weiss was fatally shot, and the verdict was justifiable homicide. The next mention of Strawhim was his encounter with Hickok.
8. Nyle H. Miller and Joseph W. Snell, "Some Notes on Kansas Cowtown Police Officers and Gun Fighters," *Kansas Historical Quarterly* (Winter 1960), p. 424.
9. Drago, *Wild Woolly and Wicked*, p. 64.
10. Streeter, *The Kaw*, p. 122. Some reports give the estimate of cattle passing through Abilene that summer as 175,000.
11. Ibid., p. 120.
12. Drago, *Wild Woolly and Wicked*, p. 65.
13. Ibid., p. 65. Mattie Silks later became famous for her fancy house in Denver on Holladay Street (changed later to Market Street). The only time she ever demonstrated her skill with a gun was against a madam from another house on Holladay Street. The quarrel was over Cort Thompson, Mattie's man. Mattie had to buy a ranch in eastern Colorado and move Thompson out there to run it in order to keep the police from putting him away for good.
14. Streeter, *The Kaw*, p. 123.
15. Ibid., p. 124.

16. Drago, *Wild Woolly and Wicked*, p. 73.
17. Streeter, *The Kaw*, p. 125.
18. Ibid., p. 126.
19. Drago, *Wild Woolly and Wicked*, p. 76.
20. Ibid., p. 80.
21. Ibid., p. 21. This herd law would in effect, stop all trail driving because it would force the cattle owners to fence in their stock to keep them out of the fields. There was no way that a herd moving up from Texas could be fenced away from fields. The fence law then in effect made it mandatory that the farmer fence the cattle out of his fields. The cattleman was not responsible if his cattle trampled a field down because the farmer hadn't securely fenced the animals out.
22. Streeter, *The Kaw*, p. 122.
23. Ibid., p. 126–128.
24. Miller and Snell, "Cowtown Police Officers," pp. 228–339.
25. The *Abilene Chronicle* of November 10, 1870, calls Tom Smith a U.S. marshal, but a search reveals no record that he ever held that office.
26. Drago, *Wild Woolly and Wicked*, p. 84.
27. George A. Forsythe, "Fossil Hunting on the Plains of Western Kansas," *Fort Wallace* (Kans.) *Bugle*, June 1976.

CHAPTER 24

HICKOK'S REIGN

As 1871 DAWNED, the *Abilene Chronicle* boasted that the town now had over five hundred permanent residents. It made no reference to the fluctuating population that filled Texas Abilene in the summer.

The spring election brought some changes. T. C. Henry had been mayor of the town since it had been organized into a city. His farming operations had grown until he was too busy to take another term. By this time Joseph McCoy had become little more than a name to be remembered as the one who brought the Texas cattle trade to Abilene. Those who had profited from the Texas cattle nominated McCoy for mayor. Henry, being a farmer, did not want the Texas trade. The cattle trampled the fields, broke fences, and generally made profitable farming almost impossible. Henry, McCoy's former friend, campaigned hard against him but to no avail. McCoy was elected.[1]

As mayor, McCoy's first job was to find a marshal to replace Tom Smith. McCoy didn't expect to find Smith's equal, but something would have to be done before Texas Abilene filled up again. By April 15 the town council was getting desperate. The wild town would erupt any day.

A man had gotten off the train from Hays just a few days before. Everyone on the council knew Bill Hickok, but a majority doubted if he was the right man for the marshal job. However, with no suitable man in sight, the council decided unanimously that Wild Bill Hickok was exactly the right man for the job, and he was offered $150 a month. He accepted.[2]

At a council meeting on May 8 two councilmen resigned. Another walked out after the resignations were accepted. Major McCoy ordered Marshal Hickok to bring the reluctant committeeman back into the meeting. When he walked out

Courtesy the Kansas State Historical Society, Topeka

James B. Hickok

again, Hickok forcibly brought him back.[3] There obviously was a lack of total harmony among the council members.

Wild Bill Hickok came to Abilene with quite a reputation. He had scouted for General Custer and the Seventh Cavalry, had been involved in many a battle where guns settled the issue, had been wounded several times, and had inflicted serious or fatal wounds on many of his adversaries.

He had good reasons for leaving Hays. At Hays he had been elected sheriff of Ellis County in a special election in August 1869, but he lost the regular election on November 2 the same year. As marshal of Hays he had been in several fights with guns.[4]

His serious trouble apparently began with some behind-the-back remarks made by both Hickok and Capt. Tom Custer. Gen. George Custer's younger brother. Captain Custer was commanding officer of M Troop of the Seventh Cavalry, and he shared none of his brother's respect for Hickok. He expressed his sentiments, and Hickok let it be known that the feeling was mutual.

Tom Custer had his bouts with the bottle, and on one such occasion he considered it prudent to shoot up the town of Hays. Hickok arrested him and made him leave town. Custer considered this an insult to himself as an army officer and to the entire M Troop. He believed that only the army had a right to chastise him.

Custer rode back into Hays with several of his men to kill Hickok and redeem the honor of M Troop. In the fight that followed, two soldiers were shot. Pvt. John Kyle died the next day; Pvt. Jeremiah Lonergan recovered from his wounds and returned to duty about five weeks later.[5]

It was this incident that persuaded Hickok to leave Hays. In his own words: "I couldn't fight the whole Seventh Cavalry."[6]

With this background he showed up in Abilene. Hays had been good training for Abilene, in case Hickok hadn't had enough training in the rough years before. The Jones and Plummer Trail, often called the Western Trail, ran through Hays on its way north to Ogallala, where the bulk of the cattle went on to ranges in eastern Montana and Wyoming or western Dakota Territory and Nebraska. Hays, being farther west than either Abilene or Ellsworth, had a much longer life as a cattle town. However, it was never the shipping point that the towns to the east were. Before the farmers cut off the road to Ellsworth (which would have made Hays the shipping point) the Santa Fe Railroad had laid its tracks many miles to the south and started the cow towns of Wichita and Dodge City. Hays was always just a "passing through" point on the western trail.

Courtesy the Kansas State Historical Society, Topeka

Fort Hays — cavalry stable, 1873

Trying to keep the lid on a town that offered the cowboy a place to let off the steam built up through two months of lonely trail-driving was a challenge to the strongest and bravest. Whether Wild Bill Hickok was either strong or brave depends on the one who evaluates his efforts. He did survive, and he put his experience to use in Abilene.

Mayor McCoy tried to reclaim Abilene for the respectable citizens. He ordered the red-light district north of the tracks closed and set aside a new area southeast of town for this segment of Texas Abilene. This section quickly became known as McCoy's Addition. Hickok had to move these people out, and he succeeded. He picked three deputies — James Gainsford, J. H. McDonald (who had backed off when Tom Smith was killed), and Tom Carson, a nephew of Kit.[7]

By midsummer respectable Abilene had a population of eight hundred. These permanent citizens backed McCoy when he put Hickok to work enforcing the new laws in Texas Abilene.[8]

Two men came to Abilene that summer who might have successfully challenged Hickok's rule. One was John Hardin, and the other was the man many called the most dangerous killer in the west, Ben Thompson.

Thompson was five feet nine inches tall, blue-eyed, and dark-skinned. A neat dresser, he made friends easily. But he was a killer. He had served in the Conferderate Army and had been the bad boy of his regiment. After the war he got into many fights and finally killed a man. That earned him two years in prison. He got out in 1870 and the next summer showed up in Abilene.[9]

John Wesley Hardin came up the trail with Colonel Wheeler's herd. While the herd was held on North Cottonwood Creek to fatten, Hardin came into town often. He already had several arrest warrants on him from Texas, and it is likely that those wanted posters had reached Abilene. If so, Hickok ignored them. He was no fool. He likely knew that in the same crew with Hardin were seven of his cousins — the four Clements brothers and three Dixon brothers. None were known for their Sunday School manners.[10]

Billy Chorn, the boss of Colonel Wheeler's trail drive, was killed by a Mexican cowboy in the crew, and Hardin got

Courtesy the Kansas State Historical Society, Topeka

Fort Hays — blockhouse, 1873

the job of going after him. He asked for a deputy sheriff's badge before starting. To all who knew Hardin, it was obvious why he asked for the badge. That badge would be protection against prosecution for murder. Two hundred miles south of Abilene Hardin found the cowboy who had killed Chorn, and he shot him. Then he came back to Abilene.[11]

Ben Thompson's friend, Phil Coe, arrived in Abilene about the time Thompson won a big stake at a gambling table. The two friends put their money together and opened their own saloon called the Bull's Head. Coe was a huge man, standing six feet four inches, and wore a full beard. The two appeared to be making a fortune in their new saloon, but they soon sold out to Tom Sheran.[12]

The year 1871 was proving to be a great one for the Abilene cattle market. It had never been better; it would never be as great again.[13] The reason for its dim future lay in two places: One was the farmers, who were crowding onto the good land around Abilene, plowing up the grass and fencing out cattle. The other lay to the west about sixty miles — Ellsworth.

Ellsworth had an established population of about twelve hundred,[14] bigger than Abilene. It was far enough west that there were no farmers. It was also closer to the Texas ranges — if the trail bosses would aim at Ellsworth as soon as they crossed into Kansas.

The town had been trying to lure some of the cattle trade away from Abilene since 1869. Two to six men had been kept on the Arkansas River to point the way to Ellsworth. In 1871 their efforts began to pay off.

After its end-of-track days Ellsworth was, first and last, a cow town. It had an unusual main street, divided in the middle by the grade and rails of the railroad. So the town had a North Main Street and South Main Street, and there was plenty of room to drive teams and wagons on either side of the track with the business places set well back from the street.

Most of the business houses faced the railroad tracks. They were one- or two-story buildings with wooden awnings. In 1871 the business section of town was about three blocks long. There was a bank, a hardware, a drugstore, lumberyard, general store, and furniture store. And, of course, enough saloons to quench the thirst of the driest cowboys. There were also several hotels and rooming houses.[15]

Ellsworth had gotten a head start on most of its sister towns because of Fort Ellsworth, established in 1864. When the fort became Fort Harker it was even bigger, and there was more reason than ever for people to move close to the fort for pro-

Courtesy the Kansas State Historical Society, Topeka

Ellsworth — Kansas Pacific Railroad

tection and to make a living by selling to the soldiers stationed there. It was established as a village in 1868, then incorporated as a third-class city in 1871.[16]

The stockyards were built in the west part of town. A few cattle were shipped out in '69 and more in '70. In '71 the total swelled to thirty-five thousand. Ellsworth felt it was on the way.[17]

Ellsworth lured Shanghai Pierce away from Abilene in 1871. Shanghai's real name was Abel, but not one man in a hundred was aware that he had any name other than Shanghai. In '71 Shanghai had directed his trail boss to point toward Abilene, and he went ahead to prepare things for the herd's arrival.

He found Abilene at its peak, with a summer population of seven or eight hundred.[18] It sported a new brick courthouse, a stone schoolhouse, a newspaper, theater, depot, two banks, four hotels, two churches, a jail, and countless saloons and bars, all open at all hours.

After watching the wild life of Abilene and feeling certain that outlaws controlled the town, Shanghai decided to move west. There were too many grangers around Abilene anyway, so he shifted to Ellsworth and sent word to his herd, still well to the south, to change its destination.[19]

Shanghai's trademark was his bullhorn voice. One man claimed that if he whispered it could be heard half a mile away. Joseph McCoy, in describing him, said: "If they are within cannon-shot of where he is, they hear his ear-splitting voice more piercing than a locomotive whistle — more noisy than a steam calliope. It is idle to try to dispute or debate with him, for he will overwhelm you with indescribable noise."

When Shanghai saw the inadequate stockyards at Ellsworth he set up a roar that was heard over all the town and prairies. The builders insisted the yards were big enough to handle all the cattle that would come to Ellsworth. Shanghai "gently" informed them that he would be back next year — and so would Print Olive, Seth Mabry, Colonel Myers, William Perryman, and many other Texas cattlemen.[20]

Abilene ended its greatest season with more cattle shipped out of its yards than anyone could accurately tally. Streeter says over two hundred thousand went through Abilene that summer. Joseph McCoy said that two hundred and thirty-seven thousand arrived in Kansas City alone and added that his figure was likely no more than half of what went through Abilene during the season.

By early October most of the herds were sold and some of the saloons were closed. About twenty Texans were having a last fling in town before heading south. This

Courtesy the Kansas State Historical Society, Topeka

Ellsworth — stockyards, 1870s

was the setting for Hickok's biggest confrontation of the season.

Hickok and Ben Thompson's partner, Phil Coe, had clashed earlier in the summer over the affections of one of Mattie Silk's girls named Jessie Hazel.[21] The rivalry continued, but the issue had not been settled. Thompson left Abilene sometime after he and Coe sold the Bull's Head Saloon. Coe stayed on to finish the season.

Coe joined his Texas buddies for the final spree on the town. It was October 5, too late in the year to expect any real trouble on the Texas Abilene side of the tracks. The celebration got out of hand when Coe shot at a dog that nipped at his heels in front of the Alamo Saloon, Wild Bill's main hangout.

Hickok rushed outside and demanded to know who had fired the shot and why. Coe seldom carried a gun, but this night he had made an exception. He told Hickok what he had done. Coe still had the gun in his hand when he faced Hickok, scarcely eight feet from him.

Either Coe made a threatening move with the gun or Hickok was sure Coe would try to settle the summer's differences now that he had a gun in his hand. Hickok drew his gun swiftly. Some observers said Coe got off the first shot and that it went through Hickok's coat. Hickok shot Coe in the stomach, and Coe's second shot went between the marshal's legs and into the board sidewalk. Hickok made the remark, "I shot too low," perhaps because Coe was such a tall man and Hickok's shot was on the level.[22]

Mike Williams, the man Hickok had recommended for the job as guard at the Novelty Theater nearby, came running around the corner to help Hickok. Hickok saw the man coming with a gun in his hand but failed to recognize him. Suspecting he was another of the Texans, he wheeled and fired, killing Williams instantly.[23]

Coe lived for two days. Hickok let it be known how much he regretted killing Williams, but he voiced no regret over the death of Phil Coe. These two men were all that Hickok killed in Abilene.

On December 12 the town council of Abilene met and passed a resolution discharging Hickok as marshal because there was no longer any need for his services. They then passed another resolution naming James A. Gauthie city marshal at $50 a month, a saving of $100 a month over Hickok's salary.[24]

Of the more than six hundred thousand head of cattle that came up the trail from Texas during the summer of 1871, many were not sold because of their poor condition. Some estimates put the total held over on the buffalo grass of western Kansas at three hundred thousand head.

The herds had barely been moved out on the buffalo grass prairies when a cold rain struck. The temperature dropped and the rain turned to ice, freezing two to three inches thick over everything. For three days a terrible wind blew; when it was over, thousands of the cattle were dead. So were many horses — and even some of the men who had been caught in the storm.

The winter of 1871–72 was severe. It was estimated that a quarter of a million cattle perished on the plains, as well as several hundred cow ponies.[25]

In the midst of this severe winter the Grand Duke Alexis of Russia came to the United States for the express purpose of hunting buffalo. The first hunt was in January, about fifty miles south of North Platte on Red Willow in Nebraska. The army sent Generals Sheridan, Forsythe, and Custer along, as well as Bill Cody as guide. The duke had his fancy, heated tents, with a complete contingent of Russian officers, secretaries, and servants. They killed some buffalo and saw some friendly Indians.[26]

The tour went on to Denver, and then returned on the Kansas Pacific. Fort Wallace supplied horses, mules, and ambulances to follow the hunt that took place in eastern Colorado. One report stated that over two hundred buffalo were killed, the biggest herd being found near Kit Carson.[27]

From there the group went east by rail. The editor of the *Ellsworth Reporter* made this comment in the next issue after the duke and his entourage had passed through: "Duke Alexis did himself the honor to pass through Ellsworth the other night, sleeping in seven palace cars. He did not call at the *Reporter* office and we don't care. It will be a good excuse for us not calling on him when we go to Russia."[28]

Abilene was struggling for survival in the cattle-shipping business, even though it had just experienced its biggest year ever. The farmers were in a majority around town.[29] T. C. Henry was their leader. He drew up a circular that the farmers signed, stating flatly that the inhabitants of Dickinson County would no longer submit to the evils of the cattle trade. The circular was sent to Texas, over the vehement protests of Joseph McCoy. But the fences put up by the farmers were a much greater deterrent to the Texas herds than the circular. Besides, Ellsworth offered as good a market as Abilene, and the trail into Ellsworth was open. It was also a few miles shorter. Abilene had had its day.

Ellsworth was a bigger town, too. That meant more things to buy, perhaps more things for the trail-weary cowboy to do. Proof that those in Abilene saw the handwriting on the wall was the moving to Ellsworth of Drover's Cottage, which had been built in Abilene by McCoy then sold to M. B. George. J. W. and Louisa Gore had been running the three-story hotel in Abilene, and they came along to operate it in Ellsworth. The hotel had to be taken apart to move. It made the trip by flatcar in good shape and was soon being set up for business in its new location.[30]

The foghorn voice of Shanghai Pierce the year before had apparently had some effect on the town planners. The stockyards west of town had been expanded until they covered many acres. There were seven chutes from which cattle could be loaded into cattle cars simultaneously. Col. R. D. Hunter was the superintendent of the yards, which the *Ellsworth Reporter* claimed were the largest in the state.[31]

The first herds arrived at Ellsworth in June 1872. Two weeks later there were twenty-eight herds fattening on the grass around town. By midsummer there were one hundred thousand head waiting to be shipped out.[32]

J. L. Councell was marshal of Ellsworth in the summer of 1872. In the early part of the season gunfights were not yet dominating the news, as this item in the May 16 issue of the *Ellsworth Reporter* proves: "The other morning we witnessed the marshal and assistant arguing a point with a woman. The point in dispute seemed to be the proper way to go to the cooler. The marshal insisted on her walking and she insisted on being carried. As is always the way, the woman came out victorious. Drunk was no name for it."[33]

In early July the town presented the look of a gawky boy growing too fast for his clothes. New stores were everywhere, including four new saloons. Drover's Cottage was open for business although still unfinished.

This hotel was one of the first things Print Olive saw when he arrived in Ellsworth on July 3. Print had stayed in Drover's Cottage in Abilene, and he immediately made it his headquarters again. His herd was being held southwest of town on the Smoky Hill River. His herd of three thousand cattle, worth $5 to $10 a head in Texas would bring $20 to $25 in

Ellsworth, which meant a good profit — as much as $45,000.[34]

Olive wouldn't sell his cattle until they had grazed about three weeks and regained the fat they had lost on the long trail. He was still in town in late July, just after selling his herd, when he got into a quarrel with a gambler named Kennedy. It ended in no more than words, since Kennedy was not armed. Later that day at the Ellsworth Billiard Saloon, it suddenly erupted again. The *Reporter* gave this account:

> Ellsworth, which has been remarkably quiet this season, had its first shooting affair this season last Saturday at about six o'clock at the Ellsworth Billiard saloon. . . . I. P. Olive was seated at a table playing cards. . . . Kennedy came into the room, went behind the bar and taking a revolver walked up in front of Olive and fired at him, telling him "to pass in his check." The second, third and fourth shots took effect, one entering the groin and making a bad wound, one in the thigh and the other in the hand.
>
> Olive could not fire, though he was armed; but someone, it seems a little uncertain who,[35] fired at Kennedy, hitting him in the hip, making a flesh wound. The difficulty arose from a game of cards in the forenoon, Kennedy accusing Olive of unfair dealing, Olive replying in language that professionals cannot bear. The affair made considerable excitement. The wounded were taken in custody and cared for. Drs. Duck & Fox extracted the bullet from Olive and a piece of his gold chain which was shot into the wound. It was feared that Olive would not survive, but the skill of the doctors saved him.[36] Kennedy was removed to South Main Street and put under the charge of three policemen, but by the aid of friends he escaped during the night from the windows and has not since been heard of.
>
> All has been quiet since the affair and is likely to remain so.[37]

The coming of the railroad and settlers and the vast herds of cattle moving north out of Texas helped push the buffalo west. The hunters were hard on their heels now. Buffalo hides were bringing about $3.50 each. Millions were killed from 1868 until the herds were decimated by 1881. Buffalo bones brought $8 a ton, and it took the bones of a hundred buffalo to make a ton. From the Kansas prairies alone there were harvested $2.5 million worth of bones. That would mean the bones of approximately thirty-one million buffalo carcasses.[38] The suddenly empty prairies were an open invitation to the cattleman and the settler.

Ellsworth had a reputation of being a rough town, first when it was the town closest to Fort Ellsworth and then Fort Harker, next when it was an end-of-track town, and finally when it was a cow town. Perhaps it was the history of violence in Ellsworth as much as the violence it actually showed during the cattle-shipping days that prompted one writer to make the remark in later years: "Abilene, the first; Ellsworth, the wickedest; Dodge, the last."[39]

With the cattle drives moving through Kansas, the railroad running all the way to Denver, and settlers moving farther west every day, it would seem that the threat posed by Indians would surely be gone. But though they were now on the reservations, receiving their dole from the government, they renewed their war against the whites whenever the opportunity presented itself.

Such a chance occurred in September 1872, approximately ninety to a hundred miles west and a little south of Ellsworth. Dick Jordon and his brother, George, were buffalo hunters. They had a young Swedish boy working for them. When they decided to go on a buffalo hunt from their home about twenty miles west of Ellis, Dick Jordon's wife asked to go along. Her four-month-old baby had recently died, and she was lonely. They agreed, since she had gone on hunts before.

They intended to hunt along the Smoky Hill River and south toward Fort Dodge, expecting to be gone six or seven weeks. Both Dick and Mrs. Jordon had relatives living in or near Ellis, and they were told about the hunt.

The Jordons had two well-equipped wagons, with all the provisions they would need. The family dog, a Newfoundland named Queen, trailed the wagons.

None of those awaiting their return expected to hear from them for several weeks. Dick Jordon's dog appeared at Jordon's father's homestead about three weeks after the hunt began, but the Jordons decided that Dick had sent the dog back for chasing buffalo, a thing that had happened before.

About the time the Jordon hunting party should have returned, a man came to Buffalo Station on the railroad with word that he had found two wagons on Walnut Creek, about twenty or twenty-five miles south of the Smoky Hill River. There was the body of a man near the wagons, and some sacks of provisions bore the name of R. Jordon.

Alarm spread through the community of Ellis when word reached there. A telegram to Fort Hays brought a sergeant and ten privates to the scene, guided by the hunter who had found the wagons.

They found Dick Jordon by the wagons, scalped. The Swedish boy, Fred Nonnan (Nelson — both names are given) was a short distance away, dead and scalped. Only the sunbonnet and apron of Mrs. Jordon were found. George Jordon was not discovered until the next trip. He was quite a distance from the others, where he had apparently tried to get to some willows.

A description of the twenty-four-year-old Mrs. Jordon was sent out, but no trace of her was ever found. It was thought that the Indians probably killed her on their way back to the reservation to get their winter rations. They certainly could not have taken her with them to the reservation.

The army was almost helpless. The Interior Department was in charge of Indian affairs, and their officials considered the Indians subdued and friendly and no threat to white settlers. Nothing could change their minds. However, the massacre of the Jordon party did little to make the citizens along the Smoky Hill River feel that the Indians were their friends.

Whether the residents of the Smoky Hill Valley lived in a wild town like Ellsworth or Abilene where outlaws could shoot up the town and anybody who got in the way or lived out on a homestead where a stray band of Indians might descend on them with rifles and scalping knives, it was not a time of blissful peace.

NOTES

1. Harry Sinclair Drago, *Wild Woolly and Wicked* (New York: Bramhall House, 1960), p. 86.
2. Ibid.; Floyd Benjamin Streeter, *The Kaw* (New York: Farrar & Rinehart, 1941), p. 129. He also got a percentage of the fines levied on

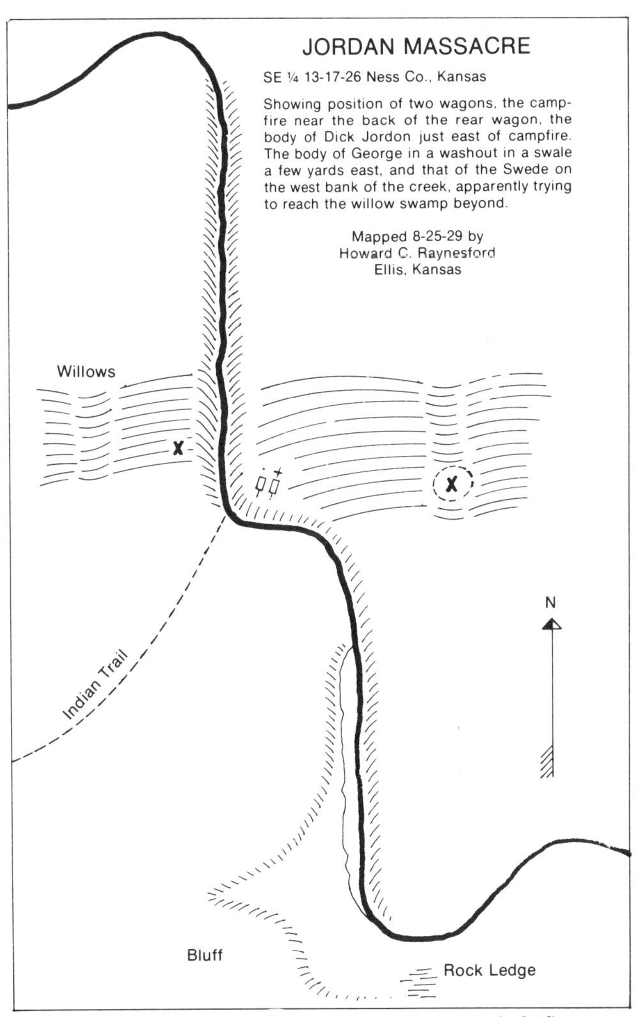

Mapped 8-25-29 by Howard C. Raynesford, Ellis, Kansas
Jordon massacre

those he arrested. One author points out that the 1871 council evidently didn't value Hickok as highly as Tom Smith, since they had paid Smith $225 a month and paid Hickok only $150.
3. Nyle H. Miller and Joseph W. Snell, "Some Notes on Kansas Cowtown Police Officers and Gun Fighters," *Kansas Historical Quarterly* (Winter 1960), p. 429. Cartoons showing Hickok carrying Councilman Burroughs into the meeting over his shoulder were carried in the newspapers of that month.
4. Ibid., p. 424. Hickok, in making his report of men who had died at Hays while he was there, listed Strawhim (also spelled Stranghan, Strawhorne, Strawhan) as having been killed in April 1870. This is obviously an error, since the Leavenworth *Times* and *Conservative* reported the killing on September 28, 1869.
5. Blaine Burkey, *Custer Come at Once* (Hays, Kans.: Thomas More Prep, 1976), p. 96.
6. Drago, *Wild Woolly and Wicked*, p. 94.
7. Miller and Snell, "Cowboy Police Officers," p. 430.
8. Drago, *Wild Woolly and Wicked*, p. 97.
9. Streeter, *The Kaw*, p. 130.
10. Drago, *Wild Wooly and Wicked*, p. 100.
11. Ibid., pp. 101–2.
12. Streeter, *The Kaw*, p. 131.
13. Drago, *Wild Woolly and Wicked*, p. 95.
14. Ibid., p. 114. Streeter gives the population of Ellsworth in '71 as about a thousand.
15. Streeter, *The Kaw*, pp. 133–4.
16. Drago, *Wild Woolly and Wicked*, p. 119.
17. Streeter, *The Kaw*, p. 135.
18. Chris Emmett, *Shanghai Pierce: A Fair Likeness* (Norman: Univ. of Oklahoma Press, 1953), p. 70. The census listed people from twenty-seven states and thirteen foreign countries during the summer months. And "no one thought to take the census in the Devil's Addition, which housed the Jezebels and Delilahs."
19. Ibid., p. 72.
20. Drago, *Wild Woolly and Wicked*, p. 116.
21. Ibid., p. 106.
22. Streeter, *The Kaw*, pp. 131–2.
23. Drago, *Wild Woolly and Wicked*, p. 109.
24. Miller and Snell, "Cowtown Police Officers," p. 439.
25. Streeter, *The Kaw*, pp. 184–5.
26. Drago, *Wild Woolly and Wicked*, p. 120. This account says the site of this hunt was "fifty miles west of North Platte," which would put it exactly on the site of Ogallala. It was actually in northern Hayes County, almost due south of North Platte.
27. Mrs. Frank C. Montgomery, "Fort Wallace and Its Relation to the Frontier," *Kansas Historical Collections, 1926–1928* 17 (1928), p. 251.
28. Drago, *Wild Woolly and Wicked*, p. 120.
29. Ibid., p. 113.
30. Harry E. Chrisman, *The Ladder of Rivers* (Denver: Sage Books, 1962), pp. 117–8.
31. Streeter, *The Kaw*, p. 135.
32. George Jelinek, "The Ellsworth Story," *Ellsworth* (Kans.) *Reporter*, 3 August 1967.
33. Miller and Snell, "Cowtown Police Officers," p. 200.
34. Chrisman, *Ladder of Rivers*, pp. 117–8.
35. Chrisman says it was Print Olive's faithful hired hand, "Nigger Jim" who fired the shot that wounded Kennedy. Jim was just outside the saloon when the shooting began, and he fired from the door at Kennedy.
36. Chrisman says Print Olive became furious after Dr. Duck and Dr. Fox had probed for thirty minutes and had not recovered either bullet. He fired them and had another physician, Dr. Minnick, brought in. It was Dr. Minnick who removed the bullets.
37. *Ellsworth Reporter*, 1 August 1872.
38. Jelinek, "Ellsworth Story."
39. Ibid.

CHAPTER 25

"HELL IS IN SESSION IN ELLSWORTH"

WILLIAM M. COX was the general livestock agent for the Kansas Pacific Railroad, and the company had a job for him to do. There was no doubt in the minds of the Kansas Pacific Railroad men through the winter of 1872–73 that their reign as the only railroad from Kansas to the east was about over. The Santa Fe Railroad was building rapidly through the southern part of the state, going past Wichita toward Dodge City.

Once the towns on the southern route were established and ready to handle cattle, Texas ranchers would likely send their cattle there because those towns were many miles closer.

Cox's job was to blaze a fast trail to Ellsworth, free of all obstacles. Cutting off the Chisholm Trail that pointed toward Abilene, Cox's trail ran north through Kingman, crossed the Arkansas at Ellinwood, then bent back a little to the northeast to Ellsworth. Cox had four Texas cattlemen with him.[1] This was the trail that they predicted would bring glory to Ellsworth in 1873.

The new trail had abundant grass and water, and it shortened the distance from Texas to Ellsworth by thirty-five miles. That could mean at least three fewer days on the trail for the herds.[2]

Ellsworth had thirteen saloons ready for the big push in '73. This was to be Ellsworth's big year, as 1871 had been for Abilene. But the people of Ellsworth had seen what happened to Abilene, and they were determined that it would not happen to them. There was already a $25 government license on each saloon and a $10 business tax. The city then added $500 to each saloon. The more undesirable businesses were relegated to an area along the riverbottom a half-mile from the center of town. This quickly earned the local name of Nauchville.[3] It was a generally accepted fact that there was no law in Nauchville.

The first herds from the south hit Ellsworth early in '73, as soon as the grass was good enough to fatten them.[4] It was the peak year for Ellsworth. Before the summer was over, many things would happen. One was the arrival of two hundred and twenty thousand Texas cattle.[5]

As fast as sales were made the cattle were shipped out, loaded from the seven loading chutes in the pens. Considering that they could crowd about twenty head into each car, it is easy to see that a great many cattle moved out of the Ellsworth stockyards each day. Loading sometimes went on much of the night, too.

The cost of shipping a carload of cattle from Ellsworth to Chicago, which included two feedings, was $90, to St. Louis $60, and to Kansas City $35.[6] Considering the better market to be found at cities where packing plants practically joined the railroad yards, shippers were more than willing to pay the freight. Often Texas owners shipped their cattle to the cities, instead of selling in Ellsworth, and went along to sell directly to the packing plants.

Ellsworth was duly proud of its loading and shipping pens. One reporter described them as ". . . the best and most complete set of yards that are to be found in the state. There are seven shoots [sic] for loading, with two pens to each, large enough for one car of cattle; also six large pens that will hold ten carloads apiece, and back of that a large yard that will hold 500 head. . . . There are also gates from one pen to another, and well fixed so as to be very handy. The small pens next to the shoots are floored with two inch plank. Eight men can load from 150 to 200 cars per day."[7]

Although Ellsworth thought it was ready for the cattle business, it hadn't anticipated two disastrous developments — a drop in the market for beef and the dry sultry weather. By June the hills around Ellsworth were black with cattle. The market was flat, the weather dry and hot. Cowboys who had expected to be heading back to Texas had to take their turns herding cattle waiting to be sold. The rest of the time they loafed in town, hundreds more than the town had expected at one time. Noses were choked with dust, bodies smothered in dry heat, tempers short — the situation was growing acute.

On June 21 the town had an election to select a new mayor. James Miller won on a platform to maintain strict order.[8] He promptly augmented the police force to three policemen to help the marshal. The marshal was Brocky ("Jack") Norton, and his three assistants were John ("Jack") DeLong, John ("Jack") Morco, and John ("Jack") Brauham. The Four Jacks, they were called.[9]

Perhaps the only decent law officer Ellsworth had was the county sheriff, Chauncey Whitney. The marshal and most of his assistants had bad records. Marshal Norton had earned his in Abilene, while Morco, apparently the worst troublemaker in the lot, had killed four men in California, apparently unarmed — men who rushed to the rescue of his wife when he was beating her.[10]

It was into this situation that Ben and Billy Thompson came to Ellsworth. Ben had tried to salvage something from his interest in the Bull's Head Saloon in Abilene but, with the shifting of the cattle trade to Ellsworth, Abilene had changed. There was nothing to be realized from his saloon interest there. Broke but determined to get into the swing of things again, the two brothers came to Ellsworth.

Ellsworth was having more trouble than just the clash of the law with the lawless. The cattle market had hit bottom. Cowboys were broke and disgusted. Grass shriveled, and men sweltered in the heat. Tempers were made shorter by the lack of activity and the poor prospects of a profit for their long drive. Ellsworth was ripe for a violent summer.[11]

Ben Thompson managed to scrape together enough money to open a gambling room in Brennan's Saloon. Texans were being arrested on the slightest provocation and dragged into court to pay $15 to $35 fines. They were getting hotter and hotter under the collar, but they lacked any leadership to oppose the laws of the town. Now they had Ben Thompson, and he was a force that even the Four Jacks had to respect.

By the first of August cowboys and their bosses were seething like a latent volcano. A reporter for one Kansas newspaper, after watching things in the town, especially on South Main Street, wrote back to his paper: "Hell is still in session in Ellworth."[12]

Half the month of August went by without unusual violence. It erupted suddenly and unexpectedly. On Friday, the fifteenth in Ben Thompson's gambling room at Joe Brennan's Saloon, a game involving Cad Pierce and Neil Cain was going on.

Pierce wanted to bet higher stakes than Cain could handle, so Ben asked a professional gambler, John Sterling, if he would take Pierce's overbets. Sterling, half drunk, agreed. He told Thompson that if he won he'd cut Ben in for half. Sterling did win quite a pile of Pierce's money, but he left without cutting Thompson in for his share. Later in the afternoon Thompson found Sterling and asked for his money. Sterling, knowing that Thompson was unarmed because the city ordinance required all guns to be checked, slapped Ben instead of paying him.

If he had been fully sober Sterling would likely have thought twice before slapping Ben Thompson. Anyone could have told him that no one slapped Thompson and lived to brag about it. Ben started for Sterling bare-handed, but Jack Morco, one of Ellsworth's policemen and a good friend of Sterling, leaped in front of Ben with a drawn pistol. Thompson stopped.

Courtesy the Kansas State Historical Society, Topeka

C. B. Whitney, Ellsworth County sheriff

He knew Morco was a killer who hated him — a feeling that was mutual. He told Morco to get Sterling out of there, and the policeman did.

No one expected Thompson to let the face slapping go unavenged. Still, it was Sterling and Morco who threw the challenge to Thompson. Sterling got a shotgun, and he and Morco went to Brennan's Saloon and yelled at the door for Thompson to come out and fight.

Thompson tried to borrow a gun but couldn't. Finally he ran to the saloon where all checked guns were kept, and there he grabbed his revolver and a rifle. Billy Thompson, already drunk, got Ben's prize shotgun, which Cad Pierce had given him, and followed Ben into the street.

By then Sterling and Morco were out of sight. Ben yelled for them to come out. Sterling and Morco didn't respond, but Sheriff Chauncey Whitney heard the commotion and came running to put a stop to it. The sheriff tried to be fair-minded. He got along with both factions in town, so he had little fear of the Thompsons. He likely wouldn't have hesitated even if he had been afraid. Chauncey Whitney had been with Forsythe's scout at the battle of Beecher Island. Few situations could be more dangerous than that.

The Thompsons agreed not to cause any trouble if Whitney would disarm Sterling and make Morco behave. They walked together to Brennan's Saloon. The details of what happened next are confused, due to the loyalties of the various reporters. Apparently Billy Thompson, still carrying Ben's shotgun on full cock, went into the saloon first, followed by Sheriff Whitney. Just as Ben Thompson was starting through the door, Bill Lanford, a Texas cowman, shouted a warning: "Look out, Ben! Here they come with guns!"

Ben wheeled around to see Sterling running toward the saloon with a pistol in his hand. Ben dived into the alley by

Beebe's General Store and waited. Langford's yell had brought Whitney back to the street. Seeing what was happening, he shouted for Sterling and Ben to stop. Sterling ignored the sheriff and kept coming.

When Sterling got close enough to see Ben, he stopped dead in his tracks. Instead of shooting, however, he dived into the door of the store; his bravery had suddenly evaporated. Ben snapped a shot at him that hit the door jamb. One historian says that was probably the poorest shooting Thompson had ever done.

Hearing the shot, Billy Thompson staggered outside, his shotgun ready to use. The two versions of the next couple of seconds are quite different. The Texans swore that Billy's shotgun accidentally discharged, hitting Whitney in the shoulder and lung. The other side said Billy deliberately fired the gun — whether he was too drunk to recognize Whitney or just didn't care was the question.

Courtesy the Kansas State Historical Society, Topeka *Bill Nye sketch*

Billy Thompson shooting Sheriff C. B. Whitney in Ellsworth

That ended the battle for the moment. Ben Thompson was furious with his brother for shooting their friend but was determined to get him out of this trouble, as he had many other times. While friends picked up Whitney and carried him to his home, Ben ordered Billy to get out of town. He gave Billy a revolver but took back his own shotgun. A paper reported that Billy rode out of town "cursing and inviting a fight."

Mayor Miller rushed down when he heard the uproar. When he saw the situation he demanded that Ben Thompson be disarmed and arrested. None of the policemen wanted to take the chance. The mayor, in a rage, fired them all. The only officer the town had then was Deputy Sheriff Ed Hogue. The mayor and Hogue finally screwed up enough courage to walk out and talk to Ben. Thompson, with Billy finally out of town, agreed to put down his gun if the mayor would take away Sterling's and Morco's arms.[13] Morco and Sterling also agreed to the terms. The crisis was over.

Word came back to town that Billy Thompson had gone no farther than Nauchville, where he was visiting his special girl friend, Molly Brennan. A few citizens formed a vigilante committee and went down to look for him. They didn't find him. Some said they didn't look very hard.

Three days later, on Monday morning, August 18, Sheriff Chauncey Whitney died from blood poisoning of the wounds he received from the shotgun blast.

As a postscript to this battle, Billy Thompson was finally arrested by Captain Sparks of the Texas Rangers in the fall of 1876. After a long legal battle extradition papers were issued, and Billy was brought back to Kansas in early 1877 for trial. By then much had been forgotten, and Texas men swore under oath that the shot had been an accident. Billy Thompson was finally declared innocent of Whitney's death.

It was the biggest battle of the summer in Ellsworth, but Sheriff Whitney was the only man killed. The killing was not over, however. The sheriff was well liked by the decent citizens of Ellsworth, and his death outraged them. A vigilante committee was formed and let it be known that certain unwanted men from the Lone Star State would be given a "white affidavit" as a warning to get out of town in twenty-four hours or suffer the consequences. Ben Thompson heard about these affidavits and left town before he could be served with one, going to Kansas City.[14]

Some of the policemen who had been fired were rehired, and Ed Crawford was added to the force. After Ben Thompson left Ellsworth, others who were certain to be on the list to receive white affidavits were uneasy. Cad Pierce, who had taken up a collection to give to Billy Thompson when he left town, was one who was sure he had been marked.

On August 20, five days after Sheriff Whitney had been killed, Pierce, Neil Cain and John Good met Ed Hogue and the new policeman, Ed Crawford, in front of Beebe's store. Pierce asked about the affidavits. Words quickly became heated, and Crawford took an active part, finally challenging Pierce to a fight. Pierce was not armed, since carrying a gun would have invited trouble with the police. However, when he reached behind him, Crawford drew his gun and shot Pierce, claiming afterward that he knew Pierce was reaching for his gun.

Pierce, wounded ran into Beebe's store. Crawford shot him again as he went through the door. Pierce collapsed, and reports said that Crawford beat him over the head with his gun until he was dead.[15]

Some newspapers said it was wonderful that the policemen were finally standing up to the Texas criminals. Others called it outright murder because Pierce was not armed. The Texans claimed that even if Crawford had thought Pierce was reaching for his gun he could have seen after one shot that he was unarmed. From that moment on, it was cold-blooded murder. The bulk of the citizens of Ellsworth, as eager as the police to get rid of the Texans, agreed that it was murder, not law and order.

The Texans were really aroused by then. They came from their camps around town, armed to the teeth, and rode through the streets shooting wildly. They didn't injure anyone, but they treed the town. Before they left they yelled that they would be back and burn the town to the ground.[16] The people of Ellsworth believed them. There were a lot of Texans on the prairies around town.

The townspeople armed themselves and patrolled the town that night in bands, ready to put out any fires that might be

Courtesy the Kansas State Historical Society, Topeka
Copied from Human Life, February 1907

Wyatt Earp

started. None were. It was apparent to the rough element that the permanent citizens of the town were prepared to fight for their homes. A pitched battle was too much for the transients to consider. They could conduct their business elsewhere without the danger of an all-out battle. They began to leave Ellsworth the next day. An item in the *Commonwealth* said: "The 21st of August will be remembered in Ellsworth for the exodus of the roughs and gamblers."[17]

The same bands of men who roamed the town to prevent fires also raided many hotel rooms occupied by gamblers and "Texas badmen," looking for a big cache of arms that was supposed to be hidden in town.

To the Texans, even to the law-abiding cattlemen, this was heaping insult on injury. Many of them turned their herds south to the Santa Fe Railroad to ship them east. The prices were no better, but the climate for Texans was. The drought had about wiped out the good grass around Ellsworth, anyway.

The newspaper pleaded with the real cattlemen to stay and sell their cattle. A few agreed — on the condition that all the police of Ellsworth be fired and new men hired. The town council, faced with the possible loss of the cattle herds, agreed. All the policemen were dismissed on August 27, just two weeks after Whitney was killed.[18]

The erstwhile policemen were ordered to turn in their guns. Two, Jack Morco and Ed Crawford, refused, leaving town instead. Morco and Crawford were given a warning to stay out of Ellsworth, but eight days after he was fired Morco returned, riding boldly up and down the street flaunting his guns. Charlie Brown, one of the new policemen, confronted Morco and demanded his guns, according to the town ordinance. Morco refused. He drew one of the guns, but Brown was too fast. He shot Morco twice, once in the heart, and then in the head as he fell. So the badge-toter the Texans hated most was finally killed by the police of Ellsworth, the body he had belonged to for so long.[19]

Ellsworth quieted down then and things looked better, although still very grim. Then on September 20 disaster struck. The New York Stock Exchange closed its doors, and panic swept the financial world. At first the effects reached the western ranges in a trickle. Then the full impact hit, bringing a complete collapse of the cattle market. Those who had not already sold their herds couldn't give them away. Many ranchers were in debt, depending on their cattle sales to pull them out. Now there was no market; they couldn't pay off their debts. The creditors, fearing they wouldn't get their money, demanded immediate payment. Ranchers who had appeared to be riding high, with huge herds waiting for the market, were suddenly dead broke.[20]

Those who could keep their cattle put them out on grass for the winter. Even this was not going to be much of a reprieve. The summer had been extremely dry. Even though the herds were moved west where cattle had not grazed all summer, there was still only short grass. Fully forty percent of the cattle around Ellsworth were pushed west onto what grass they could find and prepared to weather the winter, if possible.[21]

Ellsworth saw a dismal future, but it did not close down as early as usual in the fall because there were still many Texas herds around, waiting and hoping the market would open up just a little, enough so they could get rid of the cattle driven up from Texas last spring.

Ed Crawford, the man who had killed Cad Pierce, ignored the order to stay out of Ellsworth and came back the first of November. He soon made the headlines of the local paper. Under the heading: "Ed Crawford Shot" the story read:

Last Sunday Ed Crawford came to Ellsworth. His presence here was a surprise, as it was understood that his life would not be safe here, on account of his shooting Cad Pierce. He was warned that his life was in danger, but he "was not afraid." Thursday he was pretty full of whiskey, and Friday evening we noticed he was considerably under the influence of liquor. With some friends, or possibly decoying enemies, he went down to Nauchville and visited two houses; he was pretty drunk and rough; at the second house he visited there was a crowd of men, mostly Texans, and he had been there but a few moments before, having stepped in the hall, he was shot twice, the first ball passing through his head, the second into his body. It is not known for certain who fired the fatal shot, but it is supposed to have been one Putnam,[22] and that he did it to avenge the murder of Cad Pierce. It was reported that Crawford fired, but it was probably incorrect. He was shot down by some person secreted in the hall and he made no fight or scarcely a struggle. With this last murder we hope the chapter of crime in this city is complete for 1873, and for many years to come.[23]

The *Reporter* was to get its wish, more completely perhaps than it wanted. Crawford's murder was the last of the '73 season. A hundred miles south, Wichita was putting in stockyards and shipping pens. The herds would not come to Ellsworth again.

The drought of the summer extended into the fall. Cropland that had dried out and grassland that had been trampled by too many hungry cattle allowed the wind to pick up the dust and blow it for miles. Junction City reported: "The streets were filled all day long with so dense a cloud of dust that you couldn't see the cigar before your face; and so deep was the artificial darkness that several men who owe this establishment passed directly by the office door without seeing it. The *Lawrence Journal*, which is a standard authority on the subject of weather, says the wind blew seventy miles an hour in Lawrence."[24]

Nor was the dust the only problem. The same *Junction City Weekly Union* reported on November 22, 1873: "Monday was the big prairie fire day all over the country. At Hays City the gale got up what

Courtesy the Kansas State Historical Society, Topeka

Kansas dust storm about 1938

is called in that region a 'sand storm,' rendering it almost impossible to discern objects, and while this was at its height, a prairie fire made for the town. . . . It was with the greatest difficulty that the people in the face of the drifting, blinding sand, managed to keep the fire from entering and sweeping away the town."[25]

The November dust storms were a matter of record all over Kansas that year. The *Weather Review* for the month stated: "In the latter part of November, vast prairie fires occurred in the far west, and several dust storms, filling the air with fine and unpalpable particles, which are known to remain suspended in the air for many days, and sometimes are finally precipitated with water, forming the celebrated 'black rain.' "[26]

It was a dismal ending to the year all along the Smoky Hill River. The drought had hurt the crops of the farmers. The money panic had caused banks to close and railroads to go into receivership and had brought bankruptcy to many a rancher.

It was a particularly sad ending of a year which had started with such glowing hopes for Ellsworth. The eruption of violence in town, the money panic, closing of banks, and finally the loss of the cattle market spelled doom to the high hopes of the town. There were few dreams of a big 1874 for Ellsworth as winter closed down.

NOTES

1. Floyd Benjamin Streeter, *The Kaw*, (New York: Farrar & Rinehart, 1941), p. 107.
2. George Jelinek, "The Ellsworth Story," *Ellsworth* (Kans.) *Reporter*, 3 August 1967.
3. Harry Sinclair Drago, *Wild Woolly and Wicked*, (New York: Bramhall House, 1960), p. 120.
4. Jelinek, "Ellsworth Story."
5. Drago, *Wild Woolly and Wicked*, p. 113. Jelinek places the number to come to Ellsworth at 150,000. Streeter says there were 100,000 there by the end of May; by June 5 it had grown to 125,000, and by July the total had swelled to 177,000.
6. Jelinek, "Ellsworth Story."
7. George Jelinek, "Frontier Land," *Ellsworth* (Kans.) *Reporter*, 1973; "A description of Ellsworth"; quoted from the *Manhatten Nationalist*, 2 August 1872.
8. Ibid.; "Law Enforcement."
9. Drago, *Wild Woolly and Wicked*, p. 121.
10. Ibid., p. 124. DeLong and Brauham were virtually unknown but fit the mold of the other two. Ed Hogue was deputy sheriff under Sheriff Whitney, and his record was almost as bad as the others.
11. Jelinek, "Frontier Land"; "Law and Order."
12. Jelinek, "Ellsworth Story"; Chris Emmett, *Shanghai Pierce: A Fair Likeness* (Norman: Univ. of Oklahoma Press, 1953), p. 73.
13. Streeter, *The Kaw*, pp. 139–147; Drago, *Wild Woolly and Wicked*, pp. 127–138. Stuart Lake in his biograghy of Wyatt Earp (*Wyatt Earp, Frontier Marshal*) claims it was Wyatt Earp who disarmed Ben Thompson after Billy had fled. Few believe that Earp was even in town. No newspaper accounts of the battle in Ellsworth's South Main Street even mention Earp. He would hardly have been ignored if he had actually disarmed Ben Thompson.
14. Streeter, *The Kaw*, p. 147.
15. Drago, *Wild Woolly and Wicked*, p. 139.
16. Ibid., p. 140.
17. *Topeka Commonwealth*, 28 August 1873.
18. Jelinek, "Frontier Land"; "Law Enforcement."
19. Drago, *Wild Woolly and Wicked*, pp. 141–2.
20. Streeter, *The Kaw*, p. 186.
21. Drago, *Wild Woolly and Wicked*, p. 142.
22. The Putnams were cousins of Cad Pierce.
23. *Ellsworth Reporter*, 13 November 1873. Crawford was killed on November 7.
24. *Junction City (Kans.) Weekly Union*, 15 November 1873.
25. James C. Malin, "Dust Storms, 1861–1880," *Kansas Historical Quarterly* (August 1946), p. 271.
26. Ibid.

CHAPTER 26

THE LAST TRAIL TRAGEDY

OF THE THOUSANDS OF LONGHORNS put on the grass of western Kansas to winter, a big percentage died. The grass was short due to the dry weather the summer before, and the weather was bitter cold to the steers used to the warmer climate of Texas. Many cattle were butchered just to get tallow, which the owners could sell.

Only the cattle that had wintered in western Kansas came to Ellsworth for shipping in 1874, and the total number was eighteen thousand five hundred head. All the herds coming from Texas stopped at Wichita, saving several days of driving. As one reporter stated it: "Wichita took the trade, the toughs, and some of the merchants."[1]

Kansas had endured a severe drought in 1860, and people in the East thought that was the permanent state of weather in Kansas. Henry Worrall painted a picture showing men climbing ladders to chop ears of corn off the stalks and two men standing on one watermelon. He named his picture, "Droughty Kansas."[2]

His picture was circulated in the East and was the cause of many people moving to Kansas. Then came the dry summer of 1873, followed by an even drier 1874. An added plague in '74 was an invasion of grasshopper hordes.

They came like a cloud out of a clear sky and settled down, devouring everything they could chew. Men scraped them out of their beards and hair. Farmers rushed to their cornfields with sharpened corn knives but came back discouraged. The corn stalks were bare by the time they got to the field.

The hoppers ate everything in the garden, even hollowing out the onions, leaving an empty mold in the ground like "an uncorked bottle." They left nothing but their eggs for a new generation next year. Some farmers said, "If winter don't kill them off, it's all up with the people. There'll never be another harvest in Kansas."[3]

Newspapers reported that the men who had come from the East to get rich in the bountiful land of Kansas made long trips just "to cuss the man who got up that 'picter' " of the huge corn and melons. They admitted they had been enticed to Kansas by the picture.[4]

Grasshoppers and drought came together. The substitute editor of the *Junction City Union*, M. L. Prentice, wrote an article about the troubles of Kansas that summer of 1874:

> Misfortunes never come singly, and a "dry spell" brings with it any number of disasters and inconveniences. A drought nourishes chinch bugs, sun strokes, grasshoppers and profanity. . . . We all know that looking for rain will not bring it, nor will gazing steadfastly at the barometer affect the movements of that instrument. . . . Yet for the last six weeks . . . men have gone about with their eyes cocked at the brazen heavens after the manner of a goose going under a gate, while Hookey's barometer, the standard which tells the town when it isn't going to rain, is corralled like a bulletin board in war times.

As a matter of history we may say that at this writing the drouth which embraces the Kaw Valley (including the Smoky Hill River) from one end to the other continues without any sign of a "let up."[5]

The settlers considered luckiest along the Smoky Hill were those who lived in dugouts, not because of the elegance of their houses but because of the coolness in the summer and warmth in the winter. As one traveler described these dugouts after his first sight of them: "Simply a burrow with a pitched roof of sod, seldom having a window, the door answering this purpose, however inelegant in appearance, is truly a snug place in which to spend the blustery winter days. There your plainsman can lie back at his ease on his bed of robes, and think it a bed of roses and hear with philosophic calmness the peltings of the rude storm without."[6]

Being dug into the ground, insects and rodents took refuge in the dugouts, too, sharing the comfort with their human companions, much to the annoyance and disgust of the humans, especially the women. There was a ditty that showed the humor that kept these pioneers sane. It was dubbed "The Land of the Free."

The land of the free
The land of the bedbug, grasshopper and flea
I'll sing of its praises; I'll tell of its fame
While starving to death on my government claim.[7]

This same breed of humor prompted one man to put in verse the story that a plainsman told him about running down and punishing a mule thief.

We started arter that 'ere pup.
An' took the judge along
For fear, with all our dander up
We might do somethin' wrong.

We caught him under twenty miles,
An' tried him under trees:
The judge he passed around the "smiles"
As sort of jury fees.

"Pris'ner," says judge, "now say your say,
An' make it short an' sweet,
An' while yer at it, kneel and pray,
For Death yer can not cheat.

"No man shall hang, by this 'ere court,
Exceptin' on the square;
There's time fur speech, if so it's short,
But none to chew or swear."

An' then the thievin' rascal cursed,
An' threw his life away,
He said, "Just pony out your worst,
Your best would be foul play."

Then Judge he frowned an awful frown,
An' snapped this sentence short,
"Jones, twitch the rope, an' write this down,
Hung for contempt of court."[8]

While cattle continued to come out of Texas to the markets in southern Kansas, some poured on across western Kansas to Ogallala, where most of them went to ranges in Montana and Wyoming and the prairies of Nebraska and the Dakotas. A great many of the cattle were also stopping in Kansas. The growth of the cattle business in Kansas is revealed in the cattle census. In 1870 a little under 374,000 head were reported; in 1880 the figure was more than 1,533,000.[9]

The days of Indian raids were past for the Smoky Hill Valley, according to the newspaper reports and army bulletins. It was this false promise that likely led to the worst massacre in western Kansas. Although the tragedy culminated in September of 1874 it had its beginning in Georgia, in the Blue Ridge Mountains of Fannin County.

Their homeland devastated by guerrillas during the Civil War, John and Lydia German decided to move west. It took them five years to accumulate enough to outfit a wagon and oxteam. By 1870 they had enough to start west with their seven children, six girls and a boy.

Stopping to work to make money for travel, they moved slowly. It was four years later, on August 15, 1874, that they left Missouri on the last leg of their migration to Colorado, with a good wagon and a fresh oxteam.

By now some of the children were grown. Rebecca, the oldest, was twenty;

Stephen, the only son, was nineteen. Catherine was seventeen, Joanna was fifteen, Sophia twelve, Juliana seven, and Nancy Adelaide (Addie) was five.[10]

They drove two cows and calves, besides their oxen and the wagon loaded with the provisions they would need. They also had a feather bed and Sophia's crate of chickens. It was a big load for a wagon. John generally walked ahead, and often Stephen and two or three of the oldest girls would walk. Lydia drove the oxen.

They headed northwest to Ellsworth, Kansas, on the Smoky Hill, and from there followed the railroad past Fort Hays to Ellis. They were told at Ellis that they should go south to the river and follow the old Butterfield Overland Despatch Trail because there wasn't enough water or grass ahead if they stayed near the railroad.

Assured there was no longer any danger from Indians, they turned south to the old B.O.D. Trail. There they found plenty of water and grass for the cattle.

Just how far they had traveled on the trail by the night of September 10 is still a controversy. Late that afternoon, just as they were ready to camp, they met two men going east who told them they could reach Fort Wallace the next day.[11]

Photo by Author

Death Hollow campground at Forks of Smoky Hill River. Ruts of old B.O.D. Trail in foreground.

The place where they camped was by a dry streambed, but they dug a foot down into the sandy bed and got water for themselves and their stock. They hurried through their evening chores so they could get to bed and get an early start. John German wanted to get to Fort Wallace the next day.[12]

On the morning of September 11 they were up and had things ready to leave by sunrise. The two cows and calves were off to the north grazing, and Stephen and Catherine went to bring them back and drive them after the wagon. John led off as usual, with his rifle over his arm. Lydia drove the oxen, with Rebecca, the oldest daughter, at her side. Joanna and Sophia were in the wagon, and Julia and Addie were sitting on the tailgate with the crate of chickens.

Stephen and Catherine had just turned the cattle toward the wagon when they heard the yells of Indians. The warriors charged out of a ravine that paralleled the trail.

John was the first one to be hit. He was killed before he could use his rifle. Lydia leaped off the wagon to run to her husband and was killed by a tomahawk. Rebecca grabbed the ax in the front of the wagon and swung it at the Indian reaching for her. She hit him on the shoulder, but another Indian shot her.

Meanwhile, Stephen and Catherine turned to run toward the bluffs behind them, where they could hide. One Indian overtook Stephen and drove a lance through him. Another fired an arrow at Catherine, hitting her in the thigh and stopping her flight. The Indian leaped off his horse and jerked the arrow out of Catherine's thigh. He threw her, screaming, onto his horse and charged back to the wagon.

The war party of Indians consisted of seventeen warriors and, strangely, two squaws.[13] The leader of the party was Kicking Horse.[14] The Indians took the oxen off the wagon and put them with the two cows and calves. Others ransacked the wagon, taking anything they had any use for. Little Addie was crying uncontrollably, and one warrior brought up his gun to shoot her to put a stop to the crying. One of the two squaws in the group leaped in front of the little five-year-old and saved her. From then on the squaw claimed Addie and Julia, the seven-year-old.

The two oldest girls, Catherine and Joanna, were taken to the back of the wagon, where the Indians began arguing about them. Finally they jerked the bonnets off the two girls. Joanna was two years younger than Catherine, but she was bigger and had long hair. Catherine's hair was short. Catherine was dragged to the front of the wagon with the other girls. One shot from an Indian rifle, and Joanna's long hair became a scalp to be taken as a trophy.

The Indians took their four prisoners and headed southwest, driving the cattle and leaving the wagon in flames. After getting away from the scene they stopped and killed the cattle and had a feast.

Each girl had to ride with an Indian. It began to rain that afternoon, the first rain that had fallen on the prairies for a long time. The second day the Indians shot a buffalo, and the girls got some meat. They hadn't been able to eat that first day. The third day the Indians raided a ranch and got more cattle and some horses. From then on Catherine and Sophia had horses of their own to ride, but the two smaller girls were kept on horses with their captors.[15]

The Indians crossed the North Canadian River in Oklahoma Territory and went on to McClellan Creek in the Texas Panhandle, about two hundred and thirty miles south of Fort Wallace.[16] It was here, late in September, that the Indians took alarm at something and hurriedly broke camp, leaving the two little girls, Julia and Addie, sitting on the prairie. The two older girls lagged behind until the Indians who had been caring for the little girls caught up with the others. The little girls were not with them. Catherine and Sophia were sure the little ones had been killed.

The little girls were still alive. They had simply been left on the prairie to die. Julia, at seven, was the older, so she took charge. The two little girls wandered around until they found a wagon track and followed it to an army camp that had been abandoned only about a week. There they found some hardtack, horse corn, and meat scraps. Those tidbits, along with wild berries, grapes, and onions, made up their diet and kept them alive.

Meanwhile, a hunter along the Smoky Hill River had discovered the bodies at the massacre site. He rode directly to Sheridan, eight miles up the North Fork of the Smoky Hill from the Forks, and sent a telegram to Fort Wallace. Soldiers were sent immediately to the scene.

John H. Edwards, state senator from Ellis County, sent a letter to the *Topeka Commonwealth* as soon as he heard about it. The letter appeared in that paper on October 9, 1874. Senator Edwards got the wrong information about the number and sex of the dead, but army records show he as not confused with most of the other facts.

Ellis, Kan., October 4, 1874

To the Editor of the Commonwealth:

On Wednesday last [September 30] a hunter arrived at Sheridan from the north fork of the Smoky Hill River and reported having found the bodies of three men and one woman who had been killed by the Indians and their wagon burned. The news was telegraphed to Fort Wallace and a squad of soldiers, in charge of a lieutenant, sent down to investigate the matter. They returned on Saturday to Monument Station, bringing the bodies of the three men and the woman. They had apparently been dead ten or twelve days.[17] An axe was sticking in the woman's head, and all the bodies were more or less mutilated. They had apparently been surprised and killed without resistance. From the tracks in the vicinity, there must have been at least three or four children in the party. None of their bodies baving been found, however, the supposition is that they were carried off. The wagon had been burned and everything carried off. A Bible was found nearby, the family record of which proves the party to have come from the town of Blue Ridge, state of Georgia, and of the name of German.

John H. Edwards[18]

The soldiers sent from Fort Wallace were under the command of Lt. C. C. Hewitt, Nineteenth Infantry, a spring graduate of West Point. The names and birth dates found in the Bible at the massacre site were proof that four girls were missing. This launched one of the greatest search-and-rescue missions ever undertaken by the army of the plains. All the soldiers who could be spared from the forts along the Smoky Hill took up the search.

The two older German girls were in the main camp of the Cheyenne chief, Stone Calf. They were forced to do the work of squaws, beaten when they didn't, and ridiculed at every opportunity. Yet they fared almost as well physically as the Indians. It was a hard winter, and Stone Calf was forced to move far west on the staked Plains, apparently into eastern New Mexico, to avoid the hundreds of soldiers searching for the girls.

Fort Wallace Portraits

Cadet Christian C. Hewitt

Stone Calf got word that the army was demanding the return of the four girls. Realizing that the army had somehow learned there were four girls taken captive, he sent warriors out to find the two who had been left on the prairie.[19]

On November 7 they found the girls still alive and started with them back to Stone Calf's main camp. The following day, November 8, Lt. Frank Baldwin, patrolling in the Texas Panhandle, was told by his scouts that a band of Indians was camped near the north branch of McClellan Creek. Lieutenant Baldwin sent word to Gen. Nelson Miles but then decided he must attack at once in case the Indians might be holding some of the girls captives. His only chance to rescue them was total surprise.

With Troop D of the Sixth Cavalry and Company D of the Fifth Infantry, he charged into the camp, routing the Indians. The battle lasted for hours, but when it was over no captives were found. Then an Indian sneaked back into camp and fired his rifle at a bundle of buffalo robes. He missed, and a soldier shot and killed the Indian. The soldiers immediately investigated the roll of robes and found Julia German hiding inside. She said her sister was nearby, and they searched the camp again. They found the little five-year-old trying to build a fire. She had been sent out for fuel just before the attack and had kept right on mechanically trying to do what she had been ordered to do.[20]

The girls were taken to Camp Supply,

where officers' wives took over the task of restoring them to health. They were almost starved to death.

The older girls were aware at last that efforts were being made to get their release. The army stopped all supplies to the Cheyennes, once they discovered which tribe had the girls. With nothing to eat and their ponies starving, Stone Calf's tribe finally agreed to bargain. But Grey Beard, who had Sophia, held out for better terms, and the exchange of the girls for provisions was delayed.

The army, fearing the girls would be killed, waited. The starvation of the tribe and their ponies brought about the capitulation of the Indians, and the white girls were finally taken to the Cheyenne Agency in Indian territory and released on February 26, 1875.[21]

The girls were nothing but skin and bones, but so were the Indians. Catherine celebrated her eighteenth birthday in March at the agency and weighed only eighty pounds on that day.[22] That the girls survived is almost a miracle. All lived fairly long lives, Julia reaching ninety-two years of age.[23]

This was one of the worst Indian massacres along the Smoky Hill River and was the last raid on the Smoky Hill Trail itself. The remains of the massacred members of the German family were disinterred and brought to the Fort Wallace Cemetery, which had a section for civilian burials. The request for authority to bring the

Courtesy the Nebraska State Historical Society

First photograph of Julia (Right) and Addie (Left) German taken after their rescue November 8, 1874.

Courtesy the Nebraska State Historical Society

Sophia (Left) and Catherine (Right) German shortly after their rescue February 28, 1875.

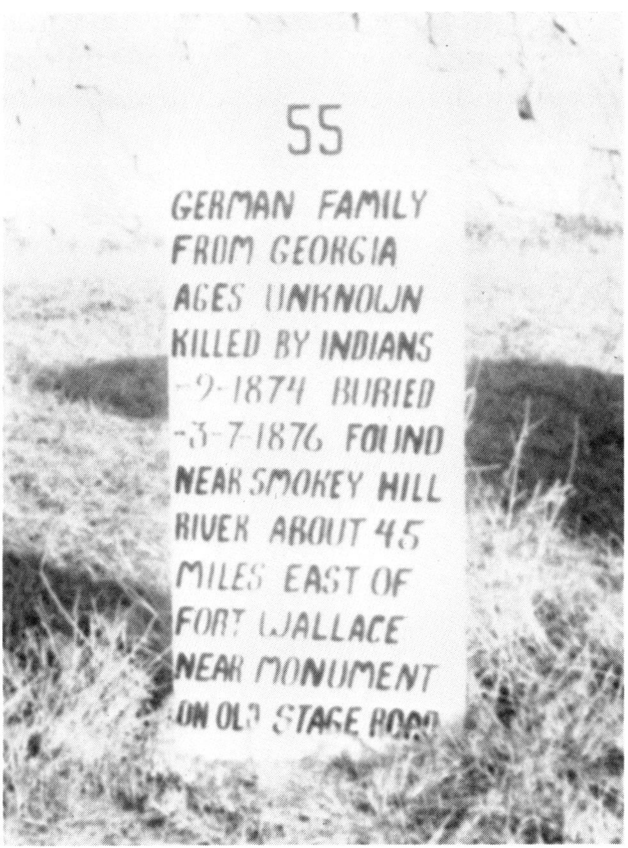

Photo by Author

Burial No. 55 in Fort Wallace Cemetery. (Note erroneous location — forty-five miles east.)

bodies to the post cemetery for proper burial was made by the commanding officer of the post of December 21, 1874 or 1875 (the writing on the official request is almost too dim to distinguish). The reason for the request is clear: "The detail sent with Lieutenant Hewitt to investigate and bury the remains were unable to give the graves a sufficient depth, having no suitable implements.[24] Graves in that part of the cemetery at this post intended for civilians could be prepared and the removal done by the transportation belonging to this post."

The actual burial of the remains in the post cemetery was not completed until March 7, 1876, according to the cemetary records of Fort Wallace.[25]

NOTES

1. Harry Sinclair Drago, *Wild Woolly and Wicked*, (New York: Bramhall House, 1960), pp. 142–3.
2. Robert Taft, "The Pictorial Record of the Old West," *Kansas Historical Quarterly* (August 1946), p. 250.
3. Robert W. Richmond and Robert W. Mardock, *A Nation Moving West* (Lincoln: Univ. of Nebraska Press, 1966), pp. 311–3; taken from *Kansas Historical Quarterly*, vol. 7.
4. Taft, "Pictorial Record," p. 250.
5. James C. Malin, "Dust Storms, 1861–1880," *Kansas Historical Quarterly* (August 1946), p. 272; quoted from *Junction City* (Kans.) *Weekly Union*, 1 August 1874.
6. Taft, "Pictorial Record," pp. 18–19.
7. Ibid., p. 19.
8. Ibid., p. 258; quoted from W. E. Webb, *Buffalo Days* (Cincinnati: Hanniford & Company, 1872).
9. Mary Einsel, "Commanche Cattle Pool," *Kansas Historical Quarterly* (Spring 1960), p. 59.
10. Mrs. Frank C. Montgomery, "Fort Wallace and Its Relation to the Frontier," *Kansas Historical Collections, 1926–1928* 17 (1928), p. 257.
11. Catherine clearly recalled this fact later — that they could get to Fort Wallace the next day — and it is reported in almost every account of the massacre. An oxteam could travel no more than twelve to fourteen miles a day — sixteen at most — pulling a wagon loaded as heavily as was the German wagon. Mrs. Montgomery quoted George Bird Grinnell as saying an average day's travel for an oxteam was from ten to twelve miles ("Fort Wallace," page 259). Alexander Majors, of Russell, Majors, and Waddell, said that an oxteam could pull a loaded wagon twelve to fifteen miles a day (*A Nation Moving West*, page 216). Some later reports said the massacre occurred as much as forty-five miles east of Fort Wallace. In view of the statement that they could have reached Fort Wallace in one day with an oxteam, this is ridiculous. Later army estimates placed it at thirty miles east of Fort Wallace. A marker has been erected about twenty-six to twenty-eight miles east of the fort site. However, reports of discovery of the bodies on "the North Fork of the Smoky" and "near the forks of the Smoky" would place the site about fourteen miles from Fort Wallace, a reasonable day's travel for an oxteam. Also, the North Fork of the Smoky at the forks is usually dry in September, but water is just below the surface so they could have dug a foot into the sandy streambed and reached water. Where the marker is erected there appears to be no place where water could be obtained in a dry season like 1874. The lay of the land as described by Catherine fits both the marker site and the Forks of the Smoky Hill. The man who found the bodies reported his discovery to Sheridan, which is only eight miles up the North Fork of the Smoky. The actual site, however, is not as important as what took place, and there is little controversy about that.
12. Vince Rogers, *The German Family Massacre* (Roseburg, Oreg.: Rogers), p. 5. Vince Rogers is the grandson of Catherine German.
13. Montgomery, "Fort Wallace," p. 259.

Photo by Author

Monument to German family in Fort Wallace Cemetery, erected in 1957.

14. David Dary, "The Saga of the Pioneer Sisters," *Kansas City Star Magazine*, 3 December 1972.
15. Rogers, *German Family Massacre*, p. 7.
16. Montgomery, "Fort Wallace," p. 260.
17. The senator was wrong in the time the victims had been dead, although he may have been quoting the estimate given by the soldiers who examined the bodies. If the hunter found them on September 30, the German family members had been dead nineteen days at that time.
18. Montgomery, "Fort Wallace," pp. 261–2; quoted from *Topeka Commonwealth*, 9 October 1874.
19. Dary, "Pioneer Sisters."
20. Montgomery, "Fort Wallace," p. 261.
21. Ibid., p. 264.
22. Ibid., p. 265.
23. Dary, "Pioneer Sisters." Catherine married Amos Swerdfeger and died in California in 1932 at age seventy-five. Sophia married Albert Feldman and died in Nebraska in 1947 at age eighty-five. Julia married first Howard Reese then Albert Brooks and died in California in 1959 at age ninety-two. Addie married first Frank Andrews then Frank Lehman, raised eleven children, and died in Kansas City in 1943 at age of seventy-four.
24. This would suggest that Senator Edwards in his early report to the *Topeka Commonwealth* was in error when he said the soldiers took the bodies to Monument for burial. It suggests instead that the bodies were buried at the site of the massacre and not taken up until they were removed to the cemetery at Fort Wallace.
25. Fort Wallace post records.

CHAPTER 27

THE LAST RAID

WESTERN KANSAS AND THE SMOKY HILL had not heard the last of the Indians who massacred the German family. While many of them escaped to the north, others apparently vanished among the many Indians camped around the agency. On April 6, 1875, some of the worst rebels of the Cheyenne broke away from the Cheyenne Agency and headed north. General Sheridan later wrote:

A party of about sixty Cheyennes, consisting of the worst criminals of the tribe, those who had murdered the German family and others, being afraid on that account to surrender with the rest, crossed the Arkansas River west of Fort Dodge and attempted to make their way to the Sioux country, north of the Platte.[1]

These Indians struck at a cattle herd on Punished Woman's Creek, about forty miles southeast of Fort Wallace. They killed more than a hundred head of cattle before they were driven off. Homer Wheeler, the sutler at Fort Wallace, owned the cattle, and when the order went out for the army to pursue the Indians, he volunteered to guide the soldiers. Lieutenant Henely, Commander of Troop H of the Sixth Cavalry, was given the job of running down the Indians.

Lieutenant Henely had served on McClellan Creek in Texas and had taken part in the rescue of the two youngest German girls. Since none of the Indians responsible for the massacre of the German family had been punished, Henely saw this as an opportunity to mete out some of the deserved punishment.

With Wheeler as guide, the troopers found the trail at Punished Woman's Creek, followed it north across the Smoky Hill River and the B.O.D. road, and crossed the railroad west of Monument. At the headwaters of the Saline River they met three hunters who told them there were Indians camped on Middle Sappa Creek. Wheeler located the camp after some searching and reported to Henely. The lieutenant brought his men into position.

The soldiers, according to one report, used the cry, "Remember the German girls," as they charged. The battle was furious, lasting three hours. Nineteen warriors were killed, including two chiefs and a medicine man. Eight squaws and children were inadvertantly killed in the battle. Two soldiers were killed, but none was wounded.[2]

Twelve lodges were destroyed after the remainder of the Indians fled north. Among the things found at the camp before the lodges were burned were some crude sketches of battles the Indians had taken part in. One was definitely identified as the massacre of the German family. One horse recovered was the horse of Private Pettyjohn, who had been killed in the battle on McClellan Creek in Texas when the little German girls were rescued.[3] The troops who had fought in that battle on McClellan Creek felt that the German family had been partly vindicated.

More than three years later after settlers and townspeople had relaxed and no longer had any fear of the Indians, the warriors struck for the last time. It was one of the bloodiest and most extensive raids in the history of western Kansas. It wasn't because there were more Indians or that they fought harder; it was simply that there were more helpless whites in their path.

The first inkling anyone along the Smoky Hill had of possible trouble was a report to the army posts along the Smoky Hill by way of the telegraph that Dull Knife and a large band of Cheyennes had escaped from Fort Reno in Indian territory and were heading north.

Copied from "The Indians Last Fight" by Collins
Cheyenne — Dull Knife

Disease had been killing the Northern Cheyennes, who were unaccustomed to the climate in the south. They had been moved a short distance from the main camp at Fort Reno, and a company of soldiers was sent to keep an eye on them. The Cheyennes had been brought down from Fort Robinson in northern Nebraska in 1876.[4] Now, in order to survive, they felt they had to get back to the country of the Sioux, with whom they were more closely aligned than with the Southern Cheyennes.

On the night of September 9, 1878, the Indians slipped out of camp, leaving their tepees standing to keep the soldiers from learning of their escape as long as possible. Two hundred and thirty-five Indians made their escape, but this number included only eighty-nine warriors. It also included thirty-four children.[5]

They headed north, getting a good start before their flight was discovered. The company that had been watching them gave pursuit, but when it caught up it was no match for the well-armed Indians — who had been allowed to keep their guns on the reservation.

Fort Dodge was alerted to the approach of the Indians, and help was called for. Lt. Col. William H. Lewis at Fort Dodge personally took command of the troops sent out to capture the runaway Cheyennes.

The Indians crossed the Arkansas River about twenty miles west of Dodge City and headed north. Colonel Lewis pursued, finally catching up with them on September 27 at Famished Woman's Creek.[6] Here the Indians went up the canyon, about thirty miles southeast of Fort Wallace. The soldiers followed and were ambushed. On outcroppings on top of the canyon walls, the Indians had built little forts of rocks and fought from behind them.

In the battle, Colonel Lewis received a wound in the thigh which cut a main artery, causing it to bleed profusely. Two other soldiers were also wounded. One Indian was found dead; the others escaped.

After the battle twenty-five soldiers put Colonel Lewis in an ambulance and dashed toward Fort Wallace, about thirty miles away. They were within about eight miles of the post when the colonel died.[7]

The Indians headed almost due north from the scene of the battle, crossing the railroad just east of Carlyle (present Oakley). Reports said the Indians killed about twenty people south of the Arkansas River and another six before they reached the railroad.[8]

Twenty men were killed in Decatur County and eleven in Rawlins County along the northern border of Kansas as the Indians raced north.[9] A scout for the army, George W. Brown, said they found every settler's house deserted and everything scattered around. Surviving settlers told them the Indians had fanned out, killing every man they could find for fifteen miles along Beaver Creek and the same on Sappa Creek. They came upon one schoolhouse and killed all the bigger boys.[10]

The killing spree extended into Nebraska. The Indians were finally stopped and captured near Fort Robinson, in northwestern Nebraska. It was the last raid in Kansas. As one writer described it, "the last war whoop."

The Indians were kept in a barracks at Fort Robinson until they could be returned to Fort Reno in Indian territory. On January 9, four months to the day from the time they had broken out of the reservation at Fort Reno, they broke out of the barracks at Fort Robinson. It was bitter cold, and the battle raged through the night as the Indians escaped into the bluffs to the north and west of the fort. When it was all over a few days later many of the Indians were dead, but Dull Knife had escaped to the Sioux camps. Wild Hog and Old Crow, Dull Knife's top chiefs, were already in irons at Fort Robinson when the breakout occurred. They were sent south again, still in irons, for trial.

Thus ended the last great raid on the plains by the Indians.

The story of the trails of the Smoky Hills could hardly be finished without a final report on the man who initiated and built the most famous of all those trails, the Butterfield Overland Despatch.

David A. Butterfield first came to Kansas in 1857 and bought a lot in Manhattan where he built a stone house.[11] In 1862 he moved to Denver. He moved back to Atchison, Kansas, in 1864 when he put into action his idea of a straight route to Denver from the Missouri. It was more than a year before the first stagecoach ran over the route to Denver, but his influential friends and employees honored him with a tablet (made by Tiffany & Co.) of gold dug from the Colorado mines. On one side is engraved: "Butterfield Overland Despatch Established by D. A. Butterfield July 5th,

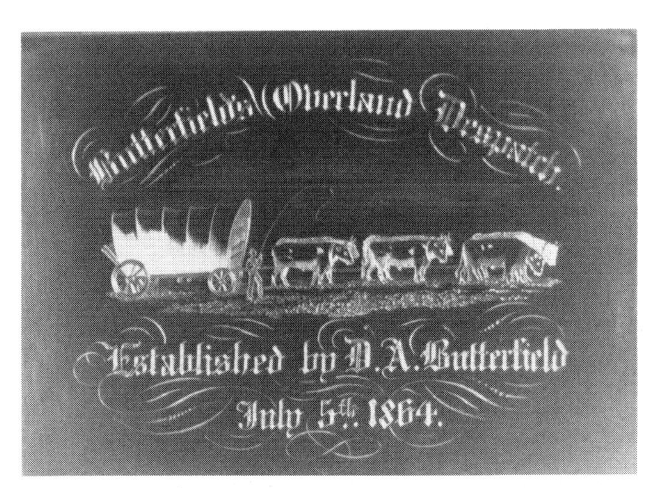

Courtesy Mrs. Harold DeBacker

Gold medal given to David Butterfield (owned now by his great-granddaughter, Mrs. Harold DeBacker, Boulder, Colorado).

Courtesy the Kansas State Historical Society, Topeka

Butterfield House, Manhattan (3070 Sage Street)

1864." On the opposite side is listed the names of the donors.[12]

Always the dreamer, the builder, the visionary, Butterfield didn't abandon his dreams of making transportation easier and faster after he sold the B.O.D. to Ben Holladay. He eventually came to Hot Springs, Arkansas, where he built a streetcar system and planned a railroad between Hot Springs and Malvern, about fifteen miles away. He had many friends in Hot Springs, and life was good for him when it ended abruptly and tragically. He died Sunday morning, March 28, 1875, at the age of forty-one, just three days past his twentieth wedding anniversary.

The March 30 issue of *The Daily Press* of Hot Springs, headlined the story, "Cowardly Murder," and gave the details.

On Saturday afternoon [March 27] about five o'clock, Col. Butterfield went into the car stable and spoke to Harry Bailey, the stock tender, about his abusing stock and told him to curry a certain horse, when Harry told him if he wanted the horse curried, he could do it himself, which exasperated Col. B. and picking up a small stick of wood nearby, he struck Harry, hitting him on the hand. At this instant, Joe Decker, who was standing at his back, picked up a stick of wood and without a word of warning struck Butterfield a fearful blow on the right side of the head, felling him to the ground instantly. The murderer stopped but a moment to view the body of him he had so brutally slain, then after climbing a fence nearby, took to his heels. Constable Parker being near at hand, followed in pursuit and overtook him when about a mile from the scene of the murder.

The body of Col. Butterfield was soon placed upon a cot, which was put into a carriage and in this way he was conveyed to his residence. Before arriving in sight of home, the sad news was gently

Courtesy Mrs. Harold DeBacker

Mary Millions Butterfield (wife of David Butterfield)

broken to his family. Drs. Hobson and Taylor, who had been called in by friends, examined the wound, with little hopes for his recovery, said as little to grieve the family as possible. He remained unconscious from the time he was struck until Sunday morning between nine and ten o'clock when he breathed his last.

Joe Decker, the murderer, is a person who was in Col. Butterfield's employ as chairman on the railroad survey between Hot Springs and Malvern. Col. B. payed him off at the office about an hour before the trouble at the stable. He is reported as being a bad character, and also that this is not the first difficulty of the kind that he has been engaged in.

The obsequies of the late Colonel D. A. Butterfield were the most grand and imposing ever witnessed in this city. First came a street car deeply draped in the sombre hues of mourning, containing the Hot Springs Brass Band, playing the dirge: "Solemn Strikes the Funeral Knell," then came the casket bearing the remains of the deceased, following which was a long line of carriages filled with mourners, while along the walk a procession of Masons, appropriately clad, filed in mournful silence, accompanying the venerated remains to their final resting place. It was indeed a sad and mournful duty the fraternity had to perform, to convey to the silent tomb the remains of him whom they had learned to love for his many virtues and sterling integrity.[13]

Thus ended the career of the instigator of the most glamorous and most dangerous of all the trails along the Smoky Hill River, the B.O.D.

NOTES

1. Mrs. Frank C. Montgomery, "Fort Wallace and Its Relation to the Frontier," *Kansas Historical Collections, 1926–1928* 17 (1928), p. 268.
2. Ibid., p. 269.
3. Ibid.
4. George W. Brown, "Kansas Indian Wars," *Kansas Historical Collections, 1926–1928* 17 (1928), p. 134.
5. Montgomery, "Fort Wallace," p. 272.
6. Famished Woman's Creek is the same as Punished Woman's Creek. One legend as to how it got its name says that an Indian squaw had disobeyed some tribal law and had been left beside the creek to starve. The name of the creek later was changed to Beaver Creek, not to be confused with the Beaver Creek in northwestern Kansas which runs into the Republican. This Beaver Creek ran into the Smoky Hill River. Its name was later changed to Ladder Creek. The site of the battle is very near El Cuartelejo, which is located in what is now Scott County Park.
7. Brown, "Kansas Indian Wars," p. 137.
8. Montgomery, "Fort Wallace," p. 274.
9. Ibid., p. 273.
10. Brown, "Kansas Indian Wars," p. 137.
11. C. W. McCampbell, "Manhattan's Oldest House Was Built by David A. Butterfield," *Kansas Historical Quarterly* (Spring 1957). This house is still standing at 307 Osage Street in Manhattan.
12. Ella A. Butterfield, "Butterfield Overland Despatch," *The Trail* (December 1925).
13. *Hot Springs* (Ark.) *Daily Press*, 30 March 1875.

Courtesy Mrs. Harold DeBacker

David Butterfield (son of David Butterfield)

Courtesy Mrs. Harold DeBacker

Maude M. Butterfield (daughter of David Butterfield)

Courtesy Mrs. Harold DeBacker

Lillie Butterfield (daughter of David Butterfield)

Courtesy Mrs. Harold DeBacker

Ella A. Butterfield (daughter of David Butterfield)

Courtesy Mrs. Harold DeBacker

Flora Butterfield (daughter of David Butterfield)

EPILOG

THIS BOOK WOULD NOT BE COMPLETE without the story of the marking of the Butterfield Overland Despatch Trail through western Kansas. The stone post markers erected in the western counties where the original B.O.D. Trail crosses the highways and county roads of today will preserve the old trail for posterity. Howard Raynesford, rapidly approaching his ninetieth birthday but as sharp of mind and as full of enthusiasm as a young man, conceived the idea of the stone post markers, got the resolution through the Kansas Legislature in 1963, and, through a series of talks on a tour through the area, raised the money for the markers and their erection.

He wrote an account of the placing of these markers, modestly playing down his own role in the work. Kansas and historians in years to come will have Howard Raynesford to thank for the marking of this important trail.

Following is his account, written in the mid-1960s when he was almost ninety:

Western-minded organizations have fairly well marked the old Santa Fe Trail, and they keep it in the limelight by staging frequent treks over it. Ezra Meeker, who went west over the Oregon Trail in 1852, retraced it in 1906 with an ox team and wagon and placed markers on it to preserve its course for posterity. But the equally historic Smoky Hill Trail has been sadly neglected and all but forgotten.

Back in the late 1920s, Mr. W. E. Connelley, then secretary of the Kansas State Historical Society, asked me to search out the old Smoky Hill Trail through western Kansas and map it for the Society. I have been working on it ever since as time and opportunity permitted until now I have it traced out, mostly by walking it, and mapped it from Fort Ellsworth through the seven counties of Ellsworth, Russell, Ellis, Trego, Gove, Logan and Wallace, to the Colorado state line, a distance of about 220 miles. I also have quite a number of the station sites accurately surveyed and mapped. It's

At Monument Works in Hays, H. C. Raynesford showing plaque to be imbedded in base.

well that it is mapped. In going over it recently, I found that in many places it was so obliterated that it could not be accurately located without reference to the maps.

Realizing that it would soon be lost, owing to the elements, agricultural activities, etc., I determined to mark it, not only to perserve its course but so it can be easily found by anyone interested. Wooden markers were suggested as being less expensive but Nyle Miller, secretary of the Kansas State Historical Society, said the Society had had to replace many of their wooden markers after only a few years. We wanted something more permanent. Of course, granite or marble markers were out of the question because of the cost. It was going to require many markers, perhaps one hundred and fifty, to mark the trail properly, and they should be uniform over the entire distance.

First marker set in Trego County at Holinger's Corner September 24, 1963. Commissioner Ward Philip leveling form.

Kansas has a native stone that has withstood the ravages of western weather for 75 to 90 years without apparent deterioration. This is the rock from which were cut the famous stone fence posts which have become such a prominent feature of Western Kansas. Authorities say that at the peak of their use, there were more than forty thousand miles of these stone-post fences. They have been the object of great curiosity especially to the out-of-state tourists, and have been described to these tourists as markers over Indian graves or small pebbles planted by early settlers which grew so luxuriently in the extremely rich western Kansas soil that they occasionally needed trimming.

Great Bend Morning Daily Tribune

Erecting first marker on Smoky Hill Trail at site of Big Creek Station on Philip Ranch.

The modern highway requires a much wider right-of-way than did the section line road of half a century ago. These wider roads forced many of these fences to be set back and, in some cases, the landowners, rather than reset these heavy posts (they weigh up to 600 pounds each), piled them and built new fences with modern treated wood or steel posts. We were able to secure all of these discarded stone posts that we needed for our purpose just for hauling them away.

These posts made into the B.O.D. markers are eight to ten inches square and are left in the rough as the posts were. They stand 30 to 36 inches tall above 21 by 24 inch cement base. One of these has been placed on the trail wherever it crosses a highway or road. On the side facing the road, a panel has been smoothed and the legend, "B O D 1865" has been sandblasted in letters large enough to be read easily by the motorists flashing by on the highway. A plaque has been inserted in the base, giving some of the Trail's history, and on top of the shaft a groove has been cut, showing in what direction the Trail ran at that particular spot.

Authorization to place these markers on highway rights-of-way was necessary from the State Legislature and that permission was granted unanimously by a Resolution introduced by State Senator Worden Howat of Wakeeney, in which the Trail was officially designated THE SMOKY HILL TRAIL. The State Highway Commission agreed to cooperate with anyone desiring to help erect the markers. The commissioners and engineers in every one of the counties in which the Trail was to be marked construed this to include them and this resulted in each of them furnishing trucks, men and material to assist in setting the markers. With this help, 20 markers were set in Ellsworth County, 30 in Russell, 32 in Ellis, 20 in Trego, 12 in Gove, 14 in Logan, and 10 in Wallace.

Since the legislature made no appropriation for this project and the handling and processing of these markers did cost money, it was necessary to seek funds. Sandblasting is expensive but James Wolf, owner of Wolf's Exclusive Memorial Co. of Ellis, generously offered to donate his time, asking only to be reimbursed for the material and power used. I presented the project before Chambers of Commerce, all kinds of clubs, historical societies, historically-minded individuals, even landowners through whose land the Trail ran, stressing the Trail's historical importance and the need to mark it to preserve its course. I pointed out its great recreational value for Boy Scout Troops, saddle clubs, etc., and its advertising possibilities to the adjacent towns. I suggested that if each town could see its way clear to sponsor at least the markers to be placed on the roads near it, the cost would be very little to each community and it would give a sense of proprietorship that would increase in value as time went by.

The response generally was good although not quite enough to cover the cost of the project. It required a lot of traveling and talking but we have set 138 of these markers on the 220 miles between old Fort Ellsworth (Fort Harker) and the Colorado state line. They have been accepted as both attractive and appropriate and, if they escape the vandals, at the end of the next century they will still be pointing out the course of this historic old SMOKY HILL TRAIL.

ACKNOWLEDGMENTS

First of all, I want to express my great appreciation of the help and encouragement of Charles A. Baougher, who at the very beginning was as interested and avid as I was in searching out the course of the old Smoky Hill Trail. We walked many miles together and it was a matter of deep regret to me that he could not stay with it to the finish.

The help of Everett Wandby of Gorham, C. C. Porter of Russell Springs, August Schutte of Ellis, and Frank Madigan of Wallace is thankfully acknowledged. I must acknowledge the expert efficiency of my son, Kirk, in the surveying and mapping, especially of the station sites.

The first load of stone posts was donated by Orville Young of LaCross and transported by James Wolf, the monument man of Ellis. Another load was furnished by Louis J. Billinger of Hays with Douglas Philip bringing them in. Other donations of posts were made by R. J. Sloan of McCracken and Fred Dirk of LaCross.

It was a matter of great satisfaction to me that the first contribution of money came from the Chamber of Commerce of my hometown of Ellis, which, upon hearing the story of the project, immediately voted a good sum to start the work.

Those making contributions were:
Ellis Chamber of Commerce
Hays Chamber of Commerce
Quinter Chamber of Commerce
Oakley Chamber of Commerce
WaKeeney Lions Club
Gove City Lions Club
Trego County Historical Society
Russell County Historical Society
Ellsworth County — through George Jelinek
City of Dorrance
Better Farm Homes Club of WaKeeney
Friendly Neighbors Club, Russell Springs
Carl Flax, Ellis
Ruby Nelson, Ellis
Hazel Merritt, Ellis
Phil Nicholson, Ellis
Douglas Philip, Hays
Al Esterdahl, Hays
Frank Schippers, Victoria
Mrs. H. A. Opdyche, Russell
W. W. Harvey, Ogallah
L. H. Raynesford, Long Beach, California
Kirk Raynesford, North Hollywood, California
Ward R. Philip, WaKeeney
Charles A. Ott, WaKeeney
John Zeman, Sr., Collyer
A. P. Weigel, Collyer
Bertrand Elevator, Monument (Don Moore)
Marjorie Wright, Russell Springs
Lorin Wilds, Quinter
Foard Darnall, Wallace
Leal Stewart, Healy
Ivan R. Mort, Hill City

BIBLIOGRAPHY

Anderson, George L. *Kansas West*. San Marino, Ca.: Golden West Books, 1963.

———. "Along the Line of the Kansas Pacific Railway in Western Kansas in 1870." *Kansas Historical Quarterly*, May 1951.

———. *The Battle of Beecher Island*. Sterling, Colo.: Royal Printing Company, 1968.

Bell, J. M. "Reminiscences." *Cavalry Journal* 10 (1897).

Bell, William A. *New Tracks in North America*. New York: Scribner, Welford & Company, 1870. Reprint. Albuquerque: Horn & Wallace, 1965.

———. *Beecher Island Annual*, Vol. 2, No. 1. Wray, Colo.: Beecher Island Battle Memorial Association, 1905.

Blue, Daniel. *Thrilling Narrative of the Adventures, Sufferings and Starvation of Pike's Peak Gold Seekers on the Plains of the West in the Winter and Spring of 1859*. Chicago: Evening Journal Steam Print, 1860. Reprint. Fairfield, Wash.: Ye Galleon Press, 1968.

Brady, Cyrus Townsend. *Indian Fights and Fighters*. McClure, Philips & Co. Reprint. Lincoln: Univ. of Nebraska Press, 1971.

Brininstool, E. A. "The Rescue of Forsythe's Scouts." *Kansas Historical Collections 1926–1928* 17 (1928).

Brown, George W. "Kansas Indian Wars." *Kansas Historical Collections 1926–1928* 17 (1928).

Burkey, Blaine. *Custer Come at Once*. Hays, Kans.: Thomas More Prep, 1976.

Butterfield, Ella A. "Butterfield Overland Despatch." *The Trail*, December 1925.

Byers, O. P. "When Railroading Outdid the Wild West Stories." *Kansas Historical Collections 1926–1928* 17 (1928).

Ceram, C. W. *The First American: A Story of North American Archeology*. New York: Harcourt Brace Jovanovich, 1971.

Chrisman, Harry E. *The Ladder of Rivers*. Denver: Sage Books, 1962.

Connelley, William E. "Life and Adventures of George W. Brown, Soldier, Pioneer Plainsman and Buffalo Hunter." *Kansas Historical Collections 1926–1928* 17 (1928).

———. "The Treaty Held at Medicine Lodge." *Kansas Historical Collections 1926–1928* 17 (1928).

———. "Wild Bill — James Butler Hickok." *Kansas Historical Collections 1926–1928* 17 (1928).

Crossen, Forest. *Western Yesterdays*. Vol. 1. Boulder, Colo.: Boulder Publishing Company, 1963.

Dary, David. "The Saga of the Pioneer Sisters." *Kansas City* (Mo.) *Star Magazine*, 3 December 1972.

Davis, E. O. *The First Five Years of the Railroad Era in Colorado*.

Davis, Theodore H. "A Stage Ride to Colorado." *Harper's New Monthly Magazine* 35:206 (July 1867).

DeLay, L. G. "Pond Creek Centennial." *Fort Wallace* (Kans.) *Bugle*, June 1965.

Drago, Harry Sinclair. *Wild Woolly and Wicked*. New York: Bramhall House, 1960.

Dunn, Ruth. *Attack on Black Kettle's Village*. Edmonton, Okla.: Herman Kolb, 1973.

Einsel, Mary. "Comanche Cattle Pool." *Kansas Historical Quarterly*, Spring 1960.

Emmett, Chris. *Shanghai Pierce: A Fair Likeness*. Norman: Univ. of Oklahoma Press, 1953.

Farley, Alan W. "Samuel Hallett and the Union Pacific Railway Company in Kansas." *Kansas Historical Quarterly*, Spring 1959.

Faulk, Odie, B. *Land of Many Frontiers*. New York: Oxford Univ. Press, 1968.

Forsythe, George A. "A Frontier Fight." *Beecher Island Annual*. St. Francis, Kans. 1960.

———. "Fossil Hunting on the Plains of Western Kansas." *Fort Wallace* (Kans.) *Bugle*, June 1976.

Gower, Calvin W. "Kansas Territory and the Pike's Peak Gold Rush: Governing the Gold Region." *Kansas Historical Quarterly*, Autumn 1966.

———. "The Pike's Peak Gold Rush and the Smoky Hill Route, 1859—1860." *Kansas Historical Quarterly*, Summer 1959.

Gray, John S. "Will Comstock, Scout: The Natty Bumpo of Kansas." *Montana Western History* 20 (Summer 1970).

Greeley, Horace. *Overland Journey*.

Hafen, LeRoy R. ed., *Overland Routes to the Gold Fields 1859*. Glendale, Ca.: Arthur H. Clark Co., 1942.

Jackson, Mrs. Ruth. "Butterfield Overland Despatch Trail Markers." *Fort Wallace* (Kans.) *Bugle*, June 1965.

Jelinek, George. "The Ellsworth Story." *Ellsworth* (Kans.) *Reporter*, 3 August 1967.

———. "Frontier Land." *Ellsworth* (Kans.) *Reporter*, 1973.

Jensen, Oliver. *The American Heritage History of Railroads in America*. New York: American Heritage Publishing Company, 1975.

Johnson, Alma D. *Trail Dust: Over the B.O.D. Through Kansas*. Detroit: Harlo Press, 1975.
Jones, Horace. "Quivira — Rive County, Kansas." *Kansas Historical Collections 1926–1928* 17 (1928).
Lee, Wayne C. "Death Hollow." *Old West Magazine*, Spring 1977.
———. *Scotty Philip: The Man Who Saved the Buffalo*. Caldwell: Caxton Printers Ltd., 1975.
Linville, Leslie. *My Life on the Kansas Plains*. Colby, Kans.: Prairie Printers, 1968.
———. *The Smoky Hill Valley and Butterfield Trail*. Colby, Kans.: LeRoy's Printing, 1974.
Loomis, Noel. *Wells Fargo*. New York: Clarkson N. Potter, Inc., 1968.
Long, Margaret. *The Smoky Hill Trail*. Denver: W. H. Kistler Company, 1943.
Malin, James C. "Dust Storms, 1861—1880." *Kansas Historical Quarterly*, August 1946.
Manion, John S. "Indian Attack." *Fort Wallace* (Kans.) *Bugle*, March 1971.
McCampbell, C. W. "Manhattan's Oldest House Was Built by David A. Butterfield." *Kansas Historical Quarterly*, Spring 1957.
Meredith, Grace E. *Girl Captives of the Cheyennes*. Los Angeles: Gem Publishing Company, 1927.
Millbrook, Minnie Dubbs. "Big Game Hunting with the Custers, 1869—1870" *Kansas Historical Quarterly*, Winter 1975.
Miller, Nyle H. and Snell, Joseph W. "Some Notes on Kansas Cowtown Police Offices and Gun Fighters." *Kansas Historical Quarterly*, Spring 1960, Summer 1960, Autumn 1960, Winter, 1960.
Montgomery, Mrs. Frank C. "Fort Wallace and Its Relation to the Frontier." *Kansas Historical Collections 1926–1928* 17 (1928).
———. "Monument Station and Its Last Commander, Colonel Conyngham." *Fort Wallace* (Kans.) *Bugle*, June 1971.
Peterson, Nancy M. "Battle of Beecher Island." *Colorado Magazine*, March-April 1974.
Putnam, John H. "A Trip to the End of the Union Pacific in 1868." *Kansas Historical Quarterly*, August 1944.
Richmond, Robert W. and Mardock, Robert W. *A Nation Moving West*. Lincoln: Univ. of Nebraska Press, 1966.
Rogers, Vince. *The German Family Massacre*. Roseberg, Ore.: Rogers.
Root, George A. and Hickman, Russell K. "Pike's Peak Express Companies." *Kansas Historical Quarterly*, August 1944, November 1944, November 1945, February 1946.
Rosa, Joseph G. *The Gunfighter: Man or Myth*. Norman: Univ. of Oklahoma Press, 1969.
Ross, Edith Connelley. "The Quivira Village." *Kansaas Historical Collections 1926–1928* 17 (1928).
Russell, Don. *The Lives and Legends of Buffalo Bill*. Norman: Univ. of Oklahoma Press, 1960.
Sandoz, Mari. *The Cattlemen*. New York: Hastings House Pubs., Inc., 1958.
Settle, Mary Lund and Settle, Raymond W. *Saddle and Spurs*. New York: Bonanza Books, 1960.
Settle,. Raymond W. and Settle, Mary Lund. "The Early Careers of William Bradford Waddell and William Hepburn Russell: Frontier Capitalists." *Kansas Historical Quarterly*, Winter 1960.
Shine, M. A. "New Chapter in Nebraska History." *Nebraska History*, January-March 1923.
———. "Smoky Trail Aflame." *Fort Wallace* (Kans.) *Bugle*, June 1965.
Snell, Joseph W. and Richmond, Robert W. "When the Union and Kansas Pacific Built through Kansas." *Kansas Historical Quarterly*, Summer 1966, Autumn 1966.
Sparks, Ray G. *Reckoning at Summit Springs*. Kansas City Mo.: Lowell Press, 1969.
Streeter, Floyd Benjamin. *The Kaw*. New York: Farrar & Rinehart, 1941.
Taft, Robert. "The Pictorical Record of the Old West." *Kansas Historical Quarterly*, February, 1946, May 1946, August 1946, November 1946.
Thomas, A. B. "The Massacre of the Villasur Expedition at the Forks of the Platte River, August 12, 1720." *Nebraska History*, July-September 1924.
Thomas, Alfred Barnaby. *After Coronado*. Norman: Univ. of Oklahoma Press, 1935.
Thompson, W. F. "Peter Robidoux: A Real Kansas Pioneer." *Kansas Historical Collections 1926–1928* 17 (1928).
Voigt, Barton R. "The Death of Lyman S. Kidder." *South Dakota History*, Winter 1975.
Webb, W. E. "Air Towns and Their Inhabitants." *Harper's New Monthly Magazine*, November 1875.
Wetmore, Helen Cody. *Buffalo Bill: Last of the Great Scouts*. Chicago: Duluth Press, 1899.
Wetzel, Charles R. "Monument Station, Gove County." *Kansas Historical Quarterly*, Autumn 1960.
Whitney, Chauncy B. "Diary of Chauncey B. Whitney." *Beecher Island Annual*. St. Francis, Kans. 1960.
Zamonski, Stanley W. and Keller, Teddy. *The Fifty-Niners: A Denver Diary*. Denver: Sage Books, 1961.

NEWSPAPERS

Abilene Chronicle
Atchison Free Press
Atchison City Directory & Business Mirror, 1865
Cherry Creek Pioneer (Denver)
Congregational Record (Lawrence, Kans.)
Ellsworth (Kans.) *Reporter*
Freedom's Champion (Atchison)
Greeley County Republican (Tribune, Kans.)
Harper's Weekly (New York)
Hays (Kans.) *Sentinel*
Hot Springs (Ark.) *Daily Press*
Junction City (Kans.) *Sentinel*
Junction City Weekly Union
(Manhattan) *Kansas Radical*
(Topeka) *Kansas Tribune*
Lawrence (Kans.) *Journal*
Lawrence Republican
(Lawrence) *Kansas Tribune*
Leavenworth Conservative
Leavenworth Herald

Leavenworth Times
Manhattan Independent
Manhattan Nationalist
New York Tribune
Rocky Mountain News (Denver)
St. Joseph (Mo.) *Gazette*
Topeka Capital
Topeka Commonwealth
Topeka State Journal
Topeka State Record
Topeka Weekly Record
Weekly Kansas Herald (Leavenworth)
Western Journal of Commerce (Kansas City)
Western Weekly Argus (Wyandotte, Kans.)
Wyandotte Commercial Gazette.

INDEX